ACCUMULATOR AND MEMORY OPERATIONS	MNEMONIC	IMMED OP	~	#	DIRECT OP	~	#	INDEX OP	~	#	EXTND OP	~	#	INHER OP	~	#	BOOLEAN/ARITHMETIC OPERATION (All register labels refer to contents)	H (5)	I (4)	N (3)	Z (2)	V (1)	C (0)
Rotate Left	ROL							69	7	2	79	6	3				M	•	•	↕	↕	⑥	↕
	ROLA													49	2	1	A	•	•	↕	↕	⑥	↕
	ROLB													59	2	1	B	•	•	↕	↕	⑥	↕
Rotate Right	ROR							66	7	2	76	6	3				M	•	•	↕	↕	⑥	↕
	RORA													46	2	1	A	•	•	↕	↕	⑥	↕
	RORB													56	2	1	B	•	•	↕	↕	⑥	↕
Shift Left, Arithmetic	ASL							68	7	2	78	6	3				M	•	•	↕	↕	⑥	↕
	ASLA													48	2	1	A	•	•	↕	↕	⑥	↕
	ASLB													58	2	1	B	•	•	↕	↕	⑥	↕
Shift Right, Arithmetic	ASR							67	7	2	77	6	3				M	•	•	↕	↕	⑥	↕
	ASRA													47	2	1	A	•	•	↕	↕	⑥	↕
	ASRB													57	2	1	B	•	•	↕	↕	⑥	↕
Shift Right, Logic.	LSR							64	7	2	74	6	3				M	•	•	↕	↕	⑥	↕
	LSRA													44	2	1	A	•	•	↕	↕	⑥	↕
	LSRB													54	2	1	B	•	•	↕	↕	⑥	↕
Store Acmltr.	STAA				97	4	2	A7	6	2	B7	5	3				A → M	•	•	↕	↕	R	•
	STAB				D7	4	2	E7	6	2	F7	5	3				B → M	•	•	↕	↕	R	•
Subtract	SUBA	80	2	2	90	3	2	A0	5	2	B0	4	3				A − M → A	•	•	↕	↕	↕	↕
	SUBB	C0	2	2	D0	3	2	E0	5	2	F0	4	3				B − M → B	•	•	↕	↕	↕	↕
Subract Acmltrs.	SBA													10	2	1	A − B → A	•	•	↕	↕	↕	↕
Subtr. with Carry	SBCA	82	2	2	92	3	2	A2	5	2	B2	4	3				A − M − C → A	•	•	↕	↕	↕	↕
	SBCB	C2	2	2	D2	3	2	E2	5	2	F2	4	3				B − M − C → B	•	•	↕	↕	↕	↕
Transfer Acmltrs	TAB													16	2	1	A → B	•	•	↕	↕	R	•
	TBA													17	2	1	B → A	•	•	↕	↕	R	•
Test, Zero or Minus	TST							6D	7	2	7D	6	3				M − 00	•	•	↕	↕	R	R
	TSTA													4D	2	1	A − 00	•	•	↕	↕	R	R
	TSTB													5D	2	1	B − 00	•	•	↕	↕	R	R

LEGEND:

OP   Operation Code (Hexadecimal);
~   Number of MPU Cycles;
#   Number of Program Bytes;
+   Arithmetic Plus;
-    Arithmetic Minus;
•   Boolean AND;
M_{SP} Contents of memory location pointed to be Stack Pointer;

+   Boolean Inclusive OR;
⊕   Boolean Exclusive OR;
$\overline{M}$ Complement of M;
→   Transfer Into;
0   Bit = Zero;
00   Byte = Zero;
H   Half-carry from bit 3;
I   Interrupt mask
N   Negative (sign bit)

Z   Zero (byte)
V   Overflow, 2's complement
C   Carry from bit 7
R   Reset Always
S   Set Always
↕   Test and set if true, cleared otherwise
•   Not Affected
CCR Condition Code Register
LS   Least Significant
MS   Most Significant

INTRODUCTION TO MICROCOMPUTER-BASED DIGITAL SYSTEMS

McGraw-Hill Series in Electrical Engineering

Consulting Editor
Stephen W. Director, Carnegie-Mellon University

Networks and Systems
Communications and Information Theory
Control Theory
Electronics and Electronic Circuits
Power and Energy
Electromagnetics
Computer Engineering and Switching Theory
Introductory and Survey
Radio, Television, Radar, and Antennas

Previous Consulting Editors

Ronald M. Bracewell, Colin Cherry, James F. Gibbons, Willis W. Harman, Hubert Heffner, Edward W. Herold, John G. Linvill, Simon Ramo, Ronald A. Rohrer, Anthony E. Siegman, Charles Susskind, Frederick E. Terman, John G. Truxal, Ernst Weber, and John R. Whinnery

Electronics and Electronic Circuits

Consulting Editor
Stephen W. Director, Carnegie-Mellon University

INTRODUCTION TO MICROCOMPUTER-BASED DIGITAL SYSTEMS

James W. Gault, Ph.D.

Department of Electrical Engineering
North Carolina State University at Raleigh

Russell L. Pimmel, Ph.D.

Department of Electrical Engineering
University of Missouri at Columbia

McGraw-Hill Book Company

New York St. Louis San Francisco Auckland Bogotá Hamburg
Johannesburg London Madrid Mexico Montreal New Delhi
Panama Paris São Paulo Singapore Sydney Tokyo Toronto

This book was set in Times Roman by Science Typographers, Inc.
The editors were T. Michael Slaughter and J. W. Maisel;
the cover was designed by Charles A. Carson;
the production supervisor was Phil Galea.
The drawings were done by ANCO/Boston.
R. R. Donnelley & Sons Company was printer and binder.

INTRODUCTION TO MICROCOMPUTER-BASED DIGITAL SYSTEMS

1 2 3 4 5 6 7 8 9 0   D O D O   8 9 8 7 6 5 4 3 2 1

ISBN 0-07-023047-1

Library of Congress Cataloging in Publication Data

Gault, James W.
    Introduction to microcomputer-based digital
systems.
    (McGraw-Hill series in electrical engineering.
Electronics and electronic circuits)
    Includes bibliographies and index.
    1. Microcomputers. I. Pimmel, Russell L.
II. Title. III. Series.
TK7888.3.G34   621.3819'5   81-8273
ISBN 0-07-023047-1   AACR2
ISBN 0-07-023048-X (Solutions manual)

CONTENTS

PREFACE

Since the invention of the integrated circuit, continued developments have led to more and more complex devices. Computer processors, memories, standard interfaces, and even entire computer systems are available as individual integrated circuits. As a result, extremely small and economical computer systems are available and can be incorporated into many electronic systems. Since there are many advantages in this approach, electronic instrumentation, control, and communication systems are making use of the microcomputer. An understanding of the operation and application of the microcomputer is so essential for an engineer today that when there is only one required course in digital systems, it must include treatment of microcomputer-based systems.

This book is intended for use in an introductory course in digital systems taught at the sophomore or junior level without prerequisites. In writing this book our objectives have been to provide the reader with (1) an introductory understanding of the vocabulary, concepts, and techniques used in analyzing and designing traditional and programmed digital systems and (2) the background and skills needed to define a hardware configuration and associated software for a simple but realistic microcomputer-based design problem.

Our decision to write a book that develops the background and skills needed to design a microcomputer-based digital system and at the same time is suitable for a one-semester course without prerequisites forced us to select our topics carefully. The book does not provide a comprehensive coverage. Many topics are presented at a very introductory level; e.g., the discussion of semiconductor technologies is little more than a list of various types and their characteristics.

Our goals also forced us to neglect any consideration of high-level languages, which are treated in other required courses in most undergraduate engineering and science curricula. In addition, the use of assembly-language programming rather than high-level languages enhances the student's understanding of the system hardware and its interaction with software.

Our objectives require that the student acquire a detailed understanding of the system bus; the architecture and interfacing of various processor, memory, and input-output elements; the instruction set; and assembly-language programming. To develop this level of understanding in one semester we focus on one microprocessor family. This is not a serious limitation since if one processor family is understood well, others can be learned easily using the conceptual framework developed in learning the first. Focusing on one processor family in an introductory course also eliminates the potential for a superficial or confusing presentation inherent in survey courses. Finally, presenting adequate details on a specific processor allows the student to deal with meaningful problems in the laboratory.

We have tried to emphasize and illuminate concepts which have some long-term value. Rapid developments in semiconductor technology will continue to lead to new devices with improved performance characteristics. For the most part, these developments will be based on the same essential concepts as their predecessors. Although the detailed data handling, complexity, operating speed, and cost may all be different, the underlying concepts will not change very rapidly. Although the microcomputer has been a tremendous success and will have an extensive impact on electronic systems, its basic operation is not so different from the computer of a generation or so ago.

The first four chapters treat traditional concepts in digital systems. Chapter 1 provides background on information coding and on the arithmetic and logical operations in binary systems. Chapters 2 and 3 describe the basic combinational and sequential elements and define models and techniques used in designing and analyzing traditional digital systems. The behavior of several important network types, some of which are elements in a microcomputer, is also described in these chapters. Chapter 4 presents two design examples to introduce the process used in translating an imprecise verbal description into a precise technical model. Timing and synchronization problems also are introduced in this chapter.

The next six chapters focus on programmable systems. In Chap. 5 the 6800 microcomputer system is described. Machine language and the relationship between software and hardware also are introduced. Chapter 6 discusses the complete instruction set for the 6800 microcomputer system. Chapter 7 extends the language concepts introduced in the previous chapters to the more symbolic assembly language and includes the analysis of assembly-language programs in terms of their memory requirements, execution time, and data flow. Chapter 8 approaches programming from a formal, structured point of view. Basic structural units are defined and used in generating assembly-language programs for several typical problems. Chapter 9 defines the 6800 hardware elements and describes how they are interconnected to configure a microcomputer system. Chapter 10, paralleling Chap. 4, deals with the design of microcomputer-based digital systems. Basic methodology is illustrated using example problems.

This book contains a wide range of material. We recognize that treating such a breadth of material may result in a superficial treatment with no real substance or a collection of specific topics with no cohesiveness. To avoid this, we relied heavily on specific behavioral objectives in writing the book. These specific objectives are included in the introduction to each chapter.

This material has been used in a one-semester required junior level electrical engineering course. It also is suitable for a two-semester sequence focusing on traditional and programmed systems if a significant design project is included in each semester. For courses not emphasizing design, Chaps. 4 and 10 could be omitted. In any event, we recommend that courses using this book be supported by a laboratory in which students use traditional logic elements and a microcomputer.

We wish to acknowledge the part played by students who contributed to, and suffered through, the development of this book. Drs. Philip Bromberg, Nino Masnari, and Larry Monteith provided support for which we are grateful.

We would also like to thank Audrey Agnell, Emily Ausband, Kathleen Leander, and Sande Maxim, who translated numerous illegible handwritten pages into typed copy.

James W. Gault
Russell L. Pimmel

INFORMATION REPRESENTATION, INTERPRETATION, AND OPERATIONS

In this chapter we introduce methods for representing information that are compatible with digital systems. After finishing this chapter the reader should be able to:

1. Define the terms in Prob. 1-1
2. Encode and decode positive decimal integers using the binary-value code and the BCD code
3. Encode and decode positive and negative decimal integer values using the binary-value twos-complement code
4. Convert binary words into octal and hexadecimal representation and vice versa
5. Encode and decode alphanumeric characters using ASCII
6. Apply the relationship between the number of bits in a code and the number of distinct code words with and without fields
7. Perform binary addition, subtraction, and logic operations using fixed-length words and define when arithmetic overflow occurs

1-1 DIGITAL SYSTEMS AND BINARY CODE WORDS

Early electronic systems were *analog systems*, in which the input and output signals, referred to as *analog signals*, varied continuously over a certain range of values. A system *input-output model* depicts the input and output signal lines of a system. An electronic amplifier is an example of an analog system, and its input-output model showing a single input and single output line is shown in Fig. 1-1. Here the input signal might be a voltage ranging from -1 to $+1$ V and the output signal a proportional voltage ranging from -10 to $+10$ V.

Figure 1-1 Input-output system model.

Figure 1-2 Input-output model of digital system.

As electronic technology evolved, *digital systems* appeared and became more common. An input-output model for a digital system with several input lines $X_1, X_2, \ldots X_n$ and output lines $Z_1, Z_2, \ldots Z_m$ is shown in Fig. 1-2. One of the primary distinctions of the digital system is that the signals on each line, called *digital signals*, can assume only a finite set of discrete values. An example is an electronic logic gate, where the input and output voltages are defined as one of two relatively narrow ranges; e.g., a low range of 0.0 to 1.0 V and a high range of 4.0 to 5.0 V. Logic gates will be discussed in more detail later.

Digital signals that are defined for one of two ranges of values are called *binary signals* or *bits*. Since binary signals assume one of only two values, it is common to use the symbols 0 and 1 to represent these levels. Digital systems typically have multiple input and output lines, as shown in Fig. 1-2. When the values of a set of binary signals are considered together, they form a *binary word*.

Binary words are called *code words* because they represent a coding of specific information. For example, if the system depicted in Fig. 1-2 has four input lines, 0010 is a possible code word representing a particular input condition or event. Binary code words may contain any number of bits. Words of 8 bits are common and are typically called a *byte*.

We shall define a *code* as the one-to-one association of elements in one set, e.g., the characters in the alphabet, with unique binary code words. The process of converting a set of elements into their corresponding code words is referred to as *encoding*; the reverse process is called *decoding*.

The first digital systems were designed and constructed to perform a specific task. Their behavior was completely determined by the type and interconnection of the electronic elements in the system. The electronic elements are referred to as hardware, and alterations in the behavior of these systems require actual physical changes. We call such systems *conventional* or *traditional digital systems*.

In contrast, modern digital computers can perform a wide assortment of tasks since their behavior is specified both by hardware and by a specific sequence of code words entered into the computer. This sequence of code words is called a *program*. Programs are referred to as *software* to distinguish them from the physical components, i.e., the *hardware*. Systems whose behavior is defined by software are referred to as *programmable digital systems*.

The greater flexibility inherent in the programmed approach offers a big advantage over conventional digital systems. As an application evolves, design changes are implemented by changing the software, which generally is much simpler than changing the hardware. This flexibility allows a general system to be tailored for each consumer's specific needs.

Until recently, the size and cost of programmable digital systems prohibited their widespread use, but developments in the manufacture of semiconductor devices have practically eliminated size and cost constraints. As a result, extremely small, economical, general-purpose computers, called *microcomputers*, are available. Modern digital systems designed around a microcomputer are referred to as *microcomputer-based digital systems*.

1-2 CODES FOR NUMERICAL INFORMATION

Numerical computations represent one of the most common tasks performed by a microcomputer-based digital system. Since the microcomputer is a binary system, all the numerical manipulations must be accomplished with binary words. Thus, it is essential to introduce codes for numerical information which associate each element in a set of binary words with a specific decimal value. We shall describe three common codes for decimal integers: the unsigned binary-value code, the signed binary-value twos-complement code, and the binary-coded-decimal (BCD) code. These codes are suitable for integer values only (we shall not deal with noninteger values, although these codes can be extended to include them). The codes are based on the binary number system, which uses the symbols 0 and 1 and has a base value of 2. Thus the binary number 1101 is interpreted as

$$1 \times 2^3 + 1 \times 2^2 + 0 \times 2^1 + 1 \times 2^0 = 8 + 4 + 0 + 1 = 13$$

1-2-1 Unsigned Binary-Value Code

With the *unsigned binary-value code*, the coded decimal integer equals the numerical value obtained by interpreting the binary word as a binary number. Encoding and decoding is accomplished using either a look-up table or a systematic procedure for converting decimal into binary numbers and vice versa. In the encoding procedure we repeatedly divide the decimal value and the resulting quotients by 2 until the quotient is 0. The remainder of each division, which will be either 0 or 1, is noted. The binary code word is formed from these remainders, the first remainder corresponding to the least significant bit. Figure 1-3 illustrates this process by encoding the decimal integer values 6 and 150 as 8-bit binary words. The value 6 is divided by 2, producing a remainder of 0 and a quotient of 3; the second division yields a remainder of 1 and a quotient of 1; and the third, a remainder of 1 and a quotient of 0, indicating the end of the process. From the sequence of remainders, we see that the corresponding binary value is 110. Thus, the 8-bit code word for 6 is obtained by attaching five leading 0s to obtain 0000 0110.† The same procedure yields 1001 0110 for 150, as shown in the figure.

Decoding a binary word using the unsigned binary-value code is the translation from a binary number into a decimal number. Decoding is accomplished by multiplying each bit by the power of 2 corresponding to its position and then

---

† We adopt the policy of writing binary numbers in groups of 4 bits to improve readability.

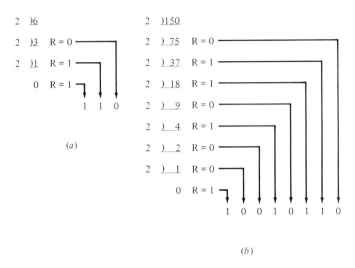

(a)

(b)

Figure 1-3 Converting decimal to binary number; 8-bit code is (a) 0000 0110 and (b) 1001 0110.

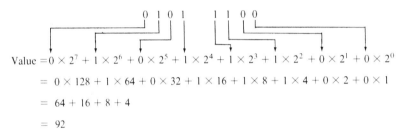

$$\text{Value} = 0 \times 2^7 + 1 \times 2^6 + 0 \times 2^5 + 1 \times 2^4 + 1 \times 2^3 + 1 \times 2^2 + 0 \times 2^1 + 0 \times 2^0$$

$$= 0 \times 128 + 1 \times 64 + 0 \times 32 + 1 \times 16 + 1 \times 8 + 1 \times 4 + 0 \times 2 + 0 \times 1$$

$$= 64 + 16 + 8 + 4$$

$$= 92$$

Figure 1-4 Converting binary into decimal numbers.

adding individual terms. Figure 1-4 illustrates decoding with the unsigned binary-value code using the word 0101 1100. The least significant bit translates into 0×2^0, the second is 0×2^1, the third is 1×2^2, and so on up to the most significant bit, which translates into 0×2^7. The equivalent decimal value is found by totaling these values to obtain 92.

1-2-2 Signed Binary-Value Codes

In general, codes to represent both positive and negative integer values use the most significant bit as a sign bit. With the most direct approach, this bit is a 0 for a positive value and a 1 for negative values; the magnitude of the number is represented by the remaining bits using the binary-value code. This approach is called the *binary-value sign-magnitude code*, and Table 1-1 shows an example using this code. Although the binary-value sign-magnitude code is the simplest to encode and decode, it requires complicated electronic hardware for simple arithmetic operations.

Table 1-1 Examples of positive and negative number codes

Value	Binary-value 8-bit code word		
	Sign-magnitude	Ones-complement	Twos-complement
+ 25	0001 1001	0001 1001	0001 1001
− 25	1001 1001	1110 0110	1110 0111

Another code for representing both positive and negative integer values is the *binary-value ones-complement code*. Positive numbers are represented using the binary-value code with the restriction that the most significant bit must be a 0. The code for a negative number is obtained by complementing each bit in the code word for the corresponding positive number. Each bit is *complemented* by changing 0 to 1 and vice versa. For example, with a 4-bit word, +4 is 0100 and − 4 is 1011. Since the most significant bit is always 0 for positive numbers, it will always be 1 for negative numbers; thus the most significant bit can still be considered a sign bit. Table 1-1 contains an additional example using this code. Although the electronic implementation for arithmetic operations with the binary-value ones-complement code is simpler than that for the binary-value sign-magnitude code, other inconveniences inhibit its use.

The most common code for representing both positive and negative integer values is the *binary-value twos-complement* code. It is similar to the binary-value ones-complement code except that the code word for a negative number is incremented by 1. For example, the 4-bit code word for −4 is 1100, which is obtained by first complementing the code word for +4, 0100, to obtain the word 1011 and then adding 1. This operation is called *negation*. Table 1-1 contains an additional example of the use of this code. As in the other two codes, the most significant bit distinguishes positive and negative numbers. With this code, arithmetic operations are comparatively easy to implement in hardware.

1-2-3 BCD Code

The third method of interpreting binary words as integer values subdivides the code word into subsegments called *fields*. This code uses a separate 4-bit field for each decimal digit, a distinct code word being defined for each decimal symbol. These symbols are coded using the binary-value code; i.e., the symbols $0, 1, 2, \ldots, 8$, and 9 are represented by the code words $0000, 0001, 0010, \ldots, 1000$, and 1001, respectively. This scheme is referred to as the *binary-coded-decimal (BCD) code*. As an example, the BCD code word for the decimal value 27 is 0010 0111. With the BCD code, the length of the binary word must be exact multiples of 4. Since 16 distinct code words can be defined with 4 bits, and since only 10 are required for the decimal symbols, 6 code words are undefined and cannot be interpreted. For example, the 4-bit word 1100 cannot be interpreted using the BCD code.

Example 1-1 Represent the decimal values $+23$ and -23 with an 8-bit code word using (a) the unsigned binary-value code, (b) the signed binary-value twos-complement code, and (c) the BCD code.

SOLUTION (a) Using the unsigned binary-value code, the code word for $+23$ is 0001 0111, obtained by the division at the right. Negative numbers cannot be represented by this code.

$$2\overline{)23}$$
$$2\overline{)11}\ 1$$
$$2\underline{)\ 5}\ 1$$
$$2\underline{)\ 2}\ 1$$
$$2\underline{)\ 1}\ 0$$
$$0\ 1$$

(b) Using the signed binary-value code, the code word for $+23$ is 0001 0111 the same as in (a). The code word for -23 is 1110 1001, obtained by complementing the code word for $+23$ and then adding 1, as shown at the right.

(c) Using the BCD code, the code word for $+23$ is 0010 0011. Negative numbers cannot be represented by this code using 8 bits.

$$\begin{array}{r} 0001\ 0111 \\ \hline 1110\ 1000 \\ 1 \\ \hline 1110\ 1001 \end{array}$$

Example 1-2 Find the greatest positive and negative numbers that can be represented in an 8-bit word using the binary-value twos-complement code.

SOLUTION The greatest positive number is 0111 1111, which represents $+127$. The greatest negative number is 1000 0000, which represents -128. This latter result is somewhat confusing since the negation of 1000 0000 produces the same code. However, the code must be interpreted, and the most consistent interpretation is -128 because the most significant bit is 1.

1-3 OCTAL AND HEXADECIMAL REPRESENTATION OF BINARY WORDS

Because it is inconvenient to deal with 8-bit, 16-bit, or larger code words on a regular basis, more compact representations are frequently used. The most common representations use the octal (base 8) and hexadecimal (base 16) number systems. In the *octal number system*, there are eight symbols $(0, 1, \ldots, 6,$ and 7) so that each symbol requires 3 bits for encoding. With these bits there are 8 patterns, and, unlike the BCD code, each is associated with an octal symbol. Converting a binary word into an octal representation is accomplished by converting 3 bits at a time starting at the right. For example, 1110 0111 is considered as 11 (the leading 0 may be added to obtain 011), 100, and 111. These translate into 3, 4, and 7 octal, respectively; thus the entire binary word is represented as 347 in octal. Conversely, 35 in octal translates into 011 and 101, which, when written as an 8-bit code word, is 0001 1101.

In the *hexadecimal number system*, there are 16 symbols $(0, 1, \ldots, 8, 9,$ A, ..., F), where the symbols A to F are single characters representing the decimal values 10 to 15, respectively. Binary representation of these symbols requires 4 bits, and all 16 patterns are associated with a hexadecimal symbol. The method for converting from a binary word into a hexadecimal representation and vice versa is analogous to that used for the octal representation except that individual hexadecimal symbols require 4 bits instead of 3 for encoding. Using the same example as above, 1110 0111 is considered as 1110 and 0111, or E7 in hexadecimal. Similarly, 35 in hexadecimal translates into 0011 0101 as an 8-bit code word. It is important to restate that for our purposes, octal and hexadecimal numbers will be used as a compact representation of binary code words regardless of whether they represent numerical information or not.

Example 1-3 An 8-bit binary code word is represented by C3 in hexadecimal notation. Decode this value using (a) the unsigned binary-value code, (b) the signed binary-value twos-complement code, and (c) the BCD code.

SOLUTION (a) In binary, C3 is 1100 0011. This binary value translates into $2^7 + 2^6 + 2^1 + 2^0 = 195$. Thus, with the unsigned binary-value code the decoded decimal value is 195.

(b) Using the signed binary-value twos-complement code, 1100 0011 represents a negative number; thus it must be negated to obtain its magnitude. This negation produces 0011 1101, which translates into $2^5 + 2^4 + 2^3 + 2^2 + 2^0 = 61$. Thus, the decoded decimal value is -61.

(c) Using the BCD code, 1100 0011 represents a two-digit decimal number. The first is an undefined code, and the second represents the symbol 3. So the code is uninterpretable.

1-4 CODES FOR NONNUMERIC INFORMATION

In addition to numerical data, there are many other types of information that must be coded as binary words for processing in digital systems. Two special problems are coding alphanumeric characters and various operations in programmable systems.

In contrast to the codes discussed in the previous section, there usually is no systematic relationship between the binary code words and the nonnumeric information. These codes represent an orderly but arbitrary assignment of a specific code word to each member in the set being encoded. The development of a code requires listing all members in the set to be encoded and the assignment of a distinct code word to each. With an N-bit binary word, there are 2^N distinct code words. For example, with a 6-bit word, there are $2^6 = 64$ distinct code words. From this information, we can define the relationship between the number of items being encoded I and the number of bits in the binary word N. We see that 2^N must be greater or equal to I. Thus N must equal the next largest integer above the value defined by $\log_2 I$. For example, 7 bits are required to code 100 items since $\log_2 100 \approx 6.64$ and the next largest integer is 7.

In many codes, certain features of the information to be encoded are treated separately in a subsegment of the binary word. As we indicated when discussing the BCD code, these subsegments are referred to as *fields*. The codes for each field are assigned independently, the number of bits in each being defined by the number of distinct ways the corresponding feature can appear. The use of fields facilitates encoding and decoding but generally increases the number of required bits.

To illustrate the development of a binary code and the advantages of using fields, let us consider representing the four colored stripes used in defining a resistance value and its tolerance. The first three stripes may be any of ten colors, and the fourth may be one of three. We first consider a code defined without the use of fields. The total number of color sequences to be represented is computed using the algebra of combinations. In this case, the number of combinations equals the product formed by multiplying the number of ways each stripe can appear; i.e., the first, second, and third stripes can occur in 10 different ways and the fourth in 3 ways, so the number of combinations in $(10)(10)(10)(3) = 3000$. Since $\log_2 3000 \approx 11.55$, 12 bits must be used in the code. The number of bits in the code also can be defined by noting that $2^{11} = 2048$ and $2^{12} = 4096$; thus 12 bits must be used to encode the 3000 combinations. To define this code we must enumerate all 3000 combinations and assign a specific binary code word to each. Every time we need to encode a color sequence or decode a binary code word to find the corresponding color sequence, the entire list must be searched.

As an alternative, we consider a code definition where each stripe is encoded separately in its own field. The first three fields, corresponding to the first three stripes, require 4 bits each, since there are ten colors which must be encoded. The

Table 1-2 Binary code for colored stripes on resistors

	Four fields of code word			
Stripe	First	Second	Third	Fourth
No. of bits	4	4	4	2

First, second, and third stripe				Fourth stripe	
Color	Code	Color	Code	Color	Code
Black	0000	Green	0101	Silver	00
Brown	0001	Blue	0110	Gold	01
Red	0010	Violet	0111	Clear	10
Orange	0011	Gray	1000		
Yellow	0100	White	1001		

For example, the pattern red-black-yellow-silver is coded as 0010 0000 0100 00.

fourth field will require 2 bits to encode the three possible colors used in the fourth stripe. Thus, the entire code word will be 14 bits (4 + 4 + 4 + 2). Code specification consists of defining binary patterns for each of the ten colors used in the first three stripes and for the three colors used in the fourth. Encoding and decoding is performed field by field and requires us to search a list of at most 10 elements. Thus, an advantage of a code defined with fields is the resulting simplification in the encoding and decoding process; the disadvantage is the need for more bits. Table 1-2 describes one code with fields for this example.

Since many digital systems process text material, codes for alphanumeric characters have been developed. One of the most common alphanumeric codes is the ASCII (American Standard Code for Information Interchange) code. The ASCII code includes the upper- and lowercase letters in the alphabet, the decimal digit symbols, the punctuation symbols, and carriage controls used in defining text. The last group includes the space (SP), carriage return (CR), line feed (LF), and so on. The 7-bit ASCII code is shown in Table 1-3. Frequently, 8 bits are used, the eighth bit set either to 0 or 1.

Example 1-4 Define the ASCII code word for each character and carriage control required to encode the message "Type (Y/N):" on one line followed by the symbol # on the next line.

SOLUTION The message requires 14 code words for the following characters and carriage controls: T, y, p, e, SP, (, Y, /, N,), :, CR, LF, and #. The corresponding code words are 54, 79, 70, 65, 20, 28, 59, 2F, 4E, 29, 3A, 0D, 0A, and 23.

Table 1-3 ASCII code for alphanumeric data

		Bits 6–4							
		0	1	2	3	4	5	6	7
	0	NUL	DLE	SP	0	@	P		p
	1	SOH	DC1	!	1	A	Q	a	q
	2	STX	DC2	"	2	B	R	b	r
	3	ETX	DC3	#	3	C	S	c	s
	4	EOT	DC4	$	4	D	T	d	t
	5	ENQ	NAK	%	5	E	U	e	u
Bits 3–0	6	ACK	SYN	&	6	F	V	f	v
	7	BEL	ETB	'	7	G	W	g	w
	8	BS	CAN	(	8	H	X	h	x
	9	HT	EM	)	9	I	Y	i	y
	A	LF	SUB	*	:	J	Z	j	z
	B	VT	ESC	+	;	K	[	k	{
	C	FF	FS	,	<	L	\	l	|
	D	CR	GS	-	=	M	]	m	}
	E	SO	RS	.	>	N	↑	n	≈
	F	SI	μs	/	?	O	←	o	DEL

Example 1-5 Five judges at a gymnastic meet score an event with an integer value from 1 to 10. How many bits are needed to encode their scores using (*a*) a code without fields and (*b*) a code where a field is assigned for each judge's vote?

SOLUTION (*a*) There are 10^5 different voting patterns. Since $\log_2 10^5 \approx 16.6$, 17 bits must be used in the code.

(*b*) In each field, 10 distinct values must be coded. Since $\log_2 10 \approx 3.32$, 4 bits must be used in each field. Thus a total of 20 bits must be used for the five fields.

Before leaving the subject of codes we should discuss two distinct ways code words are transferred from one system to another. With *parallel transmission* each bit in the code word is assigned to a wire. Thus eight wires are required to transfer an 8-bit code word using parallel transmission, as shown in Fig. 1-5*a*. Since all bits are valid during the same time interval, an entire code word is transferred during one time interval.

With *serial transmission* one wire is used to transfer all bits of the code word, as shown in Fig. 1-5*b*. Individual bits are distinguished by assigning the wire to each bit during successive time intervals. Figure 1-5*c* shows one approach in which bit 0 is assigned to the first time interval, bit 1 to the second, and so on. In this scheme it requires eight time intervals to transfer one 8-bit code word. Frequently, with serial transmission several bits are used at the beginning and end of a code word to help synchronize the transfer, making more time intervals necessary.

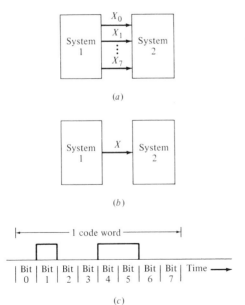

(*a*)

(*b*)

(*c*)

Figure 1-5 (*a*) Parallel transmission, (*b*) serial transmission, and (*c*) serial transmission of 0011 0010.

1-5 BINARY LOGIC AND ARITHMETIC OPERATIONS

In this section, we introduce some binary logic and arithmetic operations that can be performed in a digital system. In essence, two binary code words of specified length generate an output code word representing the result of some arithmetic or logic operation on the inputs. Possible operations include binary addition and subtraction and various logic operations, like NOT, AND, OR, EXCLUSIVE OR, NOR and NAND.

The simplest logic generation is the *logical not*. It is an operation performed on one variable, and the result is the complement of the input; i.e., if the input is 0, the result is 1 and vice versa. The NOT operation is symbolized by the overbar, for example, $\overline{A}$.

In defining logic operations involving two or more input variables, we use *truth tables* to describe the result for all possible input patterns. In generating a truth table, all input patterns are enumerated, usually with a binary counting scheme. With N inputs there are 2^N patterns, each producing a row in the truth table.

The truth tables for common logic operations on two variables are shown in Table 1-4. The two input variables are A and B. The output $A \cdot B$ represents a logical AND for which the result is 1 if, and only if, both A and B are 1. Similarly, the output $A + B$ is a logical OR, in which the result is 1 if A or B is 1. The symbol $\oplus$ defines the EXCLUSIVE OR (EOR) operation, in which the result is 1 if either input is exclusively 1. The overbar used in the output $\overline{A \cdot B}$ indicates that the result is the complement, or logical NOT, of $A \cdot B$. Similarly $\overline{A + B}$ is the complement of $A + B$. These operations are referred to as the logical NAND and NOR ("NOT AND" and "NOT OR") operations.

When these logic operations are applied to binary words, the results are determined bit by bit. For example, the logical AND of the 4-bit words 0110 and 1010 is shown in Fig. 1-6a. In the least significant position $0 \cdot 0$ is 0, in the next position $1 \cdot 1$ is 1, and in the next two positions $1 \cdot 0$ and $0 \cdot 1$ are both 0. Thus the result is 0010. Figure 1-6b shows the logical OR operation on the same two words. Again starting in the least significant position, $0 + 0$ is 0, in the next position $1 + 1$ is 1, and in the last two positions $1 + 0$ and $0 + 1$ are both 1. Thus the result is 1110.

Table 1-4 Truth tables describing logic operations

A	B	AND $A \cdot B$	OR $A + B$	EOR $A \oplus B$	NAND $\overline{A \cdot B}$	NOR $\overline{A + B}$
0	0	0	0	0	1	1
0	1	0	1	1	1	0
1	0	0	1	1	1	0
1	1	1	1	0	0	0

```
0 1 1 0              0 1 1 0
1 0 1 0              1 0 1 0
———————              ———————
0 0 1 0              1 1 1 0
```

(*a*)   (*b*)   **Figure 1-6** Examples of (*a*) logical AND and (*b*) OR operations.

Truth tables for binary addition and subtraction for a single pair of bits are shown in Table 1-5. These tables account for both input and output carries and borrows since we eventually shall apply this table when adding and subtracting binary words where carries and borrows propagate from one position to the next.

Figure 1-7 describes binary addition in a more familiar form. Each possible combination of the 2 bits being added, that is, 00, 01, 10, and 11, is shown with input carries of both 0 and 1. The input carry is shown propagating in from the less significant adjacent position, while the output carry propagates to the more significant adjacent position. The result and output carry are defined by adding the input carry with the 2 bits. Since the result must be 0 or 1, an output carry results if two or more 1s are added.

Figure 1-8 describes binary subtraction in this more familiar form. Again each possible combination of the 2 bits being subtracted is shown with input borrows of both 0 and 1. The input borrow is shown propagating in from the less significant adjacent position, while the output borrow propagates to the more significant adjacent position. In subtraction both the lower bit (the subtrahend) and the input borrow are subtracted from the upper bit (the minuend). Thus if the sum of the lower bit and the input borrow exceeds the upper bit, a borrow is propagated to the next more significant position. This borrowing increases the upper bit by 2 so that the subtraction can be performed.

The subtraction in the upper right-hand corner of Fig. 1-8 shows 1 minus 1 with the input borrow equal to 0. This means that we are subtracting 1 (the lower

Table 1-5 Truth tables for binary addition and subtraction

		A plus B					A minus B		
A	B	Input carry	Result	Output carry	A	B	Input borrow	Result	Output borrow
0	0	0	0	0	0	0	0	0	0
0	0	1	1	0	0	0	1	1	1
0	1	0	1	0	0	1	0	1	1
0	1	1	0	1	0	1	1	0	1
1	0	0	1	0	1	0	0	1	0
1	0	1	0	1	1	0	1	0	0
1	1	0	0	1	1	1	0	0	0
1	1	1	1	1	1	1	1	1	1

Carry Carry
out   in

$0 \cap 0 \cap 0$	$0 \cap 1 \cap 0$	$0 \cap 0 \cap 0$	$1 \cap 1 \cap 0$
0	0	1	1
0	1	1	0

$0 \cap 0 \cap 1$	$1 \cap 1 \cap 1$	$1 \cap 0 \cap 1$	$1 \cap 1 \cap 1$
0	0	1	1
1	0	0	1

Figure 1-7 Addition of a single pair of bits with carry.

bit plus the input borrow) from 1 (the upper bit). Thus the output borrow equals 0, and the result is 0. The subtraction in the lower right-hand corner shows 1 minus 1 with the input borrow equal to 1. This means that we are subtracting 2 (the lower bit plus the input borrow) from 1 (the upper bit). Thus the output borrow equals 1, the effective subtraction is 2 (the lower bit plus the input borrow) from 3 (the upper bit plus the 2 from the output borrow), and the result is 1. The subtraction just to the left of this one shows 0 minus 1 with the input borrow equal to 1. This means that we are subtracting 2 from 0, so that the output borrow equals 1; since the effective subtraction is 2 from 2, the result is 0. The reader is urged to work through the other combinations.

When these arithmetic operations are performed on binary words, the result is computed bit by bit, starting with the least significant bit on the far right. Resulting carries or borrows propagate to the next more significant bit. As an example, consider the addition of the two 4 bit words shown in Fig. 1-9. The input carry for the least significant bit is assumed to be 0. When these bits are added, a result of 1 with an output carry of 0 is obtained. This output carry is propagated to the next position, as shown in the small rectangle at the top. When the next two bits are added with their input carry, the result is 0 and the output carry is 1. The third bits are added with their input carry, and the result is 1 with an output carry of 1. Finally, the fourth bits and their input carry are added to obtain a result of 1 and an output carry of 0. It is common to indicate the output carry from the most significant bit.

The subtraction example shown in Fig. 1-9 is analogous to the addition example. Starting with the least significant bit, the input borrow is assumed to be 0, and the result is 1 with an output borrow of 0. Again this output borrow propagates to the next position, as indicated at the top in the small rectangle. For the second bit, the subtraction of 1 from 0 with an input borrow of 0 produces a

Borrow Borrow
out   in

$0 \cap 0 \cap 0$	$0 \cap 1 \cap 0$	$1 \cap 0 \cap 0$	$0 \cap 1 \cap 0$
0	0	1	1
0	1	1	0

$1 \cap 0 \cap 1$	$0 \cap 1 \cap 1$	$1 \cap 0 \cap 1$	$1 \cap 1 \cap 1$
0	0	1	1
1	0	0	1

Figure 1-8 Subtraction of a single pair of bits with borrow.

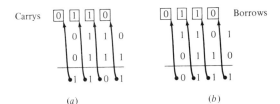

Figure 1-9 (*a*) Addition and (*b*) subtraction of two 4-bit words.

result of 1 with an output borrow of 1. For the third bit, the subtraction is 1 minus 1 with an input borrow of 1, yielding a result of 1 and an output borrow of 1. For the fourth bit, the result is a 0 with an output borrow of 0. It is common to indicate the output borrow from the most significant bit.

Since arithmetic operations almost always involve positive and negative values, the signed binary-value twos-complement code generally is used. When the result of binary addition or subtraction must be expressed in a word containing the same number of bits as the two input words, it is possible for the result to exceed the largest positive or negative value that can be represented with that number of bits (see Example 1-2). Consider the case where 0100 0001 is added to itself, to obtain 1000 0010. The two input words represent positive values, but the resulting word represents a negative value. This occurred because this addition corresponds to adding the decimal value 65 to itself; the result is 130, a value that exceeds the range of the 8-bit code. When the result of an arithmetic operation exceeds the maximum positive or negative value that can be represented by the specified number of bits, an arithmetic *overflow* has occurred.

Although an arithmetic overflow can be detected by decoding the two input words and the result, it is more convenient to examine the sign bit of the two input words and the result word for consistency. This is possible since an arithmetic overflow always produces a result with the incorrect sign.

With addition, an arithmetic overflow occurs when the two input words represent positive values and the result represents a negative value, or vice versa. These two situations are illustrated in Fig. 1-10. With subtraction there also are two situations that indicate an arithmetic overflow, as shown in Fig. 1-10. The first is a result representing a negative value that was obtained by subtracting a

Addition overflow		
Positive value	Negative value	
Positive value	Negative value	
Negative value	Positive value	

Subtraction overflow		
Positive value	Negative value	
Negative value	Positive value	
Negative value	Positive value	

Figure 1-10 Overflow conditions.

word representing a negative value from a word representing a positive value. The second is a result representing a positive value that was obtained by subtracting a word representing a positive value from one representing a negative value.

Example 1-6 For the two 8-bit words $X = 23$ and $Y = 8D$, find (a) X plus Y, (b) X minus Y, (c) Y minus X, (d) $X \cdot Y$, (e) $X + Y$, and (f) $X \oplus Y$. Express the 8-bit result as a hexadecimal value. Indicate whether an arithmetic overflow occurs.

SOLUTION (a) 0 0001 111 carry
              0010 0011
              1000 1101
              $\overline{1011\ 0000}$ → B0

(b) 1 0011 100   borrow
      0010 0011
      1000 1101
      $\overline{1001\ 0110}$ → 96†

(c) 0 1100 010 borrow
      1000 1101
      0010 0011
      $\overline{0110\ 1010}$ → 6A†

(d) 0010 0011
      1000 1101
      $\overline{0000\ 0001}$ → 01

(e) 0010 0011
    1000 1101
    $\overline{1010\ 1111}$ → AF

(f) 0010 0011
    1000 1101
    $\overline{1010\ 1110}$ → AE

† Overflow occurs.

1-6 CONCLUSION

In this chapter we have introduced information coding and binary operations. The presentation is introductory but sufficient to support our study in subsequent chapters. We have omitted many topics treated in more advanced texts, such as representation of noninteger numerical values, error-detecting codes, alternate standard alphanumeric character codes, and binary arithmetic operations with codes representing noninteger numerical values.

PROBLEMS

1-1 Define each of the following terms:

analog system	bit
analog signal	binary word
input-output model	byte
digital system	code word
digital signal	code
binary signal	encode

decode
traditional digital system
conventional digital system
program
software
programmable digital system
microcomputer-based digital system
unsigned binary-value code
signed binary-value code
signed binary-value twos-complement code
binary-coded decimal (BCD)
complement
negate

octal notation
hexadecimal notation
code field
ASCII
truth table
logical AND
logical OR
logical NOT
logical EOR
logical NAND
logical NOR
arithmetic overflow

1-2 Represent the following decimal values as 8-bit words using the unsigned binary value code:

(a) 37, 150, 325, -40, -192 (b) 43, 130, -22, -90, -150
(c) 0, 119, 76, -30, 130   (d) 28, 150, -29, -151, 0
(e) 11, 99, -99, 190, -190 (f) 62, -62, 128, -128, 0
(g) 48, -48, 127, -127, 672

1-3 Repeat Prob. 1-2 using:
(1) a 12-bit unsigned binary-value code
(2) An 8-bit signed binary-value twos-complement code
(3) A 12-bit signed binary-value twos-complement code
(4) A 16-bit signed binary-value twos-complement code
(5) An 8-bit BCD code
(6) A 12-bit BCD code
(7) A 16-bit BCD code

1-4 Interpret these binary words as decimal values using an unsigned binary value code:
(a) 0000 1001; 1000 0001; 0111 0001
(b) 0000 0000; 0101 0011; 1111 0000
(c) 1111 1111; 0111 1001; 1010 1010
(d) 0100 1101; 1100 0011; 0000 1111

1-5 Repeat Prob. 1-4 using (1) a signed binary-value twos-complement code and (2) a BCD code.

1-6 Represent the binary words in Prob. 1-4 using (1) hexadecimal and (2) octal notation.

1-7 Interpret these hexadecimal representations using an unsigned binary value code:
(a) 3F, C5, 78   (b) BE, F2, 30   (c) D2, AA, 48

1-8 Repeat Prob. 1-7 using (1) a signed binary-value twos-complement code and (2) a BCD code.

1-9 Represent the decimal values 29 and -86, using:
(a) The 8-bit unsigned binary-value code
(b) The 8-bit signed binary-value twos-complement code
(c) The BCD code
(d) The ASCII code
Compare these methods of representation for ease of conversion and number of bits required.

1-10 Find the greatest positive and negative decimal quantities that can be represented with a 16-bit binary word using (a) the unsigned binary-value code and (b) the signed binary-value twos-complement code.

1-11 Repeat Prob. 1-10 for a 12-bit word.

1-12 Four judges can vote either yes or no on an issue.
(a) Find the minimum number of bits necessary to encode the vote.
(b) Repeat for the situation where each judge can vote yes, no, or abstain.
(c) Repeat for the situation where the judge can vote with an integer value from 1 to 10.

1-13 Repeat Prob. 1-12 for the case where each judge is assigned a separate field in the code word.

1-14 Develop a binary coding scheme which will allow any of the possible single-plane tick tack toe board configurations to be described. What is the smallest number of bits that can be used? Define an approach that uses separate fields for each square. Discuss the trade-offs between them.

1-15 Define a binary information organization which will allow bicycles on campus to be cataloged. The information should include color, a six-digit frame serial number, a three-letter manufacturer's code, and the owner's social security number.

1-16 Determine a binary scheme using fields which will allow any poker hand to be defined. Determine the minimum number of bits required.

1-17 A black-and-white picture is to be encoded for processing in a digital system. The picture is divided up into small cells, and the average brightness of each cell is characterized by a gray level.

(*a*) If a 5 × 5 grid with 8 gray scales is used, how many bits are required if each cell is assigned a separate field?

(*b*) If the required resolution is to be a 5 × 5 grid, how many gray levels can be accommodated with a 100-bit code word without using fields?

(*c*) Repeat part (*b*) for the case where a field is assigned to each cell.

1-18 How many bits are required in a code for the 26 uppercase characters in the alphabet? How many are required in a code for the 26 upper- and lowercase characters in the alphabet? How many are required in a code for the 26 upper- and lowercase characters in the alphabet, the 10 integer values, and 15 punctuation marks?

1-19 Encode the message, "Now is the time for conscientious study" using the ASCII code and 1 byte for each character.

1-20 Decode the following hexadecimal characters if each pair of values is taken as a single ASCII character:

$$436F6E67726174756C6174696F6E732021$$

1-21 Encode the following 3-line message using the ASCII code:

Line 1,
Line 2,
Line 3!

1-22 Perform the AND, OR, EOR, NAND, and NOR operation using the following hexadecimal numbers. Express the result as a two-digit hexadecimal number:

(*a*) 23 and 81   (*b*) A7 and 55   (*c*) 37 and 95
(*d*) B3 and 77   (*e*) 00 and FF   (*f*) 01 and 10
(*g*) 80 and 80

1-23 For the binary words listed perform the AND, OR, EOR, NAND, and NOR operations:

(*a*) 0010 0110   (*b*) 0001 1101   (*c*) 1111 0000
    0011 0101   0010 1011   0110 1100
(*d*) 1100 1110   (*e*) 0110 0110   (*f*) 0111 0111
    1001 0111   0001 0111   0011 0000

1-24 Repeat Prob. 1-22 using the addition and subtraction (the first minus the second) operations. Indicate when an overflow occurs.

1-25 Repeat Prob. 1-23 using the addition and subtraction operations. Indicate when an overflow occurs.

1-26 For the two 8-bit words $X = 96$ and $Y = 23$, find:

(*a*) X plus Y (*b*) X minus Y (*c*) Y minus X
(*d*) $X \cdot Y$ (*e*) $X + Y$ (*f*) $X \oplus Y$

Indicate whether an arithmetic overflow occurs.

1-27 For the three 8-bit words $X = $ A3, $Y = 05$, and $Z = 17$ find:

(*a*) X plus Y (*b*) X minus Y (*c*) Y minus X
(*d*) X plus Z (*e*) Y plus Z (*f*) X minus Z
(*g*) Z minus X (*h*) Y minus Z (*i*) Z minus Y

Indicate whether an arithmetic overflow occurs.

1-28 Perform the operations of complementation and negation using the following hexadecimal numbers and express the result in hexadecimal:

(a) F3, C2, 37   (b) 2D, 7B, A8   (c) EF, B7, 6D

REFERENCES

Flores, I.: "The Logic of Computer Arithmetic," Prentice-Hall, Englewood Cliffs, N.J., 1963.
Hwang, K.: "Computer Arithmetic: Principles, Architecture, and Design," Wiley, New York, 1979.
Peterson, W. W.: "Error-Correcting Codes," MIT Press, Cambridge, Mass., 1961.
Rhyne, V. T.: "Fundamentals of Digital Systems Design," Prentice-Hall, Englewood Cliffs, N.J., 1973.
Richards, R. K.: "Arithmetic Operations in Digital Computers," Van Nostrand, Princeton, N.J., 1955.

TWO

COMBINATIONAL NETWORKS

Combinational networks are digital networks whose output depends only on the current input. Consequently, combinational networks do not have memory. After finishing this chapter the reader should be able to:

1. Define the terms in Prob. 2-1
2. Obtain the normal and minimum sum-of-products equation from a truth table
3. Convert any logic equation into normal form and define the corresponding truth table
4. Obtain a logic equation for any logic diagram
5. For any sum-of-products equation draw an efficient logic diagram using (*a*) AND, OR, and NOT gates; (*b*) NAND gates; or (*c*) NOR gates
6. Use input-output models and abbreviated voltage tables to define the behavior of representative code converters, multiplexers, demultiplexers, comparators, full adders, and arithmetic logic units.

2-1 LOGIC GATES AND DIGITAL CIRCUITS

The logic gate is the fundamental element used in constructing models of combinational networks. We shall use the term *logic gate* or simply *gate* to describe a combinational logical element whose inputs and outputs are binary variables defined by the logic values 0 or 1. Actual electronic elements used to implement the operation represented by the logic gate will be referred to as *digital circuits* or simply circuits. The input and output signals of digital circuits are defined by a low or a high voltage level. Distinguishing between gates and circuits

A	B	C	F
0	0	0	0
0	0	1	0
0	1	0	0
0	1	1	0
1	0	0	0
1	0	1	0
1	1	0	0
1	1	1	1

Figure 2-1 Truth table for three-input AND gate.

is important when voltage assumptions are discussed later. A *logic diagram* defines the interconnection of gates to form a logic network, while a *circuit diagram* defines the interconnection of digital circuits. The circuit diagram contains additional detailed information defining package types and pin-to-pin connections not available in logic diagrams.

The behavior of a logic gate is described by a truth table listing the value of the output for all combinations of input values. Truth tables for the two-input AND, OR, EOR, NAND, and NOR gates were defined in Table 1-4. The extension to gates with three, or four, or more inputs is straightforward. For example, Fig. 2-1 contains the truth table for a three-input AND gate. The NOT gate, which was not included in Table 1-4, is a single-input single-output gate in which the output is the complement of the input; i.e., a 0 at the input produces a 1 at the output and vice versa. Symbols used to represent these six common gates in logic diagrams are shown in Fig. 2-2; the algebraic symbols used to define these operations are also listed.

Digital circuits are the electronic elements used to construct digital networks. Their inputs and outputs are electric signals characterized by voltage levels. Most digital circuits are binary, with two stable voltage levels, H (the higher) and L (the lower). The specific voltage ranges used to define H and L depend on the semiconductor technology used in manufacturing the device. Usually H and L are defined by a range of values with a sizable gap separating them. For example, with transistor-transistor logic (TTL), H is defined by the range 2.0 to 5.0 V, while L is defined by the range 0 to 0.8 V.

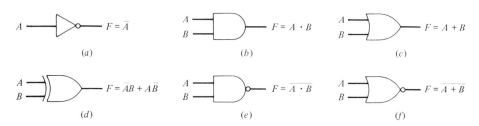

(a) (b) (c)

(d) (e) (f)

Figure 2-2 Six common logic gates: (a) NOT, (b) AND, (c) OR, (d) EOR, (e) NAND, (f) NOR.

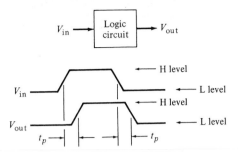

Figure 2-3 Logic-circuit timing diagram.

Because of physical limitations, the transition from one voltage level to the other requires a finite amount of time. This *propagation delay* is illustrated in Fig. 2-3. It is a characteristic of the device and limits the maximum rate at which the circuit can process information. Its magnitude depends on the semiconductor technology used in manufacturing the device, and typical values are given in Table 2-1.

Another important characteristic of a digital circuit is the power dissipation. This defines the size of the power supply or battery required by a system and the amount of heat that must be removed to keep the system at acceptable operating temperatures. Typical values for power dissipated by an individual gate are given in Table 2-1.

The behavior of electronic circuits is described by *voltage tables* defining the output voltage level for all combinations of voltage levels on the inputs. These tables are analogous to truth tables used in defining logic gates. Figure 2-4 shows the voltage tables for the two-input NAND and NOR circuits.

In using electronic circuits to implement logic gates, the voltage levels H and L must be associated with the logical values 0 and 1. There are two possible associations. The *positive-logic assumption* associates H with logic value 1 and L with logic value 0; the *negative-logic assumption* makes the opposite association.

In a complicated digital system, different voltage assumptions may be used in various subsystems. It is therefore often necessary to convert a signal based on one logic assumption into one based on the opposite. This is accomplished by

Table 2-1 Integrated-circuit (IC) families, speed, and power characteristics

Semiconductor technology	Gate propagation time, ns	Gate power dissipation, mW
Transistor-transistor logic (TTL)	10	20
Metal-oxide semiconductors:		
Positive (PMOS)	75	2.0
Negative (NMOS)	25	1.0
Complementary (CMOS)	30	0.001
Integrated injection		
logic (I^2L)	40	1.0

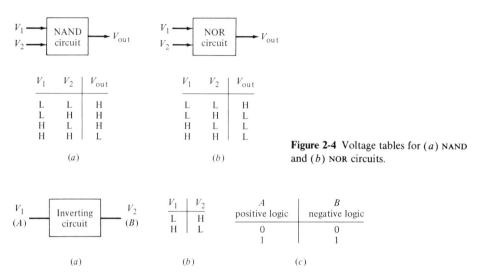

V_1	V_2	V_{out}
L	L	H
L	H	H
H	L	H
H	H	L

(a)

V_1	V_2	V_{out}
L	L	H
L	H	L
H	L	L
H	H	L

(b)

Figure 2-4 Voltage tables for (a) NAND and (b) NOR circuits.

V_1	V_2
L	H
H	L

(b)

A positive logic	B negative logic
0	0
1	1

(a)   (b)   (c)

Figure 2-5 Converting a positive- into a negative-logic assumption: (a) circuit diagram, (b) voltage table, and (c) truth table.

passing the signal through an inverting circuit, like a NOT, NAND, or NOR circuit. When a circuit is used in this way, it is interpreted as a logic-assumption converter and not as a logical NOT. Figure 2-5 illustrates the transition from a positive- to a negative-logic assumption. Electric signals V_1 and V_2 are associated with the logic variables A and B, respectively. Although the voltages V_1 and V_2 are complementary, the two logic variables A and B are equal because of the opposite logic assumptions on A and B.

2-2 LOGIC EQUATIONS AND MINIMIZATION

In the previous section we discussed the behavior of several simple logic gates; we now describe several models for representing the behavior of logic networks formed by interconnecting these gates. In general, logic networks have several input and output variables. A truth table can be used to define the value of each output for each input combination. An example is shown in Fig. 2-6, where X_1, X_2, and X_3 are input variables and Z_1 and Z_2 are output variables.

2-2-1 Logic Equations

Although the truth-table representation is adequate for networks with a limited number of variables, it becomes too cumbersome when there are a large number of variables. *Logic equations*, which describe the behavior algebraically using the AND, OR, and NOT operators, provide useful descriptions of behavior of complex networks. Representing logic behavior with algebraic equations also allows us to

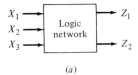

(a)

X_1	X_2	X_3	Z_1	Z_2
0	0	0	0	0
0	0	1	1	0
0	1	0	1	0
0	1	1	0	1
1	0	0	1	0
1	0	1	0	1
1	1	0	0	1
1	1	1	1	1

(b)

Figure 2-6 (a) Logic network and (b) truth table.

manipulate them according to the rules of boolean algebra. To define the relationship between the truth table and a logic equation, consider the network defined in Fig. 2-6. We note that one input combination which makes $Z_1 = 1$ is $X_1 = 0$ AND $X_2 = 0$ AND $X_3 = 1$, or alternatively, $\overline{X}_1 = 1$ AND $\overline{X}_2 = 1$ AND $X_3 = 1$. This combination can be written as $\overline{X}_1 \cdot \overline{X}_2 \cdot X_3$. The other combinations that make $Z_1 = 1$ are $\overline{X}_1 \cdot X_2 \cdot \overline{X}_3$, $X_1 \cdot \overline{X}_2 \cdot \overline{X}_3$, and $X_1 \cdot X_2 \cdot X_3$. We note that $Z_1 = 1$ if any of these conditions is 1; that is, if $\overline{X}_1 \cdot \overline{X}_2 \cdot X_3$ OR $\overline{X}_1 \cdot X_2 \cdot \overline{X}_3$ OR $X_1 \cdot \overline{X}_2 \cdot \overline{X}_3$ OR $X_1 \cdot X_2 \cdot X_3$ has a value of 1. This relationship is expressed by

$$Z_1 = \overline{X}_1 \cdot \overline{X}_2 \cdot X_3 + \overline{X}_1 \cdot X_2 \cdot \overline{X}_3 + X_1 \cdot \overline{X}_2 \cdot \overline{X}_3 + X_1 \cdot X_2 \cdot X_3 \qquad (2\text{-}1)$$

Using a similar approach, we find the equation for Z_2

$$Z_2 = \overline{X}_1 \cdot X_2 \cdot X_3 + X_1 \cdot \overline{X}_2 \cdot X_3 + X_1 \cdot X_2 \cdot \overline{X}_3 + X_1 \cdot X_2 \cdot X_3 \qquad (2\text{-}2)$$

When evaluating logic equations, logic operators are considered in the order NOT, then AND, then OR. This is analogous to the ordering of multiplication and addition in conventional algebra. As in conventional algebra, this ordering can be altered by parentheses.

Equation (2-1) indicates that the variable Z_1 is the output of a four-input OR gate and that each input to this gate is an output of a three-input AND gate. The resulting logic diagram is shown in Fig. 2-7. Although this is a valid representation of the network described by Eq. (2-1), it is not the most efficient. Boolean algebraic techniques provide methods for defining efficient representations.

Logic equations take many forms, but we shall focus on the *sum-of-products form*, which, as the term implies, is a summation in which each term is a product. As we have just seen, this means that the output variable represents the ORing of a set of variables obtained by ANDing various combinations of the input variables and their complements. The right-hand sides of Eqs. (2-1) and (2-2) are sum-of-products expressions. All logic expressions can be converted into the sum-of-products form by applying the theorems of boolean algebra.

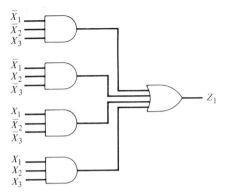

Figure 2-7 Logic diagram for Z_1 portion of the truth table in Fig. 2-6.

The theorems necessary for our purpose are shown in Table 2-2. The first four in each column describe the results when a variable is combined with the values 1 or 0, with the variable itself, or with its complement. The remainder describe basic algebraic manipulations involving two or three variables. Theorems 5–7 are identical to analogous theorems in the algebra of real numbers; Theorems 8 and 9 are not. The last pair (Theorem 9), called *De Morgan's theorems*, describe the manipulation required to eliminate complementation of an expression containing more than one variable. De Morgan's theorems must be applied to expressions containing only product terms or only sum terms. Parentheses are frequently used to convert more complex equations into one of these two forms.

As an example, let us convert Eq. (2-3) into its sum-of-products form. The first step is to apply De Morgan's theorems to eliminate all complementations involving more than one variable:

$$Z_3 = A \cdot \overline{(B + \overline{C})} + \overline{A \cdot C} \cdot (B + C) \tag{2-3}$$

$$Z_3 = A \cdot (\overline{B} \cdot C) + (\overline{A} + \overline{C}) \cdot (B + C) \tag{2-4}$$

The next step is to "multiply" using Theorem 7 to eliminate all parentheses

Table 2-2 Theorems of boolean algebra

Sum	Product
1 $X + 1 = 1$	$X \cdot 0 = 0$
2 $X + 0 = X$	$X \cdot 1 = X$
3 $X + X = X$	$X \cdot X = X$
4 $X + \overline{X} = 1$	$X \cdot \overline{X} = 0$
5 $X + Y = Y + X$	$X \cdot Y = Y \cdot X$
6 $X + (Y + Z) = (X + Y) + Z$	$X \cdot (Y \cdot Z) = (X \cdot Y) \cdot Z$
7 $X \cdot (Y + Z) = XY + XZ$	$X + (Y \cdot Z) = (X + Y)(X + Z)$
8 $X + XY = X$	$X \cdot (X + Y) = X$
9 $\overline{X + Y} = \overline{X} \cdot \overline{Y}$	$\overline{X \cdot Y} = \overline{X} + \overline{Y}$

obtaining a sum-of-products form

$$Z_3 = A \cdot \overline{B} \cdot C + \overline{A} \cdot B + \overline{A} \cdot C + \overline{C} \cdot B + \overline{C} \cdot C \tag{2-5}$$

Note that the last term, $\overline{C} \cdot C$, equals 0 by Theorem 4; it can therefore be dropped by Theorem 2. The results are

$$Z_3 = A \cdot \overline{B} \cdot C + \overline{A} \cdot B + \overline{A} \cdot C + \overline{C} \cdot B \tag{2-6}$$

Example 2-1 Apply De Morgan's theorems to obtain a sum-of-products form for $Z = \overline{(A + \overline{B}) \cdot \overline{C} \cdot D}$.

SOLUTION

$$Z = \overline{(A + \overline{B})} + \overline{\overline{C}} + \overline{D} = \overline{A} \cdot \overline{\overline{B}} + C + \overline{D}$$
$$= \overline{A} \cdot B + C + \overline{D}$$

There are many sum-of-products forms for any equation. The form in which each product term contains all the input variables either in true or complemented form is called the *normal* or *canonical form*. Equation (2-6) can be expanded into normal form by "multiplying" each term by the "sum" of the missing variable plus its complement using Theorems 4 and 7. This is illustrated by expanding Eq. (2-6) to obtain

$$Z_3 = A \cdot \overline{B} \cdot C + \overline{A} \cdot B \cdot (C + \overline{C}) + \overline{A} \cdot C \cdot (B + \overline{B}) + \overline{C} \cdot B \cdot (A + \overline{A}) \tag{2-7}$$

The first term in Eq. (2-6) contains all the variables and therefore is in the appropriate form; the second term is missing the C, so it is multiplied by $C + \overline{C}$; the third and fourth terms are treated analogously. Eliminating the parentheses leads to

$$Z_3 = A \cdot \overline{B} \cdot C + \overline{A} \cdot B \cdot C + \overline{A} \cdot B \cdot \overline{C} + \overline{A} \cdot B \cdot C + \overline{A} \cdot \overline{B} \cdot C + A \cdot B \cdot \overline{C} + \overline{A} \cdot B \cdot \overline{C}$$
$$\tag{2-8}$$

The terms $\overline{A} \cdot B \cdot C$ and $\overline{A} \cdot B \cdot \overline{C}$ appear twice in Eq. (2-8). By Theorem 3 one of each can be eliminated, and the simplified sum-of-products normal form is given by

$$Z_3 = A \cdot \overline{B} \cdot C + \overline{A} \cdot B \cdot C + \overline{A} \cdot B \cdot \overline{C} + \overline{A} \cdot \overline{B} \cdot C + A \cdot B \cdot \overline{C} \tag{2-9}$$

Although an equation can be rearranged into many sum-of-product forms, there is a unique sum-of-products normal form.

The equation for a logic variable that is a function of N independent variables may have at most 2^N product terms in its sum-of-products normal form. These product terms are called *minterms*. Each minterm is assigned a decimal number derived by replacing all true logic variables by 1 and all complemented logic variables by 0 and then interpreting this word as a binary value. For example, the term $A \cdot \overline{B} \cdot C$ is minterm 5, symbolized by m_5, since $101_2 = 5_{10}$.

Using this notation, we can rewrite Eq. (2-9) to obtain

$$Z_3(A,B,C) = m_5 + m_3 + m_2 + m_1 + m_6 \tag{2-10}$$

and after reordering the terms

$$Z_3(A,B,C) = m_1 + m_2 + m_3 + m_5 + m_6 \tag{2-11}$$

With this notation it is important to define the order of the input variables. In these equations the input variables were ordered A, B, and C, and so $Z_3(A,B,C)$ is used. Another compact notation is

$$Z_3(A,B,C) = \Sigma(1,2,3,5,6) \tag{2-12}$$

This notation states that Z_3 is the sum of minterms m_1, m_2, m_3, m_5, and m_6.

Each row in the truth table represents a minterm. For example, for the truth table in Fig. 2-6, where the rows are ordered using a binary counting scheme, the first row represents minterm m_0, the second m_1, and so on. Thus, we can write the sum-of-products normal-form equation for Z_1 and Z_2 directly from the truth table, giving

$$Z_1(X_1,X_2,X_3) = \Sigma(1,2,4,7) \tag{2-13}$$

and

$$Z_2(X_1,X_2,X_3) = \Sigma(3,5,6,7) \tag{2-14}$$

Because of this one-to-one correspondence between entries in the truth table and product terms in the normal sum-of-products form, both provide a unique representation of the logical behavior. Thus, it is convenient to use the normal sum-of-products form when comparing two logic equations for equivalency.

Example 2-2 Given the equation $Z(A,B,C) = \overline{(A \cdot \overline{B})} \cdot C$, find the normal sum-of-products expression for Z and the truth table.

SOLUTION

$$
\begin{aligned}
Z(A,B,C) &= \overline{(A \cdot \overline{B})} \cdot C = (\overline{A} + B) \cdot C \\
&= \overline{A} C + BC \\
&= \overline{A} C(\overline{B} + B) + BC(\overline{A} + A) \\
&= \overline{A}\,\overline{B}C + \overline{A} BC + \overline{A} BC + ABC \\
&= \overline{A}\,\overline{B}C + \overline{A} BC + ABC \\
&= m_1 + m_3 + m_7 \\
&= \Sigma(1,3,7)
\end{aligned}
$$

The truth table is

Minterm	ABC	Z	Minterm	ABC	Z
m_0	000	0	m_4	100	0
m_1	001	1	m_5	101	0
m_2	010	0	m_6	110	0
m_3	011	1	m_7	111	1

2-2-2 Minimization with Karnaugh Maps

One objective of design work is an efficient implementation, and in combinational network design one efficient implementation results from the so-called *minimum sum-of-products equation*. This equation form contains the smallest number of variable appearances, which, as we shall see later, corresponds to the smallest number of gate inputs.

Conceptually, a minimum sum-of-products form could be derived using the theorems of boolean algebra. Unfortunately, this approach requires considerable insight to identify the sequence of algebraic manipulations that will lead to a minimum sum-of-products expression. A graphical minimization scheme uses Karnaugh maps to accomplish these algebraic manipulations.

The *Karnaugh map*, or simply *map*, is a graphical representation of the truth table with a square representing each minterm. The minterms are ordered in an unusual pattern so that the minterms in each adjacent pair of squares are identical except that one variable appears in the true form in one minterm and in the complement form in the other. Figure 2-8 shows the arrangement of minterms in the three- and four-variable maps. To clarify the concept of adjacent squares, consider the square for m_2 in the four-variable map. Since m_2 is $\overline{X}_1 \cdot \overline{X}_2 \cdot X_3 \cdot \overline{X}_4$ and m_3 is $\overline{X}_1 \cdot \overline{X}_2 \cdot X_3 \cdot X_4$, these two minterms are identical except for X_4 and $\overline{X}_4$. The minterm m_6 is $\overline{X}_1 \cdot X_2 \cdot X_3 \cdot \overline{X}_4$, and it is identical to m_2, except for X_2 and $\overline{X}_2$.

	$\overline{X}_2\overline{X}_3$	$\overline{X}_2 X_3$	$X_2 X_3$	$X_2 \overline{X}_3$
$\overline{X}_1$	m_0	m_1	m_3	m_2
X_1	m_4	m_5	m_7	m_6

	$\overline{X}_3\overline{X}_4$	$\overline{X}_3 X_4$	$X_3 X_4$	$X_3 \overline{X}_4$
$\overline{X}_1\overline{X}_2$	m_0	m_1	m_3	m_2
$\overline{X}_1 X_2$	m_4	m_5	m_7	m_6
$X_1 X_2$	m_{12}	m_{13}	m_{15}	m_{14}
$X_1 \overline{X}_2$	m_8	m_9	m_{11}	m_{10}

Figure 2-8 Form of the three- and four-variable Karnaugh maps.

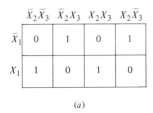

	$\bar{X}_2\bar{X}_3$	$\bar{X}_2 X_3$	$X_2 X_3$	$X_2\bar{X}_3$
$\bar{X}_1$	0	1	0	1
X_1	1	0	1	0

(a)

	$\bar{X}_2\bar{X}_3$	$\bar{X}_2 X_3$	$X_2 X_3$	$X_2\bar{X}_3$
$\bar{X}_1$	0	0	1	0
X_1	0	1	1	1

(b)

Figure 2-9 Maps for $Z_1(X_1, X_2, X_3) = \Sigma(1,2,4,7)$ and $Z_2(X_1, X_2, X_3) = \Sigma(3,5,6,7)$; corresponds to the truth table in Fig. 2-6 and Eqs. (2-13) and (2-14).

Similarly the minterm m_{10} is identical to m_2 except for X_1 and $\bar{X}_1$ and the minterm m_0 is identical to m_2 except for X_3 and $\bar{X}_3$.

The map for Z_1 and Z_2 defined by the truth table in Fig. 2-6 and by Eqs. (2-13) and (2-14) is given in Fig. 2-9. A 0 or a 1 is placed in each square depending on the value assigned to the corresponding minterm in the truth table. Figure 2-10 shows an example of a four-variable map.

Graphical minimization is based on the following algebraic manipulation:

$$F_1 = A\cdot\bar{B}\cdot\bar{C} + A\cdot\bar{B}\cdot C = A\cdot\bar{B}\cdot(\bar{C} + C) = A\cdot\bar{B} \qquad (2\text{-}15)$$

The two terms $A\cdot\bar{B}\cdot\bar{C}$ and $A\cdot\bar{B}\cdot C$ are reduced to the single term $A\cdot\bar{B}$ using Theorems 4 and 7. In a three-variable map, $A\cdot\bar{B}\cdot\bar{C}$, which is m_4, and $A\cdot\bar{B}\cdot C$, which is m_5, are adjacent squares, as shown in Fig. 2-11, the map for Eq. (2-15). The oval enclosing the two 1s represents the term $A\cdot\bar{B}$ and effectively accomplishes the algebraic simplification illustrated in Eq. (2-15).

We can expand this graphical approach to show that enclosing four 1s appearing in adjacent squares effectively applies this type of reduction repeatedly, eliminating two variables. This is illustrated in Fig. 2-12, where $F_2(A,B,C) = \Sigma(0,1,4,5)$ is reduced to $F_2 = \bar{B}$ since two variables are eliminated and $\bar{B}$ is the common variable in all enclosed minterms. This is based on the following algebraic manipulations

$$F_2 = \bar{A}\cdot\bar{B}\cdot\bar{C} + \bar{A}\cdot\bar{B}\cdot C + A\cdot\bar{B}\cdot\bar{C} + A\cdot\bar{B}\cdot C = \bar{A}\bar{B} + A\bar{B} = \bar{B} \quad (2\text{-}16)$$

Minimizing the expression $F_3(A,B,C) = \Sigma(0,2,4,5,7)$, shown in Fig. 2-13, illustrates four additional important considerations: (1) The outside squares are

	$\bar{C}\bar{D}$	$\bar{C}D$	CD	$C\bar{D}$
$\bar{A}\bar{B}$	1	0	0	0
$\bar{A}B$	1	0	1	0
AB	1	0	0	0
$A\bar{B}$	0	0	0	1

Figure 2-10 Example of a four-variable map for $F(A, B, C, D) = \Sigma(0,4,7,10,12)$.

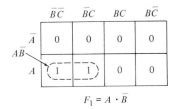

Figure 2-11 Map showing minimization of $F_1 = (A \cdot \overline{B} \cdot \overline{C} + A \cdot \overline{B} \cdot C$ [Eq. (2-15)].

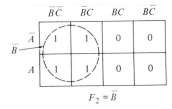

Figure 2-12 Map showing minimization of $F_2(A, B, C) = \Sigma(0, 1, 4, 5)$.

adjacent, and in this example minterms m_0 and m_2 reduce to $\overline{A} \cdot \overline{C}$. (2) It is possible to include a minterm in more than one grouping, as we did with m_0 in this example. (3) The term enclosed by the dotted oval $A \cdot \overline{B}$ does not include any minterms that are not included in the others; therefore, it is not included in the final expression. (4) The minimum sum-of-products expression is obtained by "summing" (ORing) all the essential combinations, which in this case produces $F = \overline{A} \cdot \overline{C} + \overline{B} \cdot \overline{C} + A \cdot C$.

In general this form of minimization proceeds in four steps.

1. The map is generated.
2. Minterms having a value of 1 must be grouped without including any with the value of 0. All groups must contain 1, 2, 4, 8, or 16 minterms. In grouping minterms we start by determining whether groups containing 16 minterms can be formed. Next we consider groups containing 8, 4, 2, minterms and finally only 1 minterm. A group is formed if it contains at least one minterm with the value 1 that is not already included in a group. Minterms with the value 1 can be included in more than one group and must be included in at least one group.

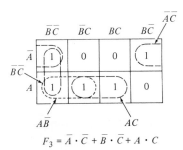

Figure 2-13 Map showing minimization of $F_3(A, B, C) = \Sigma(0, 2, 4, 5, 7)$.

3. The product representing each group is defined using the variables common to all minterms in the group.
4. The minimum sum-of-products equation is obtained by summing the products for all essential groups where an essential group is one that contains a minterm not included in any other group.

This approach represents an oversimplification but is adequate for most three- and four-variable problems. Even in problems where it does not provide an absolute minimum, it still yields an efficient solution.

This approach is applied to the four-variable maps in Fig. 2-14. In the first example, two groups of four minterms, one a row group and one a square group, are formed, and then one group of two minterms is formed. In the row group, the variables $\bar{A}$ and $\bar{B}$ are common to all four minterms, and so the product representing the group is $\bar{A} \cdot \bar{B}$. In the square group the variables A and C are common to all four minterms, and so the product is $A \cdot C$. In the two-minterm group the variables $\bar{A}$, $\bar{C}$, and $\bar{D}$ are common, and the product is $\bar{A} \cdot \bar{C} \cdot \bar{D}$.

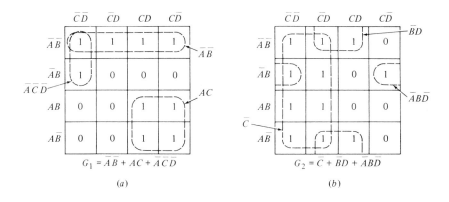

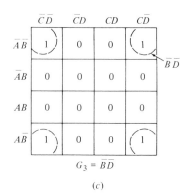

Figure 2-14 Maps showing minimization of (a) $G_1(A, B, C, D) = \Sigma(0, 1, 2, 3, 4, 10, 11, 14, 15)$, (b) $G_2(A, B, C, D) = \Sigma(0, 1, 3, 4, 5, 6, 8, 9, 11, 12, 13)$, and (c) $G_3(A, B, C, D) = \Sigma(0, 2, 8, 10)$.

In the second example (Fig. 2-14b) one group of eight, one group of four, and one group of two minterms are formed. In the group of eight only $\bar{C}$ is common to all minterms, so the product is this single variable. The square group of four is formed with two minterms in the top row and two in the bottom row; the product contains the two common variables $\bar{B}$ and D. The two-minterm group is formed with one in the leftmost column and one in the rightmost column; the product contains the three common variables $\bar{A}$, B, and $\bar{D}$.

In the third example (Fig. 2-14c) one group of four minterms is formed with the four corner minterms. The product contains two common variables $\bar{B}$ and $\bar{D}$.

Example 2-3 Find a minimum sum-of-products equation for Z.

A	B	C	Z	A	B	C	Z
0	0	0	0	1	0	0	0
0	0	1	1	1	0	1	1
0	1	0	1	1	1	0	0
0	1	1	1	1	1	1	0

SOLUTION See Fig. E2-3.

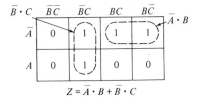

$$Z = \bar{A} \cdot B + \bar{B} \cdot C$$

Figure E2-3 K map.

2-2-3 Don't-Care Conditions

In combinational design, situations where some input combinations are undefined are common. For example, if the input to a network is a BCD-coded value, the input combinations corresponding to minterms m_{10} to m_{15} are undefined. These undefined combinations, called *don't-care conditions*, may be used to minimize the sum-of-products equation further. This advantage occurs because a don't-care condition can be treated as either a 1 or a 0, whichever is more convenient. As an example, let us minimize $H(A, B, C, D) = \Sigma(4, 5, 6, 10, 11)$ with don't-care conditions corresponding to m_2, m_3, m_7, m_8, and m_{12}. We write $d(A, B, C, D) = \Sigma(2, 3, 7, 8, 12)$ to indicate the don't-care conditions. Figure 2-15 shows the map and the minimization. In this example, it is convenient to treat the don't-care conditions represented by m_2, m_3, and m_7 as 1s and those represented by m_8 and m_{12} as 0s.

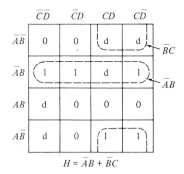

$$H = \overline{A}B + \overline{B}C$$

Figure 2-15 Map showing minimization of $H(A, B, C, D) = \Sigma(4,5,6,10,11)$ with $d(A, B, C, D) = \Sigma(2,3,7,8,12)$.

Example 2-4 Find a minimum sum-of-products equation for Z given

$$Z(A,B,C,D) = \Sigma(1,2,3,7,8,10)$$
$$d(A,B,C,D) = \Sigma(0,5,9,11,13)$$

SOLUTION See Fig. E2-4.

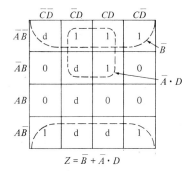

$$Z = \overline{B} + \overline{A} \cdot D$$

Figure E2-4 K map.

2-3 LOGIC DIAGRAMS

A logic diagram is a model which describes the behavior of a logic network by defining the interconnections of the logic gates. It is a convenient model since it can easily be translated into a circuit diagram. In this section we describe the procedures for generating a logic diagram from a logic equation and for obtaining an equation from a logic diagram.

2-3-1 Converting Logic Equations into Logic Diagrams

In converting a logic equation into a logic diagram, we shall limit our discussion to the sum-of-products form. Initially we focus on generating logic diagrams with AND, OR, and NOT gates; later we shall discuss converting these diagrams into NAND-gate or NOR-gate diagrams. When we exclude the NOT gates used to complement the input signals, the sum-of-products expression leads directly to a

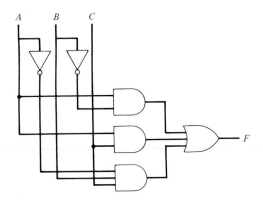

Figure 2-16 AND-OR-NOT logic diagram for $F = A \cdot \overline{B} + A \cdot C + \overline{A} \cdot B \cdot C$.

diagram with two levels of gates. AND gates are used at the first level to generate the products, and an OR gate is used at the second level to generate the sum. This is illustrated in Fig. 2-16, showing the logic diagram for $F = A \cdot \overline{B} + A \cdot C + \overline{A} \cdot B \cdot C$, where the upper AND gate generates the first product in the sum, $A \cdot \overline{B}$, the center AND gate generates the second product, $A \cdot C$, and the bottom AND gate generates the third product, $\overline{A} \cdot B \cdot C$. These products are then summed in the OR gate.†

For practical reasons we need to be able to construct logic diagrams using either NAND gates or NOR gates exclusively. We do this by defining small networks containing only NAND gates or NOR gates that are equivalent to the AND, OR, and NOT gates. By substituting these small networks into an AND, OR, and NOT logic diagram we shall obtain one that contains only NAND or NOR gates.

Let us consider NAND gates first. Since this gate is an inverting gate, it performs the NOT operation when it is used as a single-input gate, as shown in Fig. 2-17. The AND operation results if the output of a multi-input NAND gate is inverted by a second single-input NAND gate, also shown in Fig. 2-17. To obtain the OR-gate equivalent, we must first apply De Morgan's theorem to the defining equation for the NAND gate, that is, $F = \overline{A \cdot B}$, to obtain $F = \overline{A} + \overline{B}$. This equation indicates that the output of a NAND gate can be considered as the result of an OR operation on the complements of the input variables. This idea is illustrated in Fig. 2-18, where the OR-gate symbol on the right has small circles on its inputs to indicate that they are complemented before performing the OR operation. If each input to a multi-input NAND gate is first complemented by a single-input NAND gate, the resulting network is equivalent to an OR gate. This is also shown in Fig. 2-17.

Let us now consider the NOR gate. When it is used as a single-input gate, it is equivalent to a NOT gate, as shown in Fig. 2-19. A NOR-gate network equivalent to an OR gate is obtained by complementing the output of a multi-input NOR gate with a single-input NOR gate. Figure 2-19 also shows this equivalency. In order to obtain the AND-gate equivalent we must apply De Morgan's theorem to the defining equation for the NOR gate, that is, $F = \overline{A + B}$, to obtain $F = \overline{A} \cdot \overline{B}$. This

---

† We always assume that gates with the appropriate number of inputs are available.

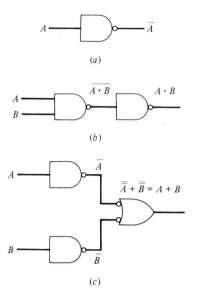

Figure 2-17 (*a*) NOT, (*b*) AND, and (*c*) OR equivalents using NAND gates.

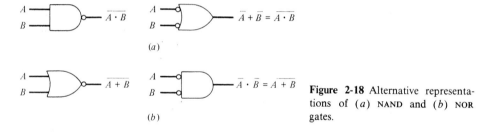

Figure 2-18 Alternative representations of (*a*) NAND and (*b*) NOR gates.

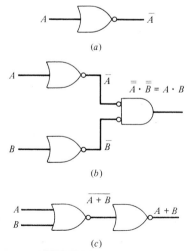

Figure 2-19 (*a*) NOT, (*b*) AND, and (*c*) OR equivalents using NOR gates.

equation indicates that the output of the NOR gate can be considered as the result of an AND operation on the complements of the input variables. This idea is illustrated in Fig. 2-18, where the AND-gate symbol on the right has small circles on its input to indicate that they are complemented before performing the AND operation. If each input to a multi-input NOR gate is first complemented by a single-input NOR gate, the resulting network is equivalent to an AND gate. This also is shown in Fig. 2-19.

Now we can use the equivalencies defined in Fig. 2-17 to convert the AND, OR, and NOT logic diagram in Fig. 2-16 into a NAND-gate logic diagram in Fig. 2-20a, where the substitution for each AND and OR gate is identified. There are several locations where two single-input gates appear in series. Since both perform NOT operations, they effectively cancel each other and therefore can be eliminated, as shown in Fig. 2-20b.

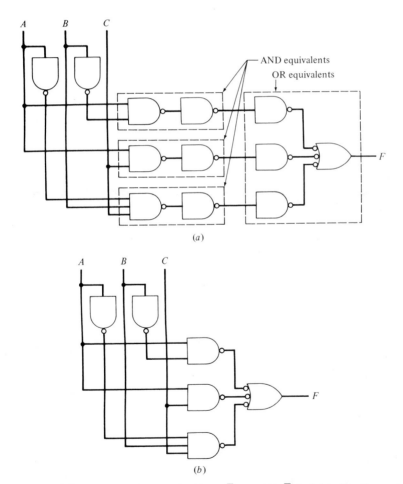

Figure 2-20 NAND logic diagrams for $F = A \cdot \bar{B} + A \cdot C + \bar{A} \cdot B \cdot C$ (a) after direct substitution and (b) after eliminating canceling gates.

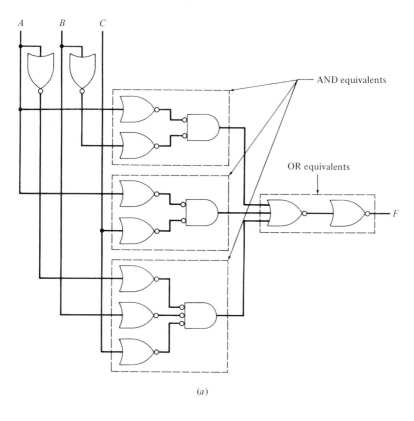

(a)

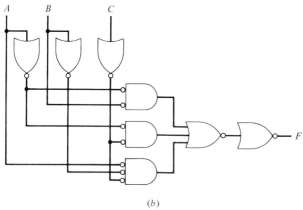

(b)

Figure 2-21 NOR logic diagram for $F = A \cdot \bar{B} + A \cdot C + \bar{A} \cdot B \cdot C$ (a) after direct substitution and (b) after eliminating canceling gates.

Figure 2-21 shows a similar development to obtain the equivalent NOR-gate logic diagram. In Fig. 2-21a NOT-, AND-, and OR-gate equivalents are identified. In this case the canceling NOT operations occur on the input signals. For example, the top input line in Fig. 2-21a is connected to the A input and then complemented in a NOT gate. This NOT gate can be eliminated by connecting this line to the $\overline{A}$ input, as shown in Fig. 2-21b. The next line down in Fig. 2-21a is connected to the $\overline{B}$ input and then complemented in a NOT gate; a more efficient arrangement is to connect this line directly to the B input, as shown in Fig. 2-21b.

In summary, a logic equation is converted into a NAND- or NOR-gate logic diagram by first converting the equation into a sum-of-products form. From this form the NOT-, AND-, and OR-gate logic diagram is constructed. Each NOT, AND, and OR is replaced by its equivalent NAND or NOR network, and canceling NOT operations are eliminated.

Example 2-5 Find an efficient NOR-gate logic diagram for a three-input network whose output is 1 when the majority of the inputs are 0s.

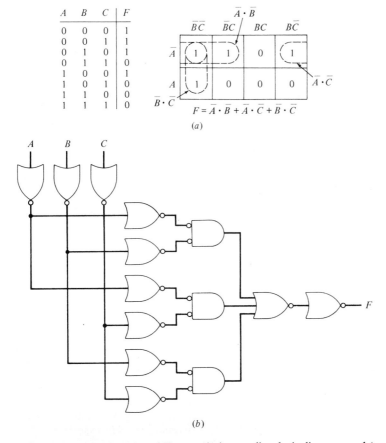

$$F = \overline{A} \cdot \overline{B} + \overline{A} \cdot \overline{C} + \overline{B} \cdot \overline{C}$$

(a)

(b)

Figure E2-5 (a) Truth table and K map, (b) intermediate logic diagrams, and (continued).

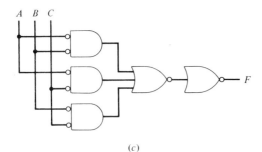

(c)

Figure E2-5 (c) final logic diagram.

SOLUTION With A, B, and C representing the inputs and F the outputs, the truth table and map are shown in Fig. E2-5a. The NOR-gate logic diagram obtained by direct substitution of equivalents is shown in Fig. E2-5b. After eliminating the canceling single-input gates, the resulting logic diagram is shown in Fig. E2-5c.

2-3-2 Converting Logic Diagrams into Logic Equations

In a logic diagram, expressions for the output signals are obtained by starting at the input and algebraically defining the output of each gate in terms of its input variables until expressions for all output signals are defined. As an example, consider the logic diagram in Fig. 2-22. Logic expressions for the signals at the outputs of the first-level gates, the AND gates, are shown. These signals are then inputs to the second-level gate, the OR gate, and its output is the sum of these expressions as shown in the figure.

The process, although identical, becomes a little more complicated when inverting gates, like the NAND gate, are used (Fig. 2-23). Note the alternative

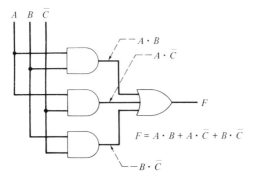

Figure 2-22 Converting an AND-OR-NOT logic diagram into a logic expression.

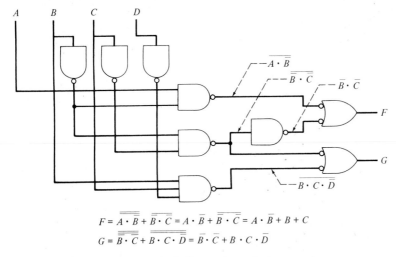

$$F = \overline{\overline{\overline{A \cdot \overline{B}}} + \overline{\overline{B} \cdot \overline{C}}} = \overline{\overline{A \cdot \overline{B}}} + \overline{\overline{\overline{B} \cdot \overline{C}}} = A \cdot \overline{B} + \overline{B} + C$$

$$G = \overline{\overline{\overline{B} \cdot \overline{C}} + \overline{B \cdot C \cdot \overline{D}}} = \overline{\overline{\overline{B} \cdot \overline{C}}} + \overline{\overline{B \cdot C \cdot \overline{D}}}$$

Figure 2-23 Converting a NAND logic diagram into a logic expression.

representation for the NAND gate at the two output gates. Expressions for the outputs of the first level gates are shown; e.g., the output of the top input gate with inputs of A and $\overline{B}$ is $\overline{A \cdot \overline{B}}$, which could be reduced to $\overline{A} + B$ by applying De Morgan's theorem. However, we have chosen to wait and simplify the final expression. Expressions for each output gate are obtained from their inputs and then simplified as shown in the figure.

Example 2-6 Does this network shown in Fig. E2-6 generate a valid output carry for a binary adder?

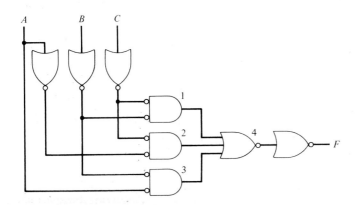

Figure E2-6 Logic diagram.

SOLUTION

$$\text{Output of gate } 1 = \overline{\overline{B} \cdot \overline{C}} = B \cdot C$$

$$\text{Output of gate } 2 = \overline{\overline{A} \cdot \overline{C}} = A \cdot C$$

$$\text{Output of gate } 3 = \overline{\overline{A} \cdot \overline{B}} = \overline{A} \cdot B$$

$$\text{Output of gate } 4 = \overline{(B \cdot C) + (A \cdot C) + (\overline{A} \cdot B)}$$

$$F = \overline{\overline{B \cdot C + A \cdot C + \overline{A} \cdot B}} = B \cdot C + A \cdot C + \overline{A} \cdot B$$

$$= (A + \overline{A}) \cdot B \cdot C + (B + \overline{B}) \cdot A \cdot C + (C + \overline{C})\overline{A} \cdot B$$

$$= A \cdot B \cdot C + \overline{A} \cdot B \cdot C + A \cdot B \cdot C + A \cdot \overline{B} \cdot C$$

$$+ \overline{A} \cdot B \cdot C + \overline{A} \cdot B \cdot \overline{C}$$

$$= \Sigma(2, 3, 5, 7)$$

The truth table for F and for the output carry (Table 1-5) is

A	B	C_{in}	F	Output carry	A	B	C_{in}	F	Output carry
0	0	0	0	0	1	0	0	0	0
0	0	1	0	0	1	0	1	1	1
0	1	0	1	0	1	1	0	0	1
0	1	1	1	1	1	1	1	1	1

Since F does not equal the output carry, the network does not generate a valid output carry.

2-4 DESIGN EXAMPLES

In this section we illustrate how to translate a verbal specification of a combinational network into a logic diagram using either NAND or NOR gates. This in essence is the design process since the logic diagram is easily converted into a circuit diagram. In these examples, we proceed systematically from the verbal specification to a truth table, from a truth table to a logic equation, and finally from a logic equation to a logic diagram.

2-4-1 Full Adder

In the first example we shall develop a logic diagram for a full adder using NOR gates. This is a network which accepts three inputs, representing the two signals to be summed and the input carry. It generates two outputs, representing the binary arithmetic sum and the output carry. Figure 2-24a shows an input-output model in which the variables are identified; this represents the first step in the design process. Figure 2-24b shows the truth table describing the relationship between the input and output variables, i.e., the behavior of this network. The first three columns represent an enumeration of all combinations of values on the inputs. Entries in the fourth and fifth columns are determined by computing the binary arithmetic sum and carry for each input combination. For example, in the first row the inputs are 0, 0, and 0, which sum to 0, so $S = 0$ and $C_{out} = 0$. In the second row, the sum of the three inputs is 1, so $S = 1$ and $C_{out} = 0$. In the last row, the sum of the three inputs is 11, so $S = 1$ and $C_{out} = 1$. Equations giving the canonical sum-of-products form for these two output variables also are shown. Figure 2-24c shows the maps used in minimizing these two equations and the minimum sum-of-products equations. Figure 2-25a shows the NOT, AND, and OR logic diagram constructed from these equations, and Figure 2-25b shows the final NOR logic diagram after removing the canceling NOT operations.

Input A ⟶
Input B ⟶ | Full adder | ⟶ Sum S
Carry in C_{in} ⟶ | | ⟶ Carry out C_{out}

(a)

Inputs			Outputs	
A	B	C_{in}	S	C_{out}
0	0	0	0	0
0	0	1	1	0
0	1	0	1	0
0	1	1	0	1
1	0	0	1	0
1	0	1	0	1
1	1	0	0	1
1	1	1	1	1

$$S(A, B, C_{in}) = \Sigma\,(1, 2, 4, 7)$$
$$C_{out}(A, B, C_{in}) = \Sigma\,(3, 5, 6, 7)$$

(b)

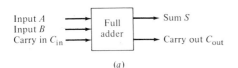

$$S = \overline{A} \cdot \overline{B} \cdot C_{in} + \overline{A} \cdot B \cdot \overline{C}_{in} + A \cdot \overline{B} \cdot \overline{C}_{in} + A \cdot B \cdot C_{in}$$

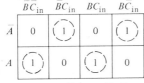

$$C_{out} = A \cdot C_{in} + A \cdot B + B \cdot C_{in}$$

(c)

Figure 2-24 Full adder: (a) input-output model, (b) truth table, and (c) maps.

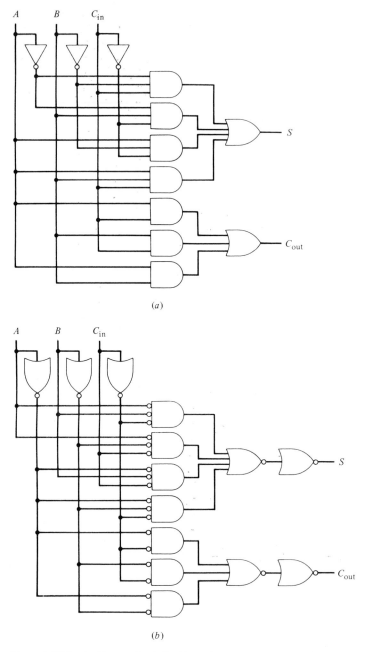

Figure 2-25 Logic diagram for full adder using (*a*) NOT, AND, and OR gates and (*b*) only NOR gates.

2-4-2 BCD-to-Seven-Segment Decoder

In the second example we consider a decoder that accepts a BCD code and generates the appropriate signals to drive a standard seven-segment display. Figure 2-26a, an input-output model of this network, indicates that there are four input signals, A representing the most significant bit of the code, B the second most significant bit, and so on. This model shows seven output signals corresponding to the seven segments in the display, as defined in Fig. 2-26b.

In the truth table for this network (Figure 2-26c) the first four columns represent an enumeration of all possible combinations of values on the inputs. The remaining seven columns indicate the desired output for each of these input combinations. The entries in these columns are defined by identifying the segments that must be activated to display the symbol corresponding to the input code word. For example, the input condition in the first row is the code word for the value 0. The corresponding display, shown in Fig. 2-26d, requires activating segments a, b, c, d, e, and f and deactivating segment g. In the truth table this condition is indicated by entering a 1 in columns a to f and a 0 in column g. The input condition in the second row is the code word for the value 1. The corresponding display, shown in Fig. 2-26d, requires activating segments b and c

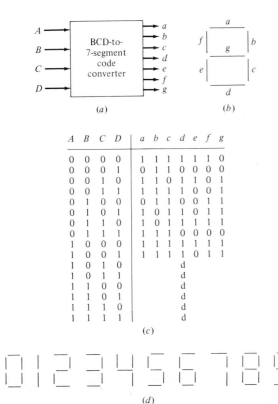

A	B	C	D	a	b	c	d	e	f	g
0	0	0	0	1	1	1	1	1	1	0
0	0	0	1	0	1	1	0	0	0	0
0	0	1	0	1	1	0	1	1	0	1
0	0	1	1	1	1	1	1	0	0	1
0	1	0	0	0	1	1	0	0	1	1
0	1	0	1	1	0	1	1	0	1	1
0	1	1	0	1	0	1	1	1	1	1
0	1	1	1	1	1	1	0	0	0	0
1	0	0	0	1	1	1	1	1	1	1
1	0	0	1	1	1	1	1	0	1	1
1	0	1	0	d						
1	0	1	1	d						
1	1	0	0	d						
1	1	0	1	d						
1	1	1	0	d						
1	1	1	1	d						

(c)

(d)

Figure 2-26 BCD-to-seven-segment decoder: (a) input-output model, (b) seven-segment display, (c) truth table, (d) display for symbols 0 through 9.

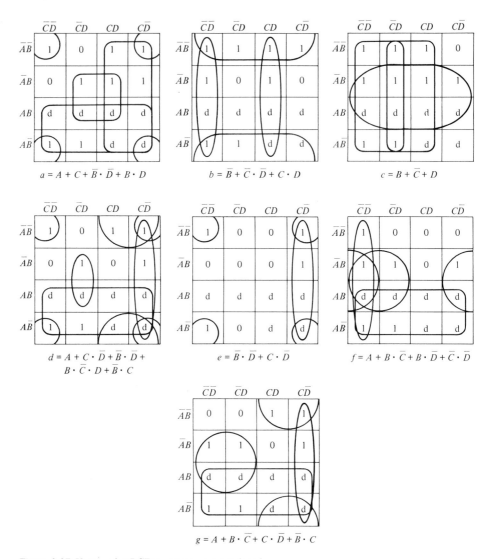

Figure 2-27 K maps for BCD-to-seven-segment decoder.

and inactivating segments a, d, e, f, and g. In the truth table, 1s are placed in columns b and c and 0s in the other five. This procedure is repeated for the third through tenth rows. In the last six rows the input condition cannot be interpreted using the BCD code, and thus these conditions are unexpected. In this design we have chosen to treat them as don't-care conditions as indicated by the d's in the truth table.

The maps for the seven output variables are shown in Fig. 2-27, which also includes the resulting sum-of-products equations. Figure 2-28 shows the NAND-gate logic diagram for this network.

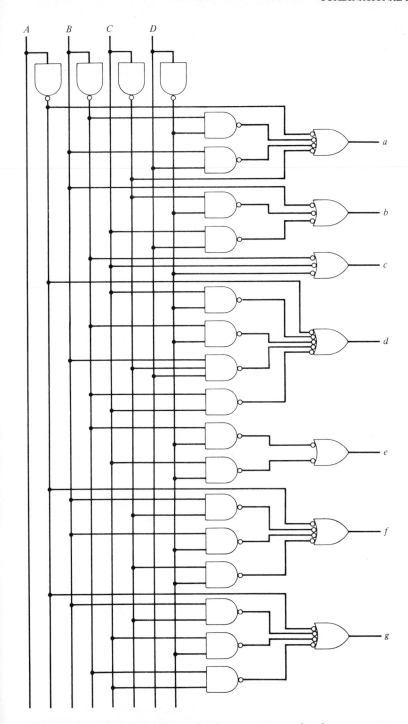

Figure 2-28 NAND-gate logic diagram for the seven-segment decoder.

2-4-3 Eight-Bit Adder-Subtracter

As a third example consider an 8-bit adder-subtracter. The network has two 8-bit inputs and a 1-bit control input, which is deactivated for addition and activated for subtraction. The outputs consist of an 8-bit result, a 1-bit arithmetic overflow signal, and a 1-bit carry-borrow signal.

Figure 2-29a shows the input-output model. The two 8-bit inputs and the 8-bit result are designated A_7 to A_0, B_7 to B_0, and R_7 to R_0, respectively. The addition-subtraction control signal, the output carry-borrow signal, and the arithmetic overflow signal are designated X, C, and V, respectively. The operation of the network is defined by indicating that if $X = 0$, then $R = A$ plus B, and if $X = 1$, then $R = A$ minus B.

The next step in our approach is to define the truth table for the network. In this case since there are 17 input variables, the truth table would have $2^{17} = 131,072$ rows. Because this represents an unmanageable number, another approach must be found. Fortunately this network has a characteristic common to many digital networks; i.e., the network can be divided into smaller identical units for processing each bit. We take advantage of this characteristic and develop a 1-bit unit and then interconnect or cascade eight of these units to form the 8-bit network.

Each 1-bit unit must accept one signal from each of the two input words A_i and B_i, an input carry-borrow signal from the previous unit C_i, and the control signal X. It must generate 1 bit of the result R_i and an output carry-borrow signal C_{i+1}. The output carry-borrow input for the first unit is connected to the low level, and the carry-borrow from the eighth unit is the carry-borrow signal for the entire adder-subtracter network. This interconnection is illustrated in Fig. 2-29b. The overflow signal V is generated in a separate, unique unit. Since arithmetic overflows are determined by the sign bit of the two inputs and the result, as discussed in Sec. 1-5, A_7, B_7, R_7, and X are inputs to the overflow unit.

Figure 2-30 shows a truth table defining the behavior of the 1-bit unit, the corresponding maps, and the minimum sum-of-products equations. In the truth table, outputs for the first eight rows with $X = 0$ are determined by performing the addition described for each row. They are identical to the truth table shown in Table 1-5. Output in the last eight rows with $X = 1$ are determined by performing the subtraction described in each row. These correspond to the combination defined in Table 1-5 and Fig. 1-8.

Figure 2-31 shows the truth table and map for the overflow unit. During addition with $X = 0$, an overflow occurs when both inputs have the same sign and the result has the opposite sign. Since A_7, B_7, and R_7 are sign bits, this occurs with minterm m_3, where the two inputs are negative and the result is positive, and with minterm m_4, where the two inputs are positive and the result negative. During subtraction with $X = 1$, an overflow occurs only when the inputs have different signs and the sign of the result is opposite that of A. This occurs with m_{10}, where a positive number is subtracted from a negative number and the result is positive, and with m_{13}, where a negative number is subtracted from a positive number and the result is negative.

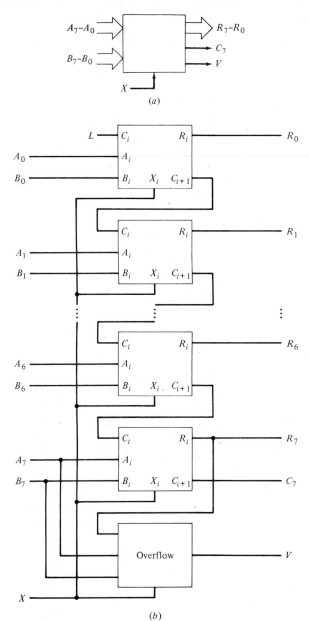

Figure 2-29 An 8-bit adder-subtracter. (*a*) Input-output model. Bit 7 is the most significant. X is the addition-subtraction control line. If X is 0, then $R = A$ plus B. If X is 1, then $R = A$ minus B. $C_7 =$ output carry or borrow; $V =$ arithmetic overflow. (*b*) Input-output model showing each stage.

The logic diagrams for the 1-bit unit and the overflow unit are shown in Fig. 2-32.

To conclude our discussion of this example, we introduce a more compact but less detailed description that will be used in the next section to define the behavior of some important combinational networks. Table 2-3 summarizes the behavior of the 8-bit adder-subtracter network. The first column shows the two

Inputs				Outputs	
X	C_i	A_i	B_i	R_i	C_{i+1}
0	0	0	0	0	0
0	0	0	1	1	0
0	0	1	0	1	0
0	0	1	1	0	1
0	1	0	0	1	0
0	1	0	1	0	1
0	1	1	0	0	1
0	1	1	1	1	1
1	0	0	0	0	0
1	0	0	1	1	1
1	0	1	0	1	0
1	0	1	1	0	0
1	1	0	0	1	1
1	1	0	1	0	1
1	1	1	0	0	0
1	1	1	1	1	1

	$\bar{A}_i\bar{B}_i$	$\bar{A}_iB_i$	A_iB_i	$A_i\bar{B}_i$
$\bar{X}\bar{C}i$	0	1	0	1
$\bar{X}C_i$	1	0	1	0
XC_i	1	0	1	0
$X\bar{C}_i$	0	1	0	1

$$R_i = C_i \cdot \bar{A}_i \cdot \bar{B}_i + C_i \cdot A_i \cdot B_i + \bar{C}_i \cdot A_i \cdot \bar{B}_i + \bar{C}_i \cdot \bar{A}_i \cdot B_i$$

	$\bar{A}_i\bar{B}_i$	$\bar{A}_iB_i$	A_iB_i	$A_i\bar{B}_i$
$\bar{X}\bar{C}_i$	0	0	1	0
$\bar{X}C_i$	0	1	1	1
XC_i	1	1	1	0
$X\bar{C}_i$	0	1	0	0

$$C_{i+1} = C_i \cdot B_i + \bar{X} \cdot C_i \cdot A_i + \bar{X} \cdot A_i \cdot B_i + X \cdot C_i \cdot \bar{A}_i + X \cdot \bar{A}_i \cdot B_i$$

Figure 2-30 Single-stage unit for the 8-bit adder-subtracter shown in Fig. 2-29.

Inputs				Outputs
X	R_7	A_7	B_7	V
0	0	0	0	0
0	0	0	1	0
0	0	1	0	0
0	0	1	1	1
0	1	0	0	1
0	1	0	1	0
0	1	1	0	0
0	1	1	1	0
1	0	0	0	0
1	0	0	1	0
1	0	1	0	1
1	0	1	1	0
1	1	0	0	0
1	1	0	1	1
1	1	1	0	0
1	1	1	1	0

(a)

	$\bar{A}_7\bar{B}_7$	$\bar{A}_7B_7$	A_7B_7	$A_7\bar{B}_7$
$\bar{X}\bar{R}_7$	0	0	1	0
$\bar{X}R_7$	1	0	0	0
XR_7	0	1	0	0
$X\bar{R}_7$	0	0	0	1

$$V = \bar{X} \cdot \bar{R}_7 \cdot A_7 \cdot B_7 + \bar{X} \cdot R_7 \cdot \bar{A}_7 \cdot \bar{B}_7 + X \cdot \bar{R}_7 \cdot A_7 \cdot \bar{B}_7 + X \cdot R_7 \cdot \bar{A}_7 \cdot B_7$$

(b)

Figure 2-31 Overflow unit for the 8-bit adder-subtracter shown in Fig. 2-29.

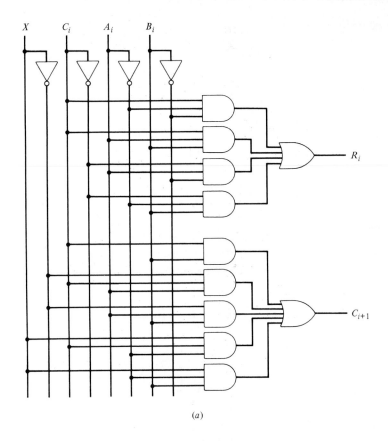

(a)

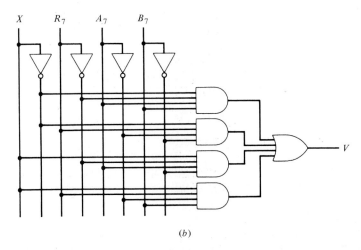

(b)

Figure 2-32 Logic diagrams for (a) single-stage unit and (b) overflow unit for the 8-bit adder-subtracter in Fig. 2-29.

Table 2-3 Eight-bit adder-subtracter

X	Result	Status signals
0	$R = A$ plus B	$C = 1$ if output carry results $V = 1$ if overflow results
1	$R = A$ minus B	$C = 1$ if output borrow results $V = 1$ if overflow results

control conditions. The second column specifies the result for each control condition; e.g., if $X = 0$, then $R = A$ plus B, indicating that the result represents the sum obtained by adding A and B. The third column specifies the condition that activates the carry-borrow signal and the arithmetic overflow signal. This column is called status signal since these two signals provide information about the status of the result; i.e., they indicate whether a carry or borrow was generated in the most significant position and whether an arithmetic overflow occurred.

2-5 IMPORTANT COMBINATIONAL NETWORKS

There are many standard combinational networks, but most fit into one of four categories: code converters, multiplexers and demultiplexers, comparators, or arithmetic logic units. All these networks can be constructed out of simple gates using the methods described in the previous sections, but they are available in a single integrated-circuit package. This section presents examples of networks in each category and introduces the use of abbreviated voltage tables to describe their behavior.

2-5-1 Code Converters

A *code converter* is a network whose inputs and outputs are binary words representing the same information in different codes. A BCD-to-decimal code converter is a simple example of this type. Figure 2-33 shows an input-output model and a voltage table for a BCD-to-decimal converter. When a positive-logic assumption is made, the first 10 input combinations correspond to the BCD code words for the decimal symbols 0 to 9. Since each of these 10 input combinations activates one output line, each of the output lines represents a decimal symbol. The last six entries, again with a positive-logic assumption, represent undefined BCD code words. In this particular case, the output lines are at the low level for these inputs. The definition of these six outputs was the choice of the designer, who could just as easily have made them all high or any combination to make most efficient use of the don't-care conditions.

Other examples of code-converter networks are the decimal-to-BCD converter, which is the counterpart of the network just described, and the BCD-to-seven-segment code converter, described in the previous section. Another

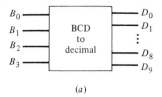

(a)

B_3	B_2	B_1	B_0	D_9	D_8	D_7	D_6	D_5	D_4	D_3	D_2	D_1	D_0
L	L	L	L	L	L	L	L	L	L	L	L	L	H
L	L	L	H	L	L	L	L	L	L	L	L	H	L
L	L	H	L	L	L	L	L	L	L	L	H	L	L
L	L	H	H	L	L	L	L	L	L	H	L	L	L
L	H	L	L	L	L	L	L	L	H	L	L	L	L
L	H	L	H	L	L	L	L	H	L	L	L	L	L
L	H	H	L	L	L	L	H	L	L	L	L	L	L
L	H	H	H	L	L	H	L	L	L	L	L	L	L
H	L	L	L	L	H	L	L	L	L	L	L	L	L
H	L	L	H	H	L	L	L	L	L	L	L	L	L
H	L	H	L	L	L	L	L	L	L	L	L	L	L
H	L	H	H	L	L	L	L	L	L	L	L	L	L
H	H	L	L	L	L	L	L	L	L	L	L	L	L
H	H	L	H	L	L	L	L	L	L	L	L	L	L
H	H	H	L	L	L	L	L	L	L	L	L	L	L
H	H	H	H	L	L	L	L	L	L	L	L	L	L

(b)

Figure 2-33 (a) Input-output model and (b) voltage table for BCD-to-decimal code converter.

important code converter is the binary-to-decimal code converter, sometimes referred to as a *decoder*. This network is an extension of the BCD-to-decimal code converter described in Fig. 2-33, but, it can have more than four inputs, and it generally has one output line for each input code word. Thus a 4-bit decoder will have four inputs defining $2^4 = 16$ distinct code words with an output line for each code word. These outputs frequently are designated lines 0 to 15.

2-5-2 Multiplexers and Demultiplexers

Multiplexers and demultiplexers are the second major category of combinational networks. The *multiplexer*, or data selector, has multiple data input lines which effectively can be connected to a single data output line. The selection is controlled by an additional set of input lines, called data-select or control lines. Figure 2-34 shows an input-output model and an abbreviated voltage table for a four-to one multiplexer. There are four data inputs D_3, D_2, D_1, and D_0, one data output Z, and two control inputs S_1 and S_0. The abbreviated voltage table indicates that the output Z is connected to the input D_0 when S_1 and S_0 are both low; it is connected to D_1 when S_1 is low and S_0 is high; and so on. Since this network has four input data lines and two input control lines for a total of six input variables, the complete voltage table would have $2^6 = 64$ rows. The abbreviated voltage table in Fig. 2-34 contains only four rows but describes the

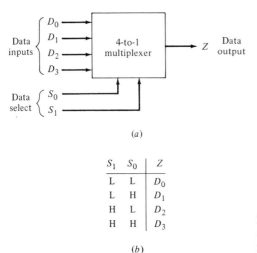

S_1	S_0	Z
L	L	D_0
L	H	D_1
H	L	D_2
H	H	D_3

(b)

Figure 2-34 (a) Input-output model and (b) abbreviated voltage table for a four-to-one multiplexer.

behavior of this network as well as a complete voltage table would. In fact it provides a clearer definition of the network's behavior because unnecessary details have been eliminated.

The behavior of a network can be characterized by a logic equation. Since equations contain binary variables which have values of 0 or 1, the characterization of a digital electronic network whose inputs and outputs are voltage levels requires a specific logic assumption. With the positive-logic assumption, the behavior of the multiplexer shown in Fig. 2-34 is given by

$$Z = \bar{S}_1 \cdot \bar{S}_0 \cdot D_0 + \bar{S}_1 \cdot S_0 \cdot D_1 + S_1 \cdot \bar{S}_0 \cdot D_2 + S_1 \cdot S_2 \cdot D_3 \qquad (2\text{-}17)$$

where the first term indicates that if $S_1 = 0$ and $S_0 = 0$, then $Z = D_0$; the second term indicates that if $S_1 = 0$ and $S_0 = 1$, then $Z = D_1$; and so on. Since with the positive-logic assumption, 0 is associated with L and 1 is associated with H, this agrees with the description in the voltage table.

The *demultiplexer* is the counterpart of the multiplexer in that it effectively connects a single input line to any of several output lines. Figure 2-35 shows the input-output model and abbreviated voltage table for a one-to-eight demultiplexer with an enable input. There are one data input (DI), eight data outputs (Z_7 to Z_0), and four control inputs, three to select the output (S_2, S_1, and S_0) and one to enable the circuit (E). The first entry in the abbreviated voltage table indicates that when the enable input is inactive (E = L), all outputs are at the low level regardless of the condition of the data-select lines or the data input line. The second entry indicates that when S_2, S_1, and S_0 are at the low level and E is at the high level, the input D is connected to Z_0, and Z_1 to Z_7 are at the low level. The third entry indicates that the input is connected to Z_1 when $S_2 = L$, $S_1 = L$, $S_0 = H$ and the enable input is active (E = H). The next six entries describe the conditions which connect the input to the remaining six outputs.

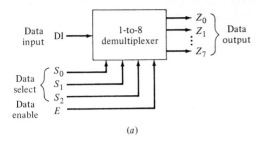

(a)

E	S_2	S_1	S_0	Z_7	Z_6	Z_5	Z_4	Z_3	Z_2	Z_1	Z_0
L	d	d	d	L	L	L	L	L	L	L	L
H	L	L	L	L	L	L	L	L	L	L	DI
H	L	L	H	L	L	L	L	L	L	DI	L
H	L	H	L	L	L	L	L	L	DI	L	L
H	L	H	H	L	L	L	L	DI	L	L	L
H	H	L	L	L	L	L	DI	L	L	L	L
H	H	L	H	L	L	DI	L	L	L	L	L
H	H	H	L	L	DI	L	L	L	L	L	L
H	H	H	H	DI	L	L	L	L	L	L	L

(b)

Figure 2-35 (a) Input-output model and (b) abbreviated voltage table for a one-to-eight demultiplexer.

The behavior of the one-to-eight demultiplexer network can also be described by logic expressions assuming a specific logic assumption. The following equations describe this network using the positive-logic assumption:

$$Z_0 = \bar{S_2} \cdot \bar{S_1} \cdot \bar{S_0} \cdot E \cdot DI \qquad Z_1 = \bar{S_2} \cdot \bar{S_1} \cdot S_0 \cdot E \cdot DI$$

$$Z_2 = \bar{S_2} \cdot S_1 \cdot \bar{S_0} \cdot E \cdot DI \qquad Z_3 = \bar{S_2} \cdot S_1 \cdot S_0 \cdot E \cdot DI$$

$$Z_4 = S_2 \cdot \bar{S_1} \cdot \bar{S_0} \cdot E \cdot DI \qquad Z_5 = S_2 \cdot \bar{S_1} \cdot S_0 \cdot E \cdot DI \qquad (2\text{-}18)$$

$$Z_6 = S_2 \cdot S_1 \cdot \bar{S_0} \cdot E \cdot DI \qquad Z_7 = S_2 \cdot S_1 \cdot S_0 \cdot E \cdot DI$$

The first of these indicates that $Z_0 = 1$ if $S_2 = 0$, $S_1 = 0$, $S_0 = 0$, $E = 1$, and $DI = 1$; this corresponds to the second row in the voltage table for $DI = 1$. The other seven equations can be interpreted in a similar way.

2-5-3 Comparators

The third category of combinational networks is the *comparator*. These networks accept two multibit binary words and generate output signals indicating the equality of the two input words and the relationship between their magnitudes. The comparison generally assumes that the two input words represent unsigned integers.

The input-output model and abbreviated voltage table for a 4-bit comparator are shown in Fig. 2-36. The two input words are represented by A_3, A_2, A_1, A_0 and B_3, B_2, B_1, B_0. The output signal is set to the high level if the two input words are equal and to the low level if the two words are unequal.

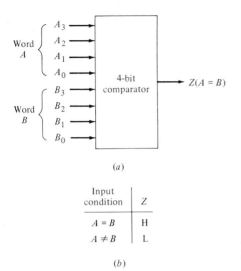

(a)

Input condition	Z
$A = B$	H
$A \neq B$	L

(b)

Figure 2-36 (a) Input-output model and (b) abbreviated voltage table for a 4-bit comparator.

Comparators are frequently connected together to increase the size of the words processed. For example, an 8-bit comparator could be formed from two 4-bit comparators. This type of interconnection is referred to as *cascading*. Since it usually is necessary to connect some outputs from the lower-order comparator into the higher-order comparator, special cascading inputs must be available.

Figure 2-37 shows an input-output model and an abbreviated voltage table for a 4-bit comparator with cascading inputs. In addition to the output signal indicating $A = B$ (Z_0), this network has two other outputs, one of which is active when $A < B$ (Z_1) while the other is active when $A > B$ (Z_2). There are cascading

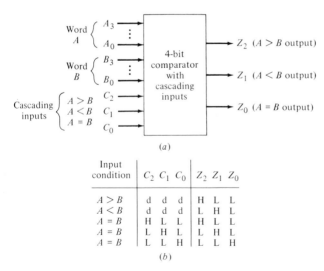

(a)

Input condition	C_2	C_1	C_0	Z_2	Z_1	Z_0
$A > B$	d	d	d	H	L	L
$A < B$	d	d	d	L	H	L
$A = B$	H	L	L	H	L	L
$A = B$	L	H	L	L	H	L
$A = B$	L	L	H	L	L	H

(b)

Figure 2-37 (a) Input-output model and (b) abbreviated voltage table for a 4-bit comparator with cascading inputs.

inputs (C_0, C_1, and C_2) corresponding to these three conditions. Since the cascading inputs are assumed to originate from a lower-order comparator, they do not affect the output signals unless the two input words are equal. The first two rows in the abbreviated voltage table indicate that Z_2 is high if $A > B$ and Z_1 is high if $A < B$, regardless of the cascading inputs. The last three rows indicate that if $A = B$, the output condition is determined by the cascading inputs.

Figure 2-38 shows the configuration for cascading four of the 4-bit comparators described in Fig. 2-37 in order to compare two 16-bit words (X_{15} to X_0 and Y_{15} to Y_0). The top 4-bit comparator operates on the four lower-order bits of X and Y. Its cascading inputs are connected to the low-level voltage L, and its outputs are connected to the cascading inputs of the next 4-bit comparator, which

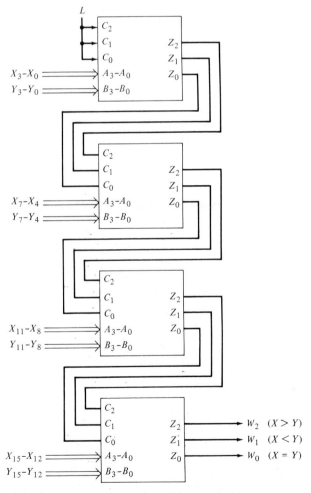

Figure 2-38 A 16-bit comparator made by interconnecting four of the 4-bit comparators shown in Fig. 2-37.

operates on bits 4 to 7 of X and Y. The third and fourth 4-bit comparators process bits 8 to 11 and 12 to 15, respectively. The output of the last 4-bit comparator indicates the relative magnitude of X and Y.

2-5-4 Arithmetic Logic Networks

The fourth category of combinational networks to be considered is arithmetic logic networks. The full adder described in Figs. 2-24 and 2-25 represents a simple example of this type. The 8-bit adder-subtracter in Fig. 2-29a and Table 2-3 represents a more complicated example.

A third example of an arithmetic logic network is shown in Fig. 2-39. This network accepts two 8-bit inputs, A_7 to A_0, and B_7 to B_0, and generates an 8-bit output R_7 to R_0. The relationship between the input variables and the output is defined by a 4-bit control input S_3 to S_0. The network also generates two status signals to indicate an arithmetic carry or borrow from the most significant bit C and arithmetic overflow V.

The table in Fig. 2-39 defines the behavior of this network, based on the positive-logic assumption. There are 16 rows corresponding to the 16 combinations on the 4-bit control input. We refer to these conditions using the hexadecimal representation; for example, $S = 0$ for the condition 0000, $S = 9$ for 1001, and $S = F$ for 1111. For each row the relationship between the two input

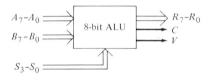

S_3	S_2	S_1	S_0	R	Comments	C	V
0	0	0	0	A		0	0
0	0	0	1	B		0	0
0	0	1	0	A plus B	Add A and B	0/1*	0/1
0	0	1	1	A minus B	Subtract B from A†	0/1	0/1
0	1	0	0	$\overline{A}$	Complement A‡	0	0
0	1	0	1	$\overline{B}$	Complement B‡	0	0
0	1	1	0	0 minus A	Negate A†	0	0
0	1	1	1	0 minus B	Negate B†	0	0
1	0	0	0	A plus 1	Increment A	0/1	0/1
1	0	0	1	B plus 1	Increment B	0/1	0/1
1	0	1	0	A minus 1	Decrement A	0/1	0/1
1	0	1	1	B minus 1	Decrement B	0/1	0/1
1	1	0	0	A AND B	AND A with B‡	0	0
1	1	0	1	A OR B	OR A with B‡	0	0
1	1	1	0	A EOR B	EOR A with B‡	0	0
1	1	1	1	max $\{A, B\}$	Select maximum	0	0

*0/1 means the value depends on the result.

†Twos complement.

‡Bit by bit.

Figure 2-39 An 8-bit ALU.

words and the output word is given symbolically in the third column and further defined in the fourth column. Each of these is referred to as an operation. The fifth column indicates how the operation affects the status signals.

For $S = 0$, the output R is set equal to A, and the carry and overflow signals will be set to 0. For $S = 1$, the output R is set equal to B; again C and V are set to 0. Arithmetic addition and subtraction operations are defined by $S = 2$ and 3, respectively. The output R represents the sum or the difference of the two input words, and C and V are set to 0 or 1, depending on the outcome of the operation.

The next four operations, corresponding to $S = 4$ to 7, produce an output that is either the complement or negative (twos-complement representation) of either input word. For these four operations the arithmetic overflow and carry signals C and V are set to 0. With the next four operations, corresponding to $S = 8$ to 11, the output R is generated by incrementing or decrementing one of the input words. Since these represent arithmetic operations, the status signals C and V are set based on the result. Operations defined by $S = 12$, 13, and 14 are logic operations, and the output R is formed bit by bit from the two input words. Status signals C and V are set to 0. For $S = 16$, the largest of the two inputs A and B is connected to the output R with C and V set to 0.

2-6 CONCLUSION

This chapter provides an introduction to, but not exhaustive coverage of, combinational networks. One major limitation of the material is that in discussing minimization with the maps we considered only three- and four-variable problems. K maps can be applied to five- and six-variable problems, but the maps become much more complex and do not markedly increase the complexity of the problem that can be solved. They have been omitted from the discussion for that reason. In practice, combinational problems of any complexity are minimized using computer techniques beyond the scope of this book.

Restricting our discussion of normal and minimum equations to the sum-of-products form is another important limitation. A similar body of material can be developed for the product-of sums form. This is not really a severe limitation because the sum of products is the most commonly used form and everything that can be done with one approach can be done with the other.

PROBLEMS

2-1 Define each of the following terms:

voltage table	negative-logic assumption
circuit diagram	logic equation
propagation delay	sum-of-products form
logic gates	normal form
logic diagram	canonical form
positive-logic assumption	minterm

minimum sum-of-products form	multiplexer
Karnaugh map	data selectors
don't-care conditions	demultiplexer
full-adder	decoder
arithmetic logic unit	comparator
code converter	cascading inputs

2-2 Derive the truth table obtained by applying the positive-logic assumption to the device described by the voltage table, and identify the resulting logical operation.

(a)

V_1	V_2	V_{out}
L	L	L
L	H	L
H	L	L
H	H	H

(b)

V_1	V_2	V_{out}
L	L	L
L	H	H
H	L	H
H	H	H

(c)

V_1	V_2	V_{out}
L	L	H
L	H	H
H	L	H
H	H	L

(d)

V_1	V_2	V_{out}
L	L	H
L	H	L
H	L	L
H	H	L

2-3 Repeat Prob. 2-2 using the negative-logic assumption.

2-4 Complete the timing diagram in Fig. P2-4 for the output signal using the circuit voltage tables in Prob. 2-2.

Figure P2-4 Timing diagram.

2-5 Write the corresponding sum-of-products normal-form algebraic equation using the m_i notation and the $\Sigma(\cdots)$ notation.

(a)

A	B	C	F
0	0	0	0
0	0	1	1
0	1	0	0
0	1	1	1
1	0	0	0
1	0	1	0
1	1	0	1
1	1	1	1

(b)

A	B	C	F
0	0	0	1
0	0	1	0
0	1	0	1
0	1	1	0
1	0	0	0
1	0	1	1
1	1	0	1
1	1	1	0

(c)

A	B	C	F
0	0	0	1
0	0	1	1
0	1	0	1
0	1	1	1
1	0	0	0
1	0	1	0
1	1	0	0
1	1	1	1

(d)

A	B	C	F
0	0	0	1
0	0	1	0
0	1	0	1
0	1	1	1
1	0	0	1
1	0	1	0
1	1	0	1
1	1	1	0

(e) $A\ B\ C\ D$	F
0 0 0 0	1
0 0 0 1	1
0 0 1 0	0
0 0 1 1	0
0 1 0 0	0
0 1 0 1	1
0 1 1 0	0
0 1 1 1	0
1 0 0 0	0
1 0 0 1	0
1 0 1 0	1
1 0 1 1	1
1 1 0 0	0
1 1 0 1	0
1 1 1 0	1
1 1 1 1	1

(f) $A\ B\ C\ D$	F
0 0 0 0	1
0 0 0 1	0
0 0 1 0	1
0 0 1 1	0
0 1 0 0	0
0 1 0 1	1
0 1 1 0	0
0 1 1 1	1
1 0 0 0	1
1 0 0 1	0
1 0 1 0	1
1 0 1 1	0
1 1 0 0	1
1 1 0 1	1
1 1 1 0	0
1 1 1 1	1

(g) $A\ B\ C\ D$	F
0 0 0 0	1
0 0 0 1	0
0 0 1 0	1
0 0 1 1	1
0 1 0 0	0
0 1 0 1	0
0 1 1 0	0
0 1 1 1	1
1 0 0 0	1
1 0 0 1	0
1 0 1 0	1
1 0 1 1	1
1 1 0 0	0
1 1 0 1	0
1 1 1 0	0
1 1 1 1	1

(h) $A\ B\ C\ D$	F
0 0 0 0	0
0 0 0 1	1
0 0 1 0	0
0 0 1 1	1
0 1 0 0	1
0 1 0 1	0
0 1 1 0	1
0 1 1 1	0
1 0 0 0	1
1 0 0 1	0
1 0 1 0	1
1 0 1 1	0
1 1 0 0	0
1 1 0 1	0
1 1 1 0	0
1 1 1 1	1

2-6 Derive the normal-form sum-of-products equation:

(a) $F(A,B,C) = A \cdot \overline{B} + A \cdot \overline{C} + B \cdot \overline{C}$

(b) $F(A,B,C) = \overline{A} + B \cdot \overline{C} + \overline{B} \cdot C$

(c) $F(A,B,C,D) = A \cdot \overline{B} \cdot C + A \cdot C \cdot \overline{D} + B \cdot D$

(d) $F(A,B,C,D) = \overline{B} + A \cdot \overline{C} \cdot D + \overline{A} \cdot B$

(e) $F(A,B,C,D) = \overline{(A + B)} + C \cdot (B + A)$

(f) $F(A,B,C,D) = \overline{(A \cdot B)} + \overline{(C + D)}$

(g) $F(A,B,C,D) = A \cdot (B \cdot \overline{C} + \overline{(A \cdot D)}) + B \cdot \overline{(A \cdot C)} + \overline{(B \cdot C)}$

(h) $F(A,B,C,D) = \overline{A \cdot B \cdot C \cdot D}$

2-7 Determine whether F_1 and F_2 are equal by expanding each to its sum-of-products normal form:

(a) $F_1(A,B,C) = \overline{\overline{A \cdot B} + A \cdot B}$
$F_2(A,B,C) = \overline{A} \cdot B + A \cdot \overline{B}$

(b) $F_1(A,B,C,D) = A \cdot \overline{B} + C \cdot \overline{D}$
$F_2(A,B,C,D) = \overline{B} \cdot D + B \cdot C + A \cdot D + A \cdot C$

(c) $F_1(A,B,C) = A \cdot \overline{B} \cdot \overline{C}$
$F_2(A,B,C) = \overline{(A \cdot (\overline{B} \cdot \overline{C}))} + \overline{A}$

(d) $F_1 = (A,B,C,D) = \overline{(A + B)} + \overline{(C + D)}$
$F_2 = (A,B,C,D) = A \cdot C \cdot \overline{D} + B \cdot C \cdot \overline{D}$

2-8 Obtain a minimum sum-of-products equation for the function defined by the truth tables in Prob. 2-5.

2-9 Obtain a minimum sum-of-products equation for F.

(a) $F(A,B,C) = m_0 + m_1 + m_2 + m_6$

(b) $F(A,B,C) = m_3 + m_4 + m_5$

(c) $F(A,B,C) = \Sigma(0,1,2,3,4,6,7)$

(d) $F(A,B,C) = \Sigma(0,1,3,4,6,7)$

(e) $F(A,B,C,D) = m_0 + m_4 + m_6 + m_8 + m_{13}$

(f) $F(A,B,C,D) = m_0 + m_4 + m_6 + m_7 + m_{12} + m_{14}$

(g) $F(A,B,C,D) = \Sigma(0,1,2,3,5,8,9,10,11,13)$

(h) $F(A,B,C,D) = \Sigma(1,3,4,5,6,9,11,12,13,14,15)$

2-10 Obtain a minimum sum-of-products equation for F using the don't-care conditions:

(a) $F(A,B,C) = m_1 + m_2 + m_3 + m_4$
$d(A,B,C) = m_6$

(b) $F(A,B,C) = \Sigma(3,5,7)$
$d(A,B,C) = \Sigma(1)$

(c) $F(A,B,C,D) = m_4 + m_5 + m_{10} + m_{11} + m_{13} + m_{15}$
$d(A,B,C,D) = m_0 + m_2 + m_3 + m_8$

(d) $F(A,B,C,D) = \Sigma(3,4,5,6,7,10,13,15)$
$d(A,B,C,D) = \Sigma(1,12)$

(e) $F(A,B,C,D) = B \cdot \bar{C} \cdot \bar{D} + \bar{A} \cdot \bar{B} \cdot D + \bar{A} \cdot C \cdot \bar{D} + B \cdot C \cdot \bar{D}$
$d(A,B,C,D) = A \cdot \bar{B} \cdot \bar{C} + A \cdot \bar{C} \cdot D + \bar{A} \cdot B \cdot D$

2-11 Without simplifying the equations draw a logic diagram using AND, OR, and NOT gates.

(a) $F(A,B,C) = \bar{A} \cdot B \cdot C + A \cdot \bar{B}$

(b) $F(A,B,C) = A \cdot \bar{B} + \bar{B} \cdot C + \bar{A}$

(c) $F(A,B,C,D) = A \cdot \bar{B} + B \cdot \bar{C} + \bar{A} \cdot D$

(d) $F(A,B,C,D) = A \cdot B \cdot \bar{C} + \bar{B} \cdot C + \bar{D}$

(e) $F(A,B,C,D) = \bar{A} \cdot B + A \cdot B \cdot C + B \cdot \bar{D}$

(f) $F(A,B,C,D) = \bar{A} \cdot B + \bar{B} \cdot C + \bar{C} \cdot D$

2-12 Repeat Prob. 2-11 and eliminate canceling gates using only (1) NAND gates and (2) NOR gates.

2-13 Find an efficient logic diagram for the truth tables in Prob. 2-5 using:
(1) AND, OR, and NOT gates
(2) Only NAND gates
(3) Only NOR gates

2-14 Find an efficient logic diagram for the logic equations in Prob. 2-6 using:
(1) AND, OR, and NOT gates
(2) Only NAND gates
(3) Only NOR gates

2-15 Find an efficient logic diagram for the logic equation given in Prob. 2-9 using:
(1) AND, OR, and NOT gates
(2) Only NAND gates
(3) Only NOR gates

2-16 Find an efficient logic diagram for the logic equations and don't-care conditions in Prob. 2-10 using:
(1) AND, OR, and NOT gates
(2) Only NAND gates
(3) Only NOR gates

2-17 Two signals using the negative-logic assumption must be ANDed to produce a signal using the positive-logic assumption. Draw a logic diagram for the required network using:
(1) AND, OR, and NOT gates
(2) Only NAND gates
(3) Only NOR gates

2-18 Repeat Prob. 2-17 for two signals that must be ORed.

2-19 Write a sum-of-products equation for Z corresponding to the logic diagram given in Fig. P2-19a and b.

2-20 (a) Write the sum-of-products equation for F in Fig. P2-20, and (b) derive the truth table for F.

2-21 (a) Write the sum-of-products equation for Z in Fig. P2-21, and (b) derive the truth table for Z.

2-22 From the logic diagram in Fig. P2-22 define the corresponding equation for:
(a) Z_1 (b) Z_2 (c) Z_3
(d) Z_4 (e) Z_5

2-23 From the logic diagram in Fig. P2-22, define the truth tables for:
(a) Z_1 (b) Z_2 (c) Z_3
(d) Z_4 (e) Z_5

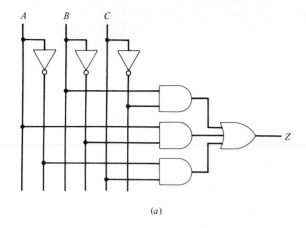

(a)

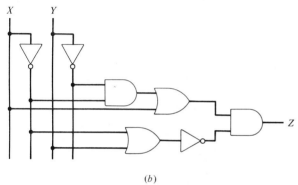

(b)

Figure P2-19 Logic diagram.

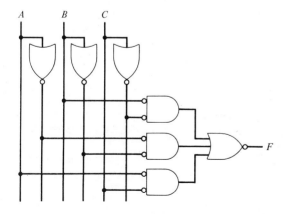

Figure P2-20 Logic diagram.

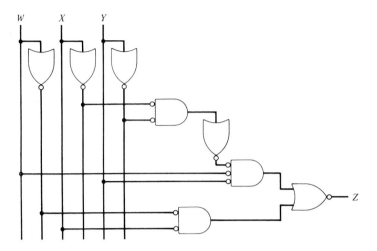

Figure P2-21 Logic diagram.

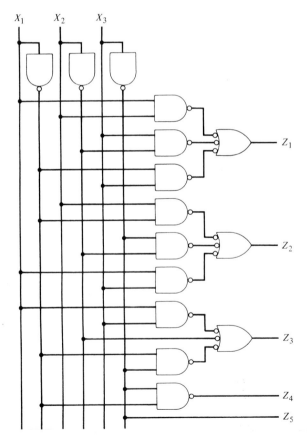

Figure P2-22 Logic diagram.

2-24 From the logic diagram in Fig. P2-24 define the corresponding equation for:

(a) Z_1 (b) Z_2 (c) Z_3 (d) Z_4 (e) Z_5

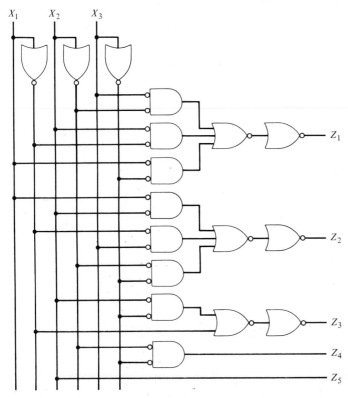

Figure P2-24 Logic diagram.

2-25 From the logic diagram in Prob. 2-24 define the truth table for:

(a) Z_1 (b) Z_2 (c) Z_3 (d) Z_4 (e) Z_5

2-26 In the circuit diagram (Fig. P2-26) define the truth table relating F to A, B, and C using a positive-logic assumption if the logic elements are (a) NAND circuits and (b) NOR circuits.

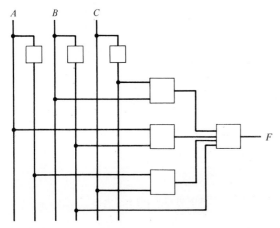

Figure P2-26 Circuit diagram.

2-27 For the logic diagram in Fig. P2-27 (1) write the corresponding equation, (2) minimize the equation, and (3) draw a logic diagram corresponding to the minimized equation using:

(*a*) AND, OR, and NOT gates

(*b*) Only NAND gates

(*c*) Only NOR gates

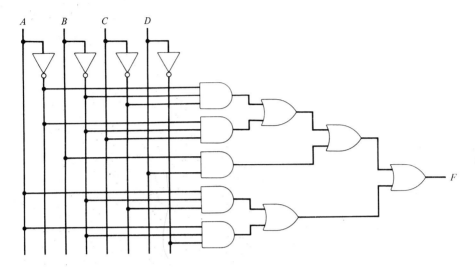

Figure P2-27 Logic diagram.

2-28 Obtain an efficient logic diagram for a full subtracter, a network that accepts two bits A and B and borrow in C_{in} and generates the difference R and a borrow out C_{out}. The difference is $A - B$. Use (*a*) NAND gates and (*b*) NOR gates.

2-29 Obtain an efficient logic diagram for a network that accepts two 2-bit words $A_1 A_0$ and $B_1 B_0$ and generates three outputs indicating that A is greater than B (Z_1), B is greater than A (Z_2), and A equals B (Z_3). The inputs are interpreted as positive-integer values. Use (*a*) NAND gates and (*b*) NOR gates.

2-30 Obtain an efficient logic diagram for a one-to-four demultiplexer with a data-enable signal similar to the one defined in Fig. 2-35 with (*a*) NAND gates and (*b*) NOR gates.

2-31 Obtain an efficient logic diagram for a network that accepts a BCD-coded digit and generates an output representing the BCD code of the difference between the input value and the decimal value 9 using (*a*) NAND gates and (*b*) NOR gates.

2-32 A certain MSI device is to be designed to accept two 4-bit values as input and produce two 4-bit outputs. If the control input is inactive, the device will output the absolute value of the two 4-bit inputs on corresponding straight-through output lines. If the control unit is active, the device will

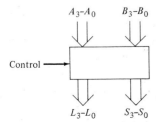

Figure P2-32 Device input-output model.

output the largest absolute value of the inputs on the L outputs and the smallest on the S outputs. An input-output model is shown in Fig. P2-32. Give an abbreviated voltage table for the device.

2-33 An MSI device performs addition and subtraction for a single digit of BCD data. The module accepts two 4-bit BCD operands and a carry input and produces a 4-bit BCD result digit and a carry output. Define the device symbol and give an abbreviated voltage table.

2-34 For the network defined in Fig. 2-39 define the outputs for each combination of select inputs with input words:

    (a) $A = 73_{16}$ and $B = 4A_{16}$
    (b) $A = 24_{16}$ and $B = 00_{16}$
    (c) $A = 19_{16}$ and $B = 19_{16}$

2-35 For the network described in Fig. 2-39, write a sum-of-products logic expression for R_0 in terms of A_0, B_0, S_0, S_1, S_2, and S_3.

2-36 For the network in Fig. 2-39 define the output voltage levels for each combination of voltage levels on the select inputs for the following input conditions:

    (a) A_7–A_0 = LLHH HLHH   (b) A_7–A_0 = LLLH LLLL
        B_7–B_0 = HHLL HHHL B_7–B_0 = LHLL LLLL
    (c) A_7–A_0 = LLLL HHHH
        B_7–B_0 = LLLL HHHH

2-37 Define the complete voltage table for a BCD-to-seven-segment code converter that operates on a negative-logic assumption. For the undefined input combinations the output should display E.

2-38 For the network described in Fig. 2-35 write a sum-of-products expression for Z_0.

2-39 Describe the input-output model and an abbreviated voltage table for a decimal-to-BCD code converter.

REFERENCES

Boole, G.: "An Investigation of the Laws of Thought, on Which Are Founded the Mathematical Theories of Logic and Probability," 1849, reprinted by Dover, New York, 1954.

Karnaugh, M.: The Map Method for Synthesis of Combinational Topic Circuits, *Trans. AIEE Commun. Electron.*, vol. 72, pt. 1, pp. 593–599, November 1953.

McCluskey, E. J.: Minimization of Boolean Functions, *Bell Syst. Tech. J.*, vol. 35, no. 6, pp. 1417–1444, November 1965.

Nagle, H. T., B. D. Carroll, and J. D. Irwin: "An Introduction to Computer Logic," Prentice-Hall, Englewood Cliffs, N.J., 1975.

Petric, S. R.: On the Minimization of Boolean Functions, *Symp. Switching Theory ICIP*, Paris, June 1959.

Quine, W. V.: A Way to Simplify Truth Functions, *Am. Math. Mon.*, vol. 62, no. 9, pp. 627–631, November 1955.

Rhyne, V. T.: "Fundamentals of Digital System Design," Prentice-Hall, Englewood Cliffs, N.J., 1973.

Su, S. Y. H., and N. T. Nam: Computer Aided Synthesis of Multiple Level NAND Networks with Fanin and Fanout Constraints, *IEEE Trans. Comput.*, vol. EC-20, no. 12, pp. 1445–1455, December 1971.

THREE

SEQUENTIAL NETWORKS

A *sequential digital* network is one whose outputs depend not only on the current inputs but also on the sequence of previous inputs. We therefore say that sequential networks have memory. By the end of this chapter the reader should be able to:

1. Define the terms in Prob. 3-1
2. Describe the behavior of various flip-flop types
3. Complete a timing diagram showing a flip-flop's response to given input waveforms
4. Convert a state table into a state diagram and vice versa
5. Define the output and state sequence resulting from an input sequence for a network described by a state table or diagram
6. Define an efficient logic diagram for a given flip-flop type and state table or diagram
7. Derive a state table or state diagram from a logic diagram
8. Define the behavior of selected counters, registers, and memory elements

3-1 THE FLIP-FLOP ELEMENT

The flip-flop is the basic sequential element. The name may be used to refer both to the electronic circuit, whose inputs and outputs are voltage levels L and H, and to the logic element, whose inputs and outputs are logic values 0 and 1, but in this text we reserve this term for the logic element and use *flip-flop circuit* for the electronic circuit. In this section we discuss the properties of both the flip-flop circuit and the flip-flop logic element.

3-1-1 Flip-Flop Circuit

The flip-flop circuit is a special electronic circuit with two output signals Q and $\overline{Q}$, as shown in Fig. 3-1. The Q output is referred to as the *true output*; $\overline{Q}$ is the *complementary* or *false output*. These signals assume one of two voltage levels and are complementary; i.e., if Q is at the high voltage level H, $\overline{Q}$ must be at the low voltage level L, and vice versa. Since the flip-flop maintains its outputs until changed by the input signals, it has two stable conditions: $Q = $ H and $\overline{Q} = $ L or $Q = $ L and $\overline{Q} = $ H. These two conditions are referred to as *states*. The first, $Q = $ H, is called the *set state*, and the second, $Q = $ L, is the *reset state*. We say that a flip-flop is *set* when it is driven into the set state, and we say that it is *reset* or *cleared* when driven into the reset state. In general, the positive-logic assumption is used with flip-flops. Thus, the set and reset states often are referred to as the 1 *state* and the 0 *state*, respectively.

We shall describe four common flip-flop circuits, the D, T, SR, and JK. Each type has a unique relationship between its input signals and the associated state transitions. This relationship is represented by a *state voltage table*, which indicates the voltage on the Q output after the clock transition for all input conditions for both the set and reset states. Figure 3-2 shows the symbol and the state voltage tables for the D, T, SR, and JK flip-flop circuits. In these tables *present state* and *next state* are used to define the condition before and after the transition.

The D flip-flop circuit has only one input signal, and the circuit assumes the state defined by this signal; i.e., the circuit is driven to the reset state when the input is low and to the set state when the input is high. The T flip-flop circuit changes states if its single input signal is high; otherwise it remains in the same state. The SR flip-flop circuit can be selectively set or reset by activating the appropriate input; i.e., the circuit is set if the S input is high and reset if the R input is high. If both inputs are low, there is no change in the state, but if both are high, the next state is undefined. The JK flip-flop circuit is similar to the SR flip-flop circuit except that the condition when both inputs are high is defined as a toggle signal; i.e., the flip-flop changes states regardless of the present state.

A flip-flop circuit is asynchronous or synchronous depending on whether a clock signal is used or not. *Asynchronous flip-flop* circuits operate without clock signals, and state transitions are initiated as soon as the input signals are altered.

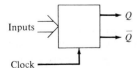

Inputs

Q

$\overline{Q}$

Clock

Figure 3-1 Flip-flop symbol.

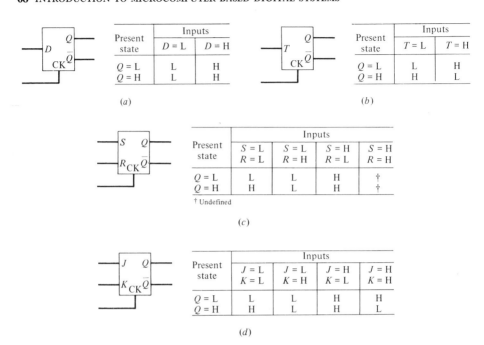

Figure 3-2 Symbol and voltage state table for (a) D flip-flop circuit, (b) T flip-flop circuit, (c) SR flip-flop circuit, and (d) JK flip-flop circuit.

Synchronous flip-flop circuits operate with a clock signal, so that the input signals are valid and the corresponding state transitions are initiated only during a specific portion of the clock signal. As a consequence, the input signals must be stable during this portion of the clock cycle. We shall consider the clock signal as a periodic pulse; the *rising* and *falling edges* provide two distinct time events which can be defined as *active phases*. Flip-flop circuits may be *edge-triggered devices*, which use the same active phase both to recognize input signals and to initiate state transitions, or *master-slave devices*, which use the rising edge of the clock pulse to recognize input signals and the falling edge of the clock pulse to initiate state transitions. The second type derives its name from the fact that it consists of two internal flip-flop circuit stages: the first stage, the master, recognizes the inputs signals and initiates its state transitions on the rising edge of the clock pulse; the second stage, the slave, accepts the outputs of the master as its input signals and initiates its state transitions on the falling edge of the clock pulse.

Figure 3-3 shows timing diagrams for a rising-edge-triggered T flip-flop circuit, for a falling-edge-triggered SR flip-flop circuit, and for a master-slave JK flip-flop circuit. In these timing diagrams we assume that the flip-flop circuits are reset initially. In Fig. 3-3a, the T input signal is low on the rising edge of the first and last clock pulses, so that the flip-flop circuit remains in the same state. With the middle two clock pulses the T input is high, so that the flip-flop circuit changes states. Just as with combinational digital circuits, there is a time delay,

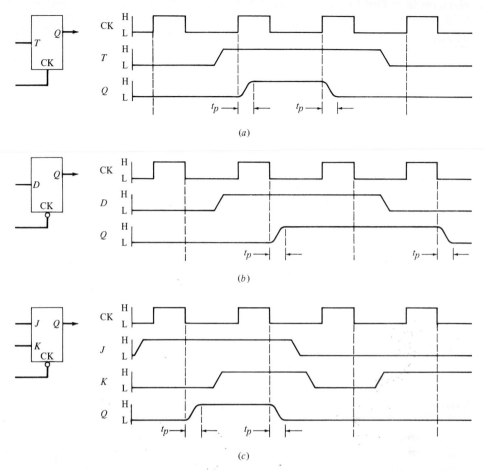

Figure 3-3 Timing diagrams: (*a*) rising-edge-triggered *T* flip-flop circuit; (*b*) falling-edge triggered *D* flip-flop circuit, and (*c*) master-slave *JK* flip-flop circuit.

referred to as the *propagation delay* t_p, before the output signal has stabilized when a transition occurs. Again, this is a characteristic of the device, and the length of delay depends on the technology used in its manufacture. With flip-flop circuits, a second important timing constraint, the flip-flop *setup time*, is an interval just before the active phase of the clock pulse during which the input signals must be stable. It also is a characteristic of the device depending on the manufacturing technology.

For the *D* flip-flop circuit in Fig. 3-3*b*, the active phase of the clock pulse is the trailing edge, as indicated by the small circle on the *C* input in the flip-flop symbol. On the first clock pulse, the *D* input is low, but since the flip-flop circuit is already reset, there is no change in state. On the second clock pulse the *D* input is high, and so the flip-flop circuit is set. There is no state change on the third clock pulse when the *D* input is high since the flip-flop circuit is already set. The flip-flop circuit is reset on the fourth clock pulse.

Table 3-1 State tables and transition tables for four flip-flop logic elements (d = Don't-care condition)

D flip-flop

State table			Transition table		

Present state	Input		Present state	Next state	D
	$D = 0$	$D = 1$			
$Q = 0$	0	1	0	0	0
$Q = 1$	0	1	0	1	1
			1	0	0
			1	1	1

T flip-flop

State table			Transition table		

Present state	Input		Present state	Next state	T
	$T = 0$	$T = 1$			
$Q = 0$	0	1	0	0	0
$Q = 1$	1	0	0	1	1
			1	0	1
			1	1	0

SR flip-flop

State table					Transition table			

Present state	Inputs SR				Present state	Next state	S	R
	0 0	0 1	1 0	1 1				
$Q = 0$	0	0	1	†	0	0	0	d
$Q = 1$	1	0	1	†	0	1	1	0
					1	0	0	1
					1	1	d	0

JK flip-flop

State table					Transition table			

Present state	Inputs JK				Present state	Next state	J	K
	0 0	0 1	1 0	1 1				
$Q = 0$	0	0	1	1	0	0	0	d
$Q = 1$	1	0	1	0	0	1	1	d
					1	0	d	1
					1	1	d	0

† Undefined.

In Fig. 3-3c, the output change is initiated on the falling edge of the clock pulse, as indicated by the circle on the C input. However, the inputs are valid on the rising edge of the clock pulse because the device is a master-slave flip-flop circuit. On the first clock pulse the J input is high and K input is low, and so the flip-flop circuit is set. Both input signals are high during the second clock pulse, and so the flip-flop circuit toggles. Nothing happens on the third clock pulse since both inputs are low. On the fourth, the inputs are defined to reset the flip-flop circuit, but since it is already reset, there is no change in its state.

3-1-2 Flip-Flop Logic Element

In associating the voltages on the flip-flop circuit inputs and outputs with binary values, we shall use the positive-logic assumption. The logic behavior of the flip-flop is described by the logic state tables or simply state tables, as shown in Table 3-1. The flip-flop state tables are analogous to the voltage state tables in Fig. 3-2 and indicate the binary value of Q after the clock pulse for all inputs conditions for both initial states ($Q = 0$ and $Q = 1$). These state tables are obtained by substituting 0 for L and 1 for H in the corresponding voltage table in Fig. 3-2.

In designing sequential networks, we use the transition table, an alternative description of the flip-flop's behavior. The *transition table*, which can be derived from the state table, defines the input condition necessary for each possible state transition. Transition tables for all four flip-flop types also are shown in Table 3-1.

We shall use the JK flip-flop to illustrate the procedure for converting a state table into a transition table. The first state transition in the table, the 0-to-0 transition, results if $J = 0$ and $K = 0$, the input condition specifying no change, or if $J = 0$ and $K = 1$, the input condition to reset the flip-flop. Thus, since K can be either 0 or 1, it can be considered a don't-care condition. Thus, the 0-to-0 transition requires that $J = 0$ and $K = $ d. For the 0-to-1 transition, the inputs must be $J = 1$ and $K = 0$, the input condition to set the flip-flop, or $J = 1$ and $K = 1$, the input condition to toggle the flip-flop. Thus, for this transition the required inputs are $J = 1$ and $K = $ d. Input requirements for the other two transitions are similarly defined.

3-2 STATE TABLES AND STATE DIAGRAMS

In describing the behavior of sequential networks containing several flip-flops we shall use the concept of states. Earlier in this chapter we defined a state as a recognizable condition and pointed out that a flip-flop has two stable states, the reset state, with $Q = 0$, and the set state, with $Q = 1$. In a network with N flip-flops the states are characterized by an N-bit binary word, where each bit is associated with one of the flip-flops. Since there are 2^N distinct patterns in an N-bit word, there are 2^N stable states.

3-2-1 Symbolic Notation

Instead of using binary code words to define the input conditions, output conditions, and states, it is sometimes convenient to define a symbolic code representing each valid input condition, output condition, and state. We shall use the symbols $I_0, I_1, I_2, \ldots, R_0, R_1, R_2, \ldots$, and $S_0, S_1, S_2, \ldots$ to represent the valid input conditions, output or response conditions, and states, respectively. Just as a flip-flop is characterized by its state table defining the next state for all combinations of inputs and present states, a sequential network, which is constructed from flip-flops, is characterized by a *network state table*, or *state table*, defining the current output condition and next state for all combinations of input conditions and present states. Alternatively, the information in the network state table can be represented by a *network state diagram*, or *state diagram*, pictorially defining the current output and next state for all combinations of input conditions and present states. Figure 3-4 shows the state table and state diagram for a sequential network. The network has two valid input conditions (I_0 and I_1), three valid output conditions (R_0, R_1, and R_2), and four valid states (S_0, S_1, S_2, and S_3).

In the state table in Fig. 3-4 the current inputs are listed across the top, and the present states are listed in the leftmost column. Entries in the internal squares define the next state and the current output for each combination of input condition and present state. For example, when the network is in state S_0 and the input is I_0, the current output is R_1 and the next state is S_1. Similarly if the input is I_1 and the present state is S_0, the current output is R_2 and the next state is S_3. As another example, for state S_3 the current output is R_0 and the next state is S_0, regardless of the input. Finally, for present state S_2 and input I_1 there is no change in state, and the current output is R_1.

In the state diagram in Fig. 3-4b, a circle represents each state, and for each input condition a directed line points to the next state. Input conditions and

Present state	Inputs I_0	I_1
S_0	S_1/R_1	S_3/R_2
S_1	S_2/R_2	S_2/R_1
S_2	S_0/R_2	S_2/R_1
S_3	S_0/R_0	S_0/R_0

(a)

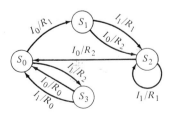

(b)

Figure 3-4 (a) Network state table and (b) state diagram.

current output conditions are defined above each directed line. In this example, there are two lines leaving state S_0, one for each valid input. If the input is I_0, the current output is R_1 and the next state is S_1; whereas if the input is I_1, the current output is R_2 and the next state is S_3. For state S_3 the next state is S_0 and the current output is R_0, regardless of the input. Also, for state S_2 with an input of I_1, there is no change in state and the current output is R_1.

Since the state table and state diagram provide the same information, it is possible to convert one into the other. In converting a state table into a state diagram a circle is drawn for each state in the leftmost column of the state table. Each internal square is translated into a directed line segment between circles. For example, for the present state S_0 in Fig. 3-4a, there are two internal squares, one for each input condition, and so there are two directed lines leaving the S_0 circle in the state diagram. For the input condition I_0, the directed line terminates on the circle for S_1 and the input and output conditions are defined by I_0/R_1. For the input condition I_1, the line is terminated on the circle for state S_3, and the input and output conditions are I_1/R_2. This same procedure would be followed for the other three present states.

The procedure for converting a state diagram into a state table is analogous. First the structure of the table is defined, a row for each state in the state diagram and a column for each unique input condition. Next each directed line is translated into an internal square. For example, for S_0 in Fig. 3-4b, the directed line for I_0 has an output of R_1 and a next state of S_1; this information is entered into the upper left internal square as S_1/R_1. The directed line for I_1 has an output of R_2 and a next state of S_3; this information is entered into the upper right square as S_3/R_2. The other three states are handled in the same way.

3-2-2 State Sequences

To illustrate that both the network state table and the network state diagram characterize the behavior of a sequential network, let us consider how the network defined in Fig. 3-4 responds to the input sequence I_1, I_1, I_0, I_1, and I_0 if the initial state is S_1. At the time of the first clock pulse, the input is I_1, and the present state is S_1. From the state table or diagram in Fig. 3-4 we see that for the combination of S_1 and I_1 the output at this clock pulse is R_1 and the next state after the clock pulse is S_2, as shown in Fig. 3-5a. For the second clock pulse, the input is specified as I_1 and the new present state defined by the transition on the previous clock pulse is S_2. From the state table or diagram we see that with the combination of I_1 and S_2 the output is R_1 and the next state is S_2. For the third clock pulse, the specified input is I_0 and the present state is S_2. This combination produces an output of R_2 and results in the new state S_0. Outputs and transition for the fourth and fifth clock pulse can be analyzed similarly.

The table in Fig. 3-5b more concisely defines the sequence of states and outputs produced by the given sequence of inputs. We may consider each vertical line to be a clock pulse, and the entries in the previous column indicate the condition at the clock pulse. For example, at the first clock pulse the valid conditions are I_1, S_1, and R_1; at the second clock pulse they are I_1, S_2, and R_1.

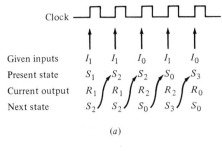

(a)

Input sequence	I_1	I_1	I_0	I_1	I_0
State sequence	S_1	S_2	S_2	S_0	S_3
Output sequence	R_1	R_1	R_2	R_2	R_0

(b)

Figure 3-5 Sequence of inputs, outputs, and states for the network defined in Fig. 3-4.

Example 3-1 A sequential network is defined by the state table below. Define the sequence of outputs and states for the input sequence I_0, I_2, I_2, I_3, and I_1. The initial state is S_2.

Present state	Input			
	I_0	I_1	I_2	I_3
S_0	S_0/R_0	S_1/R_1	S_2/R_0	S_1/R_0
S_1	S_0/R_0	S_1/R_0	S_1/R_0	S_0/R_0
S_2	S_1/R_2	S_1/R_0	S_2/R_0	S_1/R_0

SOLUTION

Input sequence	I_0	I_2	I_2	I_3	I_1
State sequence	S_2	S_1	S_1	S_1	S_0
Output sequence	R_2	R_0	R_0	R_0	R_1

3-2-3 Binary-Coded State Tables and Diagrams

State tables and state diagrams can be constructed using binary codes to represent the input conditions, output conditions, and states. Figure 3-6a describes one set of code words for the sequential network defined by the state table† and state diagram in Fig. 3-4.

---

† In all encoded state tables the next state and output variable entries are ordered with decreasing subscripts from left to right.

Coding the two input conditions requires only one binary variable, X_0. There are two choices for defining the code: letting $X_0 = 0$ for I_0 and $X_0 = 1$ for I_1 or letting $X_0 = 0$ for I_1 and $X_0 = 1$ for I_0. In Fig. 3-6a we have chosen the former.

Two variables (Z_1 and Z_0) are required for coding the three output conditions. In defining the code, there are several choices, and the only constraint is the requirement of uniqueness of the code word for each condition. The code defined in Fig. 3-6a assigns the code word 11 to the condition R_0, the code word 01 to the condition R_1, and the code word 10 to the condition R_2, the code word 00 being unassigned. These code words specify the value of the binary variables Z_1 and Z_0, Z_1 being the more significant bit. In coding the four states, we must use two binary variables, which implies that the network contains two flip-flops represented by Q_1 and Q_0. Again, there are several choices for defining the code; that used in Fig. 3-6a assigns the code word 00 to S_0, the code word 10 to S_1, the code word 11 to S_2, and the code word 01 to S_3. These code words specify the values of Q_1 and Q_0 with Q_1 the more significant.

The codes defined in Fig. 3-6a represent arbitrary choices. There are techniques for defining codes which by some criterion or other minimize the complexity of the network. We shall not be concerned with this aspect of sequential

Input code		Output code			State code		
Symbol	X_0	Symbol	Z_1	Z_0	Symbol	Q_1	Q_0
I_0	0	R_0	1	1	S_0	0	0
I_1	1	R_1	0	1	S_1	1	0
		R_2	1	0	S_2	1	1
					S_3	0	1

(a)

Present state $Q_1 Q_0$	X_0	
	0	1
0 0	10/01	01/10
1 0	11/10	11/01
1 1	00/10	11/01
0 1	00/11	00/11

$Q_1 Q_0 / Z_1 Z_0$

(b)

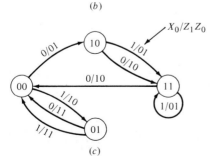

(c)

Figure 3-6 (a) One set of code words for network described by Fig. 3-4, (b) resulting encoded state table, and (c) diagram.

network design and shall limit ourselves to defining unique but arbitrary codes for each condition and state.

Figure 3-6b and c shows the encoded state table and state diagram derived from the symbolic versions in Fig. 3-4. These encoded versions are obtained by replacing each symbol by its assigned code word. For example, I_0 is replaced by 0, R_0 by 11, and S_0 by 00.

3-3 CONVERTING A STATE TABLE INTO A LOGIC DIAGRAM

In this section we describe a method for converting an encoded state table for a sequential network into an efficient logic diagram using the general structural model in Fig. 3-7. This model separates the sequential network into a combinational subnetwork and a flip-flop subnetwork. It also identifies four distinct groups of variables: network inputs X, network outputs Z, flip-flop inputs Y, and flip-flop outputs Q. Of these signals, X and Q are inputs to the combinational subnetwork, and Z and Y are outputs of this subnetwork.

Let us consider the encoded state table shown in Fig. 3-8a and develop an efficient logic diagram for it using JK flip-flops. From the state table we note that there is one input variable X_0, one output variable Z_0, and two flip-flop outputs Q_1 and Q_0. Since JK flip-flops are specified, Y contains four variables (J_1, K_1, J_0, and K_0). Figure 3-8b shows the general structural model with these variables identified explicitly. This figure points out that defining the logic diagram for this sequential network basically reduces to defining an efficient logic diagram for the combinational subnetwork. The first step in this procedure then is defining a truth table for this combinational subnetwork from the information in the state table.

The state table explicitly defines the value of Z_0 for all combinations of values for X_0, Q_1, and Q_0. Thus the truth table for Z_0 is obtained simply by rewriting the information in a more standard form. Figure 3-8c shows the resulting *output truth table*. All combinations of values for X_0, Q_1, and Q_0 were enumerated using a binary count. Each row corresponds to an internal square in the state table. For example, the first row corresponds to the upper left internal

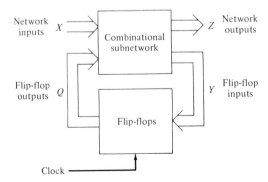

Figure 3-7 General structural model of a sequential network.

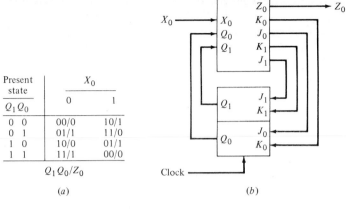

Present state / X_0 table (a):

Present state $Q_1 Q_0$	X_0	
	0	1
0 0	00/0	10/1
0 1	01/1	11/0
1 0	10/0	01/1
1 1	11/1	00/0

$Q_1 Q_0 / Z_0$

(a)

(b)

Table (c):

Input	Present state	Output
X_0	$Q_1\ Q_0$	Z_0
0	0 0	0
0	0 1	1
0	1 0	0
0	1 1	1
1	0 0	1
1	0 1	0
1	1 0	1
1	1 1	0

(c)

Table (d):

Input	Present state	Next state	Flip-flop inputs
X_0	$Q_1\ Q_0$	$Q_1\ Q_0$	$J_1\ K_1\ J_0\ K_0$
0	0 0	0 0	0 d 0 d
0	0 1	0 1	0 d d 0
0	1 0	1 0	d 0 0 d
0	1 1	1 1	d 0 d 0
1	0 0	1 0	1 d 0 d
1	0 1	1 1	1 d d 0
1	1 0	0 1	d 1 1 d
1	1 1	0 0	d 1 d 1

(d)

Figure 3-8 (*a*) State table, (*b*) structural model, (*c*) output truth table, and (*d*) extended truth table for a sequential network.

square, where the input is 0 and the present state is 00. In the state table the output for this combination is 0, which is entered under Z_0 in the first row of the truth table. The second row corresponds to the internal square where the input is 0 and the present state is 01. In the state table the output for this combination is 1, which is entered in the truth table. This procedure is repeated until all entries in the output truth table are defined.

Although the state table does not define the values for J_1, K_1, J_0, and K_0 explicitly, it does define the next state of Q_1 and Q_0, thereby indirectly defining the flip-flop inputs. Since this information is not directly available and must be derived, we use an extended truth table to transform it into the desired format.

The *extended truth table* for this problem (Fig. 3-8*d*) lists combinations of values for the input and present states, and for each combination it defines values for the associated next states and flip-flop inputs to produce the specified transition. In this table all combinations of values for X_0, Q_1, and Q_0 were enumerated by a binary count. Entries in the next-state columns were found in the corresponding internal square of the network state table, just as we found the values of Z_0 for the output truth table above. For example, the last row in the extended truth table corresponds to the internal square in the state table where the input is 1 and the present state is 11. For this combination the next state is 00, which is entered in the last row of the extended truth table. The next-to-last row in the extended truth table corresponds to the internal square in the state table where the input is 1 and the present state is 10. For this combination the next state is 01, which is entered in the extended truth table. This procedure is repeated until all next states are defined in the extended truth table.

The extended truth table now defines the present and next state for all input combinations. The next step is to define values for the flip-flop inputs to produce each transition for each flip-flop. To help complete this table we shall use the flip-flop transition table (Table 3-1), which defines the values on J and K for all possible transitions. In the first row, Q_1 undergoes a 0-to-0 transition; from the flip-flop transition table we see that $J_1 = 0$ and $K_1 = d$ produces this transition. These values are therefore entered in the first row of the extended truth table. In the last row, Q_1 undergoes a 1-to-0 transition, and so the inputs are $J_1 = d$ and $K_1 = 1$. These values are entered in the extended truth table. This procedure is repeated until J_1 and K_1 are completely defined. This procedure is then applied to define J_0 and K_0 from the specified transitions of Q_0.

The output truth table (Fig. 3-8c) and the extended truth table (Fig. 3-8d) combine to define the behavior of the combinational subnetwork. To obtain an efficient logic diagram we construct maps for Z_0, J_1, K_1, J_0, and K_0 and use the minimization techniques presented in Chap. 2 to obtain a minimum sum-of-products form for each variable. These maps and the minimization are shown in Fig. 3-9. Figure 3-10 shows the AND, OR, and NOT logic diagram implementing

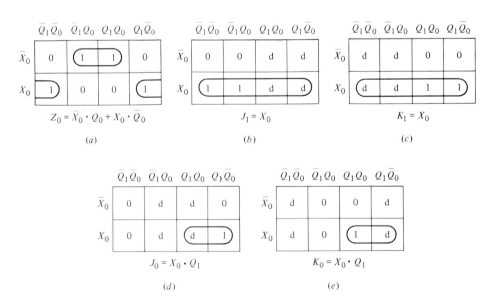

Figure 3-9 K maps for the sequential network defined in Fig. 3-8.

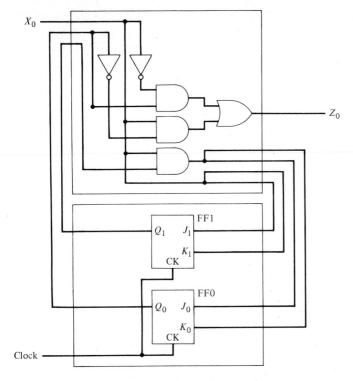

X_0

Z_0

FF1

Q_1 J_1

K_1

CK

FF0

Q_0 J_0

K_0

CK

Clock

Figure 3-10 An efficient logic diagram for the sequential network defined in Fig. 3-8.

these equations and the interconnections between logic elements in the two subnetworks. This figure emphasizes that X_0 and Z_0 are the only external signals; the flip-flop inputs and outputs are internal signals.

Example 3-2 For the state table below derive all minimum sum-of-products equations needed to construct a logic diagram using JK flip-flops.

Present state	$X_1 X_0$			
$Q_1 Q_0$	00	01	10	11
00	01/01	10/01	11/10	00/00
01	10/01	11/10	00/00	01/01
10	11/10	00/00	01/01	10/01
11	00/00	01/01	10/01	11/10

SOLUTION First we construct the standard and extended truth tables. In the latter we use the JK flip-flop transition table.

X_1	X_0	Present state Q_1	Q_0	Z_1	Z_0
0	0	0	0	0	1
		0	1	0	1
		1	0	1	0
		1	1	0	0
0	1	0	0	0	1
		0	1	1	0
		1	0	0	0
		1	1	0	1
1	0	0	0	1	0
		0	1	0	0
		1	0	0	1
		1	1	0	1
1	1	0	0	0	0
		0	1	0	1
		1	0	0	1
		1	1	1	0

X_1	X_0	Present state Q_1	Q_0	Next state Q_1	Q_0	J_1	K_1	J_0	K_0
0	0	0	0	0	1	0	d	1	d
		0	1	1	0	1	d	d	1
		1	0	1	1	d	0	1	d
		1	1	0	0	d	1	d	1
0	1	0	0	1	0	1	d	0	d
		0	1	1	1	1	d	d	0
		1	0	0	0	d	1	0	d
		1	1	0	1	d	1	d	0
1	0	0	0	1	1	1	d	1	d
		0	1	0	0	0	d	d	1
		1	0	0	1	d	1	1	d
		1	1	1	0	d	0	d	1
1	1	0	0	0	0	0	d	0	d
		0	1	0	1	0	d	d	0
		1	0	1	0	d	0	0	d
		1	1	1	1	d	0	d	0

K maps are drawn and used to define minimum sum-of-products equations (Fig. E3-2).

$$Z_1 = \overline{X}_1 \cdot \overline{X}_0 \cdot Q_1 \cdot \overline{Q}_0 + \overline{X}_1 \cdot X_0 \cdot \overline{Q}_1 \cdot Q_0 + X_1 \cdot X_0 \cdot Q_1 \cdot Q_0 + X_1 \cdot \overline{X}_0 \cdot \overline{Q}_1 \cdot \overline{Q}_0$$

$$Z_0 = \overline{X}_1 \cdot \overline{X}_0 \cdot \overline{Q}_1 + \overline{X}_1 \cdot \overline{Q}_1 \cdot \overline{Q}_0 + X_1 \cdot \overline{X}_0 \cdot Q_1 + X_1 \cdot Q_1 \cdot \overline{Q}_0$$
$$+ \overline{X}_1 \cdot X_0 \cdot Q_1 \cdot Q_0 + X_1 \cdot X_0 \cdot \overline{Q}_1 \cdot Q_0$$

$$J_1 = \overline{X}_1 \cdot X_0 + \overline{X}_1 \cdot Q_0 + X_1 \cdot \overline{X}_0 \cdot \overline{Q}_0$$

$$K_1 = \overline{X}_1 \cdot X_0 + \overline{X}_1 \cdot Q_0 + X_1 \cdot \overline{X}_0 \cdot \overline{Q}_0$$

$$J_0 = \overline{X}_0$$

$$K_0 = \overline{X}_0$$

A logic diagram can be drawn directly from these equations. The reader is encouraged to do this exercise.

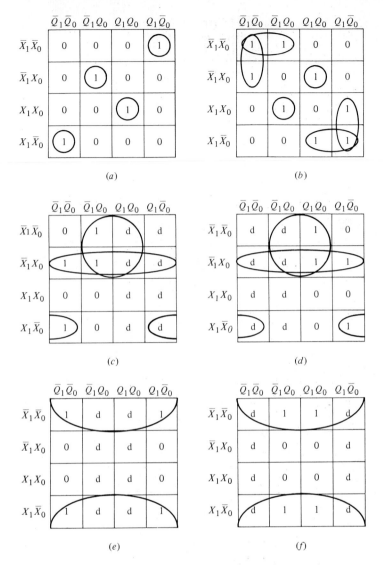

Figure E3-2 K maps: (a) Z_1, (b) Z_0, (c) J_1, (d) K_1, (e) J_0, (f) K_0.

3-4 CONVERTING A LOGIC DIAGRAM INTO A STATE TABLE

This section describes a method for converting a logic diagram for a sequential network into a state table. This conversion, the counterpart of that described in the previous section, is an essential step in the analysis of sequential networks.

Figure 3-11 shows the logic diagram for a sequential network. There are one input variable X_0, one output variable Z_0, and two T flip-flops FF0 and FF1. The

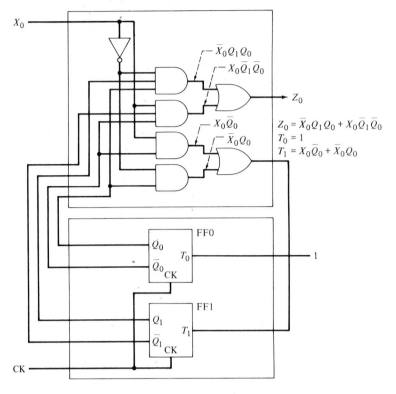

Figure 3-11 Logic diagram for a sequential network.

combinational network is described with AND, OR, and NOT gates. Z_0 and the two flip-flop inputs T_0 and T_1 can be described in terms of the combinational subnetwork inputs X_0, Q_1, and Q_0

$$Z_0 = \overline{X}_0 \cdot Q_1 \cdot Q_0 + X_0 \cdot \overline{Q}_1 \cdot \overline{Q}_0 \tag{3-1}$$

$$T_1 = X_0 \cdot \overline{Q}_0 + \overline{X}_0 \cdot Q_0 \tag{3-2}$$

$$T_0 = 1 \tag{3-3}$$

Table 3-2 shows the output truth table for the output Z_0 constructed from Eq. (3-1). The first three columns, X_0, Q_1, and Q_0, represent inputs to the combinational subnetwork, and the entries in these columns represent an enumeration of all possible combinations. As before, this enumeration is done using a binary count. Entries under Z_0 were obtained by rewriting Eq. (3-1) as $Z_0 = m_3 + m_4$ and then placing a 1 in the rows corresponding to minterms m_3 and m_4 and a 0 in all other rows.

Table 3-2 Output and extended truth tables and the state table for the sequential network defined in Fig. 3-11

Output truth table

Input X_0	Present state Q_1 Q_0		Output Z_0
0	0	0	0
0	0	1	0
0	1	0	0
0	1	1	1
1	0	0	1
1	0	1	0
1	1	0	0
1	1	1	0

Extended truth table

Input X_0	Present state Q_1 Q_0		Next state Q_1 Q_0		Flip-flop input T_1 T_0	
0	0	0	0	1	0	1
0	0	1	1	0	1	1
0	1	0	1	1	0	1
0	1	1	0	0	1	1
1	0	0	1	1	1	1
1	0	1	0	0	0	1
1	1	0	0	1	1	1
1	1	1	1	0	0	1

State table

Q_1	Q_0	X_0 0	1
0	0	01/0	11/1
0	1	10/0	00/0
1	0	11/0	01/0
1	1	00/1	10/0

Table 3-2 also shows the extended truth table for the flip-flop inputs. Entries in the input and present-state columns were enumerated just as before. Entries in the flip-flop input columns were obtained from Eqs. (3-2) and (3-3). The equation for T_1 can be rewritten as $T_1 = m_1 + m_3 + m_4 + m_6$ to define explicitly the rows where T_1 has a value of 1. Equation (3-3) indicates that T_0 is always 1, and these values are entered in the extended truth table.

This table now defines the present state and the flip-flop inputs for all combinations. Next we define the next state of each flip-flop defined by each transition. This is done in the two next state columns in the extended truth table. Entries in these columns are obtained by applying the T flip-flop state table (Table 3-1) to each specified transition for each flip-flop in each row of the extended truth table. To illustrate this technique consider FF1. In the first row $Q_1 = 0$ and $T_1 = 0$; so, from the flip-flop state table, the next state is $Q_1 = 0$; in the second row $Q_1 = 0$ and $T_1 = 1$, so the next state is $Q_1 = 1$; in the third, $Q_1 = 1$ and $T_1 = 0$, so the next state is $Q_1 = 1$; in the fourth, $Q_1 = 1$ and $T_1 = 1$, so the next is $Q_1 = 0$; and so on for the remaining four rows. Entries for FF0 are processed in the same way.

Table 3-2 also shows the state table corresponding to the two truth tables just derived. The first step in this conversion is to define the structure of the state table. The truth tables indicate that there are two state variables (Q_1 and Q_0), implying $2^2 = 4$ present states, so there are four rows in the state table. The one input variable X_0 implies $2^1 = 2$ input conditions, so the state table will have two columns. Each row in the truth tables is transferred to an internal square in the state table. For example, the first row in the truth tables represents a present state 00 and an input 0, which corresponds to the upper left internal square in the state table. From the truth tables we see that the next state is 01 and the output is 0. This information is entered as 01/0 in that square. The next row represents the present state 01 with an input of 0. Its next state 10 and the output 0 are entered into the appropriate square in the state table. This process is repeated until each row in the truth tables is transferred to the appropriate square in the state table.

Example 3-3 For the network shown in Fig. E3-3a derive the output sequence which results if the initial state is $Q_1 = 0$ and $Q_0 = 1$ and the input sequence is $X = 1, 0, 1, 1, 0$.

SOLUTION To derive the sequence of output we need to obtain the state table. First, we define equation for the output Z and the flip-flop inputs J_0, K_0, J_1, and K_1

$$Z = \left(\overline{\overline{X \cdot \overline{Q_1}}} \right) + \overline{Q_0} = X \cdot \overline{Q_1} + \overline{Q_0}$$

$$J_0 = \overline{\overline{Q_1}} + \overline{Q_0} = Q_1 + \overline{Q_0}$$

$$K_0 = \left(\overline{\overline{X \cdot \overline{Q_1}}} \right) + \overline{\overline{Q_0}} = X \cdot \overline{Q_1} + Q_0$$

$$J_1 = Q_0$$

$$K_1 = \left(\overline{X \cdot Q_0} \right) + \left(\overline{\overline{X} \cdot \overline{Q_1}} \right) = X \cdot Q_0 + \overline{X} \cdot \overline{Q_1}$$

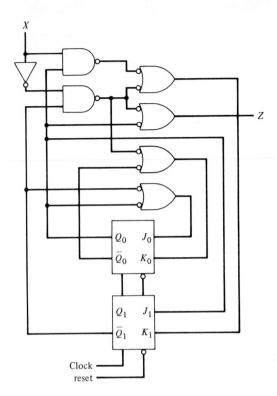

X

Z

Q_0 J_0

$\bar{Q}_0$ K_0

Q_1 J_1

$\bar{Q}_1$ K_1

Clock
reset

Figure E3-3 Logic diagram.

The output and extended truth table are now developed from these equations
and the transition table for the *JK* flip-flop.

| X | Present state | | Z |
	Q_1	Q_0	
0	0	0	1
0	0	1	1
0	1	0	1
0	1	1	0
1	0	0	1
1	0	1	0
1	1	0	1
1	1	1	0

| X | Present state | | Next state | | J_1 | K_1 | J_0 | K_0 |
	Q_1	Q_0	Q_1	Q_0				
0	0	0	0	1	0	1	1	1
0	0	1	1	0	1	1	0	1
0	1	0	1	1	0	0	1	0
0	1	1	1	0	1	0	1	1
1	0	0	0	1	0	0	1	0
1	0	1	1	0	1	1	0	1
1	1	0	1	1	0	0	1	0
1	1	1	0	0	1	1	1	1

From these tables we define the state table

Present state Q_1	Q_0	$X = 0$	$X = 1$
0	0	01/1	01/1
0	1	10/1	10/0
1	0	11/1	11/1
1	1	10/0	00/0

The sequence for the given conditions is

Input X	1	0	1	1	0
Present state Q_1Q_0	0 1	1 0	1 1	0 0	0 1
Output Z	0	1	0	1	1

3-5 DESIGN EXAMPLES

In this section we shall illustrate the process of designing simple sequential networks from a precise verbal specification. In the next chapter we shall deal with more comprehensive design problems presented with less precise specifications. Here we deal with problems whose specification translates directly into a state table or diagram.

3-5-1 Decade Counter

In the first example we shall design a decade counter using T flip-flops. This network contains four flip-flops whose outputs form a code word interpreted as a BCD-coded decimal value. On each clock pulse the coded value is incremented, and when 9 is reached, it returns to 0 on the next clock pulse. On the 9-to-0 transition the network activates an output line to indicate the counter overflowed; this signal frequently is referred to as a carry.

The first step in the design process is defining a structural model and using it to identify the input and output variables. Figure 3-12 shows such a model for the decade counter. Aside from the clock signal there are no other inputs to this network. The only output from the combinational subnetwork is the carry signal C.

The next step is to define either the state table or state diagram describing the behavior of the network. Figure 3-13a shows the state diagram for this counter. It indicates that the network has 10 acceptable states and that the sequence of states

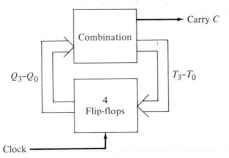

Figure 3-12 Structural model for a decade counter.

is 0000, 0001, 0010, ..., 1000, 1001, and then repeats with 0000, 0001, and so on. Since there are no inputs to the network, the values on the directed lines show only the current output associated with each state. These have a value of 0 for all valid states except 1001. Figure 3-13b shows the corresponding state table. Since the network has no inputs, there is only one internal column in the table. Note that since the next state for the six unused states 1010 to 1111 is undefined, they are designated as don't-care conditions.

Table 3-3 shows the truth table for the network output C and the extended truth table for the flip-flop inputs T_3, T_2, T_1, and T_0, obtained using the methods described in Sec. 3-3. Briefly, the present states were enumerated. Values for the output in the truth table and the next states in the extended truth table were transferred row by row from the corresponding squares in the state table or the corresponding directed line in the state diagram. Values for the flip-flop inputs were defined in order to produce each specified state transition. In defining these values we used the T flip-flop transition table (Table 3-1).

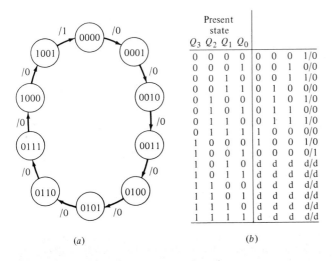

	Present state						
Q_3	Q_2	Q_1	Q_0				
0	0	0	0	0	0	0	1/0
0	0	0	1	0	0	1	0/0
0	0	1	0	0	0	1	1/0
0	0	1	1	0	1	0	0/0
0	1	0	0	0	1	0	1/0
0	1	0	1	0	1	1	0/0
0	1	1	0	0	1	1	1/0
0	1	1	1	1	0	0	0/0
1	0	0	0	1	0	0	1/0
1	0	0	1	0	0	0	0/1
1	0	1	0	d	d	d	d/d
1	0	1	1	d	d	d	d/d
1	1	0	0	d	d	d	d/d
1	1	0	1	d	d	d	d/d
1	1	1	0	d	d	d	d/d
1	1	1	1	d	d	d	d/d

(a)   (b)

Figure 3-13 (a) State diagram and (b) table for a decade counter.

Table 3-3 Output truth table and extended truth table for decade counter defined in Figs. 3-12 and 3-13

Present state Q_3 Q_2 Q_1 Q_0	Output C	Present state Q_3 Q_2 Q_1 Q_0	Next state Q_3 Q_2 Q_1 Q_0	Flip-flop input T_3 T_2 T_1 T_0
0 0 0 0	0	0 0 0 0	0 0 0 1	0 0 0 1
0 0 0 1	0	0 0 0 1	0 0 1 0	0 0 1 1
0 0 1 0	0	0 0 1 0	0 0 1 1	0 0 0 1
0 0 1 1	0	0 0 1 1	0 1 0 0	0 1 1 1
0 1 0 0	0	0 1 0 0	0 1 0 1	0 0 0 1
0 1 0 1	0	0 1 0 1	0 1 1 0	0 0 1 1
0 1 1 0	0	0 1 1 0	0 1 1 1	0 0 0 1
0 1 1 1	0	0 1 1 1	1 0 0 0	1 1 1 1
1 0 0 0	0	1 0 0 0	1 0 0 1	0 0 0 1
1 0 0 1	1	1 0 0 1	0 0 0 0	1 0 0 1
1 0 1 0	d	1 0 1 0	d d d d	d d d d
1 0 1 1	d	1 0 1 1	d d d d	d d d d
1 1 0 0	d	1 1 0 0	d d d d	d d d d
1 1 0 1	d	1 1 0 1	d d d d	d d d d
1 1 1 0	d	1 1 1 0	d d d d	d d d d
1 1 1 1	d	1 1 1 1	d d d d	d d d d

The next step is to obtain efficient equations for the output C and for the flip-flop inputs T_3, T_2, T_1, and T_0. Figure 3-14 shows the maps used in obtaining these minimum sum-of-products expressions. The logic diagram showing an AND, OR, NOT implementation corresponding to these equations is given in Fig. 3-15.

3-5-2 A 3-Bit Up-Down Binary Counter

The second example is a 3-bit up-down binary counter with one input signal, to control the direction of the count, and two output signals, one indicating the counter overflow and one indicating counter underflow. This network contains three flip-flops whose outputs form a code word interpreted as a binary value. On each clock pulse the counter increments the coded value if the input signal is active and decrements the coded value if the input signal is inactive. The output signal indicating counter overflow, sometimes called the carry signal, is active on the 111-to-000 transition. The second output signal indicating that the counter underflowed, sometimes called the borrow signal, is active on the 000-to-111 transition. We do not specify a flip-flop type since we shall stop our development after we have defined the state table.

Figure 3-16 shows the structural model for the 3-bit up-down binary counter. The input signal controlling the count is symbolized by U, the carry signal by C, and the borrow signal by B.

Figure 3-17 shows the state diagram and table for this network with the positive-logic assumption. When the input U has the value 0, the next state is

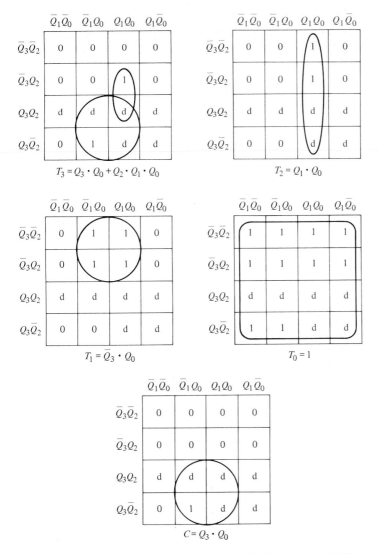

Figure 3-14 K maps for the decade counter defined in Figs. 3-12 and 3-13.

obtained by decrementing the binary value defined by the present state. This is true even for the state 000, which when decremented produces 111. On this transition the borrow signal is active and B is set to 1. When the input U has the value of 1, the next state is obtained by incrementing the binary value defined by the present state. This is also true for the state 111, which when incremented produces 000. On this transition the carry signal is active and C is set to 1.

The truth table for C and B and the extended truth table for the flip-flop inputs can be developed from either the state table or diagram using the transition table for the selected flip-flop type. From these truth tables, minimum

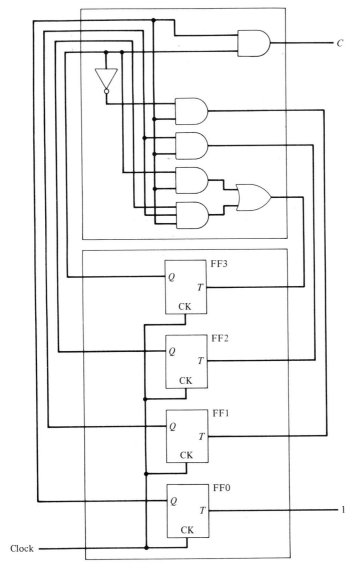

Figure 3-15 Logic diagram for the decade counter defined in Figs. 3-12 and 3-13.

sum-of-products equations can be obtained and used in drawing a logic diagram. These steps are left as an exercise for the reader.

3-5-3 A 2-Bit Shift Register

As a third example let us consider a 2-bit shift register, a sequential network that transfers the contents of each flip-flop to an adjacent one. In this example, the direction of the transfer is controlled by an input signal; the contents are shifted

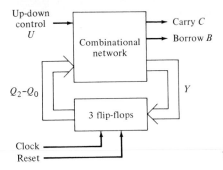

Figure 3-16 Structural model for a 3-bit up-down binary counter.

to the right if this signal is active and to the left if it is inactive. Data shifted out of the register appear on a data output line, and the value on the data input line is shifted into the register.

Figure 3-18 shows the structural model for the 2-bit shift register. The signal controlling the direction of the shift is symbolized by R; the data input and output signals are represented by DI and DO, respectively.

The behavior of this network is described by the state table in Table 3-4. Since the network has two inputs, R and DI, there are four input combinations; and since all are valid, there are four columns in the state table. There are two flip-flops, resulting in four present states, and so there are four rows in the table.

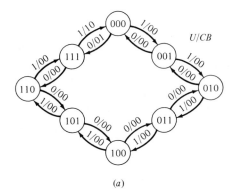

(a)

Present state Q_2 Q_1 Q_0			Input							
			0				1			
0	0	0	1	1	1/0	1	0	0	1/0	0
0	0	1	0	0	0/0	0	0	1	0/0	0
0	1	0	0	0	1/0	0	0	1	1/0	0
0	1	1	0	1	0/0	0	1	0	0/0	0
1	0	0	0	1	1/0	0	1	0	1/0	0
1	0	1	1	0	0/0	0	1	1	0/0	0
1	1	0	1	0	1/0	0	1	1	1/0	0
1	1	1	1	1	0/0	0	0	0	0/1	0

(b)

Figure 3-17 (a) State diagram and (b) table for a 3-bit up-down binary counter.

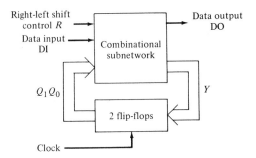

Figure 3-18 Structural model for a 2-bit shift register.

Internal entries are found by first recognizing the direction of the shift defined by R and then evaluating the output data and the effect of the shift on the contents of the register with the given input data. As an example, consider each entry in the second row where the present state is 01. We shall use Fig. 3-19 to help define the corresponding next state and output.

In the upper two examples in Fig. 3-19 where $R = 0$, a shift toward the left results. Thus, the 0 in the left position is shifted to the data output; the 1 in the right position is shifted to the left position; and the input datum, regardless of whether it is 0 or 1, is shifted to the right position. In the lower two examples in this figure, where $R = 1$, a shift toward the right results. Thus, the 1 in the right position is shifted to the data output; the 0 in the left position is shifted to the right position; and the input datum is shifted to the left position. The first example indicates that for the input condition 00 and the present state 01, the next state is 10 and the output is 0. This is entered as 10/0 in the first internal column of the second row of Table 3-4. Similarly, the second example indicates that for input condition 01 and present state 01, the next state is 11 and the output is 0. The third example indicates that for input condition 10 and present state 01, the next state is 00 and the output is 1. The fourth example indicates that for input condition 11 and present state 01, the next state is 10 and the output is 1.

Entries in the other three rows are obtained in a similar manner. This state table can be transformed into truth tables and then into a logic diagram representing a minimum sum-of-products implementation using the technique described earlier.

Table 3-4 State table for 2-bit shift register

Present State Q_1Q_0	Inputs R DI			
	0 0	0 1	1 0	1 1
00	00/0	01/0	00/0	10/0
01	10/0	11/0	00/1	10/1
10	00/1	01/1	01/0	11/0
11	10/1	11/1	01/1	11/1

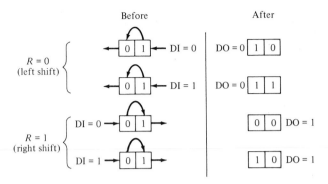

Figure 3-19 Operation of a 2-bit shift register for present state of 01.

3-5-4 An 8-Bit Shift Register

Although the approach based on the state table works with simple networks, it becomes too cumbersome as the number of flip-flops increases. Frequently the network can be divided into smaller, identical units. These can be designed using the state table; the overall network is designed by specifying their interconnection. This is analogous to our approach to complicated combinational networks.

To illustrate the use of subdivision we shall design a register which accepts 8 bits of parallel data and then shifts them out serially, i.e., bit by bit, starting with the least significant bit. This circuit is referred to as a *parallel-to-serial converter*. The circuit will have two control inputs: a data strobe signal (DS), which is active when the input parallel data is valid, and a shift-enable signal (SE), which must be active when the serial data are transferred. The first signal is active for one clock pulse to load the parallel data into the register; the second signal must be active for eight clock pulses to shift out all 8 bits. Figure 3-20a shows an input-output model for this network. The input-output model for a 1-bit unit is shown in Fig. 3-20b, and the interconnection of eight 1-bit units is shown in Fig. 3-20c.

Let us now define the state table for the identical unit. Since it contains only one flip-flop, it has just two present states. Also, it has four distinct input signals so there are sixteen input combinations. Table 3-5 shows the state table for the 1-bit unit. In the first four columns since both control inputs are 0, there is no change in state and the output is a don't-care condition. In the second four columns, DS = 0 and SE = 1, and so the data on SDI will be shifted into the flip-flop and the present state will be shifted out of the flip-flop. Thus, the next state is defined by the value of SDI and the output is defined by the present state. In the next four columns, DS = 1 and SE = 0, and so data on PDI will be loaded into the flip-flop and the condition of the output is unimportant. Thus, the next state is defined by the value of PDI and the output is a don't-care condition. In the last four columns, DS = 1 and SE = 1. Because this represents an invalid input, both the next state and the output are don't-care conditions.

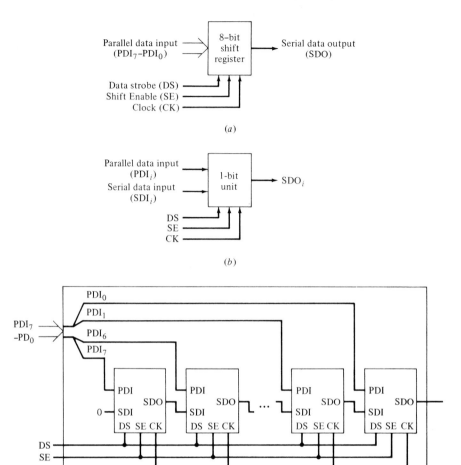

Figure 3-20 An 8-bit shift register: (a) input-output model, (b) input-output model for a 1-bit unit, and (c) diagram showing interconnections.

The state table in Table 3-5 can be transformed into a logic diagram using the techniques described in previous examples. The fact that there are four input variables and one state variable presents a small complication since we have not discussed the five-variable map. Instead we present a more intuitive approach for designing this identical unit. Note that its flip-flop must be set if both the data strobe signal DS and the parallel data input PDI are active or if both the shift-enable signal SE and the serial data input SDI are active. These conditions are summarized as

$$\text{SET} = \text{DS} \cdot \text{PDI}_i + \text{SE} \cdot \text{SDI}_i \tag{3-4}$$

Table 3-5 State table for single stage of 8-bit shift register

Present state Q	Inputs DS SE PDI SDI			
	0000	0001	0010	0011
0	0/d	0/d	0/d	0/d
1	1/d	1/d	1/d	1/d
	0100	0101	0110	0111
	0/0	1/0	0/0	1/0
	0/1	1/1	0/1	1/1
	1000	1001	1010	1011
	0/d	0/d	1/d	1/d
	0/d	0/d	1/d	1/d
	1100	1101	1110	1111
	d/d	d/d	d/d	d/d
	d/d	d/d	d/d	d/d

where SET is the signal to set the flip-flop. A similar relationship can be developed for the RESET signal:

$$\text{RESET} = \text{DS} \cdot \overline{\text{PDI}}_i + \text{SE} \cdot \overline{\text{SDI}}_i \qquad (3\text{-}5)$$

We also note that SDO_i simply represents the true output of the flip-flop. From this development we can construct a logic diagram for the single stage. Figure 3-21 shows this diagram using a *JK* flip-flop, where the logic gates implementing Eq. (3-4) are connected to the *J* input and those implementing Eq. (3-5) are connected to the *K* input.

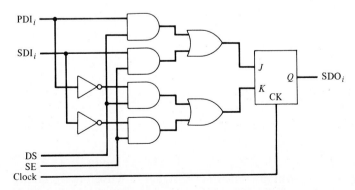

Figure 3-21 Logic diagram for the 1-bit unit of the 8-bit shift register.

3-6 IMPORTANT SEQUENTIAL NETWORKS

In this section we present examples of several important sequential networks available as single integrated circuits. They generally fit into three classes: counters, shift registers, and memory elements. Instead of the detailed models presented earlier in the chapter, we shall use abbreviated voltage tables to describe the behavior of these networks. This approach is analogous to that used in describing important combinational networks in Sec. 2-5.

3-6-1 Counters

Counters are sequential networks that proceed through a sequence of states following a counting scheme. There are two general types, decade counters and binary counters. *Decade counters* contain four flip-flops and generate the sequence corresponding to $0, 1, \ldots, 8, 9, 0, 1$, and so on. *Binary counters* may contain three, four, or more flip-flops. An N-bit binary counter generates the sequence corresponding to $0, 1, \ldots, (2^N - 1), 0, 1$, and so on.

In addition to the clock, counters have other types of inputs which are useful in various applications. One example is an input to control the direction of the counting sequence. As we saw in Sec. 3-5-2, this input is referred to as the *up-down control line*. Many counters have a *clear* input which when active resets all flip-flops in the counter. A related group of inputs allows selective setting and resetting of all flip-flops in the counter. This group contains a control input, called the *load line* or *preset control line*, which when active transfers the data on a group of *preset input lines* to the flip-flops. Thus the counter can be preset to any value by placing the appropriate pattern on the preset inputs and activating the load line.

It is common to use the negative-logic assumption on the clear and load inputs so that these signals are active when at the low voltage level. Even in synchronous counters, these inputs may be asynchronous, so that the resulting transitions occur as soon as the input becomes active. Frequently these inputs are assigned a priority to define the dominant input if both are active at the same time.

In addition to the flip-flop outputs, there may be a *carry output*, indicating counter overflow, and a *borrow output*, indicating counter underflow, as we saw in Sec. 3-5-2.

As an example of a counter, we shall consider a presettable decade counter with asynchronous clear and preset inputs. Figure 3-22 shows an input-output model of this network and an abbreviated voltage table describing its behavior. The outputs Q_3 to Q_0 represent the true outputs of the four flip-flops. The small circle on the CLEAR input indicates the negative-logic assumption, so that this input is active when at the low voltage level. The LOAD input uses the positive-logic assumption and is active at the high voltage level. The preset inputs X_3 to X_0 are connected to corresponding flip-flops. The CLOCK signal is active on the falling edge, as indicated by the small circle on this input in the model. The active phase

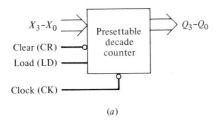

(a)

Inputs			Next state	Comments
Clear	Load	Clock		
L	d	d	L L L L	All flip-flops cleared asynchronously
H	H	d	$X_3 X_2 X_1 X_0$	All flip-flops preset asynchronously
H	L	L or H	$(Q_3 Q_2 Q_1 Q_0)$	No change
H	L	↓	$(Q_3 Q_2 Q_1 Q_0) + 1$	Incremented with active phase

(b)

Figure 3-22 Presettable decade counter; L = low voltage level, H = high voltage level, d = don't-care condition, ↓ = falling-edge-triggered.

of the clock pulse produces state transitions which correspond to incrementing the value stored in the flip-flops. Because the network is a decade counter, the sequence will correspond to $0, 1, 2, \ldots, 8, 9, 0, 1$, and so on.

The first row in the abbreviated voltage table indicates that the counter will be cleared if the CLEAR input is at the low voltage level regardless of the condition of the other inputs. Thus, the CLEAR signal has the highest priority. The second row indicates that if the CLEAR signal is inactive, i.e., at the high voltage level, and the LOAD signal is at the high voltage level, the flip-flops will be loaded or preset as defined by the preset inputs X_3 to X_0, regardless of the condition of the CLOCK signal. Thus, the LOAD signal has the second highest priority. The third row indicates that if the CLEAR and LOAD signals are inactive and the clock is stable, there will be no change in the flip-flops. The fourth row indicates that if the CLEAR and LOAD signals are inactive, the counter will increment its contents on the falling edge of the CLOCK pulse.

This network (or integrated-circuit device) can be used in many ways. Figure 3-23, a circuit containing two of these devices divides the input clock rate by 100; that is, it generates one clock pulse at the output for every 100 applied to the input. The INITIALIZE signal, generally applied at the start of operation, ensures that the flip-flops are all reset. The first 10 input clock pulses will overflow the decade counter on the left, referred to as the less significant decade counter. On the tenth pulse, its Q_3 output will fall from the high to the low voltage level, and this transition will increment the decade counter on the right, referred to as the more significant decade counter. Since the more significant decade counter will increment once for each 10 input clock pulses, it will overflow after 100 input clock pulses and generate a high- to low-voltage-level transition on its Q_3 output. When this occurs, all flip-flops in the two-decade counter are reset and ready to

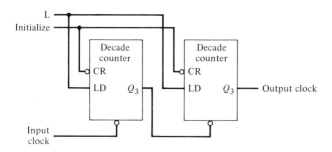

Figure 3-23 Divide-by-100 network using the presettable decade counter in Fig. 3-22.

repeat the process. Thus, the output clock rate will be one-hundredth the input rate.

Figure 3-24 shows a second application of the counter described in Fig. 3-22. This network, which divides the input clock rate by 360, makes use of the preset capability of the device. Without any presetting, a three-stage decade counter will divide by 1000; that is, there will be a high-to-low transition on Q_3 of the most significant decade counter after each 1000 input clock pulses. If the count is preset to 640, only 360 pulses will be required to produce this high-to-low transition. The preset inputs for the least significant decade counter, the one on the left, are all connected to the low voltage level; those for the middle one are arranged to preset with the value 4; while those for the most significant, the one on the right, are arranged to preset with the value 6. The preset enable signal LOAD can be activated by the INITIALIZE signal, assumed to be active when at the low level, or by an AND gate that detects when the contents of the most significant

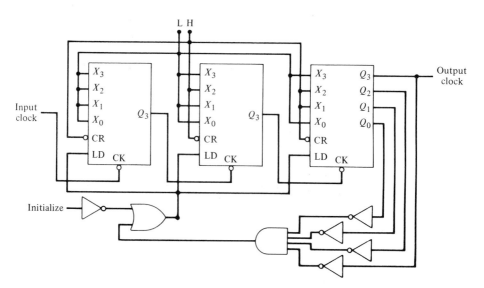

Figure 3-24 Divide-by-360 network using the presettable decade counter in Fig. 3-22.

decade counter have a value zero. The last connection is necessary so that the overall network will repeatedly generate an output for every 360 input pulses.

3-6-2 Shift Registers

The *shift register* is a sequential network in which the contents of each flip-flop are transferred to the adjacent flip-flop in the register. The value in the last flip-flop in the register is shifted out of the register, and the value on the input line is shifted into the first flip-flop in the register. Frequently, shift registers have an additional input that controls whether the shift is to the left or to the right, as we saw in Sec. 3-5-3. In many shift registers a control line is provided to enable the loading of all flip-flops in parallel from their individual inputs. It is rare to find all these inputs, outputs, and controls on a single packaged shift register, but various combinations are available.

Two important shift-register configurations represent parallel-to-serial converters and serial-to-parallel converters. When each bit in a binary word is transferred simultaneously during a single time interval using a line for each bit, a *parallel transfer* is performed. When a multibit binary word is transferred bit by bit during successive time intervals using a single line, a *serial transfer* is performed. The terms parallel and serial also are used to describe binary words and information transferred in the corresponding way. With the *parallel-to-serial converter*, the shift register has a control line that loads each flip-flop simultaneously with the input parallel word and a second control line that shifts the data out as a serial word. With the *serial-to-parallel converter*, the serial data are shifted into the shift register and then transferred out as a parallel word. Figure 3-25 shows an input-output model and abbreviated voltage table for the 8-bit serial-to-parallel converter. The network has three input signals. The CLEAR signal, which is active when low and has the highest priority, resets all eight flip-flops. The other two inputs, the CLOCK signal and the DATA INPUT (DI) signal, control the serial loading of the network. During the active phase of the CLOCK cycle, which in this case is defined by the low to high transition, the contents of all flip-flops are transferred to the right position, and the level on DI is loaded into Q_7. After eight clock cycles, an 8-bit serial word will be loaded into the register and available in parallel form at the outputs Q_7 to Q_0.

Example 3-4 The timing diagram in Fig. E3-4 describes the CLEAR (CR), DATA INPUT (DI), and CLOCK (CK) signals to clear and then transfer the ASCII code for the character A to the serial-to-parallel converter described in Fig. 3-25. Show the corresponding timing diagram for the outputs from flip-flops Q_7 to Q_0.

SOLUTION The ASCII code word is 0100 0001. Bit 0, a 1, is shifted into Q_7 on the first clock pulse, into Q_6 on the second, and so on until on the eighth clock pulse it is shifted into Q_0.

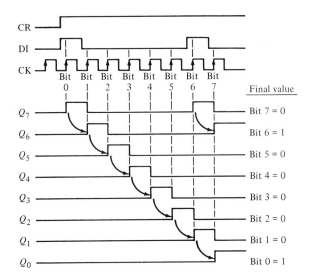

Figure E3-4 Timing diagram.

3-6-3 Memory Elements

The simplest memory element is a single register, frequently referred to as a *latch* or *data buffer*. It serves as temporary storage for a parallel word which may be valid only during a specific time interval. This type of circuit is used in interfacing digital systems. Figure 3-26 shows the input-output model and an abbreviated voltage table for a synchronous 4-bit latch. The circuit has four data inputs D_3 to D_0, each connected to a flip-flop. The voltage levels on these lines are transferred to the flip-flops during the active phase of the CLOCK signal when the STROBE

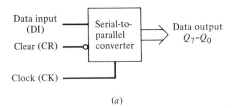

(a)

Inputs		Next state								Comments
Clear	Clock	Q_7	Q_6	Q_5	Q_4	Q_3	Q_2	Q_1	Q_0	
L	d	L	L	L	L	L	L	L	L	Clear
H	H or L	Q_7	Q_6	Q_5	Q_4	Q_3	Q_2	Q_1	Q_0	No change
H	↑	DI	Q_7	Q_6	Q_5	Q_4	Q_3	Q_2	Q_1	Shift

(b)

Figure 3-25 An 8-bit serial-to-parallel converter.

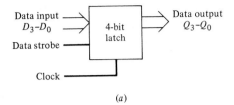

(a)

Input			Output
Strobe	Clock	D_i	Q_i
L	d	d	Q_i
H	L or H	d	Q_i
H	↑	L	L
H	↑	H	H

(b)

Figure 3-26 A 4-bit latch.

input is at the high level. The data, which are then stored in the register, are available at the outputs Q_3 to Q_0.

Integrated circuits with more than one register on the chip are available. Figure 3-27 shows the input-output model for a 4×8 *register file*, which has 32 flip-flops organized as four 8-bit words. There are eight data input lines DI_7 to DI_0, and the values on these lines can be loaded or written into any of the four 8-bit registers. There are also eight data output lines DO_7 to DO_0, and the contents of any of the four registers can be placed on these lines. The direction of data flow, i.e., whether it is written into a register or read from a register, is controlled by the Read-write (R/W) line. When this line is at the low voltage level, data will be transferred or written into the network; when it is high level, data will be transferred or read from the network. The specific register involved in the transfer is defined by the two address lines. These two lines can assume four conditions, LL, LH, HL, and HH. Each condition is used to designate one of the four registers. As an example of the operation of this network, the condition where R/W = L, A_1 = H, and A_0 = L stores or writes the value on the data input lines DI_7 to DI_0 into register 2 and holds the output lines DO_7 to DO_0 at the high voltage level. Similarly, when R/W = H, A_1 = L, A_0 = H, the contents of register 1 appear on the output lines and the data on DI_7 to DI_0 are ignored.

As semiconductor technology advanced, the size of the register files grew. This increasing complexity required more and more input and output connections. Since the number of input and output connections is a complicating factor in both the manufacture and use of the devices, methods for reducing the number of connections were introduced. An important development was the introduction of the bidirectional data line. Figure 3-28 shows the input-output model for the 4×8 register file using bidirectional data lines.

The connection of a bidirectional line to a flip-flop cell is shown in Fig. 3-29. In addition to the bidirectional data line and the read-write control line, there is another input enabling this specific cell. This signal is generated elsewhere on the integrated circuit from the input address lines. A new symbol representing a

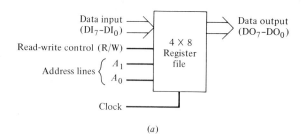

(a)

Inputs			Register contents				Output
R/W	A_1	A_2	Reg 0	Reg 1	Reg 2	Reg 3	D_o
L	L	L	DI	—	—	—	H
L	L	H	—	DI	—	—	H
L	H	L	—	—	DI	—	H
L	H	H	—	—	—	DI	H
H	L	L	—	—	—	—	Reg 0
H	L	H	—	—	—	—	Reg 1
H	H	L	—	—	—	—	Reg 2
H	H	H	—	—	—	—	Reg 3

Dash indicates no change

(b)

Figure 3-27 A 4 × 8 register file.

three-state buffer is shown in the figure. The behavior of this element is described in Fig. 3-30. Note that the output of this element has three states, the standard low and high voltage states and a third state referred to as the high-impedance state. When the circuit is in this state, its output essentially is an open circuit. If the control input is at the high level, the output is at the same level as the input. However, if the control input is at the low level, the output is in the high-impedance state. This arrangement is necessary for two reasons: (1) it coordinates the use of a single data line with the flip-flop input and output, and (2), more important, it eliminates electrical problems that could result from connecting the same data line to a large number of flip-flop cells.

Currently register files containing hundreds and even thousands of registers are available on a single integrated circuit. Because of the large storage capacity, they are called *memory elements*. Figure 3-31 shows the input-output model for a 1024 × 8 memory element requiring 10 address lines to specify uniquely the 1024 8-bit registers. In addition, there is a chip-select line that also must be activated for any data transfers.

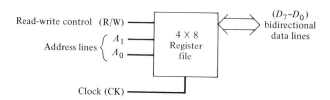

Figure 3-28 A 4 × 8 register file with bidirectional data lines.

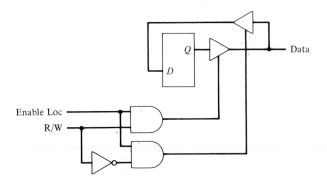

Figure 3-29 Flip-flop cell with bidirectional data lines.

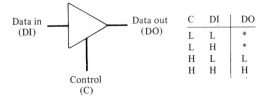

C	DI	DO
L	L	*
L	H	*
H	L	L
H	H	H

Figure 3-30 Three-state buffer; L = low voltage level, H = high voltage level, * = high-impedance state.

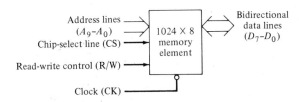

Figure 3-31 Input-output model for memory element.

3-7 CONCLUSION

This chapter is intended to provide an introduction to sequential networks. It is not a comprehensive presentation, our approach being limited to simple networks that can be handled using truth tables and K-map minimization. At the end of Chap. 2 we pointed out that there are computerized algorithms for minimizing network complexity; the same comment applies here.

In the design of sequential networks we considered only counter and shift registers. The design of controllers is a third and perhaps more important class of problems. The *controller* is a subsection of a digital system that regulates the flow of information within the remainder of the system. In general, it distinguishes a sequence of input conditions, and in response, it generates a sequence of output conditions. We shall deal with controllers in the next chapter.

In the section on important sequential networks we ended our discussion with the memory element, a major component in a computer system. We could have continued this development and introduced other components of the microcomputer, like the processor. In fact, the entire microcomputer is an important sequential network. However, we chose to save this material for later, and it will be discussed in Chap. 5.

PROBLEMS

3-1 Define each of the following terms:

flip-flop circuit	state table	parallel data transfer
synchronous flip-flop	state diagram	serial data transfer
asynchronous flip-flop	extended truth table	parallel-to-serial converter
D flip-flop	decade counter	serial-to-parallel converter
T flip-flop	binary counter	latch
SR flip-flop	synchronous input signal	register file
JK flip-flop	asynchronous input signal	three-state buffer
transition table of flip-flop	clear input	memory element
edge-triggered flip-flop	preset input	
master-slave flip-flop	shift register	

3-2 Using the clock signal and the input signals X_1 and X_2 in Fig. P3-2, draw a timing diagram showing the clock signal, the appropriate input, and the Q output. Assume that the flip-flop is reset to start.

(a) A rising-edge-triggered D flip-flop with X_1 as the input
(b) A trailing-edge-triggered D flip-flop with X_1 as the input
(c) A master-slave D flip-flop with X_1 as the input
(d) A rising-edge-triggered T flip-flop with X_1 as the input
(e) A trailing-edge-triggered T flip-flop with X_1 as the input
(f) A master-slave T flip-flop with X_1 as the input
(g) A rising-edge-triggered JK flip-flop with X_1 connected to J and X_2 to K
(h) A trailing-edge-triggered JK flip-flop with X_1 connected to J and X_2 to K
(i) A master-slave JK flip-flop with X_1 connected to J and X_2 to K

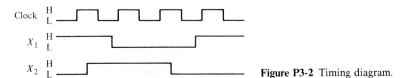

Figure P3-2 Timing diagram.

3-3 For the following state tables find the equivalent state diagram:

(a)

Present state	I_0	I_1	I_2	I_3
S_0	S_0/R_0	S_1/R_0	S_1/R_1	S_3/R_0
S_1	S_0/R_0	S_1/R_0	S_2/R_0	S_3/R_0
S_2	S_3/R_1	S_3/R_1	S_1/R_0	S_3/R_0
S_3	S_0/R_0	S_0/R_0	S_2/R_0	S_3/R_0

(b)

Present state	I_0	I_1	I_2
S_0	S_0/R_1	S_1/R_0	S_0/R_1
S_1	S_0/R_1	d	S_2/R_0
S_2	S_1/R_0	S_2/R_0	S_2/R_2

(c)

Present state	I_0	I_1
S_0	S_2/R_1	S_1/R_0
S_1	S_3/R_0	S_2/R_1
S_2	S_4/R_1	S_3/R_0
S_3	S_5/R_0	S_4/R_1
S_4	S_0/R_1	S_5/R_0
S_5	S_1/R_0	S_0/R_1

3-4 For the state diagrams in Fig. P3-4 find the equivalent state table.

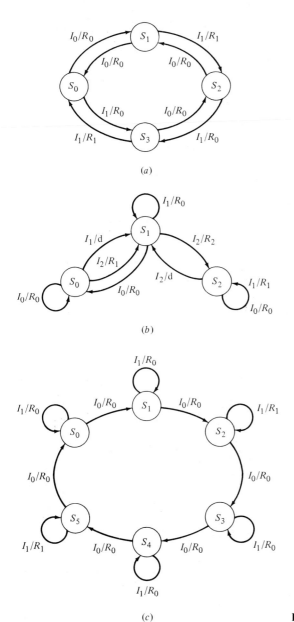

(a)

(b)

(c)

Figure P3-4 State diagrams.

3-5 For the state table in Prob. 3-3 define the sequence of states and outputs for the input sequence $I_0, I_0, I_1, I_0, I_1, I_1$. Assume that the initial state is S_0.

3-6 Repeat Prob. 3-5 for the input sequence $I_1, I_1, I_1, I_0, I_0, I_0$.

3-7 For the state diagram in Prob. 3-4, define the sequence of states and outputs for the input sequence $I_0, I_0, I_0, I_0, I_1, I_1$. Assume that the initial state is S_0.

3-8 Repeat Prob. 3-7 where the initial state is S_1.

3-9 Define an efficient logic diagram using JK flip-flops and AND, OR, and NOT gates for the encoded state tables.

(a)

Present state Q_1 Q_0	Input, X_0 0	1
0 0	01/0	11/0
0 1	01/1	10/1
1 0	01/1	10/1
1 1	00/0	10/1

(b)

Present state Q_0	Input $X_0 X_1$ 00	10	01	11
0	1/1	1/1	0/1	0/0
1	0/1	0/1	1/0	0/0

(c)

Present state Q_2 Q_1 Q_0	Input X_0 0	1
0 0 1	010/0	001/0
0 0 1	011/1	010/0
0 1 0	000/0	011/1
0 1 1	101/1	000/0
1 0 0	d	d
1 0 1	111/0	110/1
1 1 0	000/0	111/0
1 1 1	001/0	000/1

(d)

Present state Q_1 Q_0	Input $X_0 X_1$ 00	10	01	11
0 0	01/0	00/0	d	00/0
0 1	00/0	11/1	d	01/0
1 0	d	d	d	d
1 1	00/0	01/0	d	11/1

3-10 Repeat Prob. 3-9 using:
   (1) JK flip-flops and NAND gates only
   (2) JK flip-flops and NOR gates only
   (3) D flip-flops and AND, OR, and NOT gates
   (4) SR flip-flops and AND, OR, and NOT gates
   (5) T flip-flops and AND, OR, and NOT gates

3-11 Obtain an efficient logic diagram using D flip-flops and AND, OR, and NOT gates for the logic networks described by:
   (a) The state table in part (a) of Prob. 3-3 using

Symbol	Q_1	Q_0	Symbol	X_1	X_0	Symbol	Z_0
S_0	0	0	I_0	0	0	R_0	0
S_1	0	1	I_1	0	1	R_1	1
S_2	1	0	I_2	1	0		
S_3	1	1	I_3	1	1		

(*b*) The state table in part (*b*) of Prob. 3-3 using

Symbol	Q_1	Q_0	Symbol	X_1	X_0	Symbol	Z_1	Z_0
S_0	1	1	I_0	0	0	R_0	0	0
S_1	1	0	I_1	1	0	R_1	0	1
S_2	0	1	I_2	0	1	R_2	1	1

(*c*) The state table of part (*c*) of Prob. 3-3 using

Symbol	Q_2	Q_3	Q_0	Symbol	X_0	Symbol	Z_0
S_0	0	0	0	I_0	0	R_0	0
S_1	0	0	1	I_1	1	R_1	1
S_2	0	1	0				
S_3	0	1	1				
S_4	1	0	0				
S_5	1	0	1				

(*d*) The state diagram in part (*a*) of Prob. 3-4 using

Symbol	Q_1	Q_0	Symbol	X_0	Symbol	Z_0
S_0	0	0	I_0	0	R_0	0
S_1	0	1	I_1	1	R_1	1
S_2	1	0				
S_3	1	1				

(*e*) The state diagram in part (*b*) of Prob. 3-4 using the codes defined above in part (*b*)
(*f*) The state diagram in part (*c*) of Prob. 3-4 using the codes defined above in part (*c*)

3-12 Repeat Prob. 3-11 using (1) T flip-flops and (2) JK flip-flops.

3-13 Find an encoded state table for the logic diagram in Fig. P3-13*a* to *c*.

3-14 Find the encoded state diagram for the logic diagram given (*a*) in Fig. P3-14*a* and (*b*) in Fig. P3-14*b*. (*c*) Repeat part (*b*) using T flip-flops in place of the D flip-flops.

3-15 Derive the encoded state table for the logic diagrams given in Fig. P3-15*a* to *c*.

3-16 Translate the logic diagrams of Prob. 3-15 into an efficient logic diagram using D flip-flops and AND, OR, and NOT gates.

3-17 Derive efficient logic equations for the combinational subnetwork for a decade counter that increases its count by 3 on each clock pulse when a control input X is active. When X is inactive, the counter increases its count by 1 on each clock pulse. There is one output that is active when the counter contains the values 3, 6, or 9. Use AND, OR, NOT gates and:

(*a*) JK flip-flops   (*b*) D flip-flops
(*c*) SR flip-flops   (*d*) T flip-flops

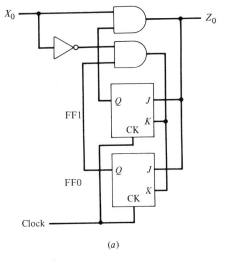

(a)

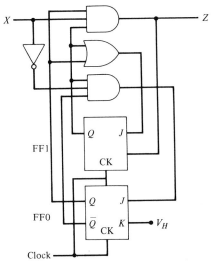

(b)

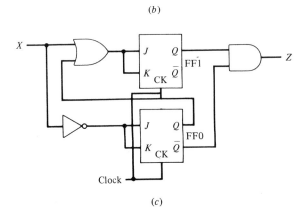

(c)

Figure P3-13 Logic diagrams.

108

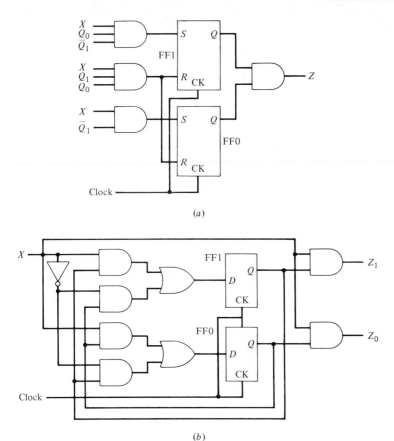

Figure P3-14 Logic diagrams.

3-18 Derive efficient logic equations describing the combinational subnetwork for a mod-5 counter that follows the sequence 000, 001, 010, 011, 100 and then repeats. In addition to the clock signal, the network has one input X and one output Z. The count is incremented when X is active and remains the same when X is inactive. The signal Z is active on the 100-to-000 transition. Use AND, OR, NOT gates and:

    (a) *JK* flip-flops   (b) *D* flip-flops

    (c) *SR* flip-flops   (d) *T* flip-flops

3-19 Derive efficient logic equations describing the combinational subnetwork for a mod-6 up-down counter. This counter follows the sequence 000, 001, 010, 011, 100, 101, and then repeats when counting up; it follows the opposite sequence when counting down. In addition to the clock signal, the network has one input X and two outputs Z_1 and Z_2. The count is incremented when X is active and decremented when X is inactive. The output Z_1 is active when the counter overflows and Z_2 is active when the counter underflows. Use AND, OR, and NOT gates and:

    (a) *JK* flip-flops   (b) *D* flip-flops

    (c) *SR* flip-flops   (d) *T* flip-flops

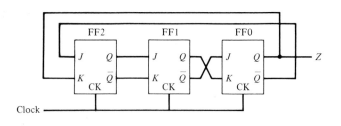

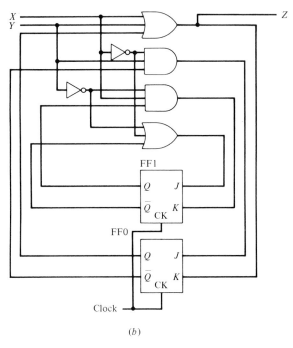

(b)

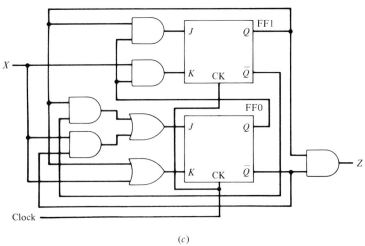

(c)

Figure P3-15 Logic diagrams.

110

3-20 Draw an efficient logic diagram for a synchronizing network which samples an input signal X and activates the output for one clock cycle each time the input becomes active. To ensure that each input transition produces only one output pulse, the input must be inactive for at least one clock cycle before the output is activated again. All signals are based on a positive logic assumption. Use:

(a) JK flip-flops and AND, OR, and NOT gates
(b) JK flip-flops and NAND gates
(c) D flip-flops and AND, OR, and NOT gates
(d) D flip-flops and NOR gates
(e) SR flip-flops and AND, OR, and NOT gates
(f) T flip-flops and AND, OR, and NOT gates

3-21 Draw a state diagram for an up-down decade counter analogous to the binary counter described in Fig. 3-17.

3-22 A sequential network accepts three input signals X_2, X_1, X_0 and generates one output signal Z. For each input, the output is activated for one clock cycle after a delay specified by the input signals. If X_0 is active, the delay is 1 cycle; if X_1 is active, the delay is 5 cycles; and if X_2 is active, the delay is 10 cycles. No output results if all three inputs are inactive, and only one input can be active at a given time. The inputs are active until the delay is complete.

(a) Using a symbolic notation, define all valid input and output conditions. Define all valid states. How many flip-flops are necessary?
(b) Derive a symbolic state table based on a positive-logic assumption.
(c) Define codes for the input and output conditions and the states.
(d) Derive an encoded state table.

3-23 A sequential network accepts five input signals; four of them (X_3, X_2, X_1 and X_0) represent a BCD-coded value, X_0 being the least significant bit. The code is valid when the fifth input X_4 is active. The network generates an output pulse each time X_4 is activated. The duration of the pulse is defined by the BCD-coded value. The inputs are active until the output becomes inactive.

(a) Using a symbolic notation, define all valid input and output conditions. Define all valid states. How many flip-flops are required?
(b) Derive a symbolic state table.
(c) Define codes for the input and output conditions and the states. Derive the encoded state table.

3-24 Referring to Fig. 3-25, describe the sequence of states for the given initial state and sequence of inputs.

CK	↑	↑	↑	↑	↑	↑	↑	↑
DI	H	L	L	H	H	L	H	H
CR	H	L	H	H	H	H	H	L
Q_7	H	—	—	—	—	—	—	—
Q_6	H	—	—	—	—	—	—	—
Q_5	H	—	—	—	—	—	—	—
Q_4	H	—	—	—	—	—	—	—
Q_3	H	—	—	—	—	—	—	—
Q_2	H	—	—	—	—	—	—	—
Q_1	H	—	—	—	—	—	—	—
Q_0	H	—	—	—	—	—	—	—

3-25 Draw an input-output model and an abbreviated voltage table for an 8×8 register file.

3-26 Draw an input-output model and an abbreviated voltage table for the 8-bit parallel-to-serial converter described in Figs. 3-20 and 3-21 and Table 3-5.

3-27 Use the presettable decade counter defined in Fig. 3-22 to design a network that divides the input clock rate by 25 using:

(a) AND, OR, and NOT gates
(b) Only NAND gates
(c) Only NOR gates

3-28 Draw the timing diagram showing the waveform for the signal DO in the circuit shown in Fig. 3-20 if the signals X_1 and X_2 from Prob. 3-2 are connected to the DI input and the C input, respectively.

3-29 For the network in Fig. 3-31 define the voltage levels on each input to write the word C3 in (a) the first and (b) the last memory location.

3-30 For the network in Fig. 3-25 show the sequence of voltage levels on the input DI to load the ASCII code word for the character Z.

REFERENCES

Blakeslee, T. R.: "Digital Design with Standard MSI and LSI," Wiley, New York, 1975.

Clare, C. R.: "Designing Logic Systems Using State Machines," McGraw-Hill, New York, 1973.

Fletcher, W. I.: "An Engineering Approach to Digital Design," Prentice-Hall, Englewood Cliffs, N.J., 1980.

Gill, A.: "Introduction to the Theory of Finite State Machines," McGraw-Hill, New York, 1962.

Hill, F. J., and G. R. Peterson: "Introduction to Switching Theory and Logic Design," Wiley, New York, 1974.

Huffman, D. A.: The Synthesis of Sequential Switching Circuits, *J. Franklin Inst.*, no. 3, 1954, pp. 161–190, no. 4, 1954, pp. 275–303.

Kohavi, Z.: "Switching and Finite Automatic Theory," McGraw-Hill, New York, 1970.

Miller, R. E.: "Switching Theory," vol. II, "Sequential Circuits and Machines," Wiley, New York, 1965.

Moore, E. F.: "Sequential Machines: Selected Papers," Addison-Wesley, Reading, Mass., 1964.

FOUR

DESIGN OF CONVENTIONAL DIGITAL NETWORKS

In this chapter we consider additional design problems. In Secs. 2-4 and 3-5 the design problems were specified in a format that directly translated into truth tables and state tables. In this chapter, we extend the design process by considering problems specified with much less precision. After finishing this chapter the reader should be able to:

1. Translate a verbal specification into (a) a list of all possible input conditions, output conditions, and states and (b) a symbolic state table defining the sequential behavior of the network
2. Define codes for the input and output conditions that are consistent with input and output signal specifications
3. Derive an encoded state table which unambiguously defines the network's desired behavior
4. Perform timing diagram analysis to verify that the system meets its timing specification

4-1 VENDING-MACHINE CONTROL UNIT

In this first example we shall design the control unit or controller for a vending machine. This control unit must interface with three auxiliary units: the coin-input unit, the change-dispensing unit, and the drink-dispensing unit, as shown in Fig.

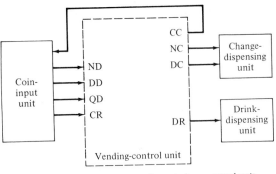

Inputs to control unit

ND = nickel deposited
DD = dime deposited
QD = quarter deposited
CR = coin return

Outputs from control unit

CC = collect coins
NC = nickel change
DC = dime change
DR = dispense drink

Figure 4-1 Input-output connections for the vending-machine control unit.

4-1. The input-output behavior of these units must be carefully considered because it directly affects the design of the control unit. A summary of the auxiliary-unit input-output signal specifications is given in Table 4-1.

Although the operation of a vending machine is familiar, let us review a typical transaction considering the activities in a more technical way. A series of coins, restricted to nickels, dimes, or quarters is inserted, one at a time, into the machine. The coin-input unit holds them in a temporary location and produces a pulse on one of its output lines indicating the denomination of each coin inserted. We define 35 cents to be the cost of a drink. The buyer may push the coin-return lever at any time before completion of a transaction, generating a signal to the controller indicating that all money has been returned. As soon as a coin input causes the sum in the present transaction to equal or exceed 35 cents, the

Table 4-1 Auxiliary-unit input-output signal specifications

Coin-input unit	Change-dispensing unit	Drink-dispensing unit
ND, DD, QD signals: unit will accept nickels, dimes, or quarters and produce 200-ms pulse (V_H) on line corresponding to that coin type; outputs will be inactive (V_L) for at least 500 ms between successive pulses CR signal: pushing coin-return button activates (V_H) coin-return line as long as button is pushed CC signal: a 50-ms pulse (V_H) on this line causes deposited coins to be collected	Unit has two input lines, one for nickels (NC) and one for dimes (DC); one coin of appropriate value is released for each input pulse (V_H) lasting longer than 50 ms; inputs must be inactive (V_L) for at least 50 ms between pulses; backlighted message USE CORRECT CHANGE indicates that change unit is out of change	Unit has single input DR and dispenses drink for each input pulse (V_H) lasting longer than 50 ms; backlighted message EMPTY indicates machine out of drinks

controller will generate output signals causing the proper change and a drink to be dispensed. In addition, a signal is generated causing the coin-input unit to transfer all coins from the temporary location to the permanent storage location.

The narrative description above, along with the information contained in Fig. 4-1 and Table 4-1, constitutes the specification for the vending-machine control unit. The design procedure consists of translating these specifications into a precise, unambiguous, technical model, namely the encoded state table. We shall use three distinct steps to accomplish this: (1) identification of the input conditions, (2) evolution of a symbolic state table, and (3) derivation of an encoded state table.

4-1-1 Identification of Input Conditions

In this step we define all possible input conditions. The vending-machine control unit receives input signals only from the coin-input unit.

The possible input conditions are no input signals active, ND active, DD active, QD active, and CR active. Table 4-2 lists these conditions and assigns an arbitrary symbol to each. This is a tentative set of input conditions. As our understanding of this problem develops, we may add or delete conditions. Eventually, the list must be complete, and each condition must be precisely defined.

4-1-2 Evolution of a Symbolic State Table

We are now ready for the second step in the design process, the derivation of a symbolic state table. In this step we first must define the initial state. This state is associated with the "rest" condition of the controller, i.e., the condition that exists after a transaction has been completed and before a new one has been initiated. We define the initial state S_0 as the condition where the total deposited is zero.

After defining the initial state we are ready to begin developing the symbolic state table, which we accomplish row by row. In the previous subsection we defined all valid input conditions in Table 4-2. Each of these results in a column in the state table. This means that the state table will have five columns and at least one row for S_0. Table 4-3 shows the form of this table. To complete it we

Table 4-2 Input-condition table for vending-machine control unit

Input-condition symbol	Description
I_0	No input active
I_1	ND active
I_2	DD active
I_3	QD active
I_4	CR active

Table 4-3 Form of state table for vending-machine control unit

Present state	Input condition				
	I_0 (no input active)	I_1 (ND active)	I_2 (DD active)	I_3 (QD active)	I_4 (CR active)
S_0 (total = 0)	For each input condition, next state and output condition must be defined				
New rows added as new states defined					

define the next state and output condition for each input condition. As we proceed, we generate two more tables, one listing all states and one listing all output conditions; they are analogous to Table 4-2, which lists the input conditions. As new states are defined, we add rows to the state table. When all entries in all rows are defined, the state table is finished (Tables 4-4 to 4-6).

Let us begin in the first row of Table 4-4 and consider the effect of each input condition in turn. For the first column, where the input condition is I_0, implying

Table 4-4 Symbolic state table for the vending-machine control unit

Present state	Input condition				
	I_0 (no inputs active)	I_1 (ND active)	I_2 (DD active)	I_3 (QD active)	I_4 (CR active)
S_0 (Total = 0)	S_0/R_0	S_1/R_0	S_2/R_0	S_3/R_0	S_0/R_0
S_1 (Total = 5¢)	S_1/R_0	S_2/R_0	S_4/R_0	S_5/R_0	S_0/R_0
S_2 (Total = 10¢)	S_2/R_0	S_4/R_0	S_6/R_0	S_0/R_1	S_0/R_0
S_3 (Total = 25¢)	S_3/R_0	S_5/R_0	S_0/R_1	S_0/R_2	S_0/R_0
S_4 (Total = 15¢)	S_4/R_0	S_6/R_0	S_3/R_0	S_0/R_3	S_0/R_0
S_5 (Total = 30¢)	S_5/R_0	S_0/R_1	S_0/R_3	S_7/R_4	S_0/R_0
S_6 (Total = 20¢)	S_6/R_0	S_3/R_0	S_5/R_0	S_0/R_4	S_0/R_0
S_7 (Owe 10¢)	S_0/R_5	S_1/R_5	S_2/R_5	S_3/R_5	S_0/R_5

Table 4-5 Output conditions for the vending-machine control unit

Output-condition symbol	Description
R_0	No activity
R_1	Dispense a drink, no change, and collect coins
R_2	Dispense a drink, 15¢ change, and collect coins
R_3	Dispense a drink, 5¢ change, and collect coins
R_4	Dispense a drink, 10¢ change, and collect coins
R_5	Dispense 10¢ change

no input activity, an output response of "no activity" is required; this condition is denoted by R_0, the first entry in Table 4-5. Furthermore, this input condition does not change the status of the transaction, and so nothing new needs to be remembered. Thus, no new state is defined, and S_0 is entered as the next state for this condition.

The second column corresponds to the input condition I_1, implying that a nickel has been deposited. Since this coin does not raise the total deposited to 35 cents, the output condition R_0 is used again. However, since this input condition does change the status of the transaction, the controller must remember that a 5-cent total has been accumulated. Therefore, a new state S_1 is defined and entered as the next state. State S_1 is the second entry in Table 4-6. The next two columns in the state table correspond to the input conditions I_2, a dime deposited, and to I_3, a quarter deposited. They are analogous to the second column and result in the definition of two new states: S_2, indicating that a 10-cent total has been accumulated, and S_3 indicating that a 25-cent total has been accumulated. Since neither is adequate to dispense a drink, the output condition R_0 is appropriate in both cases. The last column, corresponding to a coin-return

Table 4-6 State symbols for the vending-machine control unit

State symbol	Description
S_0	Total = 0
S_1	Total = 5¢
S_2	Total = 10¢
S_3	Total = 25¢
S_4	Total = 15¢
S_5	Total = 30¢
S_6	Total = 20¢
S_7	Owe 10¢

condition, requires no change in state and no output activity; thus, the entries S_0 and R_0 are appropriate.

In defining entries in the first row of the state table for the vending-machine control unit, we introduce three new states, S_1, S_2, and S_3; and so three new rows must be added to the state table. All entries in each of these rows must be defined. Most of these entries have a pattern similar to those already considered. Two new states, S_4 for the total = 15 cents and S_5 for the total = 30 cents, are introduced in the second row. An additional state, S_6 for total = 20 cents, is introduced in the third row. As these new states are defined they are entered in Table 4-6.

A new output condition must be defined for the present state S_2 and the input condition I_3, since the present total is 10 cents and the input of a quarter raises the total to the required 35 cents. In response to this present state and input condition, a new output condition to dispense a drink with no change is required. We designate this as R_1 and enter it in Table 4-5. In defining the next state for the combination of S_2 and I_3 we might introduce a new state to remember that a transaction has been completed. Alternatively, the initial state S_0 can be considered as the end of a transaction as well as the beginning of a new one. We have selected this latter option, but either choice is effective. In the remainder of the state table we shall use S_0 as the next state each time a transaction is completed.

Another interesting combination that results in a different output condition is S_3, a total of 25 cents already deposited, and I_3, an additional quarter deposited. The appropriate output condition is to dispense a drink, collect the coins, and provide a nickel and dime in change. This new output condition is represented by R_2, which also is entered in Table 4-5. Other new output conditions occur when the present state is S_4, a total of 15 cents, and the input condition is I_3, a quarter deposited, and when the present state is S_5, a total of 30 cents, and the input condition is I_3, a quarter deposited. These result in output conditions defined by R_3, dispense drink and 5 cents change, and by R_4, dispense drink and 10 cents change, defined in Table 4-5.

One entry in the table requires special attention. For the present state S_5, a total of 30 cents, and the input condition I_3, quarter deposited, the appropriate output is dispense a drink and 20 cents change. The limitations of the coin-dispensing unit make this a difficult condition to accommodate, since this unit is prepared to give, at most, one nickel and one dime for a single output condition from the control unit. Thus producing 20 cents change requires the DC line to be activated twice by the controller during two successive clock cycles. For the first clock cycle we define the output condition R_4 to dispense a drink, collect the coins, and return one dime, and we define the next state to be a new state S_7 to remember that another dime must be returned. During the next clock cycle, when the present state is S_7, the output condition is R_5, dispense a dime, regardless of the input condition. When the present state is S_7, a coin input is interpreted as the first coin of a new transaction, and so the next states are identical to those in the first row. For example, for the input condition I_1 and the present state S_7 the next state is S_1, total = 5 cents.

The other entries in the state table are straightforward but should be verified by the reader. Step 2 is complete; we have produced the symbolic state table (Table 4-4), the output condition table (Table 4-5), and the state symbol table (Table 4-6).

4-1-3 Derivation of an Encoded State Table

The final step in the design process is defining three codes to convert the symbolic state table of Table 4-4 into an encoded state table. Codes must be defined for the symbolic input conditions (Table 4-2), output conditions (Table 4-5), and states (Table 4-6). In defining these codes we must take into account the constraints placed upon input and output signals by the specification on the auxiliary units defined in Table 4-1 and Fig. 4-1.

If we were free to code the input conditions without considering external constraints, a code with a minimum of three variables could be used since there are five conditions that must be coded. Instead, the code must use the four input signals from the auxiliary units, ND, DD, QD, and CR, in a way that is consistent with the specifications of these signals. If the signals are interpreted using a positive-logic assumption, the code in Table 4-7 results. The no input active condition I_0 is represented by the code word 0000; the ND active condition I_1 is represented by 1000; and so on.† From the definition of Table 4-7 we can see that only 5 of 16 possible code words are defined. Other input code words should not occur because of the specifications of the coin input unit. For example, 1100, which corresponds to a nickel and a dime input simultaneously, would not be expected to occur. Similar reasoning can be applied to all other undefined code words.

In a similar way, if we were free to define a code for the output conditions, only three variables would be required to represent the six output conditions defined in Table 4-5. However, the code for the output conditions must be consistent with the specifications on the four signals required by the auxiliary units, as summarized in Table 4-1. For example, the output condition R_0, "no activity," requires that all output signals be inactive; thus with the positive-logic assumption the code word 0000 is associated with this condition as shown in Table 4-8. As another example, the condition R_1, "dispense drink and collect coins," requires that the signals to dispense a drink (DR) and to collect the deposited coins (CC) be active while the other two are inactive; thus the code word 0011 is associated with the condition. Code words for the other output conditions are defined in the same way. Any code word not explicitly shown in Table 4-8 is undefined.

The definition of a code for the state symbols $(S_0, S_1, \ldots, S_7)$ is not constrained by any external signal specifications. At least three variables must be used to define a code for the eight states. We shall use the minimum number since

---

† In a common code, the defined code words have exactly one active variable; they are called *one-hot codes*.

Table 4-7 Code for input conditions for vending-machine control unit†

Input condition	Description	Input variable			
		ND	DD	QD	CR
I_0	No input active	0	0	0	0
I_1	ND active	1	0	0	0
I_2	DD active	0	1	0	0
I_3	QD active	0	0	1	0
I_4	CR active	0	0	0	1

† All other code words undefined.

each variable used in the code word requires a separate flip-flop in the implementation and we wish to use as few flip-flops as possible. We shall represent these three variables with Q_2, Q_1, and Q_0. Although the exact assignment of code words to the eight states may ultimately affect the complexity of the combinational subnetwork required in the final implementation, we shall ignore this concern and seek only to produce a unique code word for each state, as shown in Table 4-9.

The three codes defined in Tables 4-7 to 4-9 are used to translate the symbolic state table given as Table 4-4 into the encoded state table shown in Table 4-10. First, the form of the encoded table is defined. Since there are three state variables, there are eight rows; the code words for them are enumerated on the left. The state symbol for each is written in parentheses; e.g., the code word

Table 4-8 Code for output conditions for vending-machine control unit†

Output condition	Description	Output variable			
		NC	DC	DR	CC
R_0	No activity	0	0	0	0
R_1	Dispense drink and collect coins	0	0	1	1
R_2	Dispense drink, collect coins, and return dime and nickel	1	1	1	1
R_3	Dispense drink, collect coins, and return nickel	1	0	1	1
R_4	Dispense drink, collect coins, and return dime	0	1	1	1
R_5	Return dime	0	1	0	0

† All other output code words undefined.

Table 4-9 Code for states for vending-machine control unit

Symbolic state	State variable			Symbolic state	State variable		
	Q_2	Q_1	Q_0		Q_2	Q_1	Q_0
S_0	0	0	0	S_4	1	0	0
S_1	0	0	1	S_5	1	0	1
S_2	0	1	0	S_6	1	1	0
S_3	0	1	1	S_7	1	1	1

000 is associated with the symbol S_0. Similarly there are four input variables, and so there are sixteen columns and the code words for them are enumerated across the top. The input condition symbols are written in parentheses with the associated code words. As before, not all the code words are defined.

Each internal entry defined in Table 4-10 is obtained by substituting the code words corresponding to the symbol for the next state and the symbol for the output condition. For example, for the present state S_0 and the input condition I_2, the next state is S_2 and an output condition is R_0. Since the code word for S_2 is 010 and the code word for R_0 is 0000, the resulting entry in the encoded state table is 010/0000. For the present state S_2 and the input condition I_3, the entry in the symbolic table is S_0/R_1. Since the code word for S_0 is 000 and the code word for R_1 is 0011, the resulting encoded entry is 000/0011. All other entries in the symbolic state table are translated analogously.

The size of the table has grown considerably and now includes many unspecified entries. For example, there are a number of unspecified input columns, corresponding to input conditions that do not occur. These entries could

Table 4-10 Encoded state table for vending-machine control unit†

Present state $Q_2Q_1Q_0$	Input variables ND, DD, QD, CR							
	0000 (I_0)	0001 (I_4)	0010 (I_3)	0011‡	0100 (I_2)	0101–0111‡	1000 (I_1)	1001–1111‡
000 (S_0)	000/0000	000/0000	011/0000		010/0000		001/0000	
001 (S_1)	001/0000	000/0000	101/0000		100/0000		010/0000	
010 (S_2)	010/0000	000/0000	000/0011		110/0000		100/0000	
011 (S_3)	011/0000	000/0000	000/1111		000/0011		101/0000	
100 (S_4)	100/0000	000/0000	000/1011		011/0000		110/0000	
101 (S_5)	101/0000	000/0000	111/0111		000/1011		000/0011	
110 (S_6)	110/0000	000/0000	000/0111		101/0000		011/0000	
111 (S_7)	000/0100	000/0100	011/0100		010/0100		001/0100	

† Output variable order is NC, DC, DR, CC.
‡ Undefined. For these entries, the next state is the same as the present state, and the output condition

be treated as don't-care conditions, but since we do not wish to dispense free drinks and change, we shall assign an output of R_0 and a next state equal to the present state for each entry to be safe. In this way, an undefined input condition produces no change in state and no active output. For clarity these entries have been omitted in Table 4-10.

The encoded state table provides a precise technical description of the vending-machine control unit and can be translated into a logic diagram using the standard techniques described earlier. Thus except for verifying timing specifications, the design is essentially complete. Before proceeding to the timing analysis, let us briefly outline the translation of the encoded state table into a logic diagram so that we can relate this example to material we have seen before.

The structural model for the vending-machine control unit using JK flip-flops is shown in Fig. 4-2. In addition to the four input signals from the coin-input unit, this figure shows two other inputs near the bottom of the picture. One is a clock whose characteristics will be discussed in the next section. The other is a reset, which must be generated when power is applied in order to ensure that the

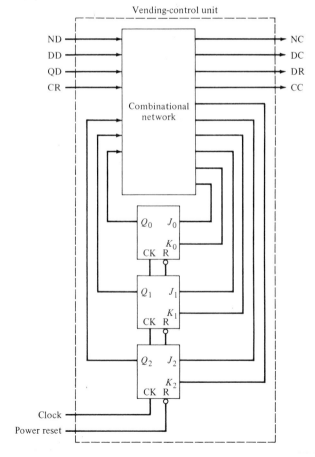

Figure 4-2 Structural model for the vending-machine control unit.

network begins in state S_0 with $Q_2 = 0$, $Q_1 = 0$, and $Q_0 = 0$. To improve the clarity of this diagram, the CLOCK and POWER RESET lines, which are connected to all flip-flops, are shown as passing behind these elements.

The vending-machine control unit involves a combinational network with seven input variables and ten output variables. K maps are not applied easily in a problem with this many input variables, but the minimization approach on which the K-map technique is based can be extended and implemented on a computer. In practice, problems of this size are handled by computer-aided techniques, which translate an encoded state table into minimum-sum-of-products equations defining the combinational subnetwork. These techniques are beyond the scope of this book.

4-1-4 Design Summary

Before continuing, let us briefly summarize what we have done with this problem. In step 1 we extracted a list of input conditions (Table 4-2) from the verbal specifications. In step 2 we defined an initial state; from it and the list of input conditions we evolved a symbolic state table (Table 4-4), which exhaustively catalogs the network's next state and output response for all valid present-state and input-condition combinations. All output conditions are listed in Table 4-5 and all symbolic states in Table 4-6. Finally, in step 3, we defined codes for all input conditions (Table 4-7), output conditions (Table 4-8), and states (Table 4-9). These codes were used to translate our symbolic state table into an encoded state table (Table 4-10), which can be considered the final design product, since all further steps required to produce a logic diagram are procedures best handled with computer help. We next consider the timing characteristics of our design.

4-1-5 Timing Considerations

The timing behavior of the vending-machine control unit is not explicitly defined by the state table discussed earlier. The predominant technique for analyzing timing behavior is the timing diagram. We use timing diagrams to establish a suitable clock period and input and output waveforms.

Clock period The minimum clock period (or maximum clock rate) is constrained by the timing specifications of the flip-flops and gates used in the implementation. The flip-flop requires two important timing specifications: (1) the setup time t_s defines the length of time during which the flip-flop inputs must be stable before the active phase of the clock pulse; (2) the propagation delay $t_{p,ff}$ defines the time required to stabilize the flip-flop outputs after the active phase of the clock pulse. For the gates in the combinational subnetwork the important timing specification is the propagation delay $t_{p,g}$, that is, the time required for the outputs to stabilize after the inputs change. As we have seen, combinational networks may contain two, three, four, or more levels of gates. In defining the

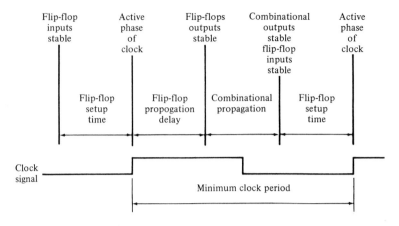

Figure 4-3 Defining minimum clock period.

delay through a combinational network, the path involving the maximum number of gates must be used to define the number of gate-propagation delays involved.

At the top of Fig. 4-3, we have identified the sequence of signal transitions for 1 clock cycle. We start when the flip-flop inputs are stable. After allowing for the flip-flop setup time t_s, the active phase of the clock pulse occurs. This initiates the transitions of the flip-flop, and their outputs are stable after the flip-flop propagation delay $t_{p,ff}$. Since the flip-flop outputs are inputs to the combinational subnetwork, the changes in the flip-flops propagate through the combinational subnetwork. After an appropriate number of gate-propagation delays, the outputs of the combinational subnetwork are stable. Thus the flip-flop inputs are again stable, and after the flip-flop setup time the active phase of the clock pulse occurs. Thus the minimum clock period is defined by the sum of the flip-flop setup time, the flip-flop propagation delay, and the propagation delay for the combinational subnetwork, which, in turn, is defined by multiplying the maximum number of gates in any path by the gate-propagation delay:

$$\text{Minimum clock period} = t_s + t_{p,ff} + \text{no. gates} \times t_{p,g} \qquad (4\text{-}1)$$

This equation defines the minimum clock period, and its reciprocal is the maximum clock rate. The actual clock rate may be slower than this maximum because of other considerations.

Input synchronization So far in our design we have made two assumptions which may not be valid: (1) we have assumed that the input signal will not change at a time which would cause an unstable input to the flip-flops during the active phase of a clock cycle, and (2) we have assumed that the duration of an input pulse is long enough to cause one change of state in the controller but not long enough to cause two or more changes. These restrictions are quite severe unless the units providing the input signals share the same clock. In this example, they do not since coin inputs are asynchronous with the controller clock.

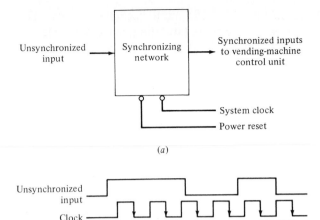

(a)

(b)

Figure 4-4 Input synchronization: (a) synchronizing-network input-output model and (b) timing relationships.

We define an input synchronization network (Fig. 4-4) to ensure the proper operation of the vending-machine control unit. With this synchronization network the input pulses occur at any time and may be any width as long as they are wider than the system clock cycle. The synchronizing network uses the same clock as the vending-machine control unit but uses the falling rather than the rising edge as an active phase, as indicated by the small circle on the clock input.

A symbolic state table describing the required behavior of the synchronization network is given in Table 4-11. This network starts in the rest state, implying that the input is inactive. As soon as an unsynchronized input occurs, the network goes to state S_1, implying an active input. It remains in state S_1 for one clock cycle and produces an active output during this cycle. From S_1 the next state is S_0 if the input pulse has gone and S_2 if it is still active. The network

Table 4-11 Symbolic state table for the synchronizing network of Fig. 4-4

R_0 = no pulse out to sync input; R_1 = pulse out to sync input

	Input condition	
Present state	I_0 (input inactive)	I_1 (input active)
S_0 (rest state)	S_0/R_0	S_1/R_0
S_1 (new input present)	S_0/R_1	S_2/R_1
S_2 (input still present)	S_0/R_0	S_2/R_0

remains in S_2 with the output inactive until the input becomes inactive. This guarantees that only one output pulse of the proper duration, one clock cycle, will be generated for each unsynchronized input of any width greater than the minimum clock period.

The procedure required to translate the symbolic state table (Table 4-11) into a logic diagram is identical to that presented in Chap. 3 and is left as an exercise. In the vending-machine control unit we must use one synchronization network for each of the four signals from the coin-input unit.

Output-pulse duration The specifications for the drink-dispensing, change-dispensing, and coin-input unit given in Table 4-1 impose explicit requirements on the duration of the vending-machine control-unit output signals. These re-

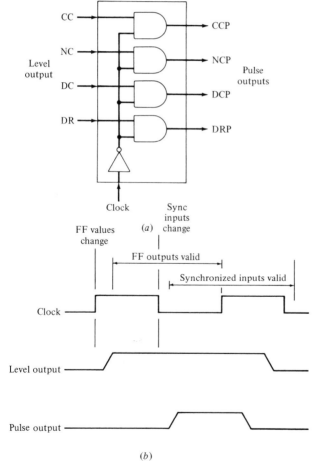

Figure 4-5 Output pulse network: (*a*) input-output model and (*b*) timing relationships.

quirements can be guaranteed most directly by defining a special output-pulse-shaping network just as we defined the input synchronization network earlier.

The output signals from the vending-machine control unit may change in response either to a change in an input signal or to a change in a flip-flop state. Theoretically, because the flip-flops change on the rising edge of the clock signal and the synchronized controlled inputs change on the falling edge of the clock signal, no spurious output pulses should be generated. Because of variation in propagation times and the number of gates in a path, however, short spurious output pulses may occur. The shape of the output pulse can be controlled more closely by ANDing the output signal with the complement of the clock, as shown in the output-pulse-shaping network of Fig. 4-5a. Figure 4-5b shows the timing relationship between the vending-machine control-unit output signals defined earlier (CC, NC, DC, and DR), the system clock, and the outputs of the pulse-shaping network, CCP, NCP, DCP, and DRP. These last signals are connected to the drink-dispensing, coin-dispensing, and coin-input units. If the low portion of the system clock cycle is made greater than 50 ms, the pulse-width specification on the output signals is met.

In summary, the timing considerations of a design are difficult to model and frequently are the most critical feature of the problem. We have defined two simple networks to provide both input-signal synchronization and output-pulse-width control. The clock period will be selected to meet the specifications on the flip-flop setup time, the flip-flop delay time, the combinational-network delay time, and the desired output-pulse width.

4-2 SIMPLE PROCESSOR

In this example we shall consider a simple processor conceptually similar to the microprocessor introduced in the next chapter. The simplicity of this processor allows us to deal with some detailed design aspects, a task that is much too complex in the realistic processor presented later. This section considers the control unit for the simple processor in detail. It is a sequential network producing a time-ordered sequence of output conditions in response to a single input condition. This behavior contrasts with the vending-machine controller, which detected a sequence of inputs and usually generated a single output.

The input-output model for the simplified processor unit is shown in Fig. 4-6. The input signal ADD/SUB is a 1-bit signal that defines the type of operation. If it is active, the processor will add the two input data words; otherwise, it will subtract the data word at B from the data word at A. The STROBE input is a timing signal indicating when the other inputs are valid. The data inputs A and B are each 8 bits long. The result R also contains 8 bits. The four single-bit output signals CARRY, OVERFLOW, MINUS, and ZERO indicate the status of the result. The READY signal is a timing signal indicating when the data output and the status outputs are valid and when the processor is ready for new input information.

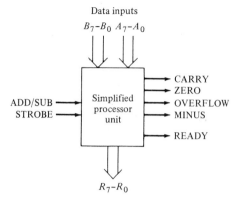

Figure 4-6 Input-output model for a simplified processor unit.

The timing relationships for the input-output signals of the simplified processor unit are shown in Fig. 4-7. The cross hatched areas indicate time intervals where the signal values are undefined. Signals shown as two parallel lines (one high and one low) indicate stable values defined as high or low, the specific value being determined by the data at the time of operation. Any external device providing input signals to the simplified processor unit must monitor the

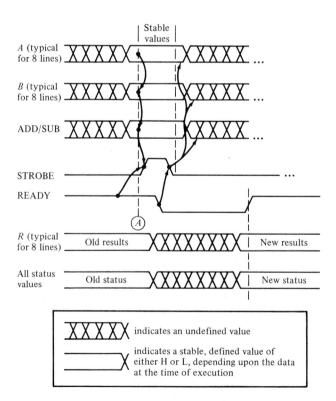

Figure 4-7 Timing relationships for the simplified processor unit.

READY output from the processor and withhold any inputs until this signal becomes active. It also must present stable values on the A lines, B lines, and the ADD/SUB line before it activates the STROBE line. The timing diagram shows directed arrows indicating the dependence of the STROBE upon the conditions of these other signals.

When a STROBE input is detected, the simple processor stores the input data and inactivates the READY line. This transition indicates that the A, B, ADD/SUB, and STROBE lines no longer need to be held stable. When the simplified processor unit has completed the specified operation, the result R and all status outputs are established before the READY signal is activated. An active READY line indicates not only that the outputs are valid but also that another transaction may begin.

This verbal description can be used to derive a block diagram of a solution, as shown in Fig. 4-8. The development of such a block diagram is not a systematic procedure but depends upon the experience and point of view of the designer. In the development of this example we shall accept Fig. 4-8 and concentrate on the design of the submodules.

The A, B, and status registers are more or less standard registers. The A register may be loaded from one of two sources by way of the multiplexer

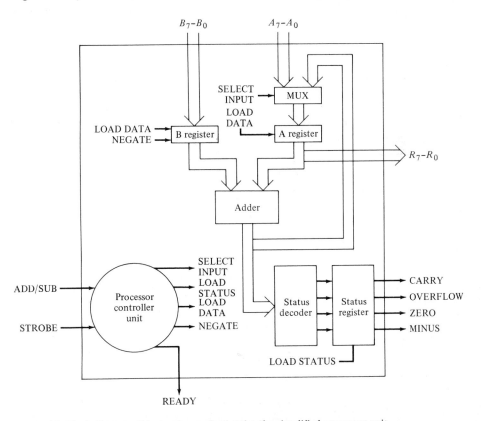

Figure 4-8 Block diagram of internal organization for the simplified processor unit.

(MUX). If the control input to the multiplexer, SELECT INPUT is high, the external input at A is selected; otherwise the output of the adder is selected. The A register is loaded when the control signal LOAD DATA is active. The B register may be loaded with external data from the B input lines, or the contents of the register may be replaced by the corresponding twos-complement value for use in subtraction. The two control inputs LOAD DATA and NEGATE define when these operations are performed. The status register is loaded with the output of the status decoder when the control signal LOAD STATUS becomes active. This register is used to store the status of the last operation; otherwise the correct status would be available only for a very short time. The adder and status decoder are combinational networks similar to the corresponding subunits in the 8-bit adder-subtracter described in Chap. 2.

All the modules described so far may be available as MSI modules or they can be designed using the procedures presented in earlier chapters. In this section we concentrate on the design of the remaining unit, the processor control unit. It produces the signals required to control the other modules, i.e., LOAD DATA, SELECT INPUT, LOAD STATUS, and NEGATE, in response to the external signals STROBE and ADD/SUB. In addition, the processor control unit produces the processor output signal READY. The procedure used in designing the vending-machine control unit will be used in designing this controller.

4-2-1 Identification of Input Conditions

As in the vending-machine control unit, we begin by identifying all valid input conditions. In this problem there are three, as described in Table 4-12. I_0 defines the condition when the STROBE signal is inactive; I_1 defines the add condition when both the STROBE and the ADD/SUB signals are active; and I_2 defines the subtract condition when the STROBE signal is active while the ADD/SUB signal is inactive.

4-2-2 Evolution of a Symbolic State Table

In the state table shown in Table 4-13 we begin with the first row, corresponding to a present state of S_0, the initial or rest state, in which the processor is ready to

Table 4-12 Input condition table for the processor control unit

Input condition symbol	Description
I_0	STROBE inactive
I_1	STROBE active and ADD operation selected
I_2	STROBE active and SUBTRACT operation selected

accept new data. The three input conditions I_0, I_1, and I_2 lead to three columns in the state table. If the condition is I_0, implying that the data inputs are not valid, the next state is the rest state and the output condition is R_0, where the input data are selected at the multiplexer and the READY signal is active. If the input condition is I_1, implying that the data words are to be added, the addition sequence is begun and a new state S_1 is defined. This combination results in a new output condition R_1, where the input data are selected at the multiplexer, the A and B registers are loaded, and the READY signal is active. Similarly, if the input condition is I_2, implying that the input data words are to be subtracted, the subtraction sequence starts and a new state S_2 is defined. The appropriate output condition is again R_1. Table 4-14 summarizes the output conditions.

We continue developing the state table by considering the entries in the second row. When the controller is in this state, the only valid input condition is I_1 because the external unit activated the STROBE line and so the STROBE and ADD/SUB signals must remain valid until the processor inactivates the READY signal. As a result we have entered a d for the input conditions I_0 and I_2. For the input condition I_1 a new output condition is needed; it is symbolized as R_2, where the adder is selected at the multiplexer and the READY line is inactive. For this combination the next state is S_3, where the addition is finished.

In the third row of the state table, the present state is S_2 (begin subtract); again only one input condition, I_2, is valid. In this state a new output condition is needed; it is defined as R_3, where the adder output is selected at the multiplexer, the contents of the B register are negated, and the READY line is inactive. Since this state provides the necessary time delay, the subtraction should be completed during the next clock cycle. Since the subtrahend has been negated in register B, subtraction is performed by adding the contents of the two registers. Thus the appropriate next state is state S_3 (finish).

In the fourth row of the state table the present state is S_3 (finish). Since the READY was inactivated during the previous states, all input conditions are possible; however, none is meaningful since the processor is still committed to a continuing operation. Thus the next state and output condition must be defined

Table 4-13 Symbolic state table for the processor control unit

	I_0 (ignore inputs)	I_1 (add inputs)	I_2 (subtract inputs)
S_0 (ready to begin)	S_0/R_0	S_1/R_1	S_2/R_1
S_1 (begin add)	d	S_3/R_2	d
S_2 (begin subtract)	d	d	S_3/R_3
S_3 (finish)	S_0/R_4	S_0/R_4	S_0/R_4

Table 4-14 Output conditions for the processor control unit

Symbol	Description
R_0	Select external data at multiplexer and indicate processor ready; do not load or negate registers
R_1	Select external data at multiplexer, load data registers; processor still ready; do not negate or load status
R_2	Select adder data at multiplexer; do not load data or status registers, do not negate, do not indicate processor ready
R_3	Negate data and select adder data at multiplexer; do not load data or status and do not indicate processor ready
R_4	Load data and status registers, select adder data at multiplexer; do not negate and do not indicate processor ready

for all input conditions. For this state a new output condition must be defined. It is symbolized by R_4, where the adder output is selected at the multiplexer; the A, B, and status registers are loaded, and the READY signal is inactive. Since loading the output of the adder into register A completes the addition or subtraction operation, the next state is the rest state S_0. This completes the derivation of a symbolic state table for the processor control unit.

4-2-3 The Encoded State Table and Timing Considerations

The code words used to define the input and output conditions for the controller are given in Tables 4-15 and 4-16, respectively. Because the input and output

Table 4-15 Input encoding for the processor control unit

	Input variables		
Input symbol	STROBE	ADD/SUB	Code† word
I_0	L	d	0d
I_1	H	H	11
I_2	H	L	10

† The positive-logic assumption H = 1, L = 0 will be used.

Table 4-16 Output encoding for the processor control unit†

Output symbol	Output variable					Code word
	READY	LOAD DATA	LOAD STATUS	NEGATE	SELECT INPUT	
R_0	H	L	L	L	H	10001
R_1	H	H	L	L	H	11001
R_2	L	L	L	L	L	00000
R_3	L	L	L	H	L	00010
R_4	L	H	H	L	L	01100

† The positive-logic assumption H = 1, L = 0 is used. All other conditions are unused.

signals are constrained by the specifications of other units in the system, there is no latitude in this definition. The codes shown are self-explanatory. The state encoding uses the minimum number of state variables and a straight binary sequence to produce a unique code word for each state symbol. For the four symbolic states we identified, two state variables Q_1 and Q_0 are required. The code is given in Table 4-17.

The input, output, and state codes are substituted into the symbolic state table of Table 4-13 resulting in the encoded state table shown in Table 4-18. Columns 00 and 01 both correspond to input condition I_0 (STROBE = L, 0d) and therefore are identical. The variables in the output code words are ordered READY, LOAD DATA, LOAD STATUS, NEGATE, and SELECT INPUT. Approaches presented in Chap. 3 can be used to convert this solution description into an implementation. The structural model for the implementation is shown in Fig. 4-9.

The control unit in the simple processor shares the same clock with all the modules it is controlling. In addition, the simple processor has a special input, the STROBE signal, and a special output, the READY signal, to synchronize the data transfers between the processor and its external units. Thus the timing considerations are much simpler than with the vending-machine control unit; they are left as an exercise.

Table 4-17 State encoding for the processor control unit

State symbol	Code words	
	Q_1	Q_0
S_0	0	0
S_1	0	1
S_2	1	0
S_3	1	1

Table 4-18 Encoded state table for the processor control unit†

Present-state state variables		Input variables STROBE, ADD/SUB			
Q_1	Q_0	$00\ (I_0)$	$01\ (I_0)$	$10\ (I_2)$	$11\ (I_1)$
0	0	00/10001	00/10001	10/11001	01/11001
0	1	d	d	d	11/00000
1	0	d	d	11/00010	d
1	1	00/01100	00/01100	00/01100	00/01100

† Order of output variables is READY, LOAD DATA, LOAD STATUS, NEGATE, SELECT INPUT.

4-3 CONCLUSIONS

We have demonstrated a design process by solving two example problems. The procedure was somewhat simplified but still representative of design methods used for many years. We have considered only restricted specifications and have ignored such issues as power, reliability, physical size, and packaging require-ments to enable us to focus upon the basic design process. We shall use this understanding to build upon as we consider the behavior of microcomputer systems and the design process used when these devices are employed as network elements.

Perhaps the most difficult aspect of design is the segmentation of a large problem into a set of meaningful and properly related subproblems, an aspect we have left untouched since it is beyond the scope of this book.

We presented the design of controllers, a most important class of systems, and the skills we have developed will be important as a basis for other design problems in later chapters. By now you should be convinced that digital systems

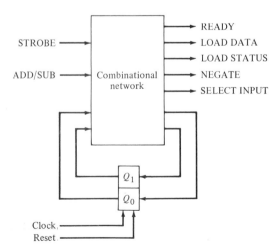

Figure 4-9 Structural model for the processor control unit.

can be designed to produce sequential behavior that varies as a function of input code words. This is one of the fundamental ideas underlying the development of all digital computers. The code words used here will become more complex instructions which can be altered to suit the problem at hand. The use of instructions to establish the specific behavior of a digital electronic system is at the heart of microcomputer-based systems, and in the next chapter we begin our discussion of these systems.

PROBLEMS

4-1 Draw the timing diagram for all output signals from the vending-machine control unit when 55 cents is deposited. Do these signals satisfy the timing specifications?

4-2 Tables 4-7 to 4-9 define codes for the input conditions, output conditions, and states in the vending-machine control unit design. Is it possible to define different codes for these conditions and states? Discuss your answer.

4-3 The vending-machine control unit is modified so that a code converter is used on the input and output signals as shown below. Define (a) the new symbolic state table and (b) the new encoded state table. Identify and discuss the advantages and disadvantages of using code converters in this way.

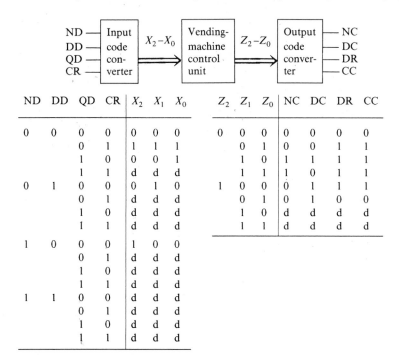

ND	DD	QD	CR	X_2	X_1	X_0
0	0	0	0	0	0	0
		0	1	1	1	1
		1	0	0	0	1
		1	1	d	d	d
0	1	0	0	0	1	0
		0	1	d	d	d
		1	0	d	d	d
		1	1	d	d	d
1	0	0	0	1	0	0
		0	1	d	d	d
		1	0	d	d	d
		1	1	d	d	d
1	1	0	0	d	d	d
		0	1	d	d	d
		1	0	d	d	d
		1	1	d	d	d

Z_2	Z_1	Z_0	NC	DC	DR	CC
0	0	0	0	0	0	0
	0	1	0	0	1	1
	1	0	1	1	1	1
	1	1	1	0	1	1
1	0	0	0	1	1	1
	0	1	0	1	0	0
	1	0	d	d	d	d
	1	1	d	d	d	d

4-4 Discuss the changes required in the vending-machine control unit if the price of a drink is raised to 40 cents.

4-5 Redesign the vending-machine control unit so that one of three brands of drinks can be selected. The cost of a drink remains at 35 cents. Develop a symbolic state table using the details described in the text. Assume that the inputs have been synchronized and are active for only one clock period.

4-6 Draw a timing diagram showing the waveform for the symbols on the ADD/SUB, STROBE, READY, LOAD DATA, LOAD STATUS, NEGATE, SELECT INPUT, Q_1, and Q_0 lines during (*a*) addition and (*b*) subtraction. Be sure to account for all propagation delays.

4-7 A sequential detector monitors a serial transmission line. The detector, if enabled, produces an output pulse whenever the ASCII code word for Q occurs. Assume that the transmitted data and your system clock are synchronized. Define the symbolic state table for this detector.

4-8 A sequential seat-belt system requires the ignition key to be inserted and then the seat-belt to be fastened, strictly in that order, before a starter-enable signal is generated. The network must remain in the enabling state until the ignition key is removed. Develop an encoded state table for this system.

4-9 The north-south primary highway has two sets of lights, one for the through lanes and one for the left-turn lanes. The east-west secondary road has one set of lights. The turn and east-west lights are activated on demand when traffic is detected by sensors. The east-west traffic takes priority over the left turn.

    (*a*) Develop a symbolic state table for the light controller

    (*b*) Define codes and develop an encoded state table for the light controller

Make reasonable assumptions to limit the complexity of the solution.

4-10 A small touch pad with five buttons (Reset, B1, B2, B3, and B4) is used to input a combination to unlock a door. The combination is B2-B3-B2-B4. Derive a symbolic state table for a sequential network that will produce signals to unlock the door if the combination is entered properly (after the system is RESET) and to sound an alarm if two consecutive errors in the combination are detected. Assume that only one button is pressed at a time and that any button input is active for only one clock period.

4-11 A two-story building has a freight elevator. There is a single request button outside the elevator on each floor and a move button inside the elevator. The door is operated manually; if it is not closed, the elevator should not move. The elevator control should monitor the door-closed sensor, move button, and the two request buttons and generate signals to move the elevator up or down. As the elevator nears the next floor, an approach signal indicates the up or down signal should be turned off, to bring the elevator to a correct stop. Assume that all inputs are active for only one clock cycle and develop a symbolic state table for the elevator control network.

4-12 An automatic bowling-pin setter has a control unit that monitors the following signals:

1. RESET, which is active when a player presses the reset button
2. BALL, which is active when a ball reaches the end of the alley
3. ALL, which is active when the pin rack detects no pins when it is lowered
4. RACK, which is active when the pin rack is in the low position

    The controller must generate the following signals:

1. SWEEP, to clear pins from the lane
2. RAISE, to lift the pin rack
3. RELEASE, to release the pins from the pin rack
4. DOWN, to lower the pin rack
5. PICK, to grab the pins standing
6. FILL, to load the rack with pins

Assume that each input condition is active during only one clock period and develop a symbolic state table for the control unit.

REFERENCES

Abd-Alla, A. M., and A. C. Meltzer: "Principles of Digital Computer Design," vol. 1, Prentice-Hall, Englewood Cliffs, N.J. 1976.

Blaauw, G.: "Digital System Implementation," Prentice-Hall, Englewood Cliffs, N.J., 1976.

Blakeslee, T. R.: "Digital Design with Standard MSI and LSI," Wiley, New York, 1975.

Chu, Y.: "Digital Computer Design Fundamentals," McGraw-Hill, New York, 1962.

Clare, C.: "Designing Logic Systems Using Finite State Machines," McGraw-Hill, New York, 1973.

Fletcher, W.: "An Engineering Approach to Digital Design," Prentice-Hall, Englewood Cliffs, N.J., 1980.

Flores, I.: "Computer Design," Prentice-Hall, Englewood Cliffs, N.J., 1967.

Gschwind, H.: "Design of Digital Computers," Springer-Verlag, New York, 1967.

Hill, F. J., and G. R. Peterson: "Digital Systems: Hardware Organization and Design," Wiley, New York, 1978.

Kohavi, Z.: "Switching and Finite Automatic Theory," McGraw-Hill, New York, 1970.

Peatman, J. B.: "The Design of Digital Systems," McGraw-Hill, New York, 1972.

Rhyne, V. T.: "Fundamentals of Digital System Design," Prentice-Hall, Englewood Cliffs, N.J., 1973.

Winkel, D., and F. Prosser: "The Art of Digital Design," Prentice-Hall, Englewood Cliffs, N.J., 1980.

6800 MICROCOMPUTER SYSTEM ARCHITECTURE

In this chapter we introduce the architecture, i.e., the organization and structure, of the 6800 microcomputer system. After finishing this chapter the reader should be able to:

1. Define the terms in Prob. 5-1
2. Draw a 6800 microcomputer system block diagram showing the four major units and describe the function of each unit
3. Define each 6800 bus signal and draw a timing diagram showing bus-read and bus-write cycles
4. Define the length and purpose of each register in the 6800 processor unit
5. Draw block diagrams for the memory, input, and output units and describe the purpose and operation of each
6. Define all addressing modes used in the 6800 and for a specific instruction define the operand or the address of the operand
7. Indicate the number of cycles required to execute a subset of the 6800 instructions, define the values on the system buses during each cycle as the instruction is executed, and describe the contents of all altered register and memory locations after the instruction has been executed
8. Define the values on the system buses during each cycle as a 6800 program is executed and indicate the contents of all registers after each instruction has been executed

5-1 INTRODUCTION TO PROGRAMMED DIGITAL SYSTEMS

In previous chapters we described models for traditional digital systems that contain such elements as logic gates, flip-flops, adders, and registers. The behavior of such networks depends on the type of elements and their interconnection, i.e., the network hardware. Thus the behavior of these traditional networks is defined completely by the hardware. In the present chapter, we begin discussing digital systems whose behavior depends not only on their hardware but also on the sequence of code words stored in the system. We refer to this sequence of code words as a *program*, and systems whose behavior depends on a program are called *programmable digital systems*. In this chapter we shall focus on the microcomputer since it is representative of most programmable digital systems.

So far in this book, the development of material has been more or less continuous, one section leading naturally into the next. The connection between this earlier material and that in the present chapter is not so apparent. Although the internal storage of a program defining the systems behavior is an important distinction, the elements used to build microcomputers represent the next stage in the evolution of semiconductor technology. In Chaps. 2 and 3 we described some complex networks, like the arithmetic logic unit and the memory element, available as integrated circuits. Integrated circuits used in microcomputer systems are very similar. They became available when semiconductor manufacturing technology advanced to allow more and more complex integrated circuits to be manufactured. This development has led to the ability to produce a single integrated-circuit implementation of a computer system. Again the major differences between this circuit and those of an earlier generation are their increased complexity and their programmability.

For several of the elements we described in earlier chapters, the relationship between the input and output data was not fixed but depended on an input control word. The arithmetic logic unit described at the end of Chap. 2 provides an example. The microcomputer is similar to the arithmetic logic unit in that during each operation the specific process it performs depends on an input control word. The microcomputer has many more possible operations than the simpler arithmetic logic unit, but each operation is defined by a specific code word and only one operation can be performed at a time.

The memory element described at the end of Chap. 3 plays an important role in the microcomputer system. These elements store the sequence of code words that define the program. The memory element allows storage of a large number of code words in memory locations with successive addresses. This means that a sequence of code words can be examined simply by altering the address applied to the memory element. A binary counter, called the program counter, provides an effective way of keeping track of the address of the next code word in the sequence. Thus each code word specifies both an operation on data and an alteration of the program counter.

We now can evolve an elementary description of the operation of a microcomputer system consisting of microprocessor, memory, input, and output units. A program, i.e., a sequence of code words, is stored in the memory unit. A counter in the microprocessor unit is initialized to point to the first code word in the sequence. The processor examines this code word, performs the specified operation, and alters the counter. This process is repeated until the program has been completed.

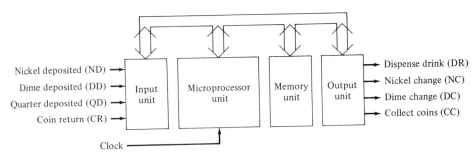

Nickel deposited (ND) →
Dime deposited (DD) →
Quarter deposited (QD) →
Coin return (CR) →

Input unit   Microprocessor unit   Memory unit   Output unit

→ Dispense drink (DR)
→ Nickel change (NC)
→ Dime change (DC)
→ Collect coins (CC)

Clock

Figure 5-1 Input-output model for a microcomputer-based vending-machine controller.

It is important for the reader to realize that the microcomputer can be used as an element in other digital systems. As an example, consider a programmed version of the vending-machine controller described in the previous chapter. Figure 5-1 shows the connection of the input and output signals to the microcomputer system. Signals from the coin-input units are connected to the microcomputer's input unit. Similarly, the microcomputer's output unit is connected to the drink dispensing, change-dispensing, and coin-input units. The memory unit would contain a sequence of code words to process the input data and to generate the appropriate output data. Table 5-1 shows a sequence of steps performing this task. In practice this sequence is converted into a sequence of binary code words, as we shall see later.

Step 1, SET TOTAL TO 0, initializes the system so that it is ready to begin a transaction and alters the program counter so that step 2 will be performed next. In step 2 the input signals are transferred to the processor unit, and the program counter is altered so that step 3 is performed next. During steps 3 to 10 the input signals are decoded and the total is adjusted to reflect the active input condition. For example, suppose a dime is deposited; the DD signal is active while QD, ND, and CR signals are inactive. In step 3 the processor alters the program counter so that step 4 is skipped since the QD signal is inactive. In contrast, during step 5, the DD signal is active so that step 6, which adds 10 to TOTAL, is performed. Since both the ND and CR signals are inactive, steps 8 and 10 are skipped.

In step 11, TOTAL is examined, and if it is less than 35, the counter is altered so that step 2 is performed next. A new sample of the input signals is taken and again decoded to adjust the total. Steps 2 to 11 are executed repeatedly until the total is equal to or greater than 35. Once this condition exists, step 12 is performed, and the signals DR and CC are activated. Steps 13 to 21 activate the appropriate change-dispensing signals. The rationale behind these nine steps is analogous to that used in decoding the input in steps 3 to 10. Since, when step 22 is reached the transaction is complete, the program counter is set to step 1 to begin a new transaction.

This description shows how the behavior of the system depends on the sequence of code words stored in the system's memory. By changing this sequence

Table 5-1 Sequence of steps for vending-machine control unit

Step	Microcomputer activity	Step	Microcomputer activity
1	Set total to 0	12	Activate DR and CC signals
2	Transfer inputs to processor	13	If total not equal 40, go to step 15; otherwise continue
3	If QD signal inactive, go to step 5; otherwise continue	14	Activate NC signal
4	Add 25 to total	15	If total not equal 45, go to step 17; otherwise continue
5	If DD signal inactive, go to step 7; otherwise continue	16	Activate DC signal
6	Add 10 to total	17	If total not equal 50, go to step 19; otherwise continue
7	If ND signal inactive, go to step 9; otherwise continue	18	Activate NC and DC signals
8	Add 5 to total	19	If total not equal 55, go to step 22
9	If CR signal inactive, go to step 11; otherwise continue	20	Activate DC signal
10	Set total to zero	21	Activate DC signal
11	If total less than 35, go to step 2; otherwise continue	22	Go to step 1

the system's behavior can be modified markedly. Thus the same hardware can be used to perform innumerable functions. This is the most important feature distinguishing programmed and traditional digital systems. The behavior of the traditional system is defined by the hardware and can be changed only by hardware modifications. In contrast the programmed system's behavior is defined by the sequence of code words, and its behavior can be changed by simply modifying these code words.

In this brief example, we suppressed many details of programmed digital system behavior which eventually must be considered. The remainder of this book develops the concepts and methods for dealing with these details. In the present chapter and the next we describe the architecture and behavior of the processor, memory, input, and output units; binary codes for each possible data transfer between these units; and the execution of these data transfers by the hardware elements. In Chaps. 7 and 8 we shall deal with programming technique for generating a sequence of code words for specific applications. In Chap. 9 we shall discuss the actual integrated circuits used in implementing programmed digital systems. Finally, in Chap. 10 we shall provide several example problems and their solution using programmed digital systems. Although we discuss the 6800 system specifically, many of the concepts are applicable to other systems.

5-2 ARCHITECTURE OF THE 6800 MICROCOMPUTER SYSTEM

In this section we describe the architecture of the 6800 microcomputer system. It consists of a system bus and four major units: the microprocessor, memory, input, and output units. In this section we present a simplified description of the architecture of each unit. In order to emphasize the operation and interaction of these units, we suppress confusing and as yet unnecessary details. Thus the architecture presented here gives not a precise picture of an actual integrated-circuit implementation but an overall view of the operation of the 6800 units. In Chap. 9 we deal with actual hardware elements and cover many of the details neglected in the present discussion.

5-2-1 The 6800 System Bus

The *system bus* consists of a set of wires connecting the four major units of the computer system. Conceptually the system-bus wires are considered as three smaller buses: the data bus, address bus, and control bus. These are discussed in the next few paragraphs and shown in Fig. 5-2.

The *data bus* is used to transfer binary words from one unit to another. These words may represent data being processed by the computer system, or they may be part of the program being executed by the computer system. The method used to distinguish these two interpretations will become apparent later when we discuss the execution of a program. During each cycle of the system clock only one binary word can be transferred on the data bus. The cycle may be a *bus-write cycle* during which data are transferred from the processor unit to one of the other units, or a *bus-read cycle*, during which data are transferred to the processor unit from one of the other units. Since the data bus is used to transfer binary words both to and from the processor unit, it is referred to as a *bidirectional bus*.

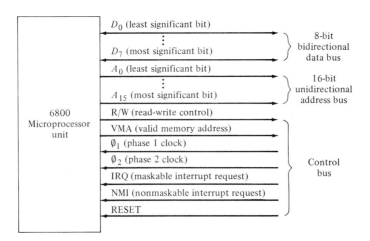

Figure 5-2 The 6800 system bus.

Typically, the number of wires in the data bus defines the word length of the computer system and the processor unit. For example, a 16-bit microprocessor has 16 wires in its data bus, i.e., 16 data lines. The 6800 is an 8-bit microprocessor and has 8 lines in its data bus. They are designated D_7 to D_0, D_7 representing the most significant bit and D_0 the least significant bit (Fig. 5-2).

The *address bus* carries a code word defining the specific register in the memory, input, or output unit that will be connected to the data bus. In simple computer systems the processor unit always provides the signals on the address bus. Therefore this bus is an input to the other three units. Since information flows in only one direction on the address bus, it is referred to as a *unidirectional bus*. In sophisticated computer systems, units other than the processor unit can drive the address bus, but we shall not discuss bidirectional address buses.

The number of wires in the address bus defines the maximum number of directly addressable locations in a computer system since a system with N wires in its address bus has 2^N unique code words for use as addresses. For example, a system with a 10-wire address bus has $2^{10} = 1024$ unique code words and can address 1024 locations. When referring to the number of addressable locations, it is common to use 1K to represent 1024 locations.† Most addresses are assigned to the memory unit, but several are also assigned to registers in the input and output units.

The 6800 microprocessor has a 16-bit address bus and can address $2^{16} = 64$K locations. The 16 lines in the address bus are designated A_{15} to A_0, representing the most significant and least significant bits, respectively (Fig. 5-2).

The *control bus* directs and synchronizes the transfer of binary words on the data and address buses. The number of wires used in the control bus varies with the sophistication of the computer system. In this presentation we shall discuss seven wires: the read-write control line, the valid-memory-address line, two timing signals, two interrupt-request lines, and the reset line.

The *read-write control signal* (R/W) defines the direction of the data transfer. This signal always originates in the processor unit. For the 6800, it is active, R/W = 1, when transferring a word to the processor unit, i.e., during a bus-read cycle. It is inactive when transferring a word from the processor unit, i.e., during a bus-write cycle. To help recall this convention, the reader should remember that R/W represents a READ-NOT-WRITE signal and therefore is active during a bus-read cycle and inactive during a bus-write cycle.

The second control signal, the *valid-memory-address signal* (VMA), also originates in the processor unit. It is activated, VMA = 1, during each clock cycle involving a bus transfer. If it is inactive, the cycle is used for internal processor operations and the signals on the data and address buses are meaningless.

The two timing signals are referred to as the phase 1 clock signal ϕ_1 and the phase 2 clock signal ϕ_2. Each completes one cycle during every cycle of the computer's clock. The two timing signals are exactly out of phase; i.e., one is

---

† The K is derived from a loose application of the abbreviation for thousand; in binary 1024 is the closest number to 1000.

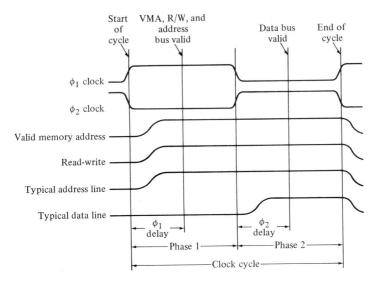

Figure 5-3 Timing diagram showing a 6800 bus-read cycle.

active while the other is inactive and vice versa. Figure 5-3, which shows a timing diagram of a bus-read cycle, illustrates the relationship between ϕ_1 and ϕ_2. At the beginning of the clock cycle ϕ_1 is activated, signifying the beginning of the first phase of the computer's clock cycle. After a specified time delay the signals on the address bus, the read-write control line, and valid-memory-address line are valid. Midway through the computer clock cycle, ϕ_1 becomes inactive and ϕ_2 becomes active, signifying the beginning of the second phase of the computer's clock cycle. After a specified time delay, the signals on the data bus are valid. Thus ϕ_1 defines when the address bus, the read-write control line, and the valid memory-address line become valid, while ϕ_2 defines when the data bus becomes valid.

The *interrupt-request signals* originate in the input and output units and are input signals to the processor unit. They can be activated by the input or output unit when a data transfer with an external device is pending. In the 6800, a request on the *nonmaskable-interrupt-request line* (NMI) cannot be ignored, or masked, by the processor unit. The processor unit can be programmed to ignore, or mask, a request on the *maskable-interrupt-request* (IRQ) line indefinitely.

The final control bus wire, the *reset signal*, is analogous to the reset signal in conventional systems. It is provided by an external source whenever power is applied to the system to ensure that the processor begins executing the correct program step.

Example 5-1 Define which lines in the system bus are active during a bus-write cycle if it transfers the ASCII code word for the character A to the memory location whose address is FF01 in hexadecimal.

SOLUTION The ASCII code word for A is 41 in hexadecimal or 0100 0001 in binary. This bit pattern must appear on D_7 to D_0; therefore D_6 and D_0 are active, and the other six lines in the data bus are inactive. The address FF01 corresponds to 1111 1111 0000 0001 in binary. Since this bit pattern appears on A_{15} to A_0, A_{15} to A_8 and A_0 are active, and A_7 to A_1 are inactive. During a bus-write cycle, VMA is active and R/W is inactive. The two timing signals ϕ_1 and ϕ_2 are active during every computer clock cycle. The IRQ, NMI, and RESET lines are controlled by external events, and their status is therefore undefined.

Example 5-2 Draw a timing diagram showing ϕ_1, ϕ_2, R/W, VMA, A_1, A_0, D_1, and D_0 during the bus-write cycle described in Example 5-1.

SOLUTION The timing diagram is shown in Fig. E5-2.

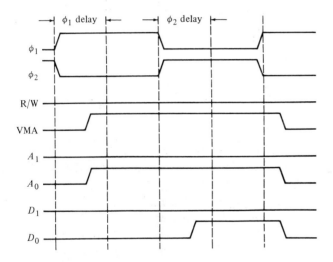

Figure E5-2 Timing diagram.

5-2-2 The 6800 Processor Unit

The essential elements in the 6800 microprocessor unit are the controller, arithmetic logic unit, and several registers, referred to as internal processor registers. This configuration is illustrated in Fig. 5-4. The controller is a sequential network conceptually similar to those discussed in Chap. 4. It accepts a code defining the operation to be executed, and it then proceeds through a sequence of states, generating a corresponding sequence of control signals. These control signals include the read-write control and valid-memory-address signals on the system's control bus. Other signals generated by the controller are connected to the

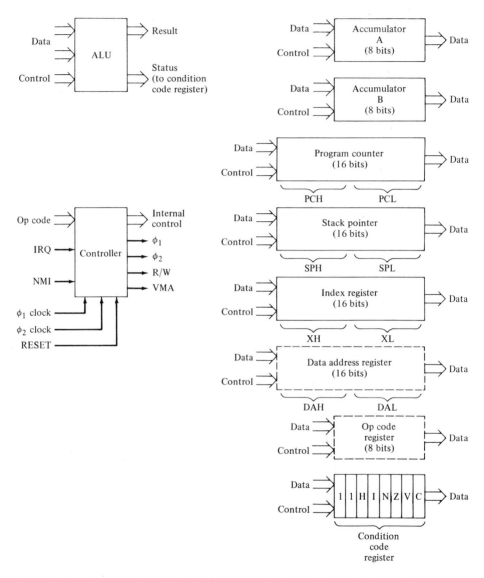

Figure 5-4 Architecture of a 6800 microprocessor. Registers drawn with dashed lines are not accessible to the user. Internal data and control lines are connected to an internal processor bus not shown for clarity.

arithmetic logic unit and the internal processor registers to regulate the flow of information in the processor and to and from the system data and address buses.

The *arithmetic logic unit* (ALU) is a combinational network like the one described in Sec. 2-5. It accepts two data words and a control word specifying the type of operation to be performed on the data. The system data bus or any of the internal processor registers can provide data words. The control word is defined by the control unit. The ALU performs the specified operation and generates an output word representing the result of the arithmetic or logic operation and a set of status signals indicating, for example, whether a carry or arithmetic overflow occurred. The result word may be directed to any of the internal registers or to the data bus. The specific destination is defined by the control unit, depending on the nature of the operation being performed. The status signals are directed to a specific internal processor register, called the condition-code register, for storage.

Internal processor registers store code words representing data, addresses, and processor status as a program is executed. Although the number and type of internal registers vary considerably among processors, all registers can be classified generally as accumulators, addressing registers, or status registers.

Accumulators store data for processing by the ALU. They usually have the same number of bits as the data bus. In the 6800 there are two 8-bit accumulators designated *accumulator A* and *accumulator B*, frequently referred to as register A and register B or simply A and B. Since the 6800 has an 8-bit data bus, these registers have 8 bits.

The accumulators are used with the data bus and the ALU in processing data. For example, two binary words can be added by loading the first into accumulator A, adding the second, loading the result into accumulator A, and then transferring the results from accumulator A to memory. During the first data transfer the data bus serves as an input to accumulator A. During the second, the ALU performs an addition in which the data bus provides one input and accumulator A the other; the output of the ALU is connected to the input of accumulator A to store the result. During the third operation the output of accumulator A is connected to the data bus so that the results are transferred to memory. Other examples of accumulator data transfers will be discussed later when we consider instruction execution.

Address registers store information defining the location of the next word in the program to be executed or the location of data to be processed. Address registers usually have the same number of bits as in the address bus, which is 16 in the 6800. The 6800 has one register, the program counter, for storing the address of the next word in the program and three registers, the data address register, the index register, and the stack pointer, for defining the address of a data word.

The *program counter* (PC) contains the address of the next word in the program.† Its output is connected to the address bus whenever a word of the program is read from memory. Every time the program counter provides an address, it is altered so that it always contains the address of the next word in the program. The operation of the program counter will be considered again when we discuss instruction execution.

The *data address register* (DA) is used for temporary storage of the address of the operand required by an instruction. Unlike most of the internal processor

---

† As shown in Fig. 5.4, the upper and lower halves of 16-bit registers are designated independently, for example PCH and PCL.

registers we shall discuss, this register cannot be examined or manipulated explicitly by the user and is essentially invisible.

The *index register* (X) is used during certain bus transfer cycles to define the location of the operand. During these transfers the index register stores a *base address*, which is added to an *address offset* contained in the program to define the address of the operand. There are special instructions for testing and manipulating the contents of the index register. The index register is useful particularly in processing lists of data, and its operation will become clearer when we consider the instruction coding and execution later.

The *stack pointer* (SP) usually is used to address a section of memory that has been reserved by the programmer for temporary data storage. This section of memory is referred to as the *stack*. The stack pointer is an *autoincrementing* and *autodecrementing* register, which means that each time it provides an address its contents are automatically either incremented or decremented. In the 6800 the stack pointer contains the address of the next empty memory location in the stack. When data are transferred to the stack, the stack pointer provides the address to the address bus for a bus-write cycle. After providing the address the stack pointer automatically decrements its contents so that it contains the address of the next empty location. When data are transferred from the stack, the stack pointer first automatically increments its contents; thus it contains the address of the last word written on the stack. It then provides this address to the address bus during a bus-read cycle. In the 6800 microcomputer the stack is used in many ways; e.g., it is used to store the return address when transferring control to subroutines or interrupt-service routines. The contents of the stack pointer also can be manipulated by special instructions. Its operation and application will be further clarified when we discuss programming examples.

Status registers contain information defining the current operation of the processor or the results of previous operations. The number of bits in a status register has no definite relationship with either the data bus or the address bus. In the 6800 there are two status registers, the op-code register and the condition-code register.

The *op-code register* (OR) contains the code word that specifies the operation currently being executed by the processor. This code word, called the operation code or op code, will be discussed further when we consider instruction coding. In the 6800 the op-code register contains 8 bits. The output of the op-code register is input to the controller to define which sequence of control signals is generated to actually execute the specified operation. Since the contents of the op-code register cannot be examined, it is invisible to the user just as the data address register is.

The *condition-code register* (CC) stores information describing the results of previous operations and information indicating whether or not the processor will acknowledge a maskable-interrupt request. This information is stored by assigning 1 bit in the register to each piece of information. In the 6800 the condition-code register contains 8 bits, but the two most significant bits are always set to 1, as shown in Fig. 5-4. The least significant bit is the *carry bit*, or C bit, set when an arithmetic carry occurs. The *overflow bit*, or V bit, is set when an arithmetic overflow occurs. The *zero bit*, or Z bit, the third bit in the condition-code register, is set when a result of zero occurs. The *negative bit*, or N bit, is set when a result is negative. The fifth bit in the condition-code register, the *interrupt-mask bit*, or I bit, is set and cleared by special instructions. If the I bit is set, the processor will ignore an interrupt request on the maskable-interrupt-request line. On the other hand, if the I bit is cleared, the request will be processed. The *half-carry bit*, or H bit, is set when a carry from bit 3 occurs. The H bit is used when performing arithmetic with BCD-coded data. The C, V, Z, N, and H bits are automatically set or cleared by the processor depending on the nature of the operation being performed and the result of that operation. In addition, the C, V, and I bits can be set or cleared by the programmer using special instructions for each bit.

Example 5-3 The internal processor registers contain the following hexadecimal values: PC = 1000, SP = 2000, X = 0F00, DA = 5050, A = 20, B = 32, OR = 9B, and CC = D2. (*a*) What is the address of the next word in the program? (*b*) What is the address of the last word placed on the stack? (*c*) Is the V bit set? (*d*) Will the processor ignore an interrupt request on the IRQ line? (*e*) Will the processor ignore an interrupt request on the NMI line?

SOLUTION (*a*) The address of the next program word is defined by the PC; it is 1000.

(*b*) Since the SP contains the address of the next empty location, the last word in the stack is in 2001.

(*c*) The V bit is the second bit from the right in the CC. The contents of CC are D2 = 1101 0010; therefore the V bit is set.

(*d*) A request on the IRQ line can be masked if the I bit is set. The I bit is the fourth bit from the left in the CC, and since this bit is set, the request will be ignored.

(*e*) A request on the NMI line cannot be ignored.

5-2-3 The 6800 Memory Unit

The memory unit is connected to the system address bus, data bus, and control bus, as shown in Fig. 5-5. The memory unit may be considered to be a large number of registers and an address decoder. Inside the memory unit the bidirectional data bus is connected to both the input and output lines of each register, as discussed in Sec. 3-6-3. These registers have the same number of bits as the data bus (8 in the 6800 bus). Each register has an input from the address decoder to enable that register and allow it to transfer a binary word either to or from the data bus. The direction of the transfer is specified by the read-write control line. When this line is active, the enabled register drives the data bus, and so a binary word is read from memory. When the read-write control line is inactive, the enabled register is loaded from the data bus, and so a binary word is written into memory.

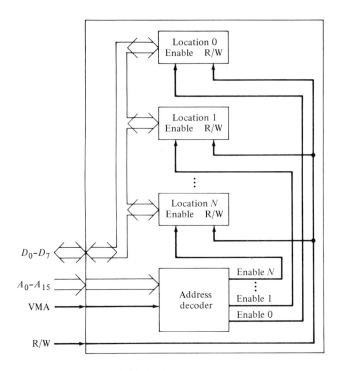

Figure 5-5 Memory-unit block diagram.

The address bus and the valid-memory-address signal are connected to the address decoder. In principle this network is an extended version of the BCD-to-decimal code converter described in Fig. 2-33. This decoder produces an enable signal for each register. During each cycle it activates the enable signal corresponding to the address on the address bus at a time when the valid-memory-address signal is active. If all 64K addresses in the 6800 system are assigned to the memory unit, there will be 64K enable lines, each connected to one of the 64K memory locations. In practice, address decoding is accomplished more efficiently by subdividing the address decoder into smaller units, discussed in Chap. 9 when we consider the actual circuits used to construct the memory unit.

Example 5-4 A particular 6800 memory unit has 4K locations. The unit is assigned consecutive addresses starting with 0000. (a) How many bits of memory does this represent? (b) What lines in the address bus must be active to write into the first location? (c) What lines in the address bus must be active to read the contents of the last location?

SOLUTION (a) Each location contains 8 bits and there are 4096 locations, so there are $8 \times 4096 = 32,768$ bits.

(b) The address of the first location is 0000 in hexadecimal or 0000 0000 0000 0000 in binary, so none of the lines in the address bus must be activated.

(c) The address of the last location is obtained by converting 4095 into a binary number. The conversion is straightforward, and the result is 0000 1111 1111 1111. Thus A_{11} to A_0 must be active to address the last location.

5-2-4 The 6800 Input Unit

The input unit is connected to the system bus and to one or more external systems. Wires connecting the input unit to the external environment are arranged in groups, the number of wires in each group usually being equal to the number of wires in the data bus. Each group of wires is referred to as an *input port*. In the 6800 an input port contains eight wires since there are eight wires in the data bus.

The essential operation of the input unit is to connect a specific input port to the data bus at a time compatible with the operation of both the computer system and the external system. Each input port is connected through an interface to the system data bus. The *input interface* is a digital network that adjusts voltage and current levels so that they are compatible and synchronizes the data transfer. In this discussion we shall assume that all external signals are electrically compatible with the input unit and focus on synchronizing the data transfer.

There are many configurations for input interfaces. We describe a relatively straightforward approach based on a data network and a status network. The data network shown in the upper part of Fig. 5-6 contains an address decoder, an AND gate, and a set of input buffers. The system address bus and the valid-memory-address line are inputs to the address decoder, which recognizes the specific address assigned to that port. The address decoder has a single output which is active when the specified address appears on the address bus while the valid memory address is active. We call this specified address the *port data address*. If the computer system has more than one input port, as shown in Fig. 5-7, each port has a unique port data address implemented in its address decoder.

The output of the address decoder is ANDed with the read-write control line to provide a signal that enables a set of input buffers identical to the three-state devices introduced in Figs. 3-29 and 3-30. When the enable signal is active, these input buffers connect the eight wires of the input port to the corresponding wires on the data bus. Thus an input transfer is performed by placing the port data address on the address bus during a bus-read cycle. This activates the output of the address decoder and enables the input buffers, thereby connecting the input port to the data bus.

The status network shown in the lower part of Fig. 5-6 contains a separate address decoder, a status flip-flop, and some logic gates. This address decoder is similar to the port-data-address decoder except that it is arranged to recognize a different address, which we shall call the *port status address*. Again, if there is more than one port, a unique port status address is assigned to each and implemented in its address-decoder circuit.

In this discussion, the status flip-flop indicates when valid data are available at the input port. As shown in Fig. 5-6, this status flip-flop has two inputs. One is a control line from the external unit indicating when the input signals at the port

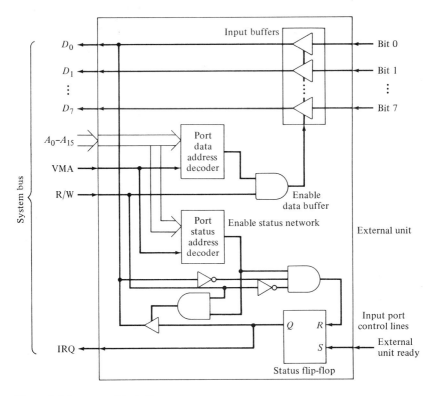

Figure 5-6 Input port block diagram.

are valid. This line, designated READY in Fig. 5-6, is connected to the S, or SET, input of the status flip-flop. Thus when the external system activates the READY line, the status flip-flop will be set. The second input to the status flip-flop originates from the D_0 line in the data bus, and it is connected to the R or RESET input. Before being applied to the status flip-flop, the signal from the data bus is complemented and then gated with the output of the status-address decoder and the complement of the read-write control signal. Thus the status flip-flop can be

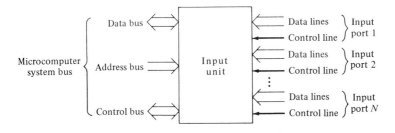

Figure 5-7 Input unit with multiple ports.

reset by placing a 0 on the D_0 line of the data bus and placing the port status address on the address bus during a bus-write cycle.

The output of the status flip-flop is buffered by a three-state device and then connected to the D_0 line of the data bus. The three-state device is controlled by an AND gate whose inputs are the enable signal from the address decoder and the read-write control line, and the resulting signal is connected to the D_0 line of the data bus. Therefore the contents of the port status flip-flop can be transferred to the D_0 line of the data bus during a bus-read cycle with the port status address on the address bus. In this way, a program anticipating input data can repeatedly test the status flip-flop to determine when the data at the input port are valid.

Frequently, the output of the status flip-flop is connected to either of the interrupt-request lines in the control bus. Thus as soon as data are valid at the input port and the READY line from the external unit is activated, an interrupt request will be generated by the input interface. If the maskable-interrupt-request line is used, depending on whether the interrupt mask bit (the I bit) in the condition code register is set or cleared, the processor will ignore or acknowledge this request, indicating valid data at the input port. If the nonmaskable-interrupt-request line is used, the processor must acknowledge the request from the input interface.

Example 5-5 In an input port with the interface defined in Fig. 5-6, the port data address is 800E and the port status address is 800F. (*a*) What lines in the address bus must be active to enable the input buffers? (*b*) What lines in

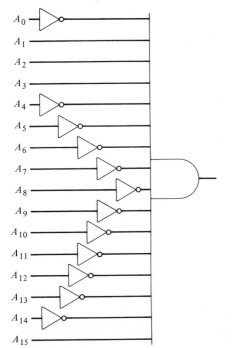

Figure E5-5 Address decoder.

the address bus must be active to test the status flip-flop? (c) What lines in the address bus must be active to clear the status flip-flop? (d) What lines in the address bus must be active to set the status flip-flop? (e) Use a 16-input AND gate and as many NOT gates as necessary to draw a logic diagram for the port-data-address decoder.

SOLUTION (a) To enable the input buffers the port data address must be placed on the address bus. This address in hexadecimal is 800E, which equals 1000 0000 0000 1110 in binary. Therefore, A_{15}, A_3, A_2, and A_1 must be active.

(b) To test the status flip-flop the port status address must be placed on the address bus. This address is 800F = 1000 0000 0000 1111; therefore, A_{15} and A_3 to A_0 must be active.

(c) Same as (b).

(d) The status flip-flop is set only by an external signal, and therefore there is no pattern on the address bus that will set the status flip-flop.

(e) The port address decoder is shown in Fig. E5-5.

5-2-5 The 6800 Output Unit

The structure and operation of the output unit are analogous to those of the input unit. The external connections are again grouped, and these groups of wires are referred to as *output ports*. Each output port has the same number of wires as the data bus, which is 8 bits in the 6800. The essential operation of the output unit is to transfer information from the processor to a specific output port using the data bus at a time compatible with the operation of the computer system and the external system.

Output ports are connected to the data bus through a digital network called the *output interface*. This network adjusts the voltage and current levels so that they are compatible and synchronizes the data transfers. Again we shall assume electrical compatibility and focus on synchronizing the data transfer.

Just as with the input interface, there are many output-interface configurations. We shall discuss one that is analogous to the input interface in Fig. 5-6. The data network of the output interface, shown in the upper part of Fig. 5-8, contains an address decoder which is arranged to recognize a specific address, called the *port data address*. The output of this address decoder is active when the specified address appears on the system address bus. The output of this decoder is ANDed with the complement of the read-write control line, and the resulting signal is used to control the loading at the *output-port data register* from the data bus. The function of this register is analogous to that of the input buffers in the input interface, but a register is used here for temporary storage of the data. Thus the contents of the data bus are transferred to the output data register by placing the port data address on the address bus during a bus-write cycle.

The status network of the output interface is very similar to that in the input interface; it contains an address decoder with a unique address, a status flip-flop, and an assortment of gates. Again, the status flip-flop is set by an external signal

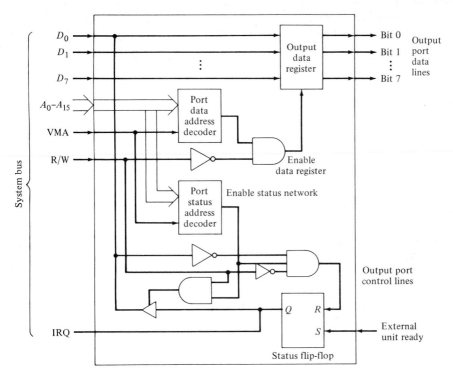

Figure 5-8 Output port.

designated READY and reset by placing a 0 on line D_0 in the data bus and the *port status address* on the address bus during a bus-write cycle. The contents of the status flip-flop can also be transferred to line D_0 in the data bus during a bus-read cycle using the port status address. Finally, the status flip-flop can be connected to one of the interrupt-request lines in the control bus.

5-3 INSTRUCTION CODING IN THE 6800

An *instruction* is the fundamental element of a program and must specify both the operation which we refer to as a boolean-arithmetic operation, and the operand. All processors are designed to execute a group of specific instructions referred to as an *instruction set*. Each instruction must be coded as binary words, and, in general, instruction code words are separated into the operand field and the operation field, as shown at the top of Fig. 5-9.

The binary pattern in the *operand field* specifies the data to be processed. This field may contain the data explicitly, the entire address locating the data, or a portion of this address. Many conventions for specifying the operand, called *addressing modes*, have been developed. Most instruction sets use several addressing modes in order to give the programmer flexibility.

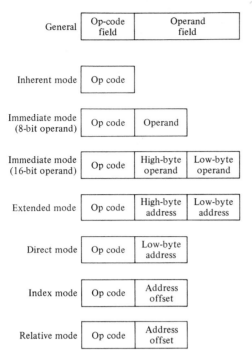

Figure 5-9 Addressing modes for the 6800.

The binary pattern in the *operation field* specifies the boolean-arithmetic operation to be performed, the internal processor registers involved, and the addressing mode that will be used in locating the data. Each combination of these three factors must have a unique code, the *operation code* or *op code* for that instruction.

Instruction codes in the 6800 instruction set may use 8, 16, or 24 bits or equivalently 1, 2, or 3 bytes. The length of the instruction code word depends on the nature of the instruction and the amount of detailed information to be represented. The first byte always contains the op code. Thus there are $2^8 = 256$ distinct op codes which can be used to specify 256 types of instruction. The second and third bytes of an instruction form the operand field. Depending on the addressing mode, they contain the operand, the complete address of the operand, a portion of the address of the operand, or an address offset.

The instruction set for the 6800 uses six addressing modes: inherent, immediate, extended, direct, indexed, and relative (Fig. 5-9).

With the *inherent addressing mode*, the operand is inherently specified by the designated boolean-arithmetic operation. For example, the instruction to clear accumulator A inherently defines an operand of 00, and the instruction to increment the index register inherently defines an operand of 01. Instructions using the inherent addressing mode are 1 byte long since no operand need be specified.

With the *immediate addressing mode* the operand is contained explicitly in the operand field of the instruction. The operand field may contain either 1 or 2 bytes, depending on the number of bytes in the internal processor register specified by the op code. Instructions using the immediate addressing mode with either of the two 8-bit accumulators require a 1-byte operand. Thus these instructions are 2 bytes long with 1 byte for the op code and 1 byte for the operand. Instructions using this addressing mode with the stack pointer and index register, which are 16-bit registers, require a 2-byte operand and thus a 3-byte instruction.

With the *extended addressing mode*, the operand is *not* contained explicitly in the instruction, but its complete address is provided in the operand field of the instruction. Since the 6800 requires a 16-bit address, the operand field with this addressing mode must have 2 bytes. Thus instructions using this addressing mode contain 3 bytes.

The *direct addressing mode* is similar to the extended addressing mode except that it is used with the first 256 memory locations whose addresses are 0000 to 00FF in hexadecimal. The operand field again contains the address of the operand, but only 1 byte is required since the most significant byte in the address is defined as 00. The use of the direct addressing mode instead of the extended addressing mode reduces the program's memory requirements and execution time, as we shall see later.

With the *indexed addressing mode* the address of the operand is obtained by adding the portion of the address provided in the instruction, referred to as the *address offset*, to the portion of the address stored in the index register, referred to as the *base address*. In the 6800, instructions using this addressing mode contain 2 bytes with only 1 byte reserved for the address offset in the operand field. Thus the address offsets may range from 00 to FF. With the indexed addressing mode the address offset always is interpreted as a positive integer, and so the range in decimal is 0 to 255. This addressing mode is particularly useful in processing lists of data, as we shall see later.

In the 6800 the *relative addressing mode* is reserved for instructions that alter the program counter. Instructions using this addressing mode are 2 bytes long, one for the op code and one for the operand field to specify the address offset, i.e., the amount the program counter is adjusted. Again the address offset ranges in hexadecimal from 00 to FF, but with the relative addressing mode the address offset is interpreted using the signed binary value twos-complement code, and so the range is -128 to 127 in decimal.

When the address offset with the relative addressing mode represents a positive integer, 00 to 7F in hexadecimal, the new contents of the program counter are found by adding the address offset to the old contents of the program counter and then incrementing twice. The double incrementation is necessary because the program counter is incremented twice in fetching the instruction, as we shall see. Thus if an instruction using the relative addressing mode is stored in memory location 1025 and the second byte of the instruction is 1A, the new contents of the program counter are obtained by adding the hexadecimal values

(PC)   1025 → 0001 0000 0010 0101
(Offset)   1A →   0001 1010
               2 →   0000 0010
                    _____
                    0001 0000 0100 0001 → 1041

                         (a)

(PC)   1025 → 0001 0000 0010 0101
(Offset) (FF)87 → 1111 1111 1000 0111
               2 →   0000 0010
                    _____
                    0000 1111 1010 1110 → OFAE

                         (b)

Figure 5-10 Computation of addresses with the relative addressing mode: (a) for positive offset; (b) for negative offset.

1025, 1A, and 2 to obtain 1041. Since the addition of hexadecimal numbers can be complicated the addition is done by converting to binary numbers, performing the binary addition, and then converting the result back to hexadecimal notation (Fig. 5-10).

When the address offset with the relative addressing mode represent a negative integer, 80 to FF in hexadecimal, the 8-bit word specifying the address offset must be converted into the corresponding 16-bit code word. This is accomplished by placing eight leading 1s or, in hexadecimal, two leading F's. For example, the program offset 87 becomes FF87 before being added to the old contents of the program counter. Manipulations associated with defining the new contents of the program counter with a negative offset are also shown in Fig. 5-10.

Example 5-6 The first word of an instruction, unspecified for this example, is stored in memory location 100, the next two bytes in the program are C3 and 05, and the index register contains 2050. Define the operand or the address of the operand as required for each of the six addressing modes available in the 6800 instruction set.

SOLUTION *Inherent mode*: The operand is specified by the op code.

Immediate mode: The operand is specified as part of the instruction; in this case it would be C3 or C305, depending on the number of bits in the internal processor register specified by the op code.

Extended mode: The operand address is C305.

Direct mode: The operand address is 00C3.

Index mode: The address is 2113, which was obtained by adding the contents of the index register to the second byte of the instruction

2050 → 0010 0000 0101 0000
  C3 →   1100 0011
       _____
       0010 0001 0001 0011 → 2113

Relative mode: The address is 00C5, which was obtained by adding the original contents of the program counter to the second byte of the instruction with the value extended to form a 16-bit word and then incremented twice

$$100 \rightarrow 0000\ 0001\ 0000\ 0000$$
$$(FF)\ C3 \rightarrow 1111\ 1111\ 1100\ 0011$$
$$2 \rightarrow \quad\quad\quad\quad\quad 10$$
$$\overline{0000\ 0000\ 1100\ 0101} \rightarrow 00C5$$

5-4 AN ABBREVIATED 6800 INSTRUCTION SET

The complete instruction set for the 6800 processor is defined in the programmer's card shown in Fig. 6-1. This instruction set is extensive and somewhat overwhelming at first glance. To focus on the concepts without worrying about all the details we shall consider an abbreviated instruction set first. The abbreviated set will be used in our initial discussion of instruction coding and execution and program coding and execution.

5-4-1 Instruction Coding

Table 5-2 contains the programmer's card for the abbreviated instruction set. For each instruction, this table defines the addressing mode, op code (OP), number of clock cycles required for execution ($\sim$), number of bytes in the instruction ($\#$), and the specified boolean-arithmetic operation using a register-transfer notation. For example, the first row of this table indicates that the instruction "clear A" uses the inherent addressing mode, has an op code of 4F, and requires two clock cycles for execution and 1 byte for coding. The register-transfer description of the specified boolean-arithmetic operation, $00 \rightarrow A$, is read "load 00 into A." The fourth row indicates that the instruction "add to A" uses the extended addressing mode, has an op code of BB, and requires four clock cycles for execution and 3 bytes for coding. The register-transfer description of the boolean-arithmetic operation $A + M \rightarrow A$ is read "load the sum of A plus the contents of the memory location M into A."

The information in Table 5-2 is very compact, and the reader needs to be able to expand this information into more explicit forms. For example, Table 5-3

Table 5-2 Programmer's card for abbreviated instruction set

Description	Addressing mode	OP	$\sim$	$\#$	Register-transfer description
Clear A	Inherent	4F	2	1	$00 \rightarrow A$
Negate A	Inherent	40	2	1	$00 - A \rightarrow A$
Load A	Immediate	86	2	2	$M \rightarrow A$
Add to A	Extended	BB	4	3	$A + M \rightarrow A$
Clear memory	Extended	7F	6	3	$00 \rightarrow M$
Store A	Extended	B7	5	3	$A \rightarrow M$

Table 5-3 Detailed instruction code word and register transfer†

Description	Addressing mode	Instruction code word	Register transfer
Clear A	Inherent	8F	$00 \to A$
Negate A	Inherent	40	$00 - \langle A \rangle \to A$
Load A	Immediate	86 H_1H_2	$H_1H_2 \to A$
Add to A	Extended	BB $H_1H_2\,H_3H_4$	$\langle A \rangle + \langle \text{LOC } H_1H_2H_3H_4 \rangle \to A$
Clear memory	Extended	7F $H_1H_2\,H_3H_4$	$00 \to \text{LOC } H_1H_2H_3H_4$
Store A	Extended	B7 $H_1H_2\,H_3H_4$	$\langle A \rangle \to \text{LOC } H_1H_2H_3H_4$

† Angle brackets $\langle \ \rangle$ indicate the contents of the enclosed register or memory location.

contains a more detailed description of the instruction and the specified register transfer. The first instruction in Table 5-2, "clear A," requires no clarification and its description transfers directly to Table 5-3. The same is true for the second instruction, "negate A," except for the angle brackets used in the register-transfer description; this notation will be used to indicate the contents of a register or memory location. In this case, $00 - \langle A \rangle \to A$ is read "00 minus the contents of A is loaded into A."

The third instruction, "load A" uses the immediate addressing mode, has an op code of 86, and contains 2 bytes. The coded instruction has the form 86 H_1H_2, where H_1 and H_2 represent hexadecimal symbols. In our earlier discussion of the immediate addressing mode we noted that the second byte contains the operand. Thus on executing the instruction 86 H_1H_2, the value H_1H_2 is loaded into accumulator A, as shown in the detailed register-transfer description in Table 5-3. This general description of the coding and execution of this instruction can be applied to specific instructions; e.g., the coded instruction 86 3C, loads the value 3C into accumulator A; that is, $3C \to A$.

As another example, the fourth instruction in Table 5-2, "add to A," uses the extended addressing mode, has an op code of BB, and contains 3 bytes. The coded instruction has the form BB $H_1H_2\,H_3H_4$, where the H_i's again represent hexadecimal symbols. In our earlier discussion of the extended addressing mode we noted that the second and third bytes define the address of an operand. Thus on executing the instruction defined by BB $H_1H_2\,H_3H_4$, the contents of memory location $H_1H_2H_3H_4$ would be added to the accumulator. The more detailed register-transfer description of the instruction is $\langle A \rangle + \langle \text{LOC } H_1H_2H_3H_4 \rangle \to A$, where the angle brackets again indicate that the contents of the enclosed register or memory location are involved. This expression is read "the contents of A plus the contents of LOC $H_1H_2H_3H_4$ are loaded into A."

This process can be repeated for the other instructions in the abbreviated set; the results are summarized in Table 5-3. The instruction to clear memory using the extended addressing mode contains 3 bytes, the second and third bytes specifying the address of the memory location to be cleared. In this case the coded instruction has the form 7F $H_1H_2\,H_3H_4$, and the specific boolean-arithmetic operation using the detailed register-transfer notation is $00 \to \text{LOC}$

$H_1H_2H_3H_4$, read "the value 00 is loaded into location $H_1H_2H_3H_4$." The store A instruction using the extended addressing mode has the form B7 H_1H_2 H_3H_4. The specified boolean-arithmetic operation using the detailed register-transfer notation is $\langle A \rangle \rightarrow$ LOC $H_1H_2H_3H_4$, which is read "the contents of A are loaded into memory location $H_1H_2H_3H_4$."

When we consider the complete instruction set, we shall give additional examples showing the translation from the compact description in Table 5-2 into the more detailed description in Table 5-3. We cannot consider every instruction in the 6800 set, however, and so the reader should understand the process and be able to apply the descriptions in these tables to specific instructions and define the effect of their execution.

Example 5-7 Define the coded form of the instruction that will (a) load the value 5 into accumulator A and (b) clear the location with the address 150.

SOLUTION (a) This instruction uses the immediate addressing mode, has an op code of 86, and contains 2 bytes, the second specifying the operand. Thus the coded instruction is 86 05.

(b) This instruction uses the extended addressing mode, has an op code of 7F, and contains 3 bytes, the second and third specifying the complete address. Thus the coded instruction is 7F 01 50.

5-4-2 Instruction Execution

Microcomputers are synchronous systems in which instructions are executed by performing a sequence of simple bus transfers and internal processor manipulations during successive clock cycles. The data transfers during these clock cycles are regulated by control signals from the controller in the processor unit. These clock cycles may be *internal cycles*, which involve only internal processor manipulation with no bus transfer, or they may be *bus-transfer cycles*, with both internal processor manipulations and a *single* bus transfer. The valid-memory-address line is used to distinguish internal and bus-transfer cycles. The controller places a 0 on the valid-memory-address line for an internal cycle and a 1 for a bus-transfer cycle. Bus-transfer cycles are either bus-read cycles or bus-write cycles, as indicated by the read-write control line. Since the execution of each instruction is accomplished by a unique sequence of internal, bus-read, and bus-write cycles, we shall describe instruction execution by defining this sequence. In doing this we shall ignore most of the internal manipulations (since they are not observable by the user) and focus on the bus-transfer cycles, simply indicating that internal cycles occur.

Instruction execution can be divided conceptually into two phases: fetch and operate.† During the *fetch phase* the instruction is transferred from memory to the

---

† The second phase is often called the execute phase, but we reserve this term for the combination of the fetch and operate phase.

processor. The fetch phase consists of one bus-read cycle to transfer the op code and one or two additional bus-read cycles to transfer the second and third bytes of the instruction if they are present. During the *operate phase* the specified boolean-arithmetic operation is performed. Although separating instruction execution into the fetch and operate phase is useful conceptually, in practice these two activities may share common clock cycles.

The execution of every instruction begins by fetching the op code, which is contained in the first byte of every instruction. This code word is stored in the op-code register and interpreted by the controller in the processor unit. The controller then generates a unique sequence of control signals in order to complete the execution of this instruction. If the instruction contains additional bytes in the operand field, they are fetched before the operate phase begins.

Table 5-4 describes the sequence of internal, bus-read, and bus-write cycles generated by the controller to execute the six instructions in the abbreviated set we have been considering. Some internal-processor-register manipulations are shown to help clarify the execution of these instructions. Transfers during the first clock cycle in the execution of all instructions are identical and consist of transferring the op code from memory to the op-code register. This is done during a bus-read cycle in which the controller places a 1 on the read-write control line $(1 \rightarrow R/W)$ and places the contents of the program counter on the system address bus $(\langle PC \rangle \rightarrow SAB)$. Since this is a bus-read cycle, the contents of the addressed location appear on the system data bus. The controller then connects the system data bus to the input of the op-code register, $\langle SDB \rangle \rightarrow OR$. Finally, the controller increments the contents of the program counter $(\langle PC \rangle + 1 \rightarrow PC)$ so that it contains the address of the next word in the program.

The first instruction in Table 5-2, "clear A," using the inherent addressing mode, contains 1 byte and requires two clock cycles for execution. The first clock cycle is the standard bus-read cycle to transfer the op code from memory to the op-code register. Since this instruction is only 1 byte long, the fetch phase is complete after the first clock cycle. Since clearing accumulator A requires no bus transfers, the second clock cycle in the sequence to execute this instruction is internal and places 00 in accumulator A.

The execution of the second instruction in this set, "negate A," is analogous to the execution of the instruction to clear A. The op code, which constitutes the entire instruction, is fetched during the first clock cycle. The second clock cycle, an internal cycle, is used to manipulate accumulator A.

From Table 5-4 we see that the third instruction in this set, "load A using the immediate addressing mode," contains 2 bytes and requires two clock cycles for execution. The first clock cycle is standard and transfers the op code from memory to the op-code register. During the second clock cycle the operand is fetched and loaded into accumulator A. This is accomplished during a bus-read cycle with the controller placing a 1 on the read-write control line and connecting the output of the program counter to the system bus $(\langle PC \rangle \rightarrow SAB)$. Since this is a bus-read cycle, the contents of the addressed location appear on the data bus. In this case this pattern represents the second byte of the instruction, and so the

Table 5-4 Sequence of cycles used to execute instructions in the abbreviated set

Instruction and addressing mode	Cycle 1	Cycle 2	Cycle 3	Cycle 4	Cycle 5	Cycle 6
Clear A, inherent	$1 \to$ R/W $\langle PC \rangle \to$ SAB $\langle SDB \rangle \to$ OR $\langle PC \rangle + 1 \to$ PC	*Internal* $00 \to A$				
Negate A, inherent	As above	*Internal* $00 - \langle A \rangle \to A$				
Load A, immediate	As above	$1 \to$ R/W $\langle PC \rangle \to$ SAB $\langle SDB \rangle \to A$ $\langle PC \rangle + 1 \to$ PC				
Add to A, extended	As above	$1 \to$ R/W $\langle PC \rangle \to$ SAB $\langle SDB \rangle \to$ DAH $\langle PC \rangle + 1 \to$ PC	$1 \to$ R/W $\langle PC \rangle \to$ SAB $\langle SDB \rangle \to$ DAL $\langle PC \rangle + 1 \to$ PC	$1 \to$ R/W $\langle DA \rangle \to$ SAB $\langle A \rangle + \langle SDB \rangle \to A$		
Clear memory, extended	As above	As above	As above	$0 \to$ R/W $\langle DA \rangle \to$ SAB $00 \to$ SDB	*Internal*	*Internal*
Store A, extended	As above	As above	As above	$0 \to$ R/W $\langle DA \rangle \to$ SAB $\langle A \rangle \to$ SDB	*Internal*	

controller connects the system data bus to the A accumulator ($\langle SDB \rangle \rightarrow A$). The controller also increments the program counter ($\langle PC \rangle + 1 \rightarrow PC$) so that it contains the address of the next word in the program.

The fourth instruction in this set, "add to A using the extended addressing mode," contains 3 bytes and requires four clock cycles for execution. The first clock cycle is standard. The next two are bus-read cycles used to transfer the upper and lower bytes of the address of the operand to the data address register. During each, the controller places a 1 on the read-write control line and connects the output of the program counter to the system address bus. During the second clock cycle in this sequence, the data bus carries the second byte of the instruction, representing the high byte of the address, and so the controller connects the system data bus to the upper half of the data address register ($\langle SDB \rangle \rightarrow DAH$). The lower half of the register, DAL, is loaded in an analogous manner during the third clock cycle. The fourth clock cycle is used for the operate phase; it is a bus-read cycle in which the controller places a 1 on the read-write control line and connects the output of the data address register to the system address bus ($\langle DA \rangle \rightarrow SAB$). The operand is read from memory and appears on the system data bus. The controller connects the system data bus and the output of accumulator A to the two inputs of the arithmetic logic unit and connects the output of the arithmetic logic unit to the input of accumulator A so that the value on the data bus is added to the current contents of the A accumulator ($\langle SDB \rangle + \langle A \rangle \rightarrow A$).

The next instruction in the abbreviated instruction set, "clear memory using the extended addressing mode," contains 3 bytes and requires six clock cycles for execution. The first three clock cycles are identical to the first three in the "add to A using the extended addressing mode." They are used to fetch the op code of the instruction and the address of the memory location that will be cleared. The last three clock cycles in the sequence to execute the instruction are devoted to the operate phase. Since only one bus-transfer cycle is required to write 00 in the specified memory location, there are two internal cycles. We adopt the convention of placing all internal cycles after the bus-transfer cycles. With this convention, the fourth clock cycle is a bus-write cycle. The controller places a 0 on the read-write control line, connects the output of the data address register to the system address bus ($\langle DA \rangle \rightarrow SAB$), and loads 00 onto the system data bus ($00 \rightarrow SDB$). Since this is a bus-write cycle, the word on the system data bus eventually is written in the addressed location. Internal cycles are listed for the fifth and sixth clock cycles required to execute this instruction.

The execution of the last instruction in the abbreviated instruction set, "store A using the extended addressing mode," is similar to that of the other two instructions using the extended addressing mode in this set. Five clock cycles are required; three are used to fetch the op codes and the address of the operand. Thus two cycles are assigned to the operate phase, and since only 1 byte must be stored, there is one bus-transfer cycle and one internal cycle. According to our convention we assign the bus transfer to the fourth clock cycle and define the fifth as an internal cycle. The fourth clock cycle is a bus-write cycle. The controller places a 0 on the read-write control line and connects the output of the data address register to the system address bus and the output of accumulator A to the system data bus. Since this is a bus-write cycle, the word on the system data bus is written into the addressed location.

We have discussed the sequence of bus transfers required to execute all six instructions in the abbreviated set. Later, when we return to our discussion of the entire 6800 instruction set, we shall see that the execution of many instructions in the complete set is analogous to that of the six instructions in the abbreviated set.

In conclusion let us outline the steps used in transforming the information in the programmer's card (Table 5-2) to the sequence of internal, bus-read, and bus-write cycles shown in Table 5-4. First we determine the total number of clock cycles required to execute the instruction from the programmer's card. Next we determine how many cycles must be used to fetch the instruction; this is equal to the number of bytes in the instruction as defined on the programmer's card. The difference between the number of clock cycles and the number of bytes in the instruction represents the number of clock cycles assigned to the operate phase of the instruction execution. The first clock cycle of every instruction execution is used to fetch the op code. Subsequent cycles are used to fetch the second and third bytes of the instruction if they exist. For the operate phase we identify all the required bus transfers and assign each to a clock cycle. We define the remainder as internal cycles. We shall review this process later in discussing the complete 6800 instruction set.

Example 5-8 The 6800 instruction set includes the instruction "load A using the extended addressing mode." This instruction has an op code of B6, contains 3 bytes, and requires four clock cycles for execution. For this instruction, define the instruction code and the more detailed register-transfer description as given in Table 5-3. Indicate the sequence of internal, bus-read, and bus-write cycles generated in executing this instruction.

SOLUTION The instruction code is B6 H_1H_2 H_3H_4, where $H_1H_2H_3H_4$ defines the address of the operand. The detailed register transfer is $\langle LOC\ H_1H_2H_3H_4\rangle \to A$. The sequence of cycles is

Cycle 1	Cycle 2	Cycle 3	Cycle 4
$1 \to R/W$	$1 \to R/W$	$1 \to R/W$	$1 \to R/W$
$\langle PC\rangle \to SAB$	$\langle PC\rangle \to SAB$	$\langle PC\rangle \to SAB$	$\langle DA\rangle \to SAB$
$\langle SDB\rangle \to OR$	$(SDB) \to DAH$	$\langle SDB\rangle \to DAL$	$\langle SDB\rangle \to A$
$\langle PC\rangle + 1 \to PC$	$\langle PC\rangle + 1 \to PC$	$\langle PC\rangle + 1 \to PC$	

Example 5-9 The program counter and accumulator A contain the hexadecimal values 1000 and C3, respectively. In location 1000 is the op code for the instruction "store A using the extended addressing mode," B7. The next two locations contain FF and 01, respectively. Define the sequence of values

on the VMA and R/W lines, the SAB, and the SDB during all clock cycles required to execute this instruction.

SOLUTION Table 5-4 defines the sequence of internal, bus-read, and bus-write cycles for this instruction. The first clock cycle is a bus-read cycle with the PC providing the address; thus VMA = 1, R/W = 1, SAB = 1000, and SDB = B7, where B7 is the contents of location 1000. The second clock cycle is similar except that the PC has been incremented; thus VMA = 1, R/W = 1, SAB = 1001, and SDB = FF, where FF is the contents of location 1001. The third cycle is also similar except that the PC has been incremented a second time; thus VMA = 1, R/W = 1, SAB = 1002, and SDB = 01, where 01 is the contents of location 1002. The fourth clock cycle is a bus-write cycle, the DA providing the address and the contents of A are placed on the SDB; thus VMA = 1, R/W = 0, SAB = FF01, and SDB = C3. The value on the SAB comes from the data address register, where the address of the operand was stored during the previous two cycles. The fifth clock cycle is an internal cycle, and so VMA = 0 and R/W, SAB, and SDB are undefined.

5-5 PROGRAM CODING AND EXECUTION

The sequence of binary words making up a program generally but not always is stored in consecutive memory locations. It is common to represent these binary words and their address in hexadecimal notation, and we adopt this convention.

Table 5-5 shows a sequence of binary words representing a short program using the instruction in Table 5-2 to clear accumulator A, load it with the value 05, negate this value, add the contents of location 2875, store the results in location 405C, and then clear location 2875. Table 5-5 indicates that the first word of the program is stored in location 010C; this is the *starting address* for the program. Locations 2875 and 405C store data used in the program.

In order to develop a better understanding of how a processor executes programs, let us trace the sequence of clock cycles used in executing this program (Table 5-6). In doing this we shall define the value on the read-write control line (R/W), the system address bus (SAB), and the system data bus (SDB) during each clock cycle and we shall indicate the contents of the program counter (PC), data address register (DA), and accumulator A after executing each instruction.

Before this program can be executed, the starting address 010C must be placed in the program counter and the controller set to its initial state. We do not discuss here how these are accomplished but assume that they have been done. When the controller is in its initial state, it generates control signals for a bus-read cycle, the program counter providing the address, in order to transfer the op code from memory to the op-code register. During first clock cycle (cycle 1) the controller places a 1 on the read-write control line and connects the output of the program counter, whose contents are 010C in this case, to the system address bus. The contents of memory location 010C, in this case 4F, are read from memory

Table 5-5 Sequence of binary words representing a program

010C	4F	Op code for "clear A"
010D	86	Op code for "load A, immediate mode"
010E	05	Operand
010F	40	Op code for "negate A"
0110	BB	Op code for "add to A, extended mode"
0111	28	High byte of address
0112	75	Low byte of address
0113	B7	Op code for "store A, extended mode"
0114	40	High byte of address
0115	5C	Low byte of address
0116	7F	Op code for "clear memory, extended mode"
0117	28	High byte of address
0118	75	Low byte of address
⋮		
2875	23	Data
⋮		
405C	A0	Data

and appear on the system data bus. The controller enables the op-code register to accept this code word from the system data bus. Once the code word is stored in the op-code register, the controller interprets it as the op code for the "clear A" instruction. During cycle 2 the controller generates control signals for an internal cycle to transfer 00 into A and then returns to its initial state. During the execution of this two-cycle instruction, the program counter was incremented once and accumulator A was cleared, so their contents are 010D and 00, respectively; the data address register was not affected by this instruction.

After cycle 2, the controller in the processor unit is again in its initial state ready to fetch the op code of the next instruction. This is accomplished by a bus-read cycle in which the controller places a 1 on the read-write control line and connects the program counter containing 010D to the address bus. The contents of the addressed memory location, 86, are read from memory and appear on the system data bus. The controller enables the op-code register to accept this code word and interprets it as an op code for a "load A using the immediate addressing mode." This instruction requires one more clock cycle, a bus-read cycle, to complete its execution, and this is performed during cycle 4. The controller places a 1 on the read-write control line and connects the output of the program counter, which was incremented after its use in cycle 3 and now contains 010E, to the system address bus. The contents of the addressed memory location, 05, are read

Table 5-6 Cycle-by-cycle execution of program in Table 5-5

		During cycle		After executing instruction		
Cycle	R/W	SAB	SDB	PC	A	DA
1	1	010C	4F			
2		INT		010D	00	
3	1	010D	86			
4	1	010E	05	010F	05	
5	1	010F	40			
6		INT		0110	FB	
7	1	0110	BB			
8	1	0111	28			
9	1	0112	75			
10	1	2875	23	0113	1E	2875
11	1	0113	B7			
12	1	0114	40			
13	1	0115	5C			
14	0	405C	1E			
15		INT		0116	1E	405C
16	1	0116	7F			
17	1	0117	28			
18	1	0118	75			
19	0	2875	00			
20		INT				
21		INT		0119	1E	2875

from memory and appear on the system data bus. The controller enables accumulator A to accept this word from the system data bus and then returns to its initial state. After executing this two-cycle instruction, the program counter, which was used and incremented twice in fetching the 2 bytes in this instruction, contains 010F. Accumulator A contains the value 05; the data address register was unaffected by this instruction.

Cycle 5 begins the execution of the third instruction, the controller is in its initial state ready to fetch an op code. The controller places a 1 on the read-write control line and transfers the contents of the program counter, 010F, to the system address bus. The contents of the addressed memory location, 40, are read from memory and appear on the data bus. The controller enables the op-code register to accept this word and interprets it as the op code for the "negate A" instruction, which requires one more clock cycle for its execution. During the next clock cycle the controller generates control signals for an internal cycle to manipulate accumulator A and then returns to its initial state. After executing this two-cycle instruction the program counter, which was incremented once, contains 0110, and accumulator A, which was negated, contains FB.

As cycle 7 begins, the controller is again ready to fetch the next op code. As before, the controller generates control signals so that the program counter provides the address (0110) and the contents of the addressed location (BB) appear on the data bus and are transferred to the op-code register. The controller interprets this as the op code for the instruction "add to A using the extended addressing mode." The instruction requires four bus-read cycles. During cycle 8 the controller places a 1 on the read-write control line and connects the output of the program counter, whose contents were incremented during the previous cycle to 0111, to the system address bus. The contents of the addressed memory location, 28, are read from memory to the system data bus and are transferred to the upper half of the data address register, which is enabled by the controller. Cycle 9 is very similar to cycle 8; the program counter, which again was incremented during the previous cycle, provides the address, 0112; and the contents of the addressed location, 75, appear on the data bus and are placed in the lower half of the data address register. During cycle 10 the controller places a 1 on the read-write control line and connects the output of the data address register, containing 2875, to the system address bus. The contents of the addressed memory location, 23, are read from memory and appear on the data bus. The controller connects the system data bus and the output of accumulator A to the inputs of the arithmetic logic unit so that the value on the system data bus is added to the current contents of accumulator A. The controller also connects the output of the arithmetic logic unit to the input of accumulator A so that the results of the addition are stored in this register. Thus during this clock cycle the value on the data bus, 23, is added to the contents of the A accumulator, FB, to obtain 1E. After executing this instruction the program counter, incremented 3 times during the fetch phase of this instruction, contains 0113; accumulator A contains 1E, representing the sum of FB and 23; and the data address register contains 2875, the address of the operand.

Cycle 11 represents the first cycle in the execution of the fifth instruction. During this cycle the program counter provides the address, 0113, and the contents of the addressed location, B7, appear on the data bus and are transferred to the op-code register. The controller recognizes this as the op code for the instruction "store A using the extended addressing mode." This is a 3-byte instruction requiring four additional clock cycles for execution with three bus-transfer cycles and one internal cycle. During cycle 12 the controller places a 1 on the read-write control line and the contents of the program counter, 0114, on the system address bus. The contents of the addressed location, 40, appear on the data bus, and the controller enables the upper half of the data address register to accept this word. Cycle 13 is analogous to cycle 12 with 0115 being placed on the address bus and 5C being transferred from memory to the lower half of the data address register. Cycle 14 is a bus-write cycle, and so the controller places a 0 on the read-write control line. It also connects the output of the data address register, containing 405C, to the system address bus and the output of accumulator A, containing 1E, to the system data bus. The value on the data bus then is written into the addressed memory location. Cycle 15 is an internal cycle. After executing this instruction, the program counter, which was incremented 3 times, contains 0116; accumulator A is unchanged; and the data address register contains 405C, the address of the operand. Also, the contents of memory location 405C were changed from A0 to 1E.

As cycle 16 begins, the controller is in its initial state and prepared to fetch the next op code. The program counter provides the address, 0116, and the contents of that location, 7F, are transferred onto the data bus and from there to the op-code register. The controller recognizes this as the op code for the instruction "clear memory using the extended addressing mode." This is a 3-byte instruction requiring five additional clock cycles for execution with three bus-transfer cycles and two internal cycles. During the cycles 17 and 18 the address is transferred to the data address register; the program counter provides the addresses 0117 and 0118, and the contents of these two locations, 28 and 75, respectively, appear on the data bus and are placed in the data address register. Cycle 19 is a bus-write cycle to clear the specified location. The controller places a 0 on the read-write control line, connects the output of the data address register, containing 2875, to the system address bus, and places 00 on the system data bus. The next two clock cycles are internal with no bus transfers. During the execution of this instruction, the program counter was incremented 3 times, so it contains 0119; accumulator A was unchanged; and the data address register was loaded with 2875. Also the contents of memory location 2875 were changed from 23 to 00.

After cycle 21, the processor is prepared to fetch the op code of the next instruction. In this discussion we are assuming that the processor stops at this point for some undefined reason. As discussed later, in practice, another instruction would be used to terminate the execution of this program and begin the execution of the next.

5-6 CONCLUSION

This chapter introduced the architecture of the 6800 microcomputer. In our discussion of the operation and structure of the four units constituting the microcomputer we suppressed many details that will surface in later chapters. The six instructions presented introduced the concepts of instruction coding and execution. The next chapter will extend these concepts and describe the complete instruction set for the 6800 microcomputer.

PROBLEMS

5-1 Define each of the following terms:

program	address bus
system bus	control bus
data bus	bidirectional bus

unidirectional bus	input port
read-write control signal	input interface
nonmaskable-interrupt-request signal	output port
maskable-interrupt-request signal	output interface
reset signal	port data address
arithmetic logic unit	port status address
internal processor register	instruction
accumulator	operand field
program counter	operation field
index register	addressing mode
stack pointer	op code
autoincrementing register	inherent addressing mode
autodecrementing register	immediate addressing mode
condition-code register	extended addressing mode
carry bit	direct addressing mode
overflow bit	indexed addressing mode
negative bit	relative addressing mode
zero bit	address offset
interrupt-mask bit	base address
half-carry bit	starting address

5-2 Define which lines of the system bus are active during a bus-write cycle used to store:

(*a*) 5B in location 109C
(*b*) A2 in location C3A1
(*c*) 01 in location 0001
(*d*) FE in location EFFE
(*e*) 91 in location 7439

5-3 Draw a timing diagram showing ϕ_1, ϕ_2, R/W, VMA, A_1, A_0, D_1, and D_0 during the bus-write cycle described in Prob. 5-2.

5-4 Define which lines of the system bus are active during a bus-write cycle that transfers the ASCII code word for the character:

(*a*) M to location OC36
(*b*) W to location 1231
(*c*) Q to location 0001
(*d*) 1 to location FFF2
(*e*) 5 to location 0039

5-5 Draw a timing diagram showing ϕ_1, ϕ_2, R/W/, VMA, A_1, A_0, D_1, and D_0 during the bus-write cycle described in Prob. 5-4.

5-6 Define which lines of the system bus are active during a bus-read cycle that transfers the ASCII code word for the character:

(*a*) Q from location 4321
(*b*) R from location 0002
(*c*) 5 from location FFFE
(*d*) 9 from location 327A
(*e*) N from location 0A02

5-7 Draw a timing diagram showing ϕ_1, ϕ_2, R/W, VMA, A_1, A_0, D_1, and D_0 during the bus-read cycle described in Prob. 5-6.

5-8 The internal processor registers contain the following hexadecimal values: PC = 0127, SP = 0105, X = 0050, DA = 3276, A = 62, B = 00, OR = 59, CC = C3.

(*a*) What is the address of the next word in the program? 1001
(*b*) What is the address for the next word pushed onto the stack? 1010
(*c*) What is the address of the last word pushed onto the stack? 1011
(*d*) What is the address of the next word pulled from the stack? 1100
(*e*) Will the processor acknowledge an interrupt request on the NMI line?
(*f*) Will the processor acknowledge an interrupt request on the IRQ line?

(*g*) Is the carry bit set?

(*h*) If the next cycle is a bus-write cycle to store the contents of A in memory, what values will appear on the SAB, SDB, and the R/W line?

(*i*) What is the op code of the current instruction?

5-9 Repeat Prob. 5-8 for PC = 5328, SP = 7100, X = 0157, DA = 0028, A = 36, B = 00, OR = 67, CC = E6.

5-10 Indicate the status of each bit in the condition-code register for the condition described in (*a*) Prob. 5-8 and (*b*) Prob. 5-9.

5-11 What modifications must be made in the 6800 processor to make it a 16-bit system?

5-12 What modifications must be made in the 6800 processor to increase the number of directly addressable locations to 512K?

5-13 A particular 6800 memory unit has 2K of memory. Define the address of the last location if the first location is assigned:

    (*a*) 0000   (*b*) 1800   (*c*) A000   (*d*) D800

    (*e*) 8800   (*f*) 1000   (*g*) 2000

5-14 What lines on the address bus must be active to select the first and last locations in the memory units defined in Prob. 5-13?

5-15 Define the first and last address used in a 6800 memory unit that has:

    (*a*) 8K of memory starting at 0000

    (*b*) 8K of memory starting at 4000

    (*c*) 16K of memory starting at 0000

    (*d*) 8K of memory in the highest address space

    (*e*) 4K of memory in the highest address space

5-16 What bits in the SAB must be active to write in the first and the last locations of the memory units defined in Prob. 5-15?

5-17 The first word of an instruction is stored in location 0572, and the next 2 bytes in the program are 6C and 93. The index register contains 372A. Define the operand or the address of the operand for all six addressing modes available on the 6800 microprocessor.

5-18 Repeat Prob. 5-17 if the first word is stored in location C372, the next two words are A3 and FD, and the index register contains 027D.

5-19 For the input port shown in Fig. 5-6 the port status address is 1025 and the port data address is 1026. Bits 0 to 6 of the port data lines are at the low level, and the other 2 bits are at the high level. The status flip-flop is set. Define the values on the SAB, SDB, and the R/W and VMA lines.

    (*a*) To test the status flip-flop

    (*b*) To transfer the input data to the processor

    (*c*) To clear the status flip-flop

    (*d*) To set the status flip-flop

    (*e*) To clear the input lines

5-20 Draw the timing diagram for the bus transfer described in Prob. 5-19. Show ϕ_1, ϕ_2, R/W, A_{15}, A_0, D_7, and D_0.

5-21 For the output port shown in Fig. 5-8 the port status address is C002, and the port data address is C003. Bit 0 of the port data line is at the high level, and all other bits are at the low level. The status flip-flop is set. Define the values on the SAB, SDB, R/W, and VMA lines:

    (*a*) To test the status flip-flop

    (*b*) To clear the status flip-flop

    (*c*) To set the status flip-flop

    (*d*) To transfer 73 to the output lines

    (*e*) To clear all the output lines

    (*f*) To transfer the pattern on the port data lines to the processor

5-22 Draw the timing diagram for the bus transfers described in Prob. 5-21. Show ϕ_1, ϕ_2, R/W, A_{15}, A_0, D_7, and D_0.

5-23 When PC = 0127 and X = 0050 define the operand or the address of the operand for all six addressing modes if the contents of locations 0128 and 0129 are:
(*a*) F3 and 72   (*b*) 27 and 63   (*c*) 00 and 42
(*d*) FF and 00   (*e*) 26 and 36

5-24 When PC = 5328 and X = 0157 define the operand or the address of the operand for all six addressing modes if the contents of locations 5329 and 532A are:
(*a*) AC and 26   (*b*) 37 and F3   (*c*) 00 and 92
(*d*) AB and 00   (*e*) 29 and A7

5-25 Define the binary code word for the instruction that will:
(*a*) Load the hexadecimal value 9 into accumulator A
(*b*) Load the hexadecimal value F3 into accumulator A
(*c*) Load the decimal value 23 into accumulator A
(*d*) Clear location A032
(*e*) Add the contents of location 1096 to accumulator A
(*f*) Store the contents of accumulator A in location 0532

5-26 Define the binary code word for the instruction that will:
(*a*) Clear location 0372
(*b*) Store A in location 17A3
(*c*) Add the contents of C372 to A
(*d*) Load the hexadecimal value 2 into A
(*e*) Load the hexadecimal value 7E into A
(*f*) Load the hexadecimal value 51 into A
(*g*) Load the decimal value 51 into A

5-27 The program counter and accumulator A contain F721 and 62, respectively. Locations F722, F723, and F724 contain F7, 24, and 09, respectively. Define the sequence of values on the SAB, SDB, and the R/W and VMA lines for one instruction if the contents of F721 are:
(*a*) 4F   (*b*) 40   (*c*) 86
(*d*) BB   (*e*) 7F   (*f*) B7

5-28 The program counter and accumulator A contain 2076 and A3, respectively. Locations 2077 and 2078 contain 10 and A3, respectively, and location 10A3 contains 5C. Define the sequence of values on the SAB, SDB, and the R/W and VMA lines for one instruction if the contents of 2076 are:
(*a*) 4F   (*b*) 40   (*c*) 86
(*d*) BB   (*e*) 7F   (*f*) B7

5-29 For the situation described in (1) Prob. 5-27 and (2) Prob. 5-28 define the contents of the program counter and the A accumulator after executing the instruction. Define the contents of all memory locations altered by the instruction.

5-30 The 6800 instruction set includes several instructions that operate on accumulator A and are analogous to the "clear A" and "negate A" instructions defined in Tables 5-2 to 5-4. Define the general instruction code word and the sequence of cycles for the instruction to:
(*a*) Complement A (the op code is 43)
(*b*) Increment A (the op code is 4C)
(*c*) Decrement A (the op code is 4A)

5-31 The 6800 instruction set includes several instructions using the immediate addressing mode to manipulate accumulator A in a way analogous to the "load A" instruction defined in Tables 5-2 to 5-4. Define the general instruction code word and sequence of cycles for the instruction that use the immediate addressing mode to:
(*a*) Add to A (the op code is 8B)
(*b*) AND with A (the op code is 84)
(*c*) Subtract from A (the op code is 80)

5-32 The 6800 instruction set includes several instructions using the extended addressing mode in a way analogous to the "add to A" instruction defined in Tables 5-2 to 5-4. Define the general instruction code word and sequence of cycles for the instruction that uses the extended addressing mode to:

(a) AND with A (the op code is B4)
(b) Load A (the op code is B6)
(c) Subtract from A (the op code is B0)

5-33 The 6800 instruction set includes several instructions using the extended addressing mode to manipulate an addressable location in a way analogous to the "clear memory" instruction defined in Tables 5-2 to 5-4. Define the general instruction code word, specified register transfer, and sequence of cycles for the instruction that uses the extended addressing mode to:

(a) Complement the contents of an addressable location (the op code is 73)
(b) Negate the contents of an addressable location (the op code is 70)
(c) Increment the contents of an addressable location (the op code is 7C)

5-34 The program counter and A accumulator contain 1027 and F3. The contents of location 2700 and 2701 are 72 and C1. Define the contents of these two registers and these two locations after executing the following instructions:

(a) 4F   (b) 40   (c) 86 03
(d) BB 27 00   (e) 7F 27 00   (f) B7 27 01
(g) BB 27 01   (h) 86 C0   (i) 86 00

5-35 Indicate the condition of the Z bit and N bit after executing the instructions defined in Prob. 5-34.

5-36 For the input port shown in Fig. 5-6 the port data and status addresses are C004 and C005, respectively. Define the instruction:
(a) To add the value on the port data lines to accumulator A
(b) To clear the status flip-flop

5-37 For the output port shown in Fig. 5-8 the port data and status addresses are 8002 and 8003, respectively. Define the instruction:
(a) To transfer the contents of A to the port data lines
(b) To clear the status flip-flop

5-38 For the output port described in Prob. 5-37, define a sequence of two instructions to transfer the ASCII code word for the character 9 to the port data lines.

5-39 A segment of a program is given below. The program counter and the A accumulator contain 1000 and 39, respectively. Locations 2000, 2001, and 2002 contain F3, 07, and 96.
(a) Define the values on the SAB, SDB, R/W, and VMA lines during all cycles required for execution.
(b) Define the contents of the program counter and accumulator A after each instruction is executed.
(c) Define the condition of the N bit and Z bit after each instruction is executed.
(d) Define the contents of all affected memory locations after executing each instruction.

Location	Contents	Location	Contents	Location	Contents	Location	Contents
1000	86	1004	00	1008	20	100C	B7
1001	00	1005	86	1009	01	100D	20
1002	B7	1006	01	100A	86	100E	02
1003	20	1007	B7	100B	02	100F	4F

5-40 Repeat Prob. 5-39 for the program segment given below. The program counter and the A accumulator contain 5099 and A3, respectively. Location 0192 contains F2.

Location	Contents	Location	Contents
5099	4F	509D	40
509A	BB	509E	B7
509B	01	509F	01
509C	92	5100	92

5-41 Repeat Prob. 5-39 for the program segment given below. The program counter contains 0027, accumulator A contains C7, and location 7F02 contains FF.

Location	Contents	Location	Contents
0027	86	002B	02
0028	01	002C	B7
0029	BB	002D	7F
002A	7F	002E	02

5-42 Repeat Prob. 5-39 for the program segment given below. The program counter contains 62FD and accumulator A contains CA.

Location	Contents	Location	Contents	Location	Contents	Location	Contents
62FA	43	62FE	62	6302	FB	6306	B7
62FB	86	62FF	FA	6303	7F	6307	62
62FC	4F	6300	BB	6304	62	6308	FB
62FD	BB	6301	62	6305	FA	6309	4F

REFERENCES

Bishop, R.: "Basic Microprocessors and the 6800," Hayden, Rochelle, N.J., 1979.

Motorola Staff: "Understanding Microprocessors," Motorola Inc., Phoenix, Ariz., 1978.

Osborne, A.: An Introduction to Microcomputers, vol. 0, "The Beginner's Book," Osborne Associates, Berkeley, Calif., 1977.

_____ : "An Introduction to Microcomputers, vol. 1, Basic Concepts," Osborne Associates, Berkeley, Calif., 1976.

Poe, E.: Using the 6800 Microprocessor, Sams, Indianapolis, Ind., 1978.

SIX

THE 6800 INSTRUCTION SET

In this chapter we consider the complete 6800 instruction set, including the coding and execution of each boolean-arithmetic operation with all available addressing modes. After finishing this chapter the reader should be able to:

1. Define all symbols used in the programmer's card in Fig. 6-1
2. Define all addressing modes used in the 6800 instructions set and for a specific coded instruction define the operand or the address of the operand
3. Indicate the number of clock cycles required to execute any 6800 instruction, define the values on all lines in the system bus during each clock cycle as the instruction is executed, and describe the contents of all altered register and addressable locations after the instruction has been executed
4. Define the values on all lines in the system bus during each clock cycle as a 6800 program is executed and indicate the contents of all registers and altered addressable locations after each instruction has been executed

6-1 PROGRAMMER'S CARD FOR THE 6800

Figure 6-1 shows a complete programmer's card for the 6800 instruction set. It contains most of the information necessary for using this instruction set. The card is divided into four sections. Instructions are divided into these sections according to the internal processor register explicitly manipulated by the instruction. Instructions in the first section manipulate one of the two accumulators or an addressable location. Instructions in the second section manipulate the index register or stack pointer. Instructions in the third section deal with the program counter and primarily represent jump and branch instructions. Instructions in the fourth section explicitly manipulate the condition-code register.

In the programmer's card the first column contains a brief verbal description of the instruction, and the second column contains a three- or four-letter mnemonic for each instruction. The next few columns indicate the addressing modes available with each instruction. Entries in these columns define the 8-bit op code for that instruction with that addressing mode (OP), the number of clock cycles required for execution ($\sim$), and the number of bytes in the instruction (#). Except for the jump and branch instructions, the next column briefly defines the boolean-arithmetic operation using a register-transfer notation. For the branch and jump instructions, which generally are conditional instructions, this column defines the test conditions in terms of specific bits in the condition-code register. More will be said about the use of test conditions in the execution of these instructions later. The last columns define how each instruction affects each bit in the condition-code register. A solid dot means that the bit is unaffected by the instruction; a double-ended vertical arrow means that the bit is set or reset according to the result of the boolean-arithmetic operation specified in the previous column; and an R or S means the bit is reset or set, respectively. Several special conditions are defined by notes to the programmer's card.

To illustrate the use of the programmer's card, consider the first row in detail. The operation is "add," which represents two different instructions, add to accumulator A (ADDA) and add to accumulator B (ADDB). Each can be used with four addressing modes: immediate, direct, indexed, and extended. The instruction "add to accumulator A using the immediate addressing mode" has an op code of 8B, requires two clock cycles for execution, and contains 2 bytes. The register-transfer description of the boolean-arithmetic operation performed by this instruction is $A + M \rightarrow A$, implying that the contents of A are added to the operand from memory and the results are stored in A.† The last column indicates that the H, N, Z, V, and C bits are set or cleared depending on the result of the specified addition and that the I bit is unaffected by this instruction.

To discuss each instruction listed in Fig. 6-1 would be very tedious. Fortunately, many instructions in this set are similar in terms of available addressing modes, specified boolean-arithmetic operation, instruction coding, and instruction execution. This allows us to group the instructions for discussion. The following sections will discuss these groups using typical instructions in each group as examples. During the discussion the reader should refer to the programmer's card to follow the development. The reader should understand these examples well enough to develop an analogous description for all other instructions in the group.

---

† Using the notation we introduced in the previous chapter, we can write this description as $\langle A \rangle + \langle M \rangle \rightarrow A$.

ACCUMULATOR AND MEMORY INSTRUCTIONS

ACCUMULATOR AND MEMORY OPERATIONS	MNEMONIC	IMMED OP	~	#	DIRECT OP	~	#	INDEX OP	~	#	EXTND OP	~	#	INHER OP	~	#	BOOLEAN/ARITHMETIC OPERATION (All register labels refer to contents)	H 5	I 4	N 3	Z 2	V 1	C 0
Add	ADDA	8B	2	2	9B	3	2	AB	5	2	BB	4	3				A + M → A	‡	•	‡	‡	‡	‡
	ADDB	CB	2	2	DB	3	2	EB	5	2	FB	4	3				B + M → B	‡	•	‡	‡	‡	‡
Add Acmltrs	ABA													1B	2	1	A + B → A	‡	•	‡	‡	‡	‡
Add with Carry	ADCA	89	2	2	99	3	2	A9	5	2	B9	4	3				A + M + C → A	‡	•	‡	‡	‡	‡
	ADCB	C9	2	2	D9	3	2	E9	5	2	F9	4	3				B + M + C → B	‡	•	‡	‡	‡	‡
And	ANDA	84	2	2	94	3	2	A4	5	2	B4	4	3				A • M → A	•	•	‡	‡	R	•
	ANDB	C4	2	2	D4	3	2	E4	5	2	F4	4	3				B • M → B	•	•	‡	‡	R	•
Bit Test	BITA	85	2	2	95	3	2	A5	5	2	B5	4	3				A • M	•	•	‡	‡	R	•
	BITB	C5	2	2	D5	3	2	E5	5	2	F5	4	3				B • M	•	•	‡	‡	R	•
Clear	CLR							6F	7	2	7F	6	3				00 → M	•	•	R	S	R	R
	CLRA													4F	2	1	00 → A	•	•	R	S	R	R
	CLRB													5F	2	1	00 → B	•	•	R	S	R	R
Compare	CMPA	81	2	2	91	3	2	A1	5	2	B1	4	3				A − M	•	•	‡	‡	‡	‡
	CMPB	C1	2	2	D1	3	2	E1	5	2	F1	4	3				B − M	•	•	‡	‡	‡	‡
Compare Acmltrs	CBA													11	2	1	A − B	•	•	‡	‡	‡	‡
Complement, 1's	COM							63	7	2	73	6	3				$\overline{M}$ → M	•	•	‡	‡	R	S
	COMA													43	2	1	$\overline{A}$ → A	•	•	‡	‡	R	S
	COMB													53	2	1	$\overline{B}$ → B	•	•	‡	‡	R	S
Complement, 2's (Negate)	NEG							60	7	2	70	6	3				00 − M → M	•	•	‡	‡	①	②
	NEGA													40	2	1	00 − A → A	•	•	‡	‡	①	②
	NEGB													50	2	1	00 − B → B	•	•	‡	‡	①	②
Decimal Adjust, A	DAA													19	2	1	Converts Binary Add. of BCD Characters into BCD Format	•	•	‡	‡	‡	③
Decrement	DEC							6A	7	2	7A	6	3				M − 1 → M	•	•	‡	‡	④	•
	DECA													4A	2	1	A − 1 → A	•	•	‡	‡	④	•
	DECB													5A	2	1	B − 1 → B	•	•	‡	‡	④	•
Exclusive OR	EORA	88	2	2	98	3	2	A8	5	2	B8	4	3				A ⊕ M → A	•	•	‡	‡	R	•
	EORB	C8	2	2	D8	3	2	E8	5	2	F8	4	3				B ⊕ M → B	•	•	‡	‡	R	•
Increment	INC							6C	7	2	7C	6	3				M + 1 → M	•	•	‡	‡	⑤	•
	INCA													4C	2	1	A + 1 → A	•	•	‡	‡	⑤	•
	INCB													5C	2	1	B + 1 → B	•	•	‡	‡	⑤	•
Load Acmltr	LDAA	86	2	2	96	3	2	A6	5	2	B6	4	3				M → A	•	•	‡	‡	R	•
	LDAB	C6	2	2	D6	3	2	E6	5	2	F6	4	3				M → B	•	•	‡	‡	R	•
Or, Inclusive	ORAA	8A	2	2	9A	3	2	AA	5	2	BA	4	3				A + M → A	•	•	‡	‡	R	•
	ORAB	CA	2	2	DA	3	2	EA	5	2	FA	4	3				B + M → B	•	•	‡	‡	R	•
Push Data	PSHA													36	4	1	A → MSP, SP − 1 → SP	•	•	•	•	•	•
	PSHB													37	4	1	B → MSP, SP − 1 → SP	•	•	•	•	•	•
Pull Data	PULA													32	4	1	SP + 1 → SP, MSP → A	•	•	•	•	•	•
	PULB													33	4	1	SP + 1 → SP, MSP → B	•	•	•	•	•	•
Rotate Left	ROL							69	7	2	79	6	3				M	•	•	‡	‡	⑥	‡
	ROLA													49	2	1	A	•	•	‡	‡	⑥	‡
	ROLB													59	2	1	B	•	•	‡	‡	⑥	‡
Rotate Right	ROR							66	7	2	76	6	3				M	•	•	‡	‡	⑥	‡
	RORA													46	2	1	A	•	•	‡	‡	⑥	‡
	RORB													56	2	1	B	•	•	‡	‡	⑥	‡
Shift Left, Arithmetic	ASL							68	7	2	78	6	3				M	•	•	‡	‡	⑥	‡
	ASLA													48	2	1	A	•	•	‡	‡	⑥	‡
	ASLB													58	2	1	B	•	•	‡	‡	⑥	‡
Shift Right, Arithmetic	ASR							67	7	2	77	6	3				M	•	•	‡	‡	⑥	‡
	ASRA													47	2	1	A	•	•	‡	‡	⑥	‡
	ASRB													57	2	1	B	•	•	‡	‡	⑥	‡
Shift Right, Logic.	LSR							64	7	2	74	6	3				M	•	•	R	‡	⑥	‡
	LSRA													44	2	1	A	•	•	R	‡	⑥	‡
	LSRB													54	2	1	B	•	•	R	‡	⑥	‡
Store Acmltr.	STAA				97	4	2	A7	6	2	B7	5	3				A → M	•	•	‡	‡	R	•
	STAB				D7	4	2	E7	6	2	F7	5	3				B → M	•	•	‡	‡	R	•
Subtract	SUBA	80	2	2	90	3	2	A0	5	2	B0	4	3				A − M → A	•	•	‡	‡	‡	‡
	SUBB	C0	2	2	D0	3	2	E0	5	2	F0	4	3				B − M → B	•	•	‡	‡	‡	‡
Subract Acmltrs.	SBA													10	2	1	A − B → A	•	•	‡	‡	‡	‡
Subtr. with Carry	SBCA	82	2	2	92	3	2	A2	5	2	B2	4	3				A − M − C → A	•	•	‡	‡	‡	‡
	SBCB	C2	2	2	D2	3	2	E2	5	2	F2	4	3				B − M − C → B	•	•	‡	‡	‡	‡
Transfer Acmltrs	TAB													16	2	1	A → B	•	•	‡	‡	R	•
	TBA													17	2	1	B → A	•	•	‡	‡	R	•
Test, Zero or Minus	TST							6D	7	2	7D	6	3				M − 00	•	•	‡	‡	R	R
	TSTA													4D	2	1	A − 00	•	•	‡	‡	R	R
	TSTB													5D	2	1	B − 00	•	•	‡	‡	R	R

LEGEND:

OP	Operation Code (Hexadecimal);	+	Boolean Inclusive OR;	Z	Zero (byte)
~	Number of MPU Cycles;	⊕	Boolean Exclusive OR;	V	Overflow, 2's complement
#	Number of Program Bytes;	$\overline{M}$	Complement of M;	C	Carry from bit 7
+	Arithmetic Plus;	→	Transfer Into;	R	Reset Always
−	Arithmetic Minus;	0	Bit = Zero;	S	Set Always
•	Boolean AND;	00	Byte = Zero;	‡	Test and set if true, cleared otherwise
MSP	Contents of memory location pointed to be Stack Pointer;	H	Half-carry from bit 3;	•	Not Affected
		I	Interrupt mask	CCR	Condition Code Register
		N	Negative (sign bit)	LS	Least Significant
				MS	Most Significant

Figure 6-1 6800 programmer's card.

INDEX REGISTER AND STACK POINTER OPERATIONS	MNEMONIC	IMMED			DIRECT			INDEX			EXTND			INHER			BOOLEAN/ARITHMETIC OPERATION	5 H	4 I	3 N	2 Z	1 V	0 C
		OP	~	#	OP	~	#	OP	~	#	OP	~	#	OP	~	#							
Compare Index Reg	CPX	8C	3	3	9C	4	2	AC	6	2	BC	5	3				$(X_H/X_L) - (M/M + 1)$	•	•	⑦	‡	⑧	•
Decrement Index Reg	DEX													09	4	1	$X - 1 \to X$	•	•	•	‡	•	•
Decrement Stack Pntr	DES													34	4	1	$SP - 1 \to SP$	•	•	•	•	•	•
Increment Index Reg	INX													08	4	1	$X + 1 \to X$	•	•	•	‡	•	•
Increment Stack Pntr	INS													31	4	1	$SP + 1 \to SP$	•	•	•	•	•	•
Load Index Reg	LDX	CE	3	3	DE	4	2	EE	6	2	FE	5	3				$M \to X_H, (M + 1) \to X_L$	•	•	⑨	‡	R	•
Load Stack Pntr	LDS	8E	3	3	9E	4	2	AE	6	2	BE	5	3				$M \to SP_H, (M + 1) \to SP_L$	•	•	⑨	‡	R	•
Store Index Reg	STX				DF	5	2	EF	7	2	FF	6	3				$X_H \to M, X_L \to (M + 1)$	•	•	⑨	‡	R	•
Store Stack Pntr	STS				9F	5	2	AF	7	2	BF	6	3				$SP_H \to M, SP_L \to (M + 1)$	•	•	⑨	‡	R	•
Indx Reg → Stack Pntr	TXS													35	4	1	$X - 1 \to SP$	•	•	•	•	•	•
Stack Pntr → Indx Reg	TSX													30	4	1	$SP + 1 \to X$	•	•	•	•	•	•

TABLE 5 – JUMP AND BRANCH INSTRUCTIONS

JUMP AND BRANCH OPERATIONS	MNEMONIC	RELATIVE			INDEX			EXTND			INHER			BRANCH TEST	5 H	4 I	3 N	2 Z	1 V	0 C
		OP	~	#	OP	~	#	OP	~	#	OP	~	#							
Branch Always	BRA	20	4	2										None	•	•	•	•	•	•
Branch If Carry Clear	BCC	24	4	2										$C = 0$	•	•	•	•	•	•
Branch If Carry Set	BCS	25	4	2										$C = 1$	•	•	•	•	•	•
Branch If = Zero	BEQ	27	4	2										$Z = 1$	•	•	•	•	•	•
Branch If ≥ Zero	BGE	2C	4	2										$N \oplus V = 0$	•	•	•	•	•	•
Branch If > Zero	BGT	2E	4	2										$Z + (N \oplus V) = 0$	•	•	•	•	•	•
Branch If Higher	BHI	22	4	2										$C + Z = 0$	•	•	•	•	•	•
Branch If ≤ Zero	BLE	2F	4	2										$Z + (N \oplus V) = 1$	•	•	•	•	•	•
Branch If Lower Or Same	BLS	23	4	2										$C + Z = 1$	•	•	•	•	•	•
Branch If < Zero	BLT	2D	4	2										$N \oplus V = 1$	•	•	•	•	•	•
Branch If Minus	BMI	2B	4	2										$N = 1$	•	•	•	•	•	•
Branch If Not Equal Zero	BNE	26	4	2										$Z = 0$	•	•	•	•	•	•
Branch If Overflow Clear	BVC	28	4	2										$V = 0$	•	•	•	•	•	•
Branch If Overflow Set	BVS	29	4	2										$V = 1$	•	•	•	•	•	•
Branch If Plus	BPL	2A	4	2										$N = 0$	•	•	•	•	•	•
Branch To Subroutine	BSR	8D	8	2											•	•	•	•	•	•
Jump	JMP				6E	4	2	7E	3	3				See Special Operations	•	•	•	•	•	•
Jump To Subroutine	JSR				AD	8	2	BD	9	3					•	•	•	•	•	•
No Operation	NOP										01	2	1	Advances Prog. Cntr. Only	•	•	•	•	•	•
Return From Interrupt	RTI										3B	10	1		—	⑩	—			
Return From Subroutine	RTS										39	5	1	See special Operations	•	•	•	•	•	•
Software Interrupt	SWI										3F	12	1		•	S	•	•	•	•
Wait for Interrupt	WAI										3E	9	1		•	⑪	•	•	•	•

TABLE 6 – CONDITION CODE REGISTER MANIPULATION INSTRUCTIONS

CONDITIONS CODE REGISTER OPERATIONS	MNEMONIC	INHER			BOOLEAN OPERATION	5 H	4 I	3 N	2 Z	1 V	0 C
		OP	~	#							
Clear Carry	CLC	0C	2	1	$0 \to C$	•	•	•	•	•	R
Clear Interrupt Mask	CLI	0E	2	1	$0 \to I$	•	R	•	•	•	•
Clear Overflow	CLV	0A	2	1	$0 \to V$	•	•	•	•	R	•
Set Carry	SEC	0D	2	1	$1 \to C$	•	•	•	•	•	S
Set Interrupt Mask	SEI	0F	2	1	$1 \to I$	•	S	•	•	•	•
Set Overflow	SEV	0B	2	1	$1 \to V$	•	•	•	•	S	•
Acmltr A → CCR	TAP	06	2	1	$A \to CCR$	—		⑫			—
CCR → Acmltr A	TPA	07	2	1	$CCR \to A$	•	•	•	•	•	•

CONDITION CODE REGISTER NOTES:

(Bit set if test is true and cleared otherwise)

① (Bit V) Test: Result = 10000000?

② (Bit C) Test: Result ≠ 00000000?

③ (Bit C) Test: Decimal value of most significant BCD Character greater than nine? (Not cleared if previously set.)

④ (Bit V) Test: Operand = 10000000 prior to execution?

⑤ (Bit V) Test: Operand = 01111111 prior to execution?

⑥ (Bit V) Test: Set equal to result of N ⊕ C after shift has occurred.

⑦ (Bit N) Test: Sign bit of most significant (MS) byte of result = 1?

⑧ (Bit V) Test: 2's complement overflow from subtraction of MS bytes?

⑨ (Bit N) Test: Result less than zero? (Bit 15 = 1)

⑩ (All) Load Condition Code Register from Stack. (See Special Operations)

⑪ (Bit I) Set when interrupt occurs. If previously set, a Non-Maskable Interrupt is required to exit the wait state.

⑫ (ALL) Set according to the contents of Accumulator A.

Figure 6-1 Continued.

179

Since instructions are coded in more or less standard format, and since the execution of all instructions is relatively standard, we have attempted to reduce repetition by omitting the following details:

1. The program counter provides the address whenever a word of an instruction is read from memory, and its contents are incremented each time it provides an address. We do not explicitly state this each time we describe fetching a byte of an instruction.
2. The controller in the processor regulates all data transfers to and from the system buses and between the internal processor registers. We do not explicitly point this out in most situations.
3. We are interested in defining how the processor registers and system buses are used in a sequential way to execute all instructions. Many instructions require internal cycles for their execution which frequently are intermingled with the bus-read and bus-write cycles in a sequence to execute the instruction most efficiently. Since this efficiency depends on the detailed operation of the controller, which is beyond the scope of this book, we shall not concern ourselves with the correct sequencing of the internal cycles. As a convention we shall simply place all internal cycles after the bus-read and bus-write cycles. However, our interests do require us to concern ourselves with the correct order of bus-read and bus-write cycles.

6-2 INSTRUCTIONS MANIPULATING A SINGLE INTERNAL PROCESSOR REGISTER

In the first group of instructions, the specified boolean-arithmetic operation manipulates the contents of a single internal processor register. This group includes instructions to clear (CLRA), complement (COMA), negate (NEGA), increment (INCA), decrement (DECA), rotate (RORA and ROLA), shift (ASLA, ASRA, and LSRA), or test (TSTA) the two accumulators;† to increment or decrement the index register (INX and DEX) or stack pointer (INS and DES); or to clear or set specific bits in the condition-code register (CLC, CLI, CLV, SEC, SEI, and SEV). All instructions in this group use the inherent addressing mode and contain 1 byte specifying the op code.

For the most part, the register-transfer description of the boolean-arithmetic operation listed in the programmer's card for this group of instructions is self-explanatory. The clear, complement, negate, increment, and decrement instructions have the obvious effect on the specified internal processor register.

The assortment of five rotate and shift instructions for the two accumulators shifts the contents from one bit position in the accumulator to the adjacent position. These five instructions differ in the direction of the shift, the source of

---

† Only the mnemonics for the instruction for accumulator A are given; there is a corresponding set for accumulator B, that is, CLRB, COMB, and so on.

the input bit, and the destination of the output bit as indicated pictorially on the programmer's card. For example, in the "rotate accumulator left" instructions (ROLA and ROLB), the carry bit provides the input for the least significant position of the accumulator and accepts the output from the most significant position. The "logical shift right" instruction (LSRA and LSRB) loads a 0 into the most significant position and transfers the contents of the least significant bit to the C bit.

The instructions to test the accumulator for zero or minus (TSTA and TSTB) set the condition-code register based on the contents of the accumulator without changing the accumulator's contents. The register-transfer description of the specified boolean-arithmetic operation on the programmer's card, 00 - A, shows no destination for the result, implying that this result is discarded.

Instructions manipulating the contents of the accumulators or the condition-code register are executed in two clock cycles. Table 6-1 describes the sequence of bus-read and internal cycles used to execute the instructions to complement accumulator A (COMA) and to clear the carry bit (CLC). For both, the first clock cycle is the standard bus-read cycle used to fetch the op code from memory. During this bus-read cycle the controller connects the output of the program counter to the system address bus and the contents of the addressed location, in this case the op code, appear on the system data bus and are transferred to the op-code register. The second clock cycle, an internal cycle, is used to perform the specified boolean-arithmetic operation and revise the condition-code register as appropriate.

Instructions manipulating the contents of the index register or stack pointer require four clock cycles for execution. Table 6-1 describes the sequence of bus-read and internal cycles used to execute the instruction to increment the index register (INX). The first clock cycle is the standard bus-read cycle to fetch

Table 6-1 Sequence of bus-read and internal cycles for example instructions manipulating a single internal processor register

Instruction	Cycle 1	Cycle 2	Cycle 3	Cycle 4
Complement A (COMA)	$1 \to R/W$ $\langle PC \rangle \to SAB$ $\langle SDB \rangle \to OR$ $\langle PC \rangle + 1 \to PC$	*Internal* $\overline{\langle A \rangle} \to A$ *Status* $\to CC$		
Clear carry bit (CLC)	$1 \to R/W$ $\langle PC \rangle \to SAB$ $\langle SDB \rangle \to OR$ $\langle PC \rangle + 1 \to PC$	*Internal* $0 \to C$		
Increment index register (INX)	$1 \to R/W$ $\langle PC \rangle \to SAB$ $\langle SDB \rangle \to OR$ $\langle PC \rangle + 1 \to PC$	*Internal* $\langle X \rangle + 1 \to X$ *Status* $\to CC$	*Internal*	*Internal*

the op code. The remaining three clock cycles are used to perform the specified boolean-arithmetic operation and revise the condition code register. Three cycles are required since the index register contains 16 bits and the arithmetic logic unit can process only 8 bits at a time. Thus incrementing or decrementing the index register or stack pointer requires more than one cycle.

Example 6-1 Indicate the sequence of values on the valid-memory-address line (VMA), the read-write control line (R/W), the system address bus (SAB), and the system data bus (SDB) required to execute the instruction specified by op code 59 (ROLB) stored in location 102C. Before the instruction is executed, the program counter, B accumulator, and condition-code register contain 102C, 51, and C7, respectively. Indicate the contents of these three processor registers after executing this instruction.

SOLUTION This instruction requires two clock cycles for execution, and its execution is analogous to the first two instructions in Table 6-1.

	Cycle 1	Cycle 2
VMA	1	0
R/W	1	*
SAB	102C	*
SDB	59	*

  * Undefined.

Since the program counter will be incremented once in fetching the 1 byte of this instruction, $\langle PC \rangle = 102D$. Before executing this instruction the C bit contains a 1 and the B accumulator contains 0101 0001; after executing the left rotation, the C bit contains a 0 and the B accumulator contains 1010 0011, or A3. The H and I bits are unaffected by this instruction. The N and Z bits are set based on the result, and, in this case, the N bit is set to 1 and the Z bit to 0 since the result of this instruction, A3, represents a negative nonzero value. Since the V bit is set based on $N \oplus C$ after execution, in this case the result is 1. Thus the condition-code register contains 1100 1010, or CA.

6-3 INSTRUCTIONS MANIPULATING TWO INTERNAL PROCESSOR REGISTERS

In the second group of instructions, the specified boolean-arithmetic operation involves two internal processor registers. This group includes instructions to add (ABA), subtract (SBA), compare (CBA), or transfer the two accumulators (TAB and TBA); to transfer the index register to the stack pointer (TXS), or vice versa (TSX), or to transfer accumulator A (TAP) to the condition-code register, or vice versa (TPA). All instructions in this group use the inherent addressing mode and thus contain only 1 byte specifying the op code.

The register-transfer descriptions of the specified boolean-arithmetic operation for the add and subtract instructions, $A + B \to A$ and $A - B \to A$, are self-explanatory. The boolean-arithmetic description of the compare-accumulator instruction, $A - B$, is similar to that for the test-accumulator instruction discussed in the previous section in that the results of the subtraction are not saved but used only to revise the condition-code register.

The transfer accumulator and condition code register instructions replace the contents of the destination register with those in the source register without changing the contents of the latter. The transfer stack pointer and index register instructions either increment or decrement the contents before the transfer, depending on the direction of the transfer.

Instructions in this group that involve the two accumulators or accumulator A and the condition-code register are executed in two cycles. Table 6-2 describes the sequence of bus-read and internal cycles to execute the instructions to add the two accumulators and to transfer the condition code register to accumulator A. For both, the first clock cycle is the standard bus-read cycle to fetch the op code. The second clock cycle is an internal cycle used to perform the specified boolean-arithmetic operation and revise the condition-code register as appropriate.

Four clock cycles are required to execute the instructions involving the index register and the stack pointer. The first is the standard bus-read cycle used to fetch the op code. The remaining three are internal cycles used to perform the specified data transfers and revise the condition-code register. Since the processor

Table 6-2 Sequence of bus-read and internal cycles for example instructions manipulating two internal processor registers

Instruction	Cycle 1	Cycle 2	Cycle 3	Cycle 4
Add accumulators (ABA)	$1 \to R/W$ $\langle PC \rangle \to SAB$ $\langle SDB \rangle \to OR$ $PC + 1 \to PC$	*Internal* $\langle A \rangle + \langle B \rangle \to A$ *Status* $\to CC$		
Transfer condition code register to accumulator A (TPA)	$1 \to R/W$ $\langle PC \rangle \to SAB$ $\langle SDB \rangle \to OR$ $\langle PC \rangle + 1 \to PC$	*Internal* $\langle CC \rangle \to A$		
Transfer stack pointer to index register (TSX)	$1 \to R/W$ $\langle PC \rangle \to SAB$ $\langle SDB \rangle \to OR$ $\langle PC \rangle + 1 \to PC$	*Internal* $\langle SP \rangle + 1 \to X$ *Status* $\to CC$	*Internal*	*Internal*

is designed to manipulate 8-bit words, the extra cycles are again required for transferring the 16-bit words used in the index register and stack pointer.

Example 6-2 Before executing an instruction the contents of the program counter (PC), index register (X), stack pointer (SP), A and B accumulators, and condition-code register (CC) are 0574, 1000, 107, 6A, 48, and C4. Indicate the contents of these registers if the contents of location 0574 are 1B (ABA).

SOLUTION The PC is incremented once to 0575; the X, SP, and B registers are unaffected. The contents of A and B are added

$$
\begin{aligned}
6A &\to 0110\ 1010 \\
48 &\to 0100\ 1000 \\
\hline
&\quad 1011\ 0010 \to B2
\end{aligned}
$$

and the result, B2, is stored in A. The H bit is set because of the carry from bit 3 to bit 4; the I bit is unaffected; the N bit is set because the result represents a negative number; the Z bit is cleared because the result is nonzero; the V bit is set because an overflow occurred since adding two positive numbers produced a negative result; and the C bit is cleared because there was no carry from bit 7. The pattern in the condition-code register is 1110 1010, or EA.

Example 6-3 Repeat Example 6-2 with 35 (TXS) in location 0574.

SOLUTION The PC is incremented once to 0575. The X, A, and B registers are unaffected. The contents of X, 1000, are decremented and the result, OFFF placed in SP. The H, I, and C bits are unaffected; the N bit is cleared since OFFF represents a positive integer when interpreted as a 16-bit code word; the Z bit is cleared; and the V bit is reset. Thus the pattern in the condition-code register is 1100 0000 or C0.

6-4 INSTRUCTIONS MANIPULATING AN ADDRESSABLE LOCATION

The third group of instructions manipulates the contents of an addressable location. This group includes instructions to clear (CLR), complement (COM), negate (NEG), increment (INC), decrement (DEC), rotate (ROL and ROR), shift (ASL, ASR, and LSR), or test (TST) the contents of any addressable location. The address of the location can be designated using either extended or indexed addressing modes.

Instructions in this group using the extended addressing mode contain 3 bytes with the op code in the first byte and the complete address in the second and third. Instructions using the indexed addressing mode contain 2 bytes, with the op code in the first and the address offset in the second. As discussed in the previous chapter, the complete address with the indexed-mode addressing is obtained by adding the address offset in the instruction to the base address in the index register.

6-4-1 Instruction Coding

Table 6-3 shows the general instruction code word and a more detailed register-transfer description of the boolean-arithmetic operation for two instructions in this group. The first, increment the contents of an addressable location using the extended addressing mode, contains 3 bytes: 7C, H_1H_2, and H_3H_4, where H_1, H_2, H_3, and H_4 represent hexadecimal symbols. The first byte, 7C, specifies the op code, while $H_1H_2H_3H_4$ defines the address of the designated location. The more detailed register-transfer description, $\langle LOC\ H_1H_2H_3H_4 \rangle + 01 \rightarrow LOC$ $H_1H_2H_3H_4$, indicates that the contents of location $H_1H_2H_3H_4$ are added to the value 01 and the results stored in location $H_1H_2H_3H_4$.

The second instruction in Table 6-3, "negate the contents of an addressable location using the indexed addressing mode," contains 2 bytes, 60 and H_1H_2. The first byte, 60, specifies the op code, and the second, H_1H_2, defines the address offset. The complete address is obtained by adding this value to the contents of X, that is, $H_1H_2 + \langle X \rangle$. The more detailed register-transfer description of the specified boolean-arithmetic operation indicates that the contents of location $(H_1H_2 + \langle X \rangle)$ are subtracted from the value 00 and the result stored in location $(H_1H_2 + \langle X \rangle)$.

6-4-2 Instruction Execution

Execution of all instructions in this group involves an arithmetic logic unit (ALU) operation. Since the processor contains this unit, data in the designated location are transferred to the processor. After the specified ALU operation, the results are transferred from the processor back to the designated location. Thus the operate phase of these instructions involves a bus-read cycle followed by a bus-write cycle.

Table 6-3 General instruction code words and detailed register-transfer description for example instructions manipulating an addressable location

Instruction	Addressing mode	Instruction code words	Detailed register transfer
Increment memory (INC)	Extended	7C $H_1H_2\ H_3H_4$	$\langle LOC\ H_1H_2H_3H_4 \rangle + 01$ $\rightarrow LOC\ H_1H_2H_3H_4$
Negate memory (NEG)	Indexed	60 H_1H_2	$00 - \langle LOC(H_1H_2 + \langle X \rangle) \rangle$ $\rightarrow LOC(H_1H_2 + \langle X \rangle)$

Table 6-4 shows the sequence of bus-read, bus-write, and internal cycles required to execute the two instructions in Table 6-3. From the programmer's card we note that the first instruction, "increment an addressable location using the extended addressing mode," requires six cycles for execution. Since there are 3 bytes in the instruction, the first 3 are bus-read cycles used to fetch the op code and the address of the designated location. During these three clock cycles the program counter provides the address, and the values on the system data bus are transferred to the op-code register, the upper half of the data address register, and the lower half of the data register in that order. The fourth clock cycle is a bus-read cycle with the output of the data address register connected to the address bus. During this clock cycle the contents of the addressed location appear on the system data bus and are added in the ALU with the value 01. The results are stored temporarily in an internal register designated as REG. During the fifth clock cycle, a bus-write cycle with the data address register again providing the address, the contents of REG are transferred to the system data bus and written into the designated location. The condition code register also is revised during this clock cycle. With the convention adopted earlier, the last clock cycle is designated as an internal cycle since no additional bus transfers are required.

The second instruction in Table 6-4, "negate an addressable location using the indexed addressing mode," requires seven clock cycles for execution. Since the

Table 6-4 Sequence of bus-read, bus-write, and internal cycles for example instructions manipulating an addressable location

Instruction	Addressing mode	Cycle 1	Cycle 2	Cycle 3	Cycle 4
Increment memory (INC)	Extended	$1 \to R/W$ $\langle PC \rangle \to SAB$ $\langle SDB \rangle \to OR$ $\langle PC \rangle + 1 \to PC$	$1 \to R/W$ $\langle PC \rangle \to SAB$ $\langle SDB \rangle \to DAH$ $\langle PC \rangle + 1 \to PC$	$1 \to R/W$ $\langle PC \rangle \to SAB$ $\langle SDB \rangle \to DAL$ $\langle PC \rangle + 1 \to PC$	$1 \to R/W$ $\langle DA \rangle \to SAB$ $01 + \langle SDB \rangle$ $\to REG$
Negate memory (NEG)	Indexed	$1 \to R/W$ $\langle PC \rangle \to SAB$ $\langle SDB \rangle \to OR$ $\langle PC \rangle + 1 \to PC$	$1 \to R/W$ $\langle PC \rangle \to SAB$ $\langle SDB \rangle + \langle X \rangle$ $\to DA$ $\langle PC \rangle + 1 \to PC$	$1 \to R/W$ $\langle DA \rangle \to SAB$ $00 - \langle SDB \rangle$ $\to REG$	$0 \to R/W$ $\langle DA \rangle \to SAB$ $\langle REG \rangle \to SDB$ *Status* $\to CC$

		Cycle 5	Cycle 6	Cycle 7
Increment memory (INC)	Extended	$0 \to R/W$ $\langle DA \rangle \to SAB$ $\langle REG \rangle \to SDB$ *Status* $\to CC$	*Internal*	
Negate memory (NEG)	Indexed	*Internal*	*Internal*	*Internal*

instruction contains 2 bytes, the first two clock cycles are bus-read cycles with the program counter providing the address. During the first the op code is transferred from memory to the op-code register. During the second clock cycle, the value on the data bus is added to the contents of the index register and the results are stored in the data address register. The third clock cycle is a bus-read cycle with the data address register providing the address. During this third clock cycle, the current contents of the designated location appear on the system data bus and are negated in the ALU; the results are temporarily stored in an internal register, again designated REG. During the fourth clock cycle, a bus-write cycle with the data address register again providing the address, the output of the internal register REG is connected to the data bus and the results are written into the addressed location. Also during this clock cycle the condition-code register is revised. Since the remaining three clock cycles do not involve any bus transfers, they are defined as internal cycles.

The extra internal cycles required for the second instruction are necessary because computing the address with the indexed addressing mode requires a 16-bit addition using the 8-bit ALU. In the sequence shown in Table 6-4 this addition is performed during the second clock cycle and the three internal cycles are at the end of the sequence according to our convention. In fact, the third, fourth, and perhaps fifth clock cycles would be internal cycles used to compute the address. Thus the bus-read and bus-write cycles transferring the data to the processor and back to the addressed location would occur during the sixth and seventh clock cycles instead of the third and fourth clock cycles.

Example 6-4 The program counter (PC) and index register (X) contain 0527 and 2036, respectively. Define the code word for the instruction that will complement the contents of memory location 2037 using the extended addressing mode. How many bus-write, bus-read, and internal cycles are required for execution? What are the contents of the program counter, and index register after executing this instruction?

SOLUTION The programmer's card indicates that this instruction has an op code of 73 (COM), requires six clock cycles for execution, and contains 3 bytes. The coded instruction is 73 20 37.

Four bus-read cycles are required; three to fetch the instruction and one to transfer the contents of location 2037 to the processor for manipulation. One bus-write cycle is required to transfer the manipulated data back to location 2037. The one remaining clock cycle is an internal cycle.

The program counter will be incremented 3 times in fetching the instruction, so that it will contain 052A. The index register is not altered.

Example 6-5 Define the sequence of bus-read, bus-write, and internal cycles required to execute the instruction to do a right arithmetic shift on the contents of an addressable location (ASR) using all available addressing modes.

SOLUTION The extended and indexed addressing modes are available. The sequence is exactly the same as that shown in Table 6-4 with the exception of cycle 4 for the extended addressing mode and cycle 3 for the indexed addressing mode during which the actual data manipulation is performed. The register transfers during these clock cycles are identical:

$$1 \to R/W$$
$$\langle DA \rangle \to SAB$$
$$\langle SDB_0 \rangle \to C \text{ bit in CC}$$
$$\langle SDB_1 \rangle \to REG_0$$
$$\vdots$$
$$\langle SDB_7 \rangle \to REG_6$$
$$\langle SDB_7 \rangle \to REG_7$$

6-5 INSTRUCTIONS MANIPULATING AN INTERNAL PROCESSOR REGISTER AND AN ADDRESSABLE LOCATION

The fourth group of instructions manipulates the contents of one of the internal processor registers and an addressable location located in the memory, input, or output units. This group includes instructions to load and store the two accumulators (LDAA and STAA),† stack pointer (LDS and STS), and index register (LDX and STX); to perform arithmetic (ADDA, ADCA, SUBA and SBCA), logic (ANDA, EORA, and ORAA), bit test (BITA), or compare (CMPA) operations with the contents of an addressable location and one of the accumulators; or to perform a compare operation with the contents of an addressable location and the contents of the index register (CPX). Although the push and pull instructions and the branch and jump instructions could be included in this group, we shall discuss them separately.

All instruction except the four that store the accumulator (STAA and STAB), index register (STX), or stack pointer (STP) use the immediate, direct, indexed, and extended addressing modes. The four store instructions use the direct, indexed, and extended addressing modes.

Instructions using the immediate addressing mode contain 2 or 3 bytes, depending on the number of bits in the internal processor register manipulated by the instruction. For those involving the 8-bit accumulators, the instructions have 2 bytes; the first specifies the op code and the second provides the 8-bit operand. For instructions involving the 16-bit stack pointer and index register, instructions have 3 bytes, the first specifying the op code and the next two providing the upper and lower halves of the 16-bit operand, respectively.

With the direct, indexed, and extended addressing modes the operand is specified by an address; thus the number of bytes in the instruction is indepen-

† Only the mnemonics for the instruction for accumulator A are given; there is a corresponding set for accumulator B, that is, LDAB, STAB, ADDB, and so on.

dent of the number of bits in the manipulated internal processor register. With the extended addressing mode the instructions contain 3 bytes. The first byte specifies the op code and the next two define the upper and lower halves of the complete address of the operand. With the direct addressing mode, the instructions contain 2 bytes. The first specifies the op code and the second provides the less significant byte of the address; the more significant byte of the address is always 00 with this addressing mode. With the indexed addressing mode, the instruction also contains 2 bytes. The second byte contains the address offset relative to the base address in the index register.

6-5-1 Instruction Coding

Table 6-5 shows the general instruction code words and a more detailed register-transfer description of the specified boolean-arithmetic operation for six instructions representative of this group. The first four are accumulator instructions; the last two are index-register-stack-pointer instructions. The first instruction, "AND with accumulator A using the immediate addressing mode," contains two bytes, 84 and H_1H_2. The first byte specifies the op code, and the second defines the operand. The register-transfer description, $\langle A \rangle \cdot H_1H_2 \to A$, indicates that a logical AND is performed using the current contents of accumulator A and the operand H_1H_2, the results being stored in accumulator A.

Table 6-5 General instruction code words and detailed register-transfer description for example instructions manipulating an internal processor register and an addressable location

Instruction	Addressing mode	Coded instruction	Detailed register transfer
AND (ANDA)	Immediate	84 H_1H_2	$\langle A \rangle \cdot H_1H_2 \to A$
Bit test (BITA)	Direct	95 H_1H_2	$\langle A \rangle \cdot \langle \text{LOC } 00\ H_1H_2 \rangle$
Subtract from B (SUBB)	Indexed	E0 H_1H_2	$\langle B \rangle - \langle \text{LOC}(\langle X \rangle + H_1H_2) \rangle \to B$
Store B (STAB)	Extended	F7 $H_1H_2H_3H_4$	$\langle B \rangle \to \text{LOC } H_1H_2H_3H_4$
Load index register (LDX)	Immediate	CE $H_1H_2H_3H_4$	$H_1H_2H_3H_4 \to X$
Store stack pointer (STS)	Direct	9F H_1H_2	$\text{SPH} \to \text{LOC } 00\ H_1H_2$ $\text{SPL} \to \text{LOC}(00\ H_1H_2 + 1)$

The second instruction, "bit test with accumulator A using the direct addressing mode," is also a 2-byte instruction. The op code, 95, is given in the first byte; the second byte, H_1H_2, provides the less significant byte of the address. The specified boolean-arithmetic operation is a logical AND between the contents of accumulator A and the contents of location 00 H_1H_2, $\langle A \rangle \cdot \langle$Loc 00 $H_1H_2 \rangle$. Since no destination register is defined, the results are not saved. Thus this instruction, like the test-accumulator and compare instructions discussed earlier, revises the condition code register without altering the contents of the accumulator.

The third instruction, "subtract from accumulator B using the indexed addressing mode," is a 2-byte instruction; the op code, E0, is given in the first byte. The second byte, H_1H_2, defines the address offset. This offset is added to the contents of the index register to define the complete address of the operand, so that the address is $(\langle X \rangle + H_1H_2)$. The register-transfer notation in Table 6-5 is $\langle B \rangle - \langle LOC(\langle X \rangle + H_1H_2) \rangle \rightarrow B$, indicating that the contents of the location specified by this address are subtracted from the contents of accumulator B and the results are stored in accumulator B.

The fourth instruction, "store accumulator B using the extended addressing mode," is a 3-byte instruction with an op code of F7. The second and third bytes, H_1H_2 and H_3H_4, provide the complete address, $H_1H_2H_3H_4$. The detailed register-transfer description indicates that this instruction transfers the contents of the B accumulator to the specified location.

The fifth instruction, "load the index register using the immediate addressing mode," contains 3 bytes, with the op code, CE, in the first byte. The second and third bytes, H_1H_2 and H_3H_4, form the 16-bit operand, which is loaded into the index register as shown in the register-transfer description in Table 6-5.

The sixth instruction, "store the stack pointer using the direct addressing mode," is a 2-byte instruction; the op code, 9F, is in the first byte. The second byte provides the less significant byte of the address, just as in the second instruction described in Table 6-5. Since the stack pointer is a 16-bit register, two memory locations are required to store the contents of this register. This instruction transfers the upper half of the stack pointer to the location specified by the address 00 H_1H_2 and the lower half to the next location, i.e., the location with the address (00 $H_1H_2 + 1$). The implicit use of two adjacent locations with this instruction is a convention used with all stack-pointer and index-register instructions.

Example 6-6 The program counter (PC), index register (X), and accumulator A contain 023C, 1052, and 76, respectively. Define the code word for the instruction that will transfer the contents of A to location 1052 using (*a*) the extended addressing mode and (*b*) the indexed addressing mode. Indicate the contents of these three registers after executing these instructions.

SOLUTION (*a*) The code word is B7 10 52. After executing this instruction, the PC, which was incremented 3 times in fetching the 3-byte instruction, contains 023F. The X and A registers were not altered during the execution of this instruction.

(*b*) The code word is A7 00. After executing this instruction the PC, which was incremented twice in fetching the 2-byte instruction, contains 023E. Again the X and A registers are unaltered.

Example 6-7 The program counter (PC) and index register (X) contain 5052 and 0001, respectively. The contents of certain memory locations are specified below with location 5052 shown containing *xx* representing various op codes. Indicate the contents of the PC, X, and A registers after executing one instruction beginning at location 5052 if *xx* is (*a*) 86, (*b*) 96, (*c*) A6, and (*d*) B6. (These are op codes for LDA instructions.)

Location	50	51	· · ·	5051	5052	5053	5054	5055
Contents	C3	97	· · ·	3F	*xx*	50	51	52

SOLUTION (*a*) Since the op code 86 defines the immediate addressing mode, the next byte, 50, is the operand. In executing this instruction the PC is incremented twice to 5054, the X register is unaffected, and the A accumulator is loaded with 50.

(*b*) The op code 96 defines the direct addressing mode, and so the next byte, 50, provides the lower half of operand's address; the upper half is 00. In executing this instruction the PC is incremented twice to 5054, the X register is unaffected, and the A accumulator is loaded with C3, the contents of location 0050.

(*c*) The op code A6 defines the indexed addressing mode, and so the next byte, 50, is the address offset. The complete address of the operand is obtained by adding this offset to the contents of X, 0001, to obtain 0051. In executing this instruction the PC is incremented twice to 5054, the X register is unaffected, and the A accumulator is loaded with 97, the contents of location 0051.

(*d*) The op code B6 defines the extended addressing mode; so the next 2 bytes 5051 define the operand's address. In executing this instruction the PC is incremented 3 times to 5055, the X register is unaltered, and the A accumulator is loaded with 3F, the contents of location 5051.

6-5-2 Instruction Execution

Table 6-6 shows the sequence of bus-read, bus-write, and internal cycles required to execute the six instructions described in Table 6-5. The first instruction, "AND with accumulator A using the immediate addressing mode," requires 2 clock cycles for execution. The first is the standard bus-read cycle to transfer the op code from memory to the op-code register. The second clock cycle is also a

Table 6-6 Sequence of bus-read, bus-write, and internal cycles for example instructions manipulating an internal processor register and an addressable location

Instruction	Addressing mode	Cycle 1	Cycle 2	Cycle 3	Cycle 4	Cycle 5
AND with A (ANDA)	Immediate	$1 \rightarrow R/W$ $\langle PC \rangle \rightarrow SAB$ $\langle SDB \rangle \rightarrow OR$ $\langle PC \rangle + 1 \rightarrow PC$	$1 \rightarrow R/W$ $\langle PC \rangle \rightarrow SAB$ $\langle SDB \rangle \cdot \langle A \rangle \rightarrow A$ $\langle PC \rangle + 1 \rightarrow PC$ $Status \rightarrow CC$			
Bit test A (BITA)	Direct	$1 \rightarrow R/W$ $\langle PC \rangle \rightarrow SAB$ $\langle SDB \rangle \rightarrow OR$ $\langle PC \rangle + 1 \rightarrow PC$	$1 \rightarrow R/W$ $\langle PC \rangle \rightarrow SAB$ $\langle SDB \rangle \rightarrow DAL$ $00 \rightarrow DAH$ $\langle PC \rangle + 1 \rightarrow PC$	$1 \rightarrow R/W$ $\langle DA \rangle \rightarrow SAB$ $\langle SDB \rangle \cdot \langle A \rangle$ $Status \rightarrow CC$		
Subtract from B (SUBB)	Indexed	$1 \rightarrow R/W$ $\langle PC \rangle \rightarrow SAB$ $\langle SDB \rangle \rightarrow OR$ $\langle PC \rangle + 1 \rightarrow PC$	$1 \rightarrow R/W$ $\langle PC \rangle \rightarrow SAB$ $\langle SDB \rangle + \langle X \rangle \rightarrow DA$ $\langle PC \rangle + 1 \rightarrow PC$	$1 \rightarrow R/W$ $\langle DA \rangle \rightarrow SAB$ $\langle B \rangle - \langle SDB \rangle \rightarrow B$ $Status \rightarrow CC$	*Internal*	*Internal*
Store B (STAB)	Extended	$1 \rightarrow R/W$ $\langle PC \rangle \rightarrow SAB$ $\langle SDB \rangle \rightarrow OR$ $\langle PC \rangle + 1 \rightarrow PC$	$1 \rightarrow R/W$ $\langle PC \rangle \rightarrow SAB$ $\langle SDB \rangle \rightarrow DAH$ $\langle PC \rangle + 1 \rightarrow PC$	$1 \rightarrow R/W$ $\langle PC \rangle \rightarrow SAB$ $\langle SDB \rangle \rightarrow DAL$ $\langle PC \rangle + 1 \rightarrow PC$	$0 \rightarrow R/W$ $\langle DA \rangle \rightarrow SAB$ $\langle B \rangle \rightarrow SDB$ $Status \rightarrow CC$	*Internal*
Load index register (LDX)	Immediate	$1 \rightarrow R/W$ $\langle PC \rangle \rightarrow SAB$ $\langle SDB \rangle \rightarrow OR$ $\langle PC \rangle + 1 \rightarrow PC$	$1 \rightarrow R/W$ $\langle PC \rangle \rightarrow SAB$ $\langle SDB \rangle \rightarrow XH$ $\langle PC \rangle + 1 \rightarrow PC$	$1 \rightarrow R/W$ $\langle PC \rangle \rightarrow SAB$ $\langle SDB \rangle \rightarrow XL$ $\langle PC \rangle + 1 \rightarrow PC$ $Status \rightarrow CC$		
Store stack pointer (STS)	Direct	$1 \rightarrow R/W$ $\langle PC \rangle \rightarrow SAB$ $\langle SDB \rangle \rightarrow OR$ $\langle PC \rangle + 1 \rightarrow PC$	$1 \rightarrow R/W$ $\langle PC \rangle \rightarrow SAB$ $\langle SDB \rangle \rightarrow DAL$ $00 \rightarrow DAH$ $\langle PC \rangle + 1 \rightarrow PC$	$0 \rightarrow R/W$ $\langle DA \rangle \rightarrow SAB$ $\langle SPH \rangle \rightarrow SDB$ $\langle DA \rangle + 1 \rightarrow DA$	$0 \rightarrow R/W$ $\langle DA \rangle \rightarrow SAB$ $\langle SPL \rangle \rightarrow SDB$ $Status \rightarrow CC$	*Internal*

bus-read cycle with the program counter providing the address. During the second clock cycle, the word on the data bus and the contents of accumulator A are combined using a logical AND operation in the ALU, and the results are stored in accumulator A. The contents of the condition-code register are revised based on the result of the AND operation as indicated by "*Status* → CC".

The second instruction in Table 6-6, "bit test with accumulator A using the direct addressing mode," requires three clock cycles for execution. The first clock cycle is used to fetch the op code. During the second clock cycle, a bus-read cycle, the second byte of the instruction is transferred to the lower half of the data address register and 00 is loaded into the upper half of this register. The third clock cycle, which is devoted to the operate phase, is a bus-read cycle with the data address register providing the address. The word on the data bus and the contents of accumulator A are combined using a logical AND in the ALU. Unlike the instruction described in the last paragraph, the results of this operation are not saved, but the contents of the condition-code register are revised based on the result of the AND operation.

The third instruction, "subtract from accumulator B using the indexed addressing mode," requires five clock cycles for execution. The first clock cycle is the standard bus-read cycle to fetch the op code. During the second clock cycle, the second byte of the instruction, which specifies the address offset, is fetched using a bus-read cycle and added to the contents of the index register; the results are placed in the data address register. The third clock cycle is a bus-read cycle used to obtain the operand. The data address register provides the address, and the operand is transferred from the addressed location to the data bus and then subtracted from the contents of accumulator B; the condition-code register is also adjusted. The fourth and fifth clock cycles are internal cycles.

The fourth instruction, "store accumulator B using the extended addressing mode," requires five clock cycles for execution. The op code is fetched during the first clock cycle. The second and third clock cycles are bus-read cycles for which the program counter provides the address. During the second clock cycle, the word on the data bus represents the more significant byte of the address, and it is loaded into the upper half of the data address register. Similarly, during the third clock cycle, the word on the data bus represents the less significant byte of the address, and it is loaded into the lower half of the data address register. Since this instruction transfers the contents of the accumulator to the addressed location, the operate phase involves a bus-write cycle. In our scheme this is performed during the fourth clock cycle in the sequence. The data address register provides the address, and the contents of the accumulator are loaded onto the data bus and written in memory; the condition code register also is adjusted. The last cycle is defined as an internal cycle.

The fifth instruction in Table 6-6, "load the index register using the immediate addressing mode," requires three clock cycles for execution. The first is the standard bus-read cycle to obtain the op code. The next two clock cycles transfer the operand, contained in the second and third bytes of the instruction, to the index register. During these bus-read cycles the program counter provides the address, and the word on the data bus is loaded into the upper and lower halves of the index register, in that order.

The sixth instruction in Table 6-6, "store the stack pointer using the direct addressing mode," requires five clock cycles for execution. The first clock cycle is the standard bus-read cycle to transfer the op code from memory to the op-code register. The second clock cycle transfers the less significant byte of the address to the lower half of the data address register and clears the upper half of this register. The third clock cycle is a bus-write cycle, for which the data address register provides the address. During this clock cycle, the contents in the upper half of the stack pointer are transferred to the data bus and then written in memory. The data address register is also incremented to point to the next higher memory location. The fourth clock cycle also is a bus-write cycle, the data address register again providing the address. This time the contents of the lower half of the stack pointer are transferred to the data bus and written in memory. The fifth clock cycle is defined as an internal cycle.

Example 6-8 Show the sequence of values on the valid-memory-address line (VMA), the read-write control line (R/W), the system address bus (SAB), and the system data bus (SDB) for the instruction execution of Example 6-7.

SOLUTION (*a*)

	CYCLE 1	CYCLE 2
VMA	1	1
R/W	1	1
SAB	5052	5053
SDB	86	50

(*b*)

	CYCLE 1	CYCLE 2	CYCLE 3
VMA	1	1	1
R/W	1	1	1
SAB	5052	5053	0050
SDB	96	50	C3

(*c*)

	CYCLE 1	CYCLE 2	CYCLE 3	CYCLE 4	CYCLE 5
VMA	1	1	1	0	0
R/W	1	1	1	*	*
SAB	5052	5053	0051	*	*
SDB	A6	50	97	*	*

* Undefined value.

(*d*)

	CYCLE 1	CYCLE 2	CYCLE 3	CYCLE 4
VMA	1	1	1	1
R/W	1	1	1	1
SAB	5052	5053	5054	5051
SDB	B6	50	51	3F

6-6 INSTRUCTIONS TRANSFERRING DATA BETWEEN THE ACCUMULATORS AND THE STACK

The fifth group of instructions are those transferring data between the two accumulators and the stack. These instructions store, or push, data onto the stack (PSHA and PSHB) and recall, or pull, data from the stack (PULA and PULB). These instructions contain 1 byte and use the inherent addressing mode since the addressed location is specified by the stack pointer.

Table 6-7 shows the general instruction code word and the detailed specified register-transfer description for two of these instructions. The first, "push data from accumulator A," is a 1-byte instruction with an op code of 36. This instruction transfers the contents of accumulator A to the location defined by the contents of the stack pointer and decrements the contents of the stack pointer *after* using it as an address. This sequence is consistent with our earlier description of the use of the stack pointer which contains the address of the next empty location and uses addresses with numerically smaller values as the stack is filled.

The second instruction in Table 6-7, "pull data for accumulator A," is also a 1-byte instruction; its op code is 32. This instruction transfers the last word in the stack to accumulator A. Since the stack pointer contains the address of the next empty location in the stack, the last word in the stack is in the location with the next higher address. Thus in executing a pull instruction, the contents of the stack pointer are incremented *before* being used as an address.

Table 6-8 shows the sequence of internal, bus-read, and bus-write cycles required to execute the two instructions defined in Table 6-7. The first, "push data from accumulator A," requires four clock cycles for execution. The first clock cycle is the standard bus-read cycle to fetch the op code. The second is a bus-write cycle to transfer the contents of accumulator A to the stack. During this clock cycle the stack pointer provides the address, and the contents of accumulator A are transferred to the data bus and then written in the addressed location. Finally the stack pointer is decremented. The last two clock cycles are defined as internal cycles.

Table 6-7 General instruction code word and detailed register-transfer description for push and pull instructions

Instruction	Coded instruction	Detailed register transfer†
Push A (PSHA)	36	$\langle A \rangle \rightarrow LOC \langle SP \rangle$ $\langle SP \rangle - 1 \rightarrow SP$
Pull A (PULA)	32	$\langle SP \rangle + 1 \rightarrow SP$ $\langle LOC \langle SP \rangle \rangle \rightarrow A$

† These transfers are performed in the order indicated.

Table 6-8 Sequence of bus-read, bus-write, and internal cycles for the push and pull instructions

Instruction	Cycle 1	Cycle 2	Cycle 3	Cycle 4
Push A (PSHA)	$1 \rightarrow R/W$ $\langle PC \rangle \rightarrow SAB$ $\langle SDB \rangle \rightarrow OR$ $\langle PC \rangle + 1 \rightarrow PC$	$0 \rightarrow R/W$ $\langle SP \rangle \rightarrow SAB$ $\langle A \rangle \rightarrow SDB$ $\langle SP \rangle - 1 \rightarrow SP$	*Internal*	*Internal*
Pull A (PULA)	$1 \rightarrow R/W$ $\langle PC \rangle \rightarrow SAB$ $\langle SDB \rangle \rightarrow OR$ $\langle PC \rangle + 1 \rightarrow PC$	$\langle SP \rangle + 1 \rightarrow SP$ $1 \rightarrow R/W$ $\langle SP \rangle \rightarrow SAB$ $\langle SDB \rangle \rightarrow A$	*Internal*	*Internal*

The second instruction in Table 6-8, "pull data for accumulator A," also requires four clock cycles for execution. The first clock cycle is the standard bus-read cycle to fetch the op code. During the second clock cycle the contents of the stack pointer are first incremented and then used as an address during a bus-read cycle. The contents of the addressed location appear on the data bus and then are transferred to accumulator A. Two internal cycles complete the execution of this instruction.

Example 6-9 Define the sequence of values on the valid-memory-address line (VMA), read-write control line (R/W), system address bus (SAB), and system data bus (SDB) as the segment of program given below is executed. When the sequence starts the program counter (PC), stack pointer (SP), and A accumulator contain 0349, 1024, and 53, respectively. Define the contents of the stack pointer after each clock cycle.

Location	0349	034A
Contents	36 (PSHA)	32 (PULA)

SOLUTION Both 36 and 32 are op codes for 1-byte instructions requiring four cycles for execution.

	Cycle 1	Cycle 2	Cycle 3	Cycle 4	Cycle 5	Cycle 6	Cycle 7	Cycle 8
VMA	1	1	0	0	1	1	0	0
R/W	1	0	*	*	1	1	*	*
SAB	0349	1024	*	*	034A	1024	*	*
SDB	36	53	*	*	32	53	*	*
SP	1024	1023	1023	1023	1023	1024	1024	1024

    * Undefined.

6-7 INSTRUCTIONS MANIPULATING THE PROGRAM COUNTER

The sixth group of instructions alters the contents of the program counter. These instructions allow programs in which the order of instruction execution is not restricted to the linear sequence defined by their storage in memory. This group includes instructions to perform an unconditional branch (BRA) or jump (JMP), a conditional branch (BCC, BCS, BEQ, BGE, BGT, BHI, BLE, BLS, BLT, BMI, BNE, BVC, BVS, BPL), a branch (BSR), or jump (JSR) to a subroutine or a return from subroutine (RTS). The unconditional branch and jump instructions always transfer a new address to the program counter; the conditional branch instructions change the program counter only if a specific bit pattern is present in the condition code register.

The branch and jump to subroutine instructions push the current contents of the program counter onto the stack before loading the program counter with a new address. The return from subroutine instruction pulls an address off the stack and loads it into the program counter. These instructions combine to allow the execution of a separate sequence of coded instructions and then the return to the appropriate place in the main sequence of coded instructions.

All branch instructions can be used only with the relative addressing mode. Branch instructions contain 2 bytes which specify the op code and the address offset, respectively. With the relative addressing mode, the address offset is added to the contents of the program counter to define the address of the next instruction. The reader should review the use of positive and negative offsets and the factor of 2, discussed in Sec. 5-3.

The two jump instructions can be used with either the indexed or extended addressing modes. With the extended addressing mode, the instruction contains 3 bytes; the first specifies the op code, while the second and third contain the complete address of the next instruction. With the indexed addressing mode, the instruction contains 2 bytes. The first again specifies the op code, and the second provides the address offset relative to the index register. The complete address of the next instruction is obtained by adding the address offset to the contents of the index register.

The return-from-subroutine instruction uses only the inherent addressing mode. Thus this instruction contains only 1 byte, the op code.

6-7-1 Instruction Coding

Table 6-9 shows the general instruction code words and detailed register-transfer description of the specified boolean-arithmetic operation for four instructions that explicitly manipulate the program counter. The first, "branch if carry clear," is representative of the conditional branch instruction. This instruction contains 2 bytes, 24 is the op code, and H_1H_2 is the address offset. The detailed register-transfer description indicates that if the test condition, in this case $C = 0$, is true, the address offset H_1H_2 is added to the program counter; otherwise nothing is done. The reader should recall that the factor 2 must be included since the

Table 6-9 General instruction code words and detailed register-transfer description for example instructions manipulating the program counter

Instruction	Addressing mode	Coded instruction	Detailed register transfer
Branch if carry clear (BCC)	Relative	$24 \ H_1 H_2$	*If* $C = 0$ $\langle PC \rangle + H_1 H_2 + 2 \rightarrow PC$ *Else* $\langle PC \rangle + 2 \rightarrow PC$
Jump (JMP)	Indexed	$6E \ H_1 H_2$	$\langle X \rangle + H_1 H_2 \rightarrow PC$
Jump to subroutine (JSR)	Extended	$BD \ H_1 H_2 H_3 H_4$	$\langle PCL \rangle \rightarrow LOC \ \langle SP \rangle$ $\langle PCH \rangle \rightarrow LOC \ (\langle SP \rangle - 1)$ $\langle SP \rangle - 2 \rightarrow SP$ $H_1 H_2 H_3 H_4 \rightarrow PC$
Return from subroutine (RTS)	Inherent	39	$\langle LOC(\langle SP \rangle + 1) \rangle \rightarrow PCH$ $\langle LOC(\langle SP \rangle + 2) \rangle \rightarrow PCL$ $\langle SP \rangle + 2 \rightarrow SP$

program counter is incremented twice in fetching the 2 bytes of this instruction. When the address offset is negative, adding the 8-bit word to the 16-bit program counter introduces one small complication since leading 1s must be placed in the most significant byte of the offset. For example, if $H_1 \geq 8$, implying a negative offset, then FF $H_1 H_2$ must be added to the program counter; similarly, if $H_1 < 8$, the offset is positive and 00 $H_1 H_2$ is added.

The second instruction in Table 6-9, the unconditional jump using the indexed addressing mode, contains 2 bytes. The op code is 6E, and the address offset is represented by $H_1 H_2$. The address offset defines the address of the next instruction relative to the index register. The execution of this instruction loads the program counter with the sum generated by adding $H_1 H_2$ and the contents of the index register.

The third instruction in Table 6-9, "jump to subroutine using the extended addressing mode," is a 3-byte instruction. The first byte, BD, specifies the op code; the second and third bytes provide the complete address of the next instruction to be executed, which is the first instruction in the subroutine. The detailed register-transfer description of the execution of this instruction shows that it differs from the branch and jump instructions in the two previous examples in that the current contents of the program counter are pushed onto the stack before the new address is placed in the program counter. This, in effect, saves the address of the next instruction in the program from which the jump is made; this address is referred to as the *return address*. The program from which the jump is made is the *calling program*. Saving the return address is defined by the register-transfer descriptions $\langle PCH \rangle \rightarrow LOC \langle SP \rangle$, $\langle PCL \rangle \rightarrow LOC \ (\langle SP \rangle - 1)$, and $\langle SP \rangle - 2 \rightarrow SP$. Loading the program counter with the address of the first instruction in the subroutine is defined by $H_1 H_2 H_3 H_4 \rightarrow PC$.

The fourth instruction in Table 6-9, "return from subroutine," essentially restores the program counter after all the instructions in the subroutine have been executed. This instruction pulls two words off the stack representing the return address and places them in the program counter. Since the stack pointer contains the address of the next empty location, these two words are stored in the locations with the next two higher addresses, LOC ($\langle SP \rangle + 1$) and LOC ($\langle SP \rangle + 2$). This instruction must be the last executable instruction in all subroutines.

Example 6-10 The contents of all programmer-accessible internal processor registers are given below. Indicate the contents of all registers after executing (*a*) the BRA instruction 20 F1, (*b*) the BEQ instruction 27 11, (*c*) the BMI instruction 2B 30, (*d*) the JMP instruction 6E 53, and (*e*) the JSR instruction BD 10 52:

$$\langle PC \rangle = 0752 \qquad \langle SP \rangle = 0063 \qquad \langle A \rangle = A3$$

$$\langle X \rangle = 1257 \qquad \langle CC \rangle = C8 \qquad \langle B \rangle = 65$$

SOLUTION (*a*) All registers but the PC are unaltered. The new contents of the PC are 0178, computed from its current contents and the offset in instruction:

$$
\begin{array}{r}
0725 \rightarrow 0000\ 0111\ 0010\ 0101 \\
(FF)F1 \rightarrow 1111\ 1111\ 1111\ 0001 \\
2 \rightarrow 0010 \\
\hline
0000\ 0111\ 0001\ 1000 \rightarrow 0718
\end{array}
$$

(*b*) All registers but the PC are unaltered. The test condition $Z = 1$ is false, so the PC is incremented twice to 0727.

(*c*) All registers but the PC are unaltered. The test condition $N = 1$ is true, so the contents of the PC become 0757, which was computed from its current contents and the offset in the instruction as shown below:

$$
\begin{array}{r}
0725 \rightarrow 0000\ 0111\ 0010\ 0101 \\
30 \rightarrow 0000\ 0000\ 0011\ 0000 \\
2 \rightarrow 0010 \\
\hline
0000\ 0111\ 0101\ 0111 \rightarrow 0757
\end{array}
$$

(*d*) All registers but the PC are unaltered. The new contents of the PC are 12AA, computed from the contents of X and the offset in the instruction as shown below:

$$
\begin{array}{r}
1257 \rightarrow 0001\ 0010\ 0101\ 0111 \\
53 \rightarrow 0000\ 0000\ 0101\ 0011 \\
\hline
0001\ 0010\ 1010\ 1010 \rightarrow 12AA
\end{array}
$$

(e) All registers but the SP and PC are unchanged. The SP is decremented twice to 0061. The PC is changed to 1052, as defined in the second and third bytes of the instruction.

6-7-2 Instruction Execution

Table 6-10 shows the sequence of bus-read, bus-write, and internal cycles required to execute the four instructions defined in Table 6-9. The first instruction, "branch if carry clear using the relative addressing mode," requires four clock cycles for execution. The first clock cycle is the standard bus-read cycle to transfer the op code from memory to the op-code register. The second clock cycle is also a bus-read cycle for which the program counter provides the address; the second byte of the instruction, the address offset, appears on the data bus. If the test condition, in this case $C = 0$, is false, this word is ignored; but if the test condition is true, the word on the data bus is added to the program counter. This addition is more complicated if the word on the data bus represents a negative offset, as discussed earlier. This complication, although not included in Table 6-10, is one reason for the two internal cycles during the third and fourth clock cycles used to execute this instruction.

The second instruction in Table 6-10, "unconditional jump using the indexed addressing mode," requires four clock cycles for execution. The first clock cycle is the standard bus-read cycle to transfer the op code from memory to the op-code register. During the second clock cycle, the address offset is transferred from memory to the data bus. This word is then added with the contents of the index register, and the resulting sum is placed in the program counter. Two internal cycles follow; they are required because the addition used to compute the new address involves a 16-bit word and must be performed with an 8-bit ALU.

The third instruction in Table 6-10, "jump to subroutine using the extended addressing mode," requires nine clock cycles for execution. The first clock cycle is the standard bus-read cycle used to fetch the op code. The second and third clock cycles are bus-read cycles for which the program counter provides the address; the two words that appear on the data bus are placed in the upper and lower half of a 16-bit internal processor register designated by REGH and REGL. The fourth clock cycle is a bus-write cycle for which the stack pointer provides the address; the lower half of the program counter is connected to the data bus, and its contents are written in memory, thereby saving the lower byte of the return address. The stack pointer is also decremented during this cycle after it provides the address. The fifth clock cycle is analogous to the fourth except that the contents of the upper half of the program counter are transferred to the stack. Also during the fifth clock cycle, the contents of the internal processor register (designated REG), which contains the address of the first instruction of the subroutine, are transferred to the program counter. Again, according to our convention, all internal cycles, four in this case, are placed at the end.

The last instruction in Table 6-10, "return from subroutine," requires five clock cycles for execution. The first clock cycle is the standard bus-read cycle to

Table 6-10 Sequence of bus-read, bus-write, and internal cycles for example instructions manipulating the program counter

Instruction	Addressing mode	Cycle 1	Cycle 2	Cycle 3	Cycle 4
Branch if carry clear (BCC)	Relative	$1 \rightarrow R/W$ $\langle PC \rangle \rightarrow SAB$ $\langle SDB \rangle \rightarrow OR$ $\langle PC \rangle + 1$ $\rightarrow PC$	$1 \rightarrow R/W$ $\langle PC \rangle \rightarrow SAB$ $\langle PC \rangle + 1 \rightarrow PC$ *If C = 0* $\langle PC \rangle + \langle SDB \rangle$ $\rightarrow PC$ *Else* nothing	*Internal*	*Internal*
Jump (JMP)	Indexed	$1 \rightarrow R/W$ $\langle PC \rangle \rightarrow SAB$ $\langle SDB \rangle \rightarrow OR$ $\langle PC \rangle + 1$ $\rightarrow PC$	$1 \rightarrow R/W$ $\langle PC \rangle \rightarrow SAB$ $\langle SDB \rangle + \langle X \rangle$ $\rightarrow PC$	*Internal*	*Internal*
Jump to subroutine (JSR)	Extended	$1 \rightarrow R/W$ $\langle PC \rangle \rightarrow SAB$ $\langle SDB \rangle \rightarrow OR$ $\langle PC \rangle + 1$ $\rightarrow PC$	$1 \rightarrow R/W$ $\langle PC \rangle \rightarrow SAB$ $\langle SDB \rangle + REGH$ $\langle PC \rangle + 1 \rightarrow PC$	$1 \rightarrow R/W$ $\langle PC \rangle \rightarrow SAB$ $\langle SDB \rangle \rightarrow REGL$ $\langle PC \rangle + 1 \rightarrow PC$	$0 \rightarrow R/W$ $\langle SP \rangle \rightarrow SAB$ $\langle PCL \rangle \rightarrow SDB$ $\langle SP \rangle - 1 \rightarrow SP$
Return from subroutine (RTS)	Inherent	$1 \rightarrow R/W$ $\langle PC \rangle \rightarrow SAB$ $\langle SDB \rangle \rightarrow OR$ $\langle PC \rangle + 1$ $\rightarrow PC$	$1 \rightarrow R/W$ $\langle SP \rangle + 1 \rightarrow SP$ $\langle SP \rangle \rightarrow SAB$ $\langle SDB \rangle \rightarrow PCH$	$1 \rightarrow R/W$ $\langle SP \rangle + 1 \rightarrow SP$ $\langle SP \rangle \rightarrow SAB$ $\langle SDB \rangle \rightarrow PCL$	*Internal*

Instruction	Addressing mode	Cycle 5	Cycle 6	Cycle 7	Cycle 8	Cycle 9
Branch if carry clear (BCC)	Relative					
Jump (JMP)	Indexed					
Jump to subroutine (JSR)	Extended	$0 \rightarrow R/W$ $\langle SP \rangle \rightarrow SAB$ $\langle PCH \rangle \rightarrow SDB$ $\langle SP \rangle - 1 \rightarrow SP$ $\langle REG \rangle \rightarrow PC$	*Internal*	*Internal*	*Internal*	*Internal*
Return from subroutine (RTS)	Inherent	*Internal*				

fetch the op code. The second and third clock cycles are bus-read cycles for which the stack pointer provides the address after first being incremented. The two words that appear on the data bus during these two bus-read cycles are placed in the upper and lower halves of the program counter, respectively. This is consistent with the order with which the 2 bytes of the return address were stored on the stack by the jump-to-subroutine instruction described in the previous paragraph. The remaining two clock cycles are defined as internal cycles.

Example 6-11 The contents of all user-accessible processor registers are given below. Define the sequence of values on the valid-memory-address line (VMA), the read-write control line (R/W), the system address bus (SAB), and the system data bus (SDB) required to execute the next instruction, a JSR instruction, if the contents of 2034 and the next two memory locations are BD, 27, and 52. What are the contents of all registers after executing this instruction?

$$\langle PC \rangle = 2034 \qquad \langle X \rangle = 0205 \qquad \langle A \rangle = 39$$

$$\langle SP \rangle = 00A3 \qquad \langle CC \rangle = C2 \qquad \langle B \rangle = 67$$

SOLUTION This instruction requires nine clock cycles for execution.

	Cycle 1	Cycle 2	Cycle 3	Cycle 4	Cycle 5	Cycle 6	Cycle 7	Cycle 8	Cycle 9
VMA	1	1	1	1	1	0	0	0	0
R/W	1	1	1	0	0	*	*	*	*
SAB	2034	2035	2036	00A3	00A2	*	*	*	*
SDB	BD	27	52	37	20	*	*	*	*

* Undefined.

All registers but the PC and SP are unaltered. The PC contains 2752, as defined in the instruction. The SP, decremented twice in pushing the 2 bytes of the return address on the stack, contains 00A1.

6-8 INSTRUCTIONS ASSOCIATED WITH INTERRUPTS

The seventh group of instructions consists of three instructions used with interrupts (RTI, SWI, and WAI). Before discussing these instructions, we describe how the 6800 processor control unit handles an interrupt. In the system an interrupt may occur in one of three ways: (1) the controller acknowledges a request on the maskable-interrupt-request line (IRQ), (2) the controller acknowledges a request on the nonmaskable-interrupt-request line (NMI), or (3) a special instruction (SWI) is executed. They are referred to as a *maskable interrupt*, a *nonmaskable interrupt*, and a *software interrupt*, respectively. For all three, the processor is designed so that the program that is interrupted will continue correctly after dealing with the interrupt. Thus the contents of all programmer-controlled internal processor registers must be saved so that after the interrupt has been dealt with, they can be restored to the same condition and the interrupted program continued. In the 6800 the contents of the program counter, index register, accumulators A and B, and the condition code register are pushed onto the stack when an interrupt is begun.

After saving the contents of the internal processor registers, the program counter is loaded with the starting address of a special program, called the *interrupt-service routine*. In practice there are three interrupt-service routines, one for each way an interrupt can occur. In the 6800 the addresses of these routines are stored in specific locations at the very end of memory (Table 6-11).

Table 6-12 shows the sequence of nine bus transfers that occur once a maskable interrupt begins. During the first clock cycle, a bus-write cycle with the stack pointer providing the address, the lower half of the program counter is pushed onto the stack; after providing the address, the stack pointer is decremented. The next six clock cycles are similar except that the contents of different processor registers are transferred to the stack. The eighth and ninth clock cycles are bus-read cycles using fixed addresses to place the starting address of the appropriate interrupt-service routine in the program counter. Table 6-12 shows the values used for an interrupt resulting from a request on the maskable-interrupt-request line. If the interrupt occurred in another way, these values would have been different, as indicated in the footnotes to Table 6-12. After these nine cycles the contents of all internal processor registers have been saved and the program counter has been loaded with the address of the first instruction in the interrupt-service routine so that the first instruction in that routine will be fetched during the next clock cycle.

Let us now return to the three instructions used with interrupts. All three are 1-byte instructions and use the inherent addressing mode. Table 6-13 shows the

Table 6-11 Locations of interrupt-service-routine addresses†

Location	Contents
FFF8	Maskable interrupt—upper byte
FFF9	Maskable interrupt—lower byte
FFFA	Software interrupt—upper byte
FFFB	Software interrupt—lower byte
FFFC	Nonmaskable interrupt—upper byte
FFFD	Nonmaskable interrupt—lower byte
FFFE	Restart—upper byte
FFFF	Restart—lower byte

† The table also shows the location of addresses of the restart routine, a program used to place the computer in a standard initial state. This restart routine is executed each time the reset line in the control bus is activated, as defined in Sec. 5-2.

Table 6-12 Sequence of bus-read, bus-write, and internal cycles for an interrupt resulting from a maskable-interrupt request

Cycle 1	Cycle 2	Cycle 3
$0 \rightarrow R/W$ $\langle SP \rangle \rightarrow SAB$ $\langle PCL \rangle \rightarrow SDB$ $\langle SP \rangle - 1 \rightarrow SP$	$0 \rightarrow R/W$ $\langle SP \rangle \rightarrow SAB$ $\langle PCH \rangle \rightarrow SDB$ $\langle SP \rangle - 1 \rightarrow SP$	$0 \rightarrow R/W$ $\langle SP \rangle \rightarrow SAB$ $\langle XL \rangle \rightarrow SDB$ $\langle SP \rangle - 1 \rightarrow SP$

Cycle 4	Cycle 5	Cycle 6
$0 \rightarrow R/W$ $\langle SP \rangle \rightarrow SAB$ $\langle XH \rangle \rightarrow SDB$ $\langle SP \rangle - 1 \rightarrow SP$	$0 \rightarrow R/W$ $\langle SP \rangle \rightarrow SAB$ $\langle A \rangle \rightarrow SDB$ $\langle SP \rangle - 1 \rightarrow SP$	$0 \rightarrow R/W$ $\langle SP \rangle \rightarrow SAB$ $\langle B \rangle \rightarrow SDB$ $\langle SP \rangle - 1 \rightarrow SP$

Cycle 7	Cycle 8	Cycle 9
$0 \rightarrow R/W$ $\langle SP \rangle \rightarrow SAB$ $\langle CC \rangle \rightarrow SDB$ $\langle SP \rangle - 1 \rightarrow SP$	$1 \rightarrow R/W$ FFF8† $\rightarrow SAB$ $\langle SDB \rangle \rightarrow PCH$	$1 \rightarrow R/W$ FFF9† $\rightarrow SAB$ $\langle SDB \rangle \rightarrow PCL$

† For software interrupt the values would be FFFA and FFFB; for a nonmaskable-interrupt request the values would be FFFC and FFFD.

detailed register transfers associated with each of these three instructions. The first instruction, "wait for interrupt," prepares the processor to accept an interrupt by pushing the contents of the program counter, index register, accumulators, and condition-code register onto the stack. This prepares the processor so that when an interrupt request occurs, the only task remaining is to load the program counter with the address of the appropriate interrupt-services routine. The second instruction, "software interrupt," saves the contents of all internal registers and loads the program counter with the address of the software interrupt-service routine. The third instruction, "return from interrupt," restores the contents of the internal processor register by pulling them off the stack. This instruction is analogous to "return from subroutine" and must be the last executable instruction in an interrupt-service routine.

The sequence of bus-read, bus-write, and internal cycles required to execute these instructions is similar to the sequence shown in Table 6-12. A major difference exists with the "return from interrupt" instruction, which essentially is the reverse process. Thus its execution consists of a sequence of pull operations representing the reverse of the sequence of push operations shown in Table 6-12.

Example 6-12 Repeat Example 6-11 for the case where the contents of 2034 are 3F, the op code for the SWI instruction. The address of the interrupt-

Table 6-13 Detailed register-transfer description for instructions to control interrupts

Instruction	Register transfers
Wait for interrupt (WAI)	$\langle PCL \rangle \to LOC \langle SP \rangle$ $\langle PCH \rangle \to LOC (\langle SP \rangle - 1)$ $\langle XL \rangle \to LOC (\langle SP \rangle - 2)$ $\langle XH \rangle \to LOC (\langle SP \rangle - 3)$ $\langle A \rangle \to LOC (\langle SP \rangle - 4)$ $\langle B \rangle \to LOC (\langle SP \rangle - 5)$ $\langle CC \rangle \to LOC (\langle SP \rangle - 6)$ $\langle SP \rangle - 7 \to SP$
Software interrupt (SWI)	$\langle PCL \rangle \to LOC \langle SP \rangle$ $\langle PCH \rangle \to LOC (\langle SP \rangle - 1)$ $\langle XL \rangle \to LOC (\langle SP \rangle - 2)$ $\langle XH \rangle \to LOC (\langle SP \rangle - 3)$ $\langle A \rangle \to LOC (\langle SP \rangle - 4)$ $\langle B \rangle \to LOC (\langle SP \rangle - 5)$ $\langle CC \rangle \to LOC (\langle SP \rangle - 6)$ $\langle SP \rangle - 7 \to SP$ $\langle LOC\ FFFA \rangle \to PCH$ $\langle LOC\ FFFB \rangle \to PCL$
Return from interrupt (RTI)	$\langle LOC(\langle SP \rangle + 1) \rangle \to CC$ $\langle LOC(\langle SP \rangle + 2) \rangle \to B$ $\langle LOC(\langle SP \rangle + 3) \rangle \to A$ $\langle LOC(\langle SP \rangle + 4) \rangle \to XH$ $\langle LOC(\langle SP \rangle + 5) \rangle \to XL$ $\langle LOC(\langle SP \rangle + 6) \rangle \to PCH$ $\langle LOC(\langle SP \rangle + 7) \rangle \to PCL$ $\langle SP \rangle + 7 \to SP$

service routine for a software interrupt is 1300, and it is stored in locations FFFA and FFFB.

SOLUTION This instruction requires 12 clock cycles for execution.

Cycle	VMA	R/W	SAB	SDB	Cycle	VMA	R/W	SAB	SDB
1	1	1	2034	3F	7	1	0	009E	67
2	1	0	00A3	35	8	1	0	009D	C2
3	1	0	00A2	20	9	1	1	FFFA	13
4	1	0	00A1	05	10	1	1	FFFB	00
5	1	0	00A0	02	11	0	*	*	*
6	1	0	009F	39	12	0	*	*	*

* Undefined.

All registers except the SP and PC, although pushed onto the stack, are unaltered. The PC contains 1300, and the SP contains 009C.

Example 6-13 Repeat Example 6-11 for the case where the contents of location of 2034 are (*a*) 39, the RTS instruction, and (*b*) 3B, the RTI instruction. The contents of certain memory locations are listed below:

Location	00A3	00A4	00A5	00A6	00A7	00A8	00A9	00AA
Contents	51	C2	73	84	95	A6	B7	C8

SOLUTION (*a*) This instruction requires five clock cycles for execution.

Cycle	VMA	R/W	SAB	SDB
1	1	1	2034	39
2	1	1	00A4	C2
3	1	1	00A5	73
4	0	*	*	*
5	0	*	*	*

* Undefined.

All registers but the PC and the SP are unchanged. The PC contains the return address pulled from the stack, C273; the SP is incremented twice to 00A5.

(*b*) This instruction requires 10 clock cycles for execution.

Cycle	VMA	R/W	SAB	SDB	Cycle	VMA	R/W	SAB	SDB
1	1	1	2034	3B	6	1	1	00A8	A6
2	1	1	00A4	C2	7	1	1	00A9	B7
3	1	1	00A5	73	8	1	1	00AA	C8
4	1	1	00A6	84	9	0	*	*	*
5	1	1	00A7	95	10	0	*	*	*

* Undefined

All registers except the SP are restored from the stack. The SP is incremented 7 times to 00AA. The contents of the other registers are

$$\langle PC \rangle = B7C8 \qquad \langle A \rangle = 84 \qquad \langle CC \rangle = C2$$

$$\langle X \rangle = 95A6 \qquad \langle B \rangle = 73$$

6-9 PROGRAM EXECUTION

Up to this point we have been considering the coding and execution of individual instructions. Now we extend these concepts to describe the coding and execution of programs containing several instructions. The approach is identical to that presented at the end of Chap. 5 except that the number of possible instructions is much greater. As an example, let us trace the execution of the program listed in Table 6-14. We shall indicate the values on the valid-memory-address line (VMA), the read-write control line (R/W), the system address bus (SAB), and the system data bus (SDB) during each cycle. We shall also define the contents of the program counter (PC), stack pointer (SP), accumulator A, data address register (DA), and the Z bit in the condition-code register after executing each instruction. When we begin, the program counter and index register contain 3002 and 2000, respectively. Table 6-15 shows the result of this analysis.

The first clock cycle (cycle 1) is a read cycle, for which the program counter provides the address, 3002. The contents of this location appear on the data bus and are transferred to the op-code register. The controller recognizes this as the op code for the instruction to load the stack pointer using the extended address-

Table 6-14 Example program

Location	Contents	Comment
:		
:		
0251	01	Data
:		
:		
08A3	02	Data
08A4	50	Data
:		
:		
3002	BE	Op code for LDS, extended mode
3003	08	High byte of address
3004	A3	Low byte of address
3005	32	Op code for PULA
3006	27	Op code for BEQ
3007	05	Address offset
3008	A7	Op code for STAA, index mode
3009	6A	Address offset
300A	44	Op code for LSRA
300B	20	Op code for BRA
300C	F9	Address offset
300D	BD	Op code for JSR, extended mode
300E	1C	High byte of address
300F	3D	Low byte of address
3010	86	Op code for LDA, immediate mode
:		
:		

Table 6-15 Sequence of bus-read, bus-write, and internal cycles for execution of the program in Table 6-14

Initially $\langle PC \rangle = 3002$ and $\langle X \rangle = 2000$

	Values during cycle				Contents after instruction executed				
Cycle	VMA	R/W	SAB	SDB	PC	SP	A	DA	Z
1	1	1	3002	BE					
2	1	1	3003	08					
3	1	1	3004	A3					
4	1	1	08A3	02					
5	1	1	08A4	50	3005	0250	*	08A4	0
6	1	1	3005	32					
7	1	1	0251	01					
8	0	*	*	*					
9	0	*	*	*	3006	0251	01	08A4	0
10	1	1	3006	27					
11	1	1	3007	05					
12	0	*	*	*					
13	0	*	*	*	3008	0251	01	08A4	0
14	1	1	3008	A7					
15	1	1	3009	6A					
16	1	0	206A	01					
17	0	*	*	*					
18	0	*	*	*					
19	0	*	*	*	300A	0251	01	206A	0
20	1	1	300A	44					
21	0	*	*	*	300B	0251	00	206A	1
22	1	1	300B	20					
23	1	1	300C	F9					
24	0	*	*	*					
25	0	*	*	*	3006	0251	00	206A	1
26	1	1	3006	27					
27	1	1	3007	05					
28	0	*	*	*					
29	0	*	*	*	300D	0251	00	206A	1
30	1	1	300D	BD					
31	1	1	300E	1C					
32	1	1	300F	3D					
33	1	0	0251	10					
34	1	0	0250	30					
35	0	*	*	*					
36	0	*	*	*					
37	0	*	*	*					
38	0	*	*	*	1C3D	024F	00	206A	1

* Undefined.

ing mode, an instruction that contains two additional bytes and requires four additional clock cycles for execution. Two of these clock cycles are required to fetch the second and third bytes in the instruction, and two are required to transfer the 2-byte operand to the 16-bit stack pointer. During cycles 2 and 3 the second and third bytes of this instruction are fetched and placed in the data address register. During cycle 4 the contents of the data address register provide the address, 08A3, to transfer the high byte of the operand, 02, to the data bus and then to the upper half of the stack pointer. Also during cycle 4 the data address register is incremented so that it contains the address of the low byte of the operand. Cycle 5 is used to transfer this value, 50, to the lower half of the stack pointer. During the execution of this instruction, the program counter was incremented 3 times to 3005, the stack pointer was loaded with 0250, and the Z bit was cleared because the 16-bit operand, 0250, was not zero. The data address register contains 08A4, the address of the lower bytes of the 16-bit operand.

In cycle 6 the controller is in its initial state; therefore the program counter provides the address, 3005, and the value on the data bus, 32 is transferred to the op-code register. The controller recognizes this as the op code for a pull A instruction, a 1-byte instruction requiring three additional cycles for execution. Since the instruction contains only 1 byte, and since only one additional bus-transfer cycle is required to transfer the operand from the stack to accumulator A, there are two internal cycles, which, according to our convention, we place after the two bus-transfer cycles. During cycle 7 the stack pointer is incremented to 0251 and then connected to the system address bus; the value on the data bus, 01, is transferred into accumulator A. Cycles 8 and 9 are internal. During the execution of this instruction, the program counter and stack pointer were incremented to 3006 and 0251, respectively; accumulator A was loaded with 01 and the Z bit was cleared because the operand, 01, was not zero.

In cycle 10 the controller is in its initial state; therefore the program counter provides the address, 3006, and the contents of this location, 27, are transferred to the op-code register. The controller recognizes this as the op code for the conditional branch instruction with the test condition $Z = 1$. This instruction contains one additional byte and requires three additional cycles for execution. One of these cycles is used to fetch the second byte of the instruction; the other two are internal cycles. During cycle 10 the second byte of the instruction, 05, representing the address offset, is fetched. Since $Z = 0$, the test condition is false and the offset is not added to the program counter. Thus the execution of this instruction simply increments the program counter twice.

In cycle 14 a new op code, A7, is transferred to the op-code register. The controller recognizes this as the op code for the instruction to store accumulator A using the indexed addressing mode, an instruction that contains one additional byte and requires five additional cycles for execution. One of these cycles is used to fetch the second byte of the instruction, one is used to transfer the contents of accumulator A to the addressed location, and three are internal cycles. During cycle 15, the program counter provides the address, the contents, 6A, of that location are transferred on the data bus and added with the value, 2000, in the index register, and the results of the addition, 206A, are placed in the data address register. During cycle 16 this register provides the address, the output of accumulator A is connected to the data bus, and the read-write control line is inactivated. This transfers 01, the contents of accumulator A, to the location 206A. During the execution of this instruction the program counter was incremented twice to 300A, the data address register was loaded with 206A, 01 was transferred to location 206A, and the Z bit was cleared since the operand, 01, was not zero.

In cycle 20 a new op code, 44, is transferred to the op-code register and is recognized as the op code for the instruction for a logical shift of the contents of accumulator A to the right. This is a 1-byte instruction, requiring one additional cycle, an internal cycle, for execution. During the execution of this instruction, the program counter was incremented once, accumulator A was shifted so that its contents changed from 01 to 00, and since the result in accumulator A had a zero value, the Z bit was set.

In cycle 22 a new op code, 20, is transferred to the op-code register. This is recognized as the op code for the unconditional branch instruction which contains one additional byte and requires three additional cycles for execution. One of these is used to fetch the second byte; the other two are internal. Cycle 23 fetches the second byte, F9, representing the address offset. Since the most significant bit is set, this represents a negative offset, so that the address of the next instruction is defined by $300B + FFF9 + 0002 = 3006$, which is placed in the program counter. This manipulation of the program counter means that the next instruction executed departs from the linear sequence of instructions in memory. All other registers are unchanged by the execution of the branch instruction.

In cycle 26 the contents of the program counter, 3006, are used as an address in transferring 27 to the op-code register. This is recognized as the conditional branch instruction with the test condition $Z = 1$. It is a 2-byte instruction requiring three additional cycles, one to fetch the second byte and two internal. Since the test condition is true, the branch will be performed. The second byte of the instruction, 05, represents a positive offset, so the address of the next instruction is defined by $3006 + 0005 + 0002 = 300D$. This value is placed in the program counter, and again the execution of this branch instruction forces a departure from the linear sequence of instructions in memory. All other registers are unaltered by this instruction.

During cycle 30 a new op code, BD, is fetched using 300D as an address. The controller recognizes this as the op code for the instruction to jump to a subroutine using the extended addressing mode. This instruction contains two additional bytes and requires eight additional cycles for execution. Two of these cycles are used to fetch the second and third bytes of the instruction, two are used to transfer the contents of the program counter, i.e., the return address, to the stack, and four are internal. During cycles 31 and 32 the program counter provides the address, and the values on the data bus are the high and low bytes of the address of the first instruction in the subroutine. During cycle 33 the stack pointer provides the address and is then decremented, the lower half of the program counter is connected to the data bus, and the read-write control line is inactive. This places 10 in location 0251. Cycle 34 is similar except that the upper half of the program counter is connected to the data bus; this transfers 30 to location 0250. Cycles 34 to 38 are internal cycles. During the execution of this instruction the program counter was loaded with 1C3D, the address of the first instruction in the subroutine, the stack pointer was decremented twice, and the return address was pushed onto the stack.

After cycle 38 the controller is in its initial state and prepared to fetch the op code of the next instruction. The contents of the program counter, 1C3D, would be placed on the address bus, and whatever appeared on the data bus would be loaded into the op-code register—but we stop our analysis at this point.

6-10 CONCLUSION

This chapter reads like a catalog and contains many important but repetitious details concerning the format and execution of 6800 instructions. We have not discussed every operation and every addressing-mode combination but have grouped the operations and discussed each addressing mode with one representative operation for the group. From this reduced treatment and with the programmer's card the reader should be able to extend the concepts to any operation with any addressing mode.

It is important to be able to understand instruction execution well enough to be able to define the sequence of bus-read and bus-write cycles required for execution. We have simplified the presentation of instruction-cycle behavior by adopting the convention that all internal cycles come at the end of execution of the instruction. This simplification helps clarify the discussion and should still allow the reader to understand the actual organization if and when it becomes important to do so. Explicit instruction-cycle organization is available in the manufacturer's literature.

PROBLEMS

6-1 In the programmer's card in Fig. 6-1 define the meaning of:
  (a) The symbols OP, ~ , and # under the heading ADDRESSING MODES
  (b) The symbols ·, ↕ , R, and S under the heading COND. CODE REG.

6-2 The contents of the program counter (PC), A accumulator, and B accumulator are 304C, 84, and 76; and the carry bit (C) is set. Indicate the contents of the program counter, the A and B accumulators and the N, Z, V, and C bits in the condition-code register after executing the following instructions:
  (a) 4F (CLRA)   (b) 40 (NEGA)   (c) 53 (COMB)
  (d) 5D (TSTB)   (e) 4C (INCA)   (f) 56 (RORB)
  (g) 59 (ROLB)   (h) 48 (ASLA)   (i) 57 (ASRB)
  (j) 44 (LRSA)

6-3 The contents of the PC, X, SP, CC, A, and B registers are 1099, 0137, 9AAC, F2, 81, and F0. The C bit is cleared. Indicate the contents of these registers after executing the following instructions:

(*a*) 43 (COMA)   (*b*) 49 (ROLA)   (*c*) 58 (ASLB)
(*d*) 50 (NEGB)   (*e*) 08 (INX)   (*f*) 31 (INS)
(*g*) 0E (CLI)   (*h*) 0D (SEC)   (*i*) 4D(TSTA)
(*j*) 40 (NEGA)

6-4 Define the values on the SAB, SDB, and the R/W and VMA lines during each cycle required to execute the instructions in Prob. 6-2.

6-5 Define the values on the SAB, SDB, and the R/W and VMA lines during each cycle required to execute the instructions in Prob. 6-3.

6-6 How many cycles are required to execute each instruction described in (1) Prob. 6-2? (2) Prob. 6-3?

6-7 Define the single 6800 instruction to increment the A accumulator, the B accumulator, the index register, stack pointer, condition-code register, and program counter.

6-8 Define the single 6800 instruction to decrement the A accumulator, B accumulator, the index register, stack pointer, condition-code register, and program counter.

6-9 The contents of accumulator A are 86, and the C bit is set. Define the contents of A and the C bit after executing each of the five 6800 instructions to shift or rotate accumulator A.

6-10 Define the general sequence of bus-read, bus-write, and internal cycles used to execute the following 6800 instructions. Use the format in Table 6-1.

(*a*) Clear A (CLRA)   (*b*) Decrement B (DECB)
(*c*) Clear overflow (CLV)   (*d*) Increment X (INX)
(*e*) Increment SP (INS)   (*f*) Rotate A right (RORA)
(*g*) Test A (TSTA)   (*h*) Negate B (NEGB)

6-11 Define the single 6800 instruction to transfer:

(*a*) The contents of A to B
(*b*) The contents of B to A
(*c*) The contents of A to the condition-code register
(*d*) The contents of the condition-code register to A
(*e*) The contents of B to the condition-code register
(*f*) The contents of A to the index register
(*g*) The contents of the index register to the stack pointer
(*h*) The contents of the stack pointer to the index register

6-12 If accumulators A and B contain 62 and 97, respectively, define the results after executing the following instructions:

(*a*) Add accumulators   (*b*) Compare accumulators
(*c*) Transfer A to B   (*d*) Transfer B to A
(*e*) Subtract accumulators

6-13 The contents of location 1024 are AA, and the C bit is set. Define the contents of this location and the C bit after executing each of the five 6800 instructions to shift or rotate this memory location.

6-14 Only two cycles are required to execute the instruction to negate A, but six or seven cycles are required to execute the instruction to negate a memory location. Discuss this difference.

6-15 In the program segment shown below the value xx in memory location C372 represents an op code. Before executing the instruction, the contents of the PC, X, A, and CC registers contain C372, 100, 9A, and A3, respectively. Indicate the contents of these registers and the contents of all manipulated addressable locations after executing the following instructions.

(*a*) $xx = 7F$ (CLR)   (*b*) $xx = 60$ (NEG)   (*c*) $xx = 6A$ (DEC)
(*d*) $xx = 78$ (ASL)   (*e*) $xx = 64$ (LSR)   (*f*) $xx = 44$ (LSRA)
(*g*) $xx = 7D$ (TST)   (*h*) $xx = 4D$ (TSTA)

Location	$\cdots$	100	101	$\cdots$	C372	C373	C374
Contents	$\cdots$	83	0F	$\cdots$	xx	01	00

6-16 Define the values of the SAB, SDB, and the R/W and VMA lines during each cycle required to execute the instruction defined in Prob. 6-15.

6-17 Define the general sequence of bus-read, bus-write, and internal cycles used to execute the following 6800 instruction with all available addressing modes. Use the format presented in Table 6-4.

   (*a*) Complement memory (COM)   (*b*) Rotate memory right (ROR)
   (*c*) Test memory (TST)   (*d*) Shift memory right (LSR)
   (*e*) Increment memory (INC)   (*f*) Increment A (INCA)

6-18 In the program segments shown below, the value xx in memory location 500 in the 6800 microprocessor represents the op code for an accumulator instruction. Before executing this instruction the contents of the program counter, A accumulator, index register, and condition-code register, are 500, 90, 2000, and C3, respectively. Indicate the contents of the program counter, the A accumulator and the condition-code register after executing the instruction.

   (*a*) xx = 86 (LDAA)   (*b*) xx = 96 (LDAA)   (*c*) xx = A6 (LDAA)
   (*d*) xx = B6 (LDAA)   (*e*) xx = 8B (ADDA)   (*f*) xx = 94 (ANDA)
   (*g*) xx = AB (ADDA)   (*h*) xx = B4 (ANDA)   (*i*) xx = B8 (EORA)
   (*j*) xx = A5 (BITA)   (*k*) xx = 98 (EORA)   (*l*) xx = 85 (BITA)
   (*m*) xx = A0 (SUBA)   (*n*) xx = B1 (CMPA)   (*o*) xx = 80 (SUBA)
   (*p*) xx = 91 (CMPA)   (*q*) xx = 9A (ORAA)   (*r*) xx = 89 (ADCA)
   (*s*) xx = BA (ORAA)   (*t*) xx = A9 (ADCA)   (*u*) xx = 82 (SBCA)
   (*v*) xx = 92 (SBCA)

Location	20	...	500	501	502	...	2020	2021
Contents	40	...	xx	20	21	...	80	73

6-19 In the program segment shown below, the value xx in memory location 1929 represents the op code for an instruction in 6800 microprocessor. Before executing this instruction the contents of the program counter, A accumulator, index register, and condition-code register are 1929, 3C, 3001, and C0. Indicate the contents of these registers and altered addressable locations after executing this instruction

   (*a*) xx = 08 (INX)   (*b*) xx = CE (LDX)   (*c*) xx = DE (LDX)
   (*d*) xx = EE (LDX)   (*e*) xx = FE (LDX)   (*f*) xx = 86 (LDAA)
   (*g*) xx = 96 (LDAA)   (*h*) xx = A6 (LDAA)   (*i*) xx = B6 (LDAA)
   (*j*) xx = 8C (CPX)   (*k*) xx = 9C (CPX)   (*l*) xx = AC (CPX)
   (*m*) xx = BC (CPX)   (*n*) xx = 20 (BRA)

Location	...	30	31	...	1929	192A	192B	192C	...	3030	3031	3032
Contents	...	10	20	...	xx	30	32	32	...	40	50	60

6-20 Define the values on the SAB, SDB, and R/W and VMA lines during each cycle required to execute the instructions described in (1) Prob. 6-18 and (2) Prob. 6-19.

6-21 Define the 6800 instructions to load:

   (*a*) The value 10 into accumulator A, accumulator B, the index register, and the stack pointer
   (*b*) The contents of location 10 into these registers
   (*c*) The contents of location 1010 into these registers

6-22 How many cycles are required to execute each instruction defined in Prob. 6-21?

6-23 Define the single 6800 instruction to add 72 to:

   (*a*) Accumulator A   (*b*) Accumulator B
   (*c*) The index register (*d*) The stack pointer
   (*e*) Location 96

6-24 How many cycles are required to execute each instruction in Prob. 6-23?

6-25 Define the general sequence of bus-read, bus-write, and internal cycles to execute the following 6800 instructions with all available addressing modes. Use a format similar to that given in Table 6-4.

    (*a*) Load A (LDAA)   (*b*) Load X (LDX)   (*c*) Load SP (LDS)
    (*d*) Store A (STAA)   (*e*) Store X (STX)   (*f*) Store SP (STS)
    (*g*) Subtract A (SUBA)   (*h*) Compare B (CMPB)   (*i*) Compare X (CMPX)
    (*j*) AND A (ANDA)

6-26 Define the single 6800 instruction that will:

    (*a*) Clear all bits except bit 0 in accumulator A without changing bit 0
    (*b*) Set bits 3 to 0 in accumulator A without changing the other 4 bits
    (*c*) Clear all bits in accumulator A
    (*d*) Set all bits in accumulator A
    (*e*) Complement bit 0 in accumulator A without changing the other bits

6-27 Define the single 6800 instruction that will:

    (*a*) Clear bits 7 to 4 in accumulator B without changing the other 4 bits
    (*b*) Set bit 5 without changing the other 7 bits
    (*c*) Set all bits in accumulator B
    (*d*) Set the even-numbered bits in accumulator B and clear the odd-numbered bits
    (*e*) Complement all bits in accumulator A except bit 7

6-28 Discuss the similarities and differences in the following groups of instructions:

    (*a*) CMPA and SUBA   (*b*) ANDA and BITA
    (*c*) CMPA, BITA, and TSTA   (*d*) ADDA and ADCA
    (*e*) SUBA and SBCA

6-29 The instructions to increment and decrement the accumulators require two cycles for execution, the corresponding instructions for the index register require four cycles, and the corresponding instructions for an addressable location require six or seven cycles. Explain these differences.

6-30 The immediate addressing mode is available on all instructions manipulating the contents of one of the accumulators and a memory location except for the store instruction. Discuss why there is no immediate addressing mode for the store A instructions.

6-31 Examine the 8-bit operation code for the instructions ADDA, ADDB, LDAA, and LDAB and determine, at least for these instructions, which bit(s) are used to distinguish register A operations from register B operations. What bit(s) are used to distinguish the four relevant addressing modes? From the bits that remain, how many unique operations (not counting register designation and addressing modes) are possible?

6-32 Indicate the contents of the program counter (PC) after executing the branch or jump instruction whose operation code is stored in Location 1155 in a 6800 microcomputer. The value in the condition code register is C5.

(*a*)
Location	1155	1156	1157	1158
Contents	20	10	2D	AB

(*b*)
Location	1155	1156	1157	1158
Contents	BD	01	53	F7

(*c*)
Location	1155	1156	1157	1158
Contents	20	FC	35	22

(*d*)
Location	1155	1156	1157	1158
Contents	2D	88	92	73

(e) Location	1155	1156	1157	1158
Contents	27	93	30	55
(f) Location	1155	1156	1157	1158
Contents	7E	90	33	AA
(g) Location	1155	1156	1157	1158
Contents	26	05	62	FE

6-33 Repeat Prob. 6-32 if the value in the condition code register is (1) EA before the branch or jump instruction is executed; (2) F0.

6-34 Define the values on the SAB, SDB, and the R/W and VMA lines during each cycle required to execute the instructions described in Prob. 6-32.

6-35 The program counter, stack pointer, and A and B accumulator contain 537C, 0092, 62, and D3, respectively and locations 0090 through 0095 contain 72, C7, 3A, 44, 6D, and A6, respectively. Define the contents of these registers and addressable locations after executing the following instruction:

(a) 32 (PULA)   (b) 36 (PSHA)   (c) 33 (PULB)
(d) 37 (PSHB)   (e) 01 (NOP)   (f) 20 D3 (BRA)
(g) 8D 92 (BSR)   (h) BD 42 C7 (JSR)

6-36 Define the value on the SAB, SDB, and R/W and VMA during each cycle required to execute the instructions defined in Prob. 6-35.

6-37 In a 6800 microcomputer system locations 0050 to 0060 contain 00 to 0F; locations FFF8 to FFFF contain 10, 00, 20, 00, 30, 00, 40, and 00 respectively; and the contents of the internal processor registers are PC = 9296, X = 01C3, SP = 0057, A = 35, B = 62, and CC = D4. Define the contents of all registers and altered addressable locations after executing the following instructions:

(a) 8D E7 (BSR)   (b) 7E 82 CD (JMP)   (c) AD 53 (JSR)
(d) 39 (RTS)   (e) 3F (SWI)   (f) 3B (RTI)
(g) 3E (WAI)   (h) 01 (NOP)

6-38 Define the value on the SAB, SDB, and R/W and VMA lines during each cycle required to execute the instructions described in Prob. 6-37.

6-39 For the conditions defined in Prob. 6-35, define the contents of all altered registers and addressable locations after the processor has responded to an active signal on the following lines:

(a) NMI   (b) IRQ   (c) RESET

6-40 Define the values on the SAB, SDB, R/W, and VMA lines during each cycle required to execute the 6800 program listed below. Also indicate the contents of all altered processor registers after each instruction is executed. Use the form shown in Table 6-15. The first executable instruction is in memory location 12.

Location	Contents	Comment
10	40	Data
11	04	Data
12	86	Op code for "load A," immediate mode
13	33	Operand
14	9B	Op code for "add to A," direct mode
15	10	Address
16	97	Op code for "store A," direct mode
17	11	Address

6-41 Repeat Prob. 6-40 for the program listed below. The first executable instruction is in memory location 800.

Location	Contents	Comment
800	86	Op code for "load A," immediate mode
801	7F	Operand
802	40	Negate A
803	97	Op code for "store A," direct mode
804	50	Address
805	7F	Op code for "clear memory," extended mode
806	01	Address
807	0E	Address

6-42 Repeat Prob. 6-40 for the program listed below. The first executable instruction is in memory location 100.

Location	Contents	Comment
FF	44	Data
100	96	Op code for "load A," direct mode
101	FF	Address
102	49	Op Code for "rotate A left"
103	2D	Op code for "branch if less than zero"
104	01	Offset
105	4F	Op code for "clear A"
106	97	Op code for "store A," direct mode
107	FF	Address

6-43 Repeat Prob. 6-40 for the program listed below. The first executable instruction is in memory location 200.

Location	Contents	Comments
200	CE	Op code for "load X," immediate mode
	FF	Operand
	FC	Operand
	6F	Op code for "clear memory," index mode
	00	Offset
	08	Op code for "increment X"
	BD	Op code for "jump to subroutine," extended mode
	06	Address
	01	Address

6-44 For the following program segments show the values on the system address bus (SAB), system data bus (SDB) and the read-write line (R/W) during each cycle and indicate the contents of all processor registers after each instruction has been executed. Use the form shown in Table 6-15. The value 35 and 87 are stored in memory locations 10 and 120, respectively. The first instruction is located in memory location FA. Mnemonics are given in parentheses by each operation code.

(a) 86 (LDAA)	(b) 96 (LDAA)	(c) 4F (CLRA)
25	10	BB (ADDA)
48 (ASLA)	47 (ASRA)	01
97 (STAA)	BA (ORAA)	20
32	01	84 (ANDA)
B4 (ANDA)	20	10
01	97 (STAA)	97 (STAA)
20	FA	50

(d) B6 (LDAA)	(e) 86 (LDAA)	(f) CE (LDX)
01	15	20
20	90 (SUBA)	00
94 (ANDA)	10	6F (CLR)
10	BA (ORAA)	00
8B (ADDA)	01	08 (INX)
05	20	6F (CLR)
B7 (STAA)	B7 (STAA)	50
01	07	DF (STX)
50	25	33

(g) 4F (CLRA)	(h) BE (LDS)	(i) 8E (LDS)
9A (ORAA)	01	10
10	20	20
80 (SUBA)	96 (LDAA)	32 (PULA)
55	10	43 (COMA)
B7 (STAA)	36 (PSHA)	36 (PSHA)
01	44 (LSRA)	40 (NEGA)
50	36 (PSHA)	36 (PSHA)

(j) 96 (LDAA)	(k) B6 (LDA)	(l) 8E (LDS)
10	01	00
26 (BNE)	20	10
02	2C (BGE)	32 (PULA)
5C (INCB)	01	8B (ADDA)
4F (CLRA)	43 (COMA)	FF
97 (STAA)	B7 (STAA)	36 (PSHA)
99	01	
	20	

(m) 8E (LDS)	(n) FE (LDX)	(o) 8E (LDS)
F0	01	01
00	20	20
96 (LDAA)	86 (LDAA)	33 (PULB)
10	56	01 (NOP)
36 (PSHA)	A7 (STAA)	96 (LDAA)
4C (INCA)	00	10
36 (PSHA)	43 (COMA)	36 (PSHA)
9F (STS)	A7 (STAA)	AF (STS)
60	01	FF

REFERENCES

See References to Chap. 5

M6800 Programming Reference Manual, Motorola, Inc., Phoenix, Ariz.
The Complete Microcomputer Data Library, Motorola, Inc., Phoenix, Ariz.

SEVEN

ASSEMBLY-LANGUAGE INSTRUCTIONS

An *assembly language* is a programming language that uses symbols in place of the binary code words in machine language. In this chapter we introduce an assembly language for the 6800 microcomputer system and discuss the conversion of an assembly-language program into an equivalent machine-language version and the analysis of assembly-language programs. After finishing this chapter readers should be able to:

1. Define the terms in Prob. 7-1
2. Write the equivalent machine-coded instruction for any assembly-language instruction
3. Translate any assembly-language program into the corresponding machine-language version
4. Define the memory requirements for any program
5. Define the number of computer clock cycles required to execute any program
6. Trace the contents of the internal processor registers and affected memory locations as any assembly-language program is executed
7. Identify the most common support programs and their purpose

7-1 ASSEMBLY LANGUAGE

An *assembly-language program* is a set of assembly-language statements that can be converted into an executable machine-language program. These statements fit into three categories: (1) *executable instructions*, equivalent to the machine-language instruction discussed in the previous chapters; (2) *data descriptors*, used to define constant values and reserve data memory locations needed in the program; and (3) *assembler directives*, used to provide information for converting the assembly-language program into a machine-language version. The form and content of these instructions, generally referred to as *syntax*, are rigidly defined. In the next three subsections we discuss the syntax used in these three types of assembly-language statements. Then we discuss the form used in arranging these statements into a program, or *program syntax*.

7-1-1 Executable Instructions

Each executable assembly-language instruction is a symbolic representation of a single machine-language instruction. Thus the assembly-language instruction must define the boolean-arithmetic operation; the addressing mode; and the operand, address, or address offset when appropriate. In addition, executable assembly-language instructions often contain a statement or comment indicating the rationale behind the instruction. Finally, it is common to assign a label, or name, to an instruction to make it easy to refer to. All this information is organized into four fields: the label, operation, operand, and comment fields. Figure 7-1 defines these fields using a highly restricted fixed format. In reality, instruction can be represented using a more variable format, the only requirement being that entries in each field be separated by a blank space. However, for ease of reading it is common to use a more restricted fixed format where entries in each field are placed with the same margins but without the precise spacing defined in Fig. 7-1.

The *label field* is used to assign a symbolic name to an instruction. Once defined, this label can be used in other instructions when referring to the labeled instruction, e.g., in a branch or jump instruction. A label may contain as many as six alphanumeric characters, but the first character must be a letter. These rules and others governing labels are summarized in Table 7-1.

The *operation field* contains a mnemonic describing the boolean-arithmetic operation specified by the instruction. Entries in this field are restricted to the mnemonics for executable instructions summarized in the programmer's card in Fig. 6-1. No other groups of characters can be used in this field in an executable instruction, but other mnemonics can be used in this field in data descriptors and assembler directives, as we shall see later (Tables 7-3 and 7-4).

The *operand field* defines both the addressing mode and the operand, the address, or the address offset. The entry in the operand field can take one of four forms: a numerical value, an ASCII code word for an alphanumeric character, a label, or a simple algebraic expression involving numerical values and labels. Numerical values can be specified using decimal, hexadecimal, octal, or binary

6 characters   4 characters   10 characters

Label field   Operation field   Operand field   Comment field

Figure 7-1 Highly restricted fixed format for executable assembly-language instructions.

Table 7-1 Rules for labels

1. Maximum number of characters is 6
2. First character must be a letter
3. No special characters or blanks allowed
4. No reserved words (that is, A, B, X, ADDA, and
   so on) can be used
5. All labels must be unique

notation. Special symbols are used to distinguish these four possibilities. Decimal values are indicated by the lack of any special symbol. Hexadecimal values are preceded by a dollar sign ($); for example, $10 is a hexadecimal value corresponding to the decimal value 16. Octal and binary values are preceded by the symbol @ and the percent sign %, respectively. Thus @10 is the octal value corresponding to the decimal value 8 and %10 is the binary value correspondiing to decimal value 2. The ASCII code word for alphanumeric characters is indicated by a pair of single quotation marks enclosing the characters. For example, 'A' in the operand field is the same as $41 since this hexadecimal value represents the ASCII code for the character A. These special symbols are defined in Table 7-2.

The addressing mode also is defined by the form of the entry in the operand field. Instructions using the inherent addressing mode require no operand, and so in an assembly-language instruction using this addressing mode, the operand field is blank. Examples of instructions using the inherent mode addressing are

INST	CLRA	CLEAR ACC A
	INX	INCREMENT INDEX

With both the extended and direct addressing modes, the instruction explicitly contains the address of the operand. In assembly-language instructions, no special symbol is used to indicate this mode, so unless a special symbol is present, entries in the operand field are interpreted as addresses. Examples of instructions

Table 7-2 Symbols used in the operand field

Symbol	Meaning
$	Hexadecimal value
@	Octal value
%	Binary value
' '	Represent the alphanumeric characters by ASCII code words
#	Immediate addressing mode
,X	Indexed addressing mode

using either extended or direct addressing modes are

INST   ADDB $1027   ADD CONTENTS OF LOC $1027

          STX   SAVE   STORE INDEX IN LOCATION SAVE

With the immediate addressing mode, the instruction explicitly contains the operand. In an assembly-language instruction, this addressing mode is indicated by the symbol #, implying that what follows is interpreted as an operand. Examples of instructions using the immediate addressing mode are

INST   ADDA   # 100   ADD DECIMAL VALUE 100 TO ACC A

          LDAA   # 'Y'   LOAD A WITH ASCII FOR Y

With the indexed addressing mode, the instruction contains the address offset relative to the index register, and the index register contains the base address. In assembly-language instructions this addressing mode is indicated by placing a comma followed by an X at the end of the operand field. This notation implies that what precedes the comma is the address offset. Examples of instructions using the indexed addressing mode are

INST   LDAB   0,X   LOAD B FROM LOC (X + 0)

          STS   1,X   STORE SP IN LOC (X + 1)

Since all branch instructions use only the relative addressing mode, no special symbol is used to indicate this mode in an assembly-language instruction. With the branch instruction, however, it is conventional to use the operand field to define the address of the next instruction that will be executed if the test condition for the branch instruction is true. The address offset for the corresponding machine-language instruction is computed during the assembly process. Examples of branch instruction using the relative addressing mode are

TEST   BEQ   NEXT   BRA TO INST LABELED NEXT

          BRA   REPEAT   BRA TO INST LABELED REPEAT

The final field in an assembly-language instruction is the *comment field*, which is used to describe the rationale of the instruction. There are no restrictions on entries in this field other than the total number of characters in the line. Additional comments can be inserted by placing an asterisk (*) at the beginning of the line, in which case the entire line is interpreted as a comment.

Example 7-1 For the following list of executable instructions identify all errors in syntax, indicate the addressing mode used in each, and define the operand, address, or address offset.

    (*a*) LABEL1   LDAA   # 50
    (*b*)   ADDA   50
    (*c*) START   CLR $3C72
    (*d*)   LDX   TABLE1

(e) AND	ANDB	#MASK2
(f)	ROL	$50,X
(g) LABEL20	STS	SAVE
(h)	STAA	#97
(i)	SUBT	$100

SOLUTION (a) Syntax correct; uses immediate addressing mode with the decimal value 50 as an operand.

(b) Syntax correct; uses direct addressing mode since the address is $0032.

(c) Syntax correct; uses extended addressing mode since the address is $3C72.

(d) Syntax correct; uses either direct or extended addressing mode depending on the value assigned to the label TABLE1.

(e) Syntax error; AND is reserved word and cannot be used as label; uses immediate addressing mode with the value assigned to MASK2 as the operand.

(f) Syntax correct; uses indexed addressing mode with an address offset of $50.

(g) Syntax error; LABEL20 contains seven characters; uses either direct or extended mode depending on value assigned to label SAVE.

(h) Syntax error; immediate-mode addressing is not valid with STAA instruction.

(i) Syntax error; SUBT is not a standard mnemonic; uses extended addressing mode.

7-1-2 Data Descriptors

Data descriptors are assembly-language statements used to define constant values and reserve memory locations needed in a program. These statements use the same form as the executable instructions with a label, operation, operand, and comment field. The rules for labels are the same as those given earlier in Table 7-1. These statements allow a programmer to reserve memory locations required by the program and to assign labels to constant values or memory locations used in executable instructions. In the data descriptor, the operation field is used to indicate the type of data description performed by the statement. Four types will

Table 7-3 Data descriptors

Mnemonic	Description	Operand field
FCB	Form constant bytes	One or more 1-byte constants
FDB	Form double bytes	One or more 2-byte constants
FCC	Form constant characters	One or more alphanumeric characters
RMB	Reserve memory bytes	Number bytes to be reserved

be discussed (Table 7-3). The operand field is used to indicate the constant values being defined or the number of memory locations being reserved.

The first data descriptor in Table 7-3 uses the mnemonic FCB, FORM CONSTANT BYTE. It is used to define constant values that are represented by 8-bit words or 1 byte. The operand field may contain a single constant or a string of constants separated by commas. These constants may be expressed as decimal, hexadecimal, octal, or binary values by using the symbols defined in Table 7-2. Two examples using this data descriptor are

DATA1   FCB $10

            FCB   10, $98, @77, %1

The first statement defines a single 1-byte constant value and assigns the label DATA1 to the address of this location. The second defines four 1-byte constant values which in hexadecimal are 0A, 98, 3F, and 01.

The second data descriptor in Table 7-3 uses the mnemonic FDB, FORM DOUBLE BYTE. It is similar to FORM CONSTANT BYTE except that it is used to define constant values represented by 16-bit words (2 bytes). An example using this data descriptor is

DATA15   FDB $725C, $A0, 1024

This statement defines three 2-byte constant values which in hexadecimal notation are 725C, 00A0, and 0200. It also assigns the label DATA15 to the address of the first.

The third data descriptor in Table 7-3 uses the mnemonic FCC, FORM CONSTANT CHARACTER. It is also similar to FORM CONSTANT BYTE except that it is used to define constant values that are ASCII code words for alphanumeric characters. Single characters or strings of characters can be defined using standard alphanumeric symbols and punctuation marks enclosed by single quotation marks. An example using this data descriptor is

MESSAG   FCC   'ERROR!'

This statement defines six ASCII code words, one for each character between the quotation marks including the exclamation point. It also assigns the label MESSAG to the address of the first.

The fourth data descriptor in Table 7-3 uses the mnemonic RMB, RESERVE MEMORY BYTE. This descriptor differs from the other three. It is used to reserve a number of memory locations. The number of locations is specified in the operand field. An example using this directive is

TABLE   RMB   100

This statement reserves 100 (decimal value) memory locations for use in the program. The address of the first of these 100 locations is assigned to the label TABLE.

7-1-3 Assembler Directives

Assembler directives are assembly-language statements used to provide information needed in converting the assembly-language program into an executable machine-language version. These statements use the same form as the executable instructions with a label and operation, operand, and comment field, although certain fields must be blank with some assembler directives. The four assembler directives we shall discuss are listed in Table 7-4.

The first, NAME PROGRAM (mnemonic NAM) is used to define the beginning of an assembly-language program and to assign a name to it. It must be the first statement in any assembly-language program. With this directive the label field must be blank, but the operand field must contain the name assigned to the program.

The second assembler directive, ORIGINATE LOCATION COUNTER (ORG), is used to define addresses that will be assigned to subsequent executable instructions or data locations. It can be used at the beginning of a program or subroutine or before a data descriptor to define their starting address explicitly. With this directive the label field must be blank and the operand field must have an entry.

The third assembler directive, END OF PROGRAM (END), is used to define the end of an assembly-language program. This directive must be the last statement in any assembly-language program. With this assembler directive both the label and operand fields must be blank.

The fourth assembler directive in this group, EQUATE (EQU), is used to assign a value to a label or to define two labels as synonyms. With this assembler directive, there must be entries in both the label and operand fields.

7-1-4 Program Syntax

In this subsection we discuss the organization, or syntax, used in grouping the three types of assembly-language statements to form a program. The program COUNTA (Table 7-5) will be used to illustrate these concepts. This program counts the number of times the ASCII code for the character A occurs in a group of words defined in the statement with the label DATA.

Table 7-4 Assembler directives

Mnemonic	Description	Comment
NAM	Name program	First statement; no label
ORG	Originate location counter	No label
END	End program	Last statement; no label
EQU	Equate label	Label required

Table 7-5 Assembly-language program COUNTA

	NAM	COUNTA	
	ORG	$50	
TALLY	RMB	1	
COUNT	RMB	1	
MASK	FCC	'A'	
NUMBER	EQU	5	
DATA	FCB	72,67,65,96,50	
	ORG	$1000	
COUNTA	CLR	TALLY	SET TALLY TO ZERO
	LDX	#DATA	PLACE ADDRESS OF FIRST IN INDEX
	LDAA	#NUMBER	GET NUMBER OF DATA WORDS
	STAA	COUNT	STORE NUMBER IN LOOP COUNTER
LOOP	BEQ	EXIT	EXIT LOOP
	LDAA	0,X	GET ONE DATA WORD
	SUBA	MASK	TEST TO SEE IF "A"
	BNE	SKIP	BRANCH IF NOT "A"
	INC	TALLY	INCREMENT TALLY IF "A"
SKIP	INX		INCREMENT ADDRESS TO NEXT ELEMENT
	DEC	COUNT	DECREMENT LOOP COUNTER
	BRA	LOOP	BRANCH TO TOP OF LOOP
EXIT	RTS		RETURN TO CALLING PROGRAM
	END		

All instructions in the program COUNTA have the correct instruction syntax. In addition, the program meets the requirement that the first and last statements be the NAM and END directives, respectively.

For ease of reading, programs generally are arranged in an orderly fashion. This orderliness includes placing the first characters in all fields directly below each other. Frequently all data descriptors are grouped at the beginning of the program with the executable instructions grouped below these statements. These features are illustrated in the program in Table 7-5. In addition it is common to assign data and machine-language executable programs to different regions of the memory space. The second statement in the program COUNTA is an ORG directive specifying that what follows is assigned to location 0050, 0051, and so on. Since the next several statements are data descriptors, these memory locations are used for data. After the last data descriptor, a second ORG directive specifies that what follows is assigned to locations 1000, 1001, and so on. Since all subsequent statements are executable instructions, these locations are used for the machine-language executable instructions.

The correct and effective use of labels is an important part of a program. Labels may be used to name an instruction, a data word, or the address of a data word. Although labels may be attached to any instruction, they are almost always used with an instruction that will be executed after a branch or jump instruction. With this convention the label appears in the operand field of the branch or jump instruction and in the label field of the instruction that will be executed after the branch or jump has been executed. The program COUNTA has four examples of the use of labels on an instruction. LOOP BEQ EXIT is paired with the third to last statement, BRA LOOP; SKIP INX is paired with the statement BNE SKIP, and EXIT RTS is paired with LOOP BEQ EXIT. With these conditional branch instructions the label in the operand field defines the instruction that will be executed next if the test condition is true. The fourth example, COUNTA CLR TALLY, does not appear to be matched with a branch or jump instruction, but the program COUNTA actually is a subroutine and in another program there is a statement JSR COUNTA or BSR COUNTA. This last example illustrates an important point: the first executable instruction in any subroutine must have a label.

Labels may be assigned to data words, and then the label can be used in the operand field of other statements in place of the code word. In the program COUNTA this is illustrated by the assembler directive NUMBER EQU 5, which assigns the decimal value 05 to the label NUMBER. Later in the program, the executable instruction, LDAA #NUMBER uses this label in its operand field. This instruction is equivalent to the statement LDAA #5, in which case the assembler directive would be superfluous. Although the approach used in COUNTA requires an extra statement, it provides a clearer explanation of the program operation and makes it easier to change the number of words in the list to be searched. Changes are easier since they are implemented by modifying the assembler directive without searching the entire program to identify all operands that must be changed. In this simple program that may not appear to be an important consideration, but in larger, more complicated programs it would be.

Labels can be assigned to addresses of data words, and then these labels can be used in the operand field of other statements in place of the address. The use of TALLY, COUNT, MASK, and DATA in the program COUNTA are examples. These labels are defined by the data descriptors and represent addresses where data words are stored. For example, TALLY represents the address where the number of A's will be totaled, MASK represents the location where the ASCII code for A is stored, and DATA represents the address of the first word in the list to be searched. These labels appear in the operand fields of instructions that operate on these locations. For example, COUNTA CLR TALLY at the beginning of the executable statements sets the contents of this location to zero at the start, and INC TALLY increments the contents of this location each time an A is identified.

The label DATA is used in a slightly different way in the instruction LDX #DATA. This program uses the index register and indexed-mode addressing to process each element in the list. In this scheme the address of the first element is placed in the index register, an element is obtained using the indexed addressing mode, and then the index register is incremented. Thus the instruction LDX #DATA uses the immediate addressing mode to place the value assigned to the label DATA, that is, the address of the first element in the list in the index register.

7-2 ASSEMBLING PROGRAMS

Assembly-language programs are not executable directly in a computer system; they must first be translated into machine language. In this section we describe a systematic, step-by-step procedure for translating an assembly-language program into an executable machine-language version. This process is called *assembling* a program, and we say that we assemble a program when we perform this translation. Simple programs can be assembled manually, but with moderately complicated programs manual assembly becomes extremely tedious and is prone to error. To overcome these problems computer manufacturers frequently supply a special computer program, called an *assembler*, that translates assembly-language programs into executable machine-language versions. In the following paragraphs we shall discuss the assembling process from the point of view of the assembler, which may be either a reader operating manually or a computer program operating automatically.

Assembling a program is done in a systematic step-by-step procedure where each statement—in fact, each field in each statement—is processed sequentially. In this process all words representing data and machine-language instructions are assigned addresses. A counter, called the *location counter*, is used by the assembler in defining these addresses. The location counter contains the address that will be assigned to the next word encountered in the assembling process. After an address is assigned, the location counter is incremented so that it contains the address of the next location. The contents of the location counter are changed when an ORG directive appears in the assembling process; the value specified in the operand field of this statement is placed in the location counter. If no ORG directive is used at the beginning of a program, the default value in the location counter is 0000.

The first step in processing an assembly-language statement is to examine the label field. If a label is present in this field, the assembler assigns a value to it. If the statement is an EQU directive, the assembler assigns the value specified in the operand field to the label. With all other types of statements the value in the location counter is assigned to the label. Thus all labels are assigned values when they occur in the label field. The label and its assigned value are then entered in the so-called *label table* or *symbol table*, used subsequently to determine the value assigned any label encountered in an operand field.

The next step is to translate the assembly-language statement into the corresponding code words and assign an address from the location counter to each code word. The nature of this translation depends on the specific mnemonic in the operation field of the statement, and we shall discuss several examples in the next few paragraphs.

The assembler directives NAM and END simply define the first and last instruction in an assembly-language program. As such, their translation does not adjust the location counter, generate any code words, or define any labels. As we discussed earlier, translating the ORG directive only loads the location counter with the value specified in the operand field. The directive EQU assigns the value in the operand field to the label contained in the directive.

With regard to data descriptors, the RMB statement assigns the current value of the location counter to its label, if present, and then adds the value in the operand field to the location counter to save the specified number of memory locations. The translation of the other three data descriptor statements, FCB, FDB, and FCC, assigns the current value in the location counter to their label, if present, generates code words corresponding to the data specified in the operand field, and assigns these code words to the addresses specified by the location counter, which is incremented once for each code word.

Translating an executable instruction assigns the current value in the location counter to the statement's label, generates the corresponding 1, 2, or 3 bytes of machine-language code words, and assigns these code words to the addresses specified by the location counter, which is incremented once for each code word. The number of bytes in the machine-language instruction depends on the arithmetic logic operation specified by the mnemonic in the operation field and on the addressing mode specified in the operand field. Once they have been determined, the number of bytes in the machine-language instruction and the first byte, i.e., the op code, are specified. The second and third bytes, if they exist, are obtained from the information in the operand field. If this field contains a numerical value or alphanumeric character, the corresponding code word is used. If the operand field contains a label, the label table will be searched to find the value assigned to the label. If the label is not in the table, i.e., if the label has not yet been defined in the assembling process, the assembler will reserve space, continue the assembling process, and return later to complete the translation after all labels have been assigned values.

7-2-1 Assembling the Program EXAMPL

Let us now consider assembling the program shown in the left-hand side of Table 7-6†; although this program does nothing useful, it makes use of several addressing modes and methods for specifying the operand. Let us now translate this program instruction by instruction. In the right-hand side of the table the resulting machine-language version is presented. Since we always express machine-language code words and the values in the location counter in hexadecimal notation, we omit the dollar sign symbol in listings of an assembled program.

The first seven statements are assembler directives or data descriptors. The first statement is the NAM directive, and its processing results in no activity; note, however, that the location counter contains the default value, 0000. The second statement, an ORG directive, adjusts the location counter to 0050. In

---

† In the remainder of this chapter we have omitted the comments in the assembly language listings for brevity. This should not mislead the reader concerning the importance of comments. In Chaps. 8, 9, and 10 we regularly use comments.

Table 7-6 Assembling subroutine EXAMPL

Assembly language			Location counter	Machine language		
				Byte 1	Byte 2	Byte 3
	NAM	EXAMPLE	0000			
	ORG	$50	0000			
ADATA	FCB	$86, $27	0050	86	27	
BDATA	RMB	3	0052			
	ORG	$F006	0055			
CDATA	FCB	$FC	F006	FC		
	ORG	$1005	F007			
INST1	CLRA		1005	4F		
INST2	INCA		1006	4C		
INST3	LDAA	#$65	1007	86	65	
INST4	LDAA	#65	1009	86	41	
INST5	LDAA	#'M'	100B	86	4D	
INST6	LDAA	#ADATA	100D	86	50	
INST7	LDAA	$65	100F	96	65	
INST8	LDAA	ADATA	1011	96	50	
INST9	LDAA	ADATA+1	1013	96	51	
INST10	LDAA	CDATA	1015	B6	F0	06
INST11	LDAA	3,X	1018	A6	03	
INST12	LDAA	ADATA,X	101A	A6	50	
	END		101C			

Label table

ADATA = 0050	INST4 = 1009	INST9 = 1013
BDATA = 0052	INST5 = 100B	INST10 = 1015
INST1 = 1005	INST6 = 100D	INST11 = 1018
INST2 = 1006	INST7 = 100F	INST12 = 101A
INST3 = 1007	INST8 = 1011	CDATA = F006

Table 7-6 we indicate the value of the location counter before the statement is translated; thus the value is 0000 before translating ORG $50 but becomes 0050 after this statement has been translated. The third statement, an FCB data descriptor, assigns the value 0050 to the label ADATA as shown in the label table at the bottom of Table 7-6. It also generates the two code words specified in the operand field, 86 and 27, assigns them to the addresses 0050 and 0051, and increments the location counter twice. The fourth statement, an RMB data descriptor, assigns the value 0052 to the label BDATA and adds 3, the value specified in the operand field, to the location counter in order to reserve three memory bytes. The resulting value in the location counter is 0055. The next statement ORG $F006, changes the location counter. Translating CDATA FCB $FC assigns the value F006 to the label CDATA, generates a code word FC, assigns it to the address F006, and increments the location counter to F007. The next statement, the third ORG directive, changes the location counter to 1005.

The next statement begins the executable instructions. The first two, with labels INST1 and INST2, use the inherent addressing mode since the operand field is blank; thus the instructions contain only 1 byte.

The op code for CLRA is 4F, and that code word is assigned to the address 1005. The location counter is incremented once to 1006. Similarly, INCA results in one code word, 4C, assigned to the address 1006. The location counter is incremented to 1007. The labels INST1 and INST2 are assigned values 1005 and 1006, respectively.

The next four statments, with the labels INST3 to INST6, use the immediate addressing mode as indicated by the special symbol (#) in the operand field. The op code for LDAA using the immediate addressing mode is 86, and the instruction contains 2 bytes. For the instruction with the label INST3 the operand field contains # $65, a hexadecimal value. Thus the second byte in the machine-language instruction will be 65. For the next instruction, the operand field contains # 65, a decimal value, which must be converted into its hexadecimal equivalent before being translated into machine language. Thus the second byte of the machine language instruction is 41. In the next instruction, the operand field contains # 'M', which represents the ASCII code for the character M. Thus the second byte in the machine-language instruction is 4D. In the next instruction, with the label INST6, the operand field contains # ADATA. Since earlier the label ADATA was assigned the value 0050, the second byte in the machine-language instruction is 50. As each instruction is translated, the location counter is incremented twice since each is a 2-byte instruction. Finally, the labels INST3, INST4, INST5, and INST5 are assigned the values, 1007, 1009, 100B, and 100D, respectively.

The next four statements, with the labels INST7 to INST10, use either the direct or extended addressing modes since the entry in the operand field contains neither of the two special symbols indicating the immediate or indexed addressing modes. The choice between the direct and extended addressing modes depends on whether the address provided in the operand field consists of 1 or 2 bytes. For the instruction with the label INST7, the address is given by the value $65, a 1-byte value. Thus the direct addressing mode is appropriate. For the LDAA instruction with the direct addressing mode, the op code is 96, and the instruction contains 2 bytes. Thus the machine code is 96 65. The instructions with the labels INST8 and INST9 are similar except that the address in the operand field is given by the label ADATA and by a function of this label, ADATA + 1. Since ADATA earlier was assigned the hexadecimal value 50, the second bytes of these two instructions are 50 and 51, respectively. As each of these three instructions is translated, the location counter is incremented twice since each contains 2 bytes. Also, the labels INST7, INST8, and INST9 are assigned values 100F, 1011, and 1013, respectively.

The instruction with the label INST10 has the label CDATA in its operand field. Since this label was assigned the value of F006, this instruction uses the extended addressing mode. The op code for the LDAA instruction with the extended addressing mode is B6, and this instruction contains 3 bytes. Thus the machine-language instruction is B6 F0 06. The location counter is incremented three times in assemblying this instruction. The label INST10 is assigned the value 1015.

The next two instructions, those with the labels INST11 and INST12, use the indexed addressing mode as indicated by the ,X in the operand field. The op code for the LDAA instruction with the indexed addressing mode is A6, and the machine-language instruction contains 2 bytes. The second byte is the address offset, which is specified by the decimal value 3 in the first case and by the label ADATA, which was assigned value 50, in the second. Thus these two instructions are translated as A6 03 and A6 50, respectively. In processing them the location counter is incremented twice. Also, the labels INST11 and INST12 are assigned the values 1018 and 101A. The last statement is the END directive, indicating the last line in the program, and so the assembly process is complete.

7-2-2 Assembling the Program YESNO

Let us now consider assembling a more realistic program. Table 7-7 shows an assembly-language subroutine to transfer a sequence of ASCII code words for either the message "YES" or the message "NO" depending on whether accumulator A has the value zero or not. This table also contains the corresponding machine code and label table generated by assembling this program. We now discuss the translation of each line into the corresponding machine-language version.

The first nine statements are either assembler directives or data descriptors. The ORG directive adjusts the location counter to 0010. The EQU directive assigns the value 8007 to the label PORTA, as shown in the label table. The third statement, YCOUNT FCB 3, assigns the current value of the location counter, 0010, to the label YCOUNT, generates a 1-byte code word, 03, corresponding to the single entry in the operand field, assigns it to the address 0010, and increments the location counter. The fourth statement, YMESS FCC 'YES', assigns the current value of the location counter, 0011, to the label YMESS. It also generates three code words, 59 45 53, corresponding to the ASCII codes for the characters Y, E, and S, assigns them to the addresses 0011 through 0013, and increases the location counter by 3. The next statement, NCOUNT FCB 2, assigns the value 0014 to the label NCOUNT and generates one code word, 02, corresponding to the entry in the operand field. It also increments the location counter. NMESS FCC 'NO' assigns the value 0015 to the label NMESS, and generates two code words, 4E and 4F, corresponding to the ASCII codes for N and O. The location counter is increased by 2. The next statement COUNT RMB 1 assigns the value 0017 to the label COUNT and increments the location counter once in order to reserve one memory location. The second ORG directive adjusts the location counter to 0500.

The next statement, YESNO TSTA, the first executable instruction, uses the inherent addressing mode since the operand field is blank. The op code for TSTA is 4D, and the corresponding machine-language instruction contains 1 byte.

Table 7-7 Assembling subroutine YESNO

Assembly language			Location counter	Machine language		
				Byte 1	Byte 2	Byte 3
	NAM	YESNO	0000			
	ORG	$10	0000			
PORTA	EQU	$8007	0010			
YCOUNT	FCB	3	0010	03		
YMESS	FCC	'YES'	0011	59	45	53
NCOUNT	FCB	2	0014	02		
NMESS	FCC	'NO'	0015	4E	4F	
COUNT	RMB	1	0017			
	ORG	$500	0018			
YESNO	TSTA		0500	4D		
	BNE	SKIP	0501	26	⑦	
	LDX	#YMESS	0503	CE	00	11
	LDAA	YCOUNT	0506	96	10	
	BRA	STORE	0508	20	⑤	
SKIP	LDX	#NMESS	050A	CE	00	15
	LDAA	NCOUNT	050D	96	14	
STORE	STAA	COUNT	050F	97	17	
REPEAT	BEQ	EXIT	0511	27	⓪B	
	LDAA	0,X	0513	A6	00	
	STAA	PORTA	0515	B7	80	07
	INX		0518	08		
	DEC	COUNT	0519	7A	00	17
	BRA	REPEAT	051C	20	Ⓕ3	
EXIT	RTS		051E	39		
	END		051F			

Label table

PORTA = 8007	NMESS = 0015	STORE = 050F
YCOUNT = 0010	COUNT = 0017	REPEAT = 0511
YMESS = 0011	YESNO = 0500	EXIT = 051E
NCOUNT = 0014	SKIP = 050A	

Translating this instruction assigns the current value in the location counter, 0500, to the label YESNO, and generates 1 byte in the machine-language program, 4D. It also increments the location counter.†

The next instruction, BNE SKIP, is a branch instruction always using the relative addressing mode. The op code is 26, and the corresponding machine-language instruction contains 2 bytes, the op code and the address offset. The

† From now on we shall not state explicitly the number of times the location counter is incremented as an executable instruction is translated.

assembly-language instruction provides this offset indirectly since the label in the operand field, SKIP, identifies the next instruction to be executed if the branch condition is true. Thus we must calculate the difference between the two locations to define the offset. This computation is further complicated since the label SKIP is undefined at this point in the assembling process. Thus the computation of the offset must be delayed. With the branch and jump instructions, it is common to find labels in the operand field that are defined later in the program. To deal with this we shall adopt the convention of simply saving space for the second byte and, with certain jump instructions, the third byte. After assembling the remainder of the program, we return and define these bytes. When we apply this convention to the translation of the BNE SKIP instruction, we see that it generates 2 bytes; the first is the op code 26; the second, shown encircled, is the offset which, although it is shown in the table, is still undefined at this point.

The next instruction, LDX #YMESS, uses the immediate addressing mode; the op code is CE, and the corresponding machine-language instruction contains 3 bytes. They are CE, the op code, and 00 11, the value assigned to the label YMESS. The LDA YCOUNT uses either the direct or the extended addressing mode, and since YCOUNT was assigned the value 0010, the direct addressing mode is chosen. The corresponding machine-language instruction contains 2 bytes, the op code, 96, and the least significant byte of the address, 10. The BRA STORE instruction has an op code of 20 and is translated into 2 bytes; using our convention, we shall define the second later.

Translating the next instruction SKIP LDX #NMESS assigns the value 050A to the label SKIP and generates a 3-byte machine-language instruction containing the op code for the LDX instruction using the immediate addressing mode, CE, and the 2-byte value assigned to the label NMESS, 00 15. The next instruction, LDA NCOUNT, uses the direct addressing mode since earlier the label NCOUNT was assigned the value 0014. The next instruction, STORE STAA COUNT, uses the direct addressing mode since earlier the label COUNT was assigned the value 0017. Translating this instruction assigns the value 050F to the label STORE and generates a 2-byte machine-language instruction containing the op code, 97, and the least significant byte of the address, 17. The next instruction, REPEAT BEQ EXIT, is a branch instruction using the relative addressing mode. Its translation assigns the value 0511 to the label REPEAT and generates a 2-byte machine-language instruction; the first is the op code, 27, and the second defines the address offset, which we shall compute later.

The next instruction, LDAA 0,X, uses the indexed addressing mode. Its translation generates a 2-byte machine-language instruction containing the op code, A6, and the address offset specified in the operand field of the assembly language instruction, 00. STAA PORTA uses the extended addressing mode since earlier the value 8007 was assigned to the label PORTA. The translation of this instruction results in 3 bytes corresponding to the op code, B7, and to the full address, 80 07. Translating the BRA REPEAT instruction generates a 2-byte machine-language instruction; the first is 20, the op code, while the second defines the offset, which will be computed later. The EXIT RTS instruction uses the inherent addressing mode. Its translation assigns the value 051E to the label EXIT and generates a 1-byte machine-language instruction containing the op code 39. The final statement is the END directive, indicating that all instructions have been translated.

Let us now return and define the second byte in the four branch instructions. As indicated in the last chapter, the address offset with the relative addressing mode may be positive, implying a branch forward, or negative, implying a branch backward. In computing the address offset we must take into account the factor of 2. To compute the offset we subtract the value assigned to the label in the operand field of the assembly-language instruction from the address assigned to the op code of the branch instruction and then subtract 2. For the first branch instruction in the program, BNE SKIP, the label SKIP was assigned 050A and the BNE op code was assigned the address 0501. Thus the offset is 050A − 0501 − 2 = 07. This subtraction is more readily done by first converting the numbers into their corresponding binary representation

$$
\begin{array}{rl}
050A \rightarrow & 0000\ 0101\ 0000\ 1010 \\
-\ 0501 \rightarrow & -\ 0000\ 0101\ 0000\ 0001 \\
\hline
& 0000\ 0000\ 0000\ 1001 \\
-\ 2 \rightarrow & -\ 0000\ 0000\ 0000\ 0010 \\
\hline
& 0000\ 0000\ 0000\ 0111 \rightarrow 07
\end{array}
$$

For the next branch instruction, BRA STORE, the label STORE was assigned the value 050F and the BRA op code was assigned the address 0508; the offset is therefore 050F − 0508 − 2 = 05. For the third branch instruction, BEQ EXIT, the label EXIT was assigned the value 051E and the op code was assigned the address 0511; thus the offset is 051E − 0511 − 2 = 0B. For the last branch instruction, BRA REPEAT, the label REPEAT was assigned the value 0511 and the op code was assigned the address 051C; thus the offset is 0511 − 051C − 2 = F3. Since this result is less obvious, the subtraction using binary numbers is shown:

$$
\begin{array}{rl}
0511 \rightarrow & 0000\ 0101\ 0001\ 0001 \\
-\ 051C \rightarrow & -\ 0000\ 0101\ 0001\ 1100 \\
\hline
& 1111\ 1111\ 1111\ 0101 \\
-\ 2 \rightarrow & -\ 0000\ 0000\ 0000\ 0010 \\
\hline
& 1111\ 1111\ 1111\ 0011 \rightarrow FFF3
\end{array}
$$

Note that the most significant byte, FF, is dropped, so that the offset is F3.

Example 7-2 Assemble the subroutine shown below.

SOLUTION

Assembly language			Location counter	Machine language		
				Byte 1	Byte 2	Byte 3
	NAM	DELAY	0000			
	ORG	$2000	0000			
DELAY	PSHA		2000	36		
	PSHB		2001	37		
	LDAA	#100	2002	86	64	
LOOPA	BEQ	EXITA	2004	27	0A	
	LDAB	#100	2006	C6	64	
LOOPB	BEQ	EXITB	2008	27	03	
	DECB		200A	5A		
	BRA	LOOPB	200B	20	FB	
EXITB	DECA		200D	4A		
	BRA	LOOPA	200E	20	F4	
EXITA	PULB		2010	33		
	PULA		2011	32		
	RTS		2012	39		
	END		2013			

7-3 PROGRAM ANALYSIS

In Sec. 7-2 we discussed assembling programs to obtain an executable machine-language program from an assembly-language version. In the present section we shall consider methods for defining (1) the amount of memory required to store a program, (2) the order in which program instructions are executed, (3) the contents of the internal processor register and addressable locations as a program is executed, and (4) the program execution time measured in clock cycles. We refer to these activities as *program analysis.*

As indicated in the previous section, we always use hexadecimal values when referring to an address, a machine-language instruction, a data word, or a label value. In the present section we also use hexadecimal values when referring to the contents of a register or addressable location. We choose this convention since these values actually represent binary words. However, when we define either the number of memory locations required to store a program or the number of computer cycles required to execute a program, we shall use a decimal value since these items are actual quantities. In short, we shall use hexadecimal values when referring to binary words interpreted as code words for addresses, instructions, or data, and we shall use decimal values when referring to a quantity, e.g., a number of memory locations or clock cycles.

7-3-1 Memory Requirements

Memory locations are required to store both the executable machine-language instructions and the binary data processed by the program. It is common to determine the subtotals for each since they generally are stored in different types of physical memory devices.

The approach for defining the number of required memory locations is simply to define the number of locations required for each assembly-language data descriptor and executable instruction and then compute the total. Since assembly-language directives do not translate into any code words, they have no memory requirements. Let us illustrate this approach by an example. The subroutine shown in Table 7-8 transfers a set of 100 (a decimal value since it defines a quantity) binary words from an input port assigned the address 8005 (a hexadecimal value since it defines an address) to a table in memory. The subroutine then transfers a string of ASCII code words corresponding to the message "DATA IN" to an output port assigned the address 8007. The last column in Table 7-8 shows the number of memory locations for each assembly-language instruction.

Table 7-8 Memory requirements for assembly-language subroutine DATA IN

	Program		Memory required
	NAM	DATAIN	0
PORT5	EQU	$8005	0
PORT7	EQU	$8007	0
	ORG	$50	0
TABLE	RMB	100	100
LENGTH	FCB	100	1
MESSAG	FCC	'DATA IN !'	9
STOP	FCB	0	1
	ORG	$1000	0 Total = 111
DATAIN	LDX	#TABLE	3
	LDAA	LENGTH	2
LOOP1	BEQ	EXIT1	2
	LDAB	PORT5	3
	STAB	0,X	2
	INX		1
	DECA		1
	BRA	LOOP1	2
EXIT1	LDX	#MESSAG	3
LOOP2	LDAA	0,X	2
	BEQ	EXIT2	2
	STAA	PORT7	3
	INX		1
	BRA	LOOP2	2
EXIT2	RTS		1
	END		0 Total = 30

The first four statements are assembler directives and require no memory locations. The data descriptor, TABLE RMB 100, requires 100 memory locations. LENGTH FCB 100 requires only one location since there is only one entry in its operand field, i.e., the hexadecimal value 64 corresponding to the decimal value 100. The directive MESSAG FCC 'DATA IN !' requires nine memory locations since the ASCII code words for nine characters, including two spaces and the exclamation point, must be stored. STOP FCB 0 requires one location to store 00. This represents all the data descriptor statements, and so a total of 111 memory locations are required for data storage.

The number of memory locations required for each executable instruction is defined by the number of bytes in the corresponding machine-language instruction. This in turn depends on the boolean-arithmetic operation and the addressing mode, as indicated in the programmer's card (Fig. 6-1). In the subroutine shown in Table 7-8, the first executable instruction, DATAIN LDX #TABLE, uses the immediate addressing mode, and the LDX instruction using this addressing mode contains 3 bytes; thus it requires three memory locations. LDAA LENGTH uses the direct addressing mode since the label LENGTH is assigned the hexadecimal value B4; thus this instruction requires two memory locations. The value B4 was obtained by adding 64 to 50. All branch instructions use the relative addressing mode and require two memory locations. LDAB PORT5 and STAA PORT7 use the extended addressing mode since the values assigned to these labels are 8005 and 8007, respectively; thus, these instructions require three memory locations. Both STAB 0,X and LOOP2 LDAA 0,X use the indexed addressing mode and require two memory locations apiece. All instructions using the inherent addressing mode, INX, DECA, and RTS, require only one memory location. The total number of memory locations for the executable instructions is 30.

Example 7-3 Define the memory requirements for the program listed in Table 7-7.

SOLUTION Eight memory locations are required for the data: one for each of the two FCB data descriptors, three for the FCC 'YES' data descriptor, two for the FCC 'NO' data descriptor, and one for the RMB 1 data descriptor.

A total of 31 memory locations are required for the executable instructions: 1 for TSTA, 2 for BNE SKIP, 3 for LDX #YMESS, 2 for LDAA YCOUNT, 2 for BRA STORE, 3 for LDX #NMESS, 2 for LDAA NCOUNT, 2 for STAA COUNT, 2 for BEQ EXIT, 2 for LDAA 0,X, 3 for STAA PORTA, 1 for INX, 3 for DEC COUNT, 2 for BRA REPEAT, and 1 for RTS.

7-3-2 Program Tracing

In this section we discuss a method for defining the order in which instructions in a program are executed and for determining the contents of the internal processor registers and affected memory locations as these instructions are executed. This procedure, called *program tracing*, is useful in identifying programming errors.

The basic procedure is to examine one instruction at a time and adjust the contents of all affected processor registers, including the condition-code register, and all affected addressable locations. The programmer's card (Fig. 6-1) contains a general description of the effect of each instruction, including its effect on each bit in the condition code register. This general information is used to define the specific effects of executing a specific instruction.

In tracing a program certain initial information must be provided. Either the contents of the program counter must be defined, or the first instruction to be executed must be identified. Frequently the contents of other internal processor registers and addressable locations are defined. As before an asterisk will mean that the contents of a register or addressable location are undefined.

When the analysis of the first instruction is complete, the next instruction to be executed is defined and the procedure repeated. Except for the branch and jump instructions, the next instruction executed always will be the next one in the assembly-language listing. For an unconditional branch or jump instruction, the next instruction executed is defined by the entry in the operand field. For conditional branch instructions, the appropriate bits in the condition-code register are examined to determine whether the test condition is true or false. If it is false, the next instruction executed will be the next one in the assembly-language listing. If it is true, the next instruction executed is defined by the entry in the operand field.

To illustrate program tracing we shall use the subroutine listed in Table 7-7. We shall begin our trace with the program counter, containing the address of the TSTA instruction, and accumulator A, containing 01. Since this subroutine manipulates accumulator A and the index register (X), we shall trace the contents of these two registers. Also, since the test condition for both conditional branch instructions is based on the Z bit, we shall trace the contents of this bit in the condition-code register. In tracing the program we shall ignore the assembled version given in Table 7-7 since the machine-language version generally is not essential for this analysis. However, it is convenient to have the translation for the data descriptors defining data and addresses. In general, if these statements are not translated, their translation is the first step in tracing a program.

Table 7-9 shows the tracing of the subroutine listed in Table 7-7. The dash is used to indicate that the contents of the register are unaltered by the execution of an instruction. The asterisk indicates undefined contents. TSTA, the first instruction executed, does not alter the contents of accumulator A, but it does clear the Z bit since the value in accumulator A is not zero. The contents of the index register are undefined.

The next instruction in the assembly-language listing, BNE SKIP, is executed next. Since branch and jump instructions alter only the program counter, there is no change in accumulator A, the index register, or the Z bit when BNE SKIP is executed. This instruction is a conditional branch instruction that will cause a branch if $Z = 0$. In this case, the test condition is true, and so the instruction with the label SKIP is executed next.

Table 7-9 Trace of subroutine in Table 7-7

Instruction			A	X	Z	Memory
YESNO	TSTA		01	*	0	
	BNE	SKIP	—	—	—	
SKIP	LDX	#NMESS	—	0015	0	
	LDAA	NCOUNT	02	—	0	
STORE	STAA	COUNT	—	—	0	02 → LOC 0017
REPEAT	BEQ	EXIT	—	—	—	
	LDAA	0,X	4E	—	0	
	STAA	PORTA	—	—	0	4E → LOC 8007
	INX		—	0016	0	
	DEC	COUNT	—	—	0	01 → LOC 0017
	BRA	REPEAT	—	—	—	
REPEAT	BEQ	EXIT	—	—	—	
	LDAA	0,X	4F	—	0	
	STAA	PORTA	—	—	0	4F → LOC 8007
	INX		—	0017	0	
	DEC	COUNT	—	—	1	00 → LOC 0017
	BRA	REPEAT	—	—	—	
REPEAT	BEQ	EXIT	—	—	—	
EXIT	RTS		—	—	—	

The instruction with label SKIP loads the index register with the value assigned to the label NMESS, that is, 0015, and it resets the Z bit since this value is not zero. Following this the next instruction in the assembly-language listing, LDAA NCOUNT, is executed; it loads accumulator A with 02, the contents of the location defined by the label NCOUNT, and again the value is not zero so the Z bit is reset. STORE STAA COUNT, the next instruction in the sequence, transfers the value in accumulator A to the location defined by the label COUNT, that is location 0017; this instruction also resets the Z bit.

The next instruction in the listing, REPEAT BEQ SKIP, has no effect on the registers we are tracing. It is a conditional branch instruction with the test condition Z = 1, which in this case is false so no branch is performed. Thus the next instruction in the listing, LDAA 0,X, is executed next.

LDAA 0,X adds the specified offset, 00, to the current contents of the index register, 0015, to obtain the address of the data. The contents of location 0015, that is, 4E, are transferred to accumulator A, and the Z bit is reset since 4E is not zero. The next instruction of the listing, STAA PORTA, transfers the contents of accumulator A to the location defined by the label PORTA, that is, location 8007; it also resets the Z bit. INX increments the contents of the index register and resets the Z bit. DEC COUNT decrements the contents of the location defined by the label COUNT, that is, 0017, and resets the Z bit.

BRA REPEAT, the next instruction in the listing, is an unconditional branch instruction and as such does not affect any of the registers we are tracing. This instruction always causes a branch, so the instruction with the label REPEAT will be executed next. Thus REPEAT BEQ EXIT, a conditional branch instruction with the test condition Z = 1, is executed next. In this case the test condition is false, so the next instruction in the listing, LDAA 0,X, is executed next.

LDAA 0,X transfers the contents of the location with the address 00 + 0016 = 0016 to accumulator A. Note that the index register was incremented after the first execution of this instruction so the second ASCII code, 4F, is transferred this time. STAA PORTA transfers this value to location 8007. The execution of INX and DEC COUNT is similar to that described earlier; except when the contents of the location defined by the label COUNT are decremented, the value becomes 00, so the Z bit is set.

The next instruction, BRA REPEAT, leaves the registers we are tracing unaltered but adjusts the program counter so the instruction with the label REPEAT will be executed next. When REPEAT BEQ EXIT is executed this time, Z = 1, so that it will cause a branch; thus the instruction with the label EXIT will be executed next. EXIT RTS returns to the calling program.

Example 7-4 Trace the execution of 10 instructions in the subroutine listed in Table 7-8 from the situation where the program counter contains the address of the LDAB PORT5 instruction. Accumulator A contains 01, accumulator B contains C3, and the index register contains 00B3.

SOLUTION Since this subroutine manipulates both accumulators and the index register, we shall trace their contents. Also, since all conditional branch instructions use the Z bit as a test condition, we shall trace its contents.

Before actually tracing the program the data descriptor statements are translated. The labels PORT5 and PORT7 are assigned the values 8005 and 8007, respectively. The RMB descriptor assigns the value 0050 to the label TABLE and reserves the address from 0050 to 00B3. The label LENGTH and MESSAG are assigned the values 00B4 and 00B5, respectively. Locations with the addresses 00B6 through 00BE contain the ASCII codes for the D, A, T, A, space, I, N, space, !.

	Instruction		A	B	X	Z	Addressable locations
	LDAB	PORT5	01	*	00B3	*	
	STAB	0,X	—	—	—	*	* → LOC 00B3
	INX		—	—	00B4	0	
	DECA		00	—	—	1	
	BRA	LOOP1	—	—	—	—	
LOOP1	BEQ	EXIT1	—	—	—	—	
EXIT1	LDX	#MESSAG	—	—	00B5	0	
AGAIN	LDAA	0,X	44	—	—	0	
	BEQ	EXIT2	—	—	—	—	
	STAA	PORT7	—	—	—	0	44 → LOC 8007

7-3-3 Execution Time

Another important analysis problem is determining the amount of time required to execute a program. Execution time frequently is specified by the number of clock cycles required to execute a program, since program execution time is obtained by multiplying the number of clock cycles by the period of the clock.

The number of clock cycles for executing a program is determined by defining the number of times each instruction is executed and the number of clock cycles required each time the instruction is executed. The programmer's card (Fig. 6-1) defines the number of clock cycles required to execute each instruction with each available addressing mode. Determining the number of times each instruction is executed is more complicated and requires an analysis of the program.

For programs containing no branch instruction, determining the number of times an instruction is executed is straightforward since each instruction is executed once. However, when a program contains a branch or jump instruction, this determination becomes more complicated since an instruction may be skipped entirely, or it may be executed repeatedly. In dealing with problems we shall consider two general program structures using branch and jump instructions, which will be discussed more formally in Chap. 8. The first of these structures involves two alternate instruction sequences, only one of which is executed. The second involves an instruction sequence which is executed repeatedly in a loop.

The subroutine in Table 7-10 is a simple example of a program containing two alternate instruction sequences. Before examining them let us define how many cycles are required to execute each instruction once. LDAA PORTA uses the extended addressing mode since the label PORTA is assigned the value C001, and so this instruction is executed in four cycles. RORA requires two cycles. All the branch instructions use four cycles. LDAA #'E' and LDAA #'O' use the immediate addressing mode, and thus each is executed in two cycles. INC ECOUNT, INC OCOUNT, and INC COUNT require six cycles each. This information is summarized in Table 7-10.

In defining the number of times each instruction is executed, we shall use the schematic diagram of the subroutine's structure shown in Fig. 7-2. The first three instructions and the last two are always executed, but in the middle are two alternate instruction sequences; the first is LDAA #'E', INC ECOUNT, and BRA CONTNU, and the second is LDAA #'O' and INC OCOUNT. To define the maximum number of cycles required to execute this subroutine, we determine which of the two alternate sequences requires more clock cycles for execution. In this example the sequence starting with LDAA #'E' requires twelve clock cycles, while the other sequence requires only eight. Thus the first would be included in computing the maximum number of clock cycles required to execute this subroutine, as shown in Table 7-10.

Table 7-11 lists a subroutine containing an instruction sequence that is executed repeatedly. Again, in defining the execution time in clock cycles, the first step is to determine the number of cycles required to execute each instruction once. The results are shown in Table 7-11.

Table 7-10 Determining execution time in a subroutine containing alternate instruction sequences

Assembly-language program			Number of cycles per execution	Number of executions	Total number of cycles
	NAM	ODDEVN	0		
	ORG	$100	0		
PORTA	EQU	C001	0		
CHAR	RMB	1	0		
ECOUNT	RMB	1	0		
OCOUNT	RMB	1	0		
COUNT	RMB	1	0		
ODDEVN	LDAA	PORTA	4	1	4
	RORA		2	1	2
	BCC	ODD	4	1	4
	LDAA	#'E'	2	1	2
	INC	ECOUNT	6	1	6
	BRA	CONTNU	4	1	4
ODD	LDAA	#'O'	2	0	0
	INC	OCOUNT	6	0	0
CONTNU	INC	COUNT	6	1	6
	RTS		5	1	5
	END		0		
Total				Total	33

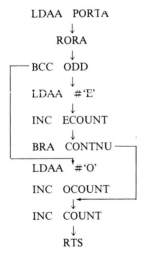

```
LDAA  PORTA
       ↓
      RORA
       ↓
 BCC  ODD
       ↓
LDAA  #'E'
       ↓
INC  ECOUNT
       ↓
BRA  CONTNU
       ↓
LDAA  #'O'
       ↓
INC  OCOUNT
       ↓
INC  COUNT
       ↓
      RTS
```

Figure 7-2 Schematic diagram showing structure of subroutine listed in Table 7-10.

242

Table 7-11 Determining execution time in a subroutine containing a loop

Assembly-language program			Number of cycles per execution	Number of executions	Total number of cycles
	NAM	MOVE	0		
	ORG	$500	0		
NUMBER	FCB	4	0		
ADDRSS	FDB	$1000	0		
PORT5	EQU	$4002	0		
COUNT	RMB	1	0		
MOVE	LDX	ADDRSS	5	1	5
	LDAA	NUMBER	4	1	4
	STAA	COUNT	5	1	5
LOOP	BEQ	EXIT	4	5	20
	LDAB	0,X	5	4	20
	STAB	$FF,X	6	4	24
	INX		4	4	16
	DEC	COUNT	6	4	24
	BRA	LOOP	4	4	16
EXIT	LDAA	#1	2	1	2
	STAA	PORT5	5	1	5
	RTS		5	1	5
	END		0		
				Total	146

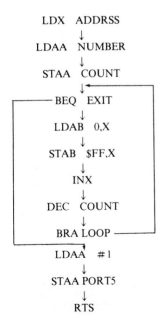

LDX   ADDRSS
↓
LDAA   NUMBER
↓
STAA   COUNT
↓
BEQ   EXIT
↓
LDAB   0,X
↓
STAB $FF,X
↓
INX
↓
DEC   COUNT
↓
BRA LOOP
LDAA   #1
↓
STAA PORT5
↓
RTS

Figure 7-3 Schematic diagram showing the structure of the subroutine listed in Table 7-11.

Figure 7-3 shows schematically the structure of the subroutine listed in Table 7-11. The first three instructions and last three instructions are executed once each time the subroutine is executed, but the instruction sequence from LOOP BEQ EXIT through BRA LOOP are executed repeatedly. We refer to this structure as a *loop*. In this loop the contents of the location with the label COUNT are used to control the number of times the loop is executed. We shall refer to this location as the *loop counter*. In this case when the loop counter contains the value 4, the sequence will be started and completed the first time; similarly when the loop counter contains 3, 2, and 1, respectively, the sequence will be started and completed the second, third and fourth times. When the loop counter contains 0, the sequence will be started, but on this iteration the instruction LOOP BEQ EXIT will cause a branch out of the loop to the instruction with the label EXIT. Thus all instruction in the sequence except LOOP BEQ EXIT will be executed 4 times as defined by the initial value in the loop counter. The first instruction in the sequence, LOOP BEQ EXIT, is executed 1 additional time, for a total of 5 times. The number of times each instruction is executed along with the total number of clock cycles required for each instruction is summarized in Table 7-11.

From this example, we can generalize the method for defining the number of times instructions contained in a loop will be executed. First there is generally a loop counter used to control the number of iterations. This counter may be a memory location or an internal processor register. Also, this counter may be

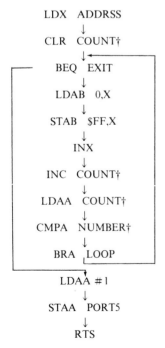

LDX   ADDRSS
↓
CLR   COUNT†
↓
BEQ   EXIT
↓
LDAB   0,X
↓
STAB $FF,X
↓
INX
↓
INC   COUNT†
↓
LDAA   COUNT†
↓
CMPA   NUMBER†
↓
BRA   LOOP
↓
LDAA #1
↓
STAA   PORT5
↓
RTS

† Modified instruction.

Figure 7-4 Schematic diagram showing an alternate structure for the subroutine shown in Fig. 7-3.

initialized to the desired number of iterations and decremented on each iteration, as in the previous example, or it may be initialized to zero and incremented on each iteration. In the first case, the looping is terminated when the loop counter reaches zero; in the second, it is terminated when the loop counter reaches the desired number of iterations.

Figure 7-4 shows the structure of a subroutine in which the counter is initialized to zero and then incremented. This subroutine performs the same function as that shown in Fig. 7-3 and listed in Table 7-11. The entire sequence of instructions in the loop is executed 4 times; the LOOP BEQ EXIT is executed 5 times. If the contents of NUMBER are changed to 10 in either program, the entire sequence will be executed 10 times with the LOOP BEQ EXIT instruction executed 1 additional time. From this we can generalize and note that the maximum value in the loop counter, whether it is initialized to it or used to terminate the looping, defines the number of times the sequence of instructions in the loop is executed. The conditional branch instruction at the beginning of the sequence is executed one extra time. Although these two structures are very common, the reader should be aware that other structures exist and that this generalization may not apply exactly in all cases.

Let us now consider a slightly more complicated example with two loops, one inside the other. Table 7-12 lists a subroutine that generates a time delay. Figure 7-5 shows the structure of this subroutine. The sequence of three instructions from BLOOP BEQ EXIT to BRA BLOOP forms a loop in which the accumulator B is the loop counter and is initialized to 100, the desired number of iterations. Thus each time this loop is entered, BLOOP BEQ BEXIT will be executed 101

Table 7-12 Determining the execution time for the subroutine DELAY1

Assembly-language program			Number of cycles per execution	Number of executions	Total number of cycles
	NAM	DELAY1	0		
	ORG	$500	0		
ACOUNT	RMB	1	0		
DELAY	CLR	ACOUNT	6	1	6
ALOOP	LDAA	ACOUNT	4	11	44
	CMPA	#10	2	11	22
	BEQ	AEXIT	4	11	44
	LDAB	#100	2	10	20
BLOOP	BEQ	BEXIT	4	10 × 101	4,040
	DECB		2	10 × 100	2,000
	BRA	BLOOP	4	10 × 100	4,000
BEXIT	INC	ACOUNT	6	10	60
	BRA	ALOOP	4	10	40
AEXIT	RTS		5	1	5
	END		0		
				Total	10,281

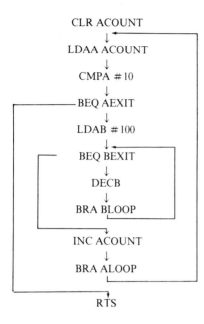

Figure 7-5 Structure of the subroutine listed in Table 7-12.

times and the other two instructions will be executed 100 times. The larger loop contains the sequence of instruction from ALOOP LDAA ACOUNT through BRA ALOOP, and it includes the inner loop. The addressable location with the label ACOUNT serves as the loop counter for the larger loop, and it is initialized to zero. The looping is terminated when the loop counter reaches 10. Thus instructions ALOOP LDAA ACOUNT through BEQ AEXIT are executed 11 times, and the remainder of the sequence is executed 10 times. This means that the inner loop will be entered 10 times so that BLOOP BEQ BEXIT will be executed $10 \times 101 = 1010$ times and DECB and BRA BLOOP will be executed $10 \times 100 = 1000$ times. This information is summarized in the right-hand side of Table 7-12.

Example 7-5 Determine the number of computer cycles required to execute the subroutine listed in Table 7-5.

SOLUTION The first two instructions are executed once. The instruction sequence LOOP1 BEQ EXIT1 to BRA LOOP1 is in a loop with the loop counter initialized to 100. Thus LOOP1 BEQ EXIT1 is executed 101 times and the rest of the instructions are executed 100 times. EXIT1 LDX #MES-SAG is executed once. The instruction sequence LOOP2 LDAA 0,X to BRA LOOP2 is in a loop with a different structure from that discussed. The sequence is started and completed until a data word of 00 occurs. When it

Table 7-13 Execution analysis

Program listing			Number of cycles per execution	Number of executions	Total number of cycles
	NAM	DATAIN	0		
PORT5	EQU	$8005	0		
PORT7	EQU	$8007	0		
	ORG	$10	0		
TABLE	RMB	100	0		
LENGTH	FCB	100	0		
MESSAG	FCC	'DATA IN !'	0		
STOP	FCB	0	0		
	ORG	$1000	0		
DATAIN	LDX	#TABLE	3	1	3
	LDAA	LENGTH	3	1	3
LOOP1	BEQ	EXIT1	4	101	404
	LDAB	PORT5	4	100	400
	STAB	0,X	6	100	600
	INX		4	100	400
	DECA		2	100	200
	BRA	LOOP1	4	100	400
EXIT1	LDX	#MESSAG	3	1	3
LOOP2	LDAA	0,X	5	10	50
	BEQ	EXIT2	4	10	40
	STAA	PORT7	5	9	45
	INX		4	9	36
	BRA	LOOP2	4	9	36
EXIT2	RTS		5	1	5
	END		0		
				Total	2625

does, the first two instructions in the sequence are executed and BEQ EXIT2 causes a branch out of the loop. The data words encountered are the ASCII codes for the nine characters in the message 'DATA IN !' and the 00 stored in the next location. Thus LOOP2 LDA 0,X and BEQ EXIT2 are executed 10 times, while STAA PORT7, INX, and BRA LOOP2 are executed 9 times. Finally RTS is executed once. This information is summarized in Table 7-13.

7-4 SPECIAL PROGRAMMING PROBLEMS

In this section we want to analyze assembly-language programs representative of two important general classes of programs. One class deals with subroutine linkage while the other class is concerned with synchronizing input and output transfers. The development of similar programs will be considered later. However,

Table 7-14 Assembling a program using subroutines

Program listing			Location counter	Machine language Byte 1	Byte 2	Byte 3
	NAM	EXAMPL	0000			
	ORG	$50	0000			
ADDRSS	FDB	$200	0050	02	00	
	ORG	$2000	0052			
	RMB	$100	2000			
STACK	EQU	$20FF	2100			
	ORG	$1000	2100			
EXAMPL	LDS	#STACK	1000	8E	20	FF
	LDX	ADDRSS	1003	DE	50	
	JSR	SUB1	1005	BD	(00)	(A0)
	JSR	SUB2	1008	BD	(00)	(A3)
	STX	ADDRSS	100B	DF	50	
HERE	BRA	HERE	100D	20	(FE)	
	ORG	$A0	100E			
SUB1	LDAA	0,X	00A0	A6	00	
RETRN1	RTS		00A2	39		
SUB2	COMA		00A3	43		
	JSR	SUB3	00A4	BD	(50)	(00)
	INX		00A7	08		
RETRN2	RTS		00A8	39		
	ORG	$5000	00A9			
SUB3	STA	0,X	5000	A7	00	
RETRN3	RTS		5002	39	—	
	END		5003			

Label table

ADDRSS = 0050	SUB1 = 00A0	RETRN2 = 00A8
STACK = 20FF	RETRN1 = 00A2	SUB3 = 5000
EXAMPL = 1000	SUB2 = 00A3 ⁻	RETRN3 = 5002
HERE = 100D		

we want to point out a few ideas in the context of assembly-language program analysis.

7-4-1 Subroutine Linkage

Table 7-14 contains a listing of a main program that in turn uses several subroutines. This program is of no practical value except for use as an illustration of subroutine linkage. We shall assemble and later trace the execution of this program. Table 7-14 also summarizes the machine code obtained by assembling this program.

The first seven instructions are assembler directives or data descriptors. ADDRSS FDB $200 assigns the value 0050 to the label ADDRSS and generates two code words, 02 and 00. The next three directives combine to reserve memory space for the stack; the 256 locations with the addresses 2000 through 20FF are reserved, and the label STACK is assigned the value 20FF.

The first executable instruction, EXAMPL LDS #STACK, assigns the value 1000 to the label EXAMPL and generates a 3-byte machine-language instruction containing the op code, 8E, and the full operand, 20FF. LDX ADDRSS generates a 2-byte machine-language instruction containing the op code, DE, and the lower byte of the address, 50. The translation of JSR SUB1 produces a 3-byte machine-language instruction containing the op code, BD, and the address of the first instruction of the subroutine SUB1. Since the label SUB1 is not yet defined in the assembling process, we simply reserve two locations and return to define their contents after assembling the remainder of the program. The next instruction, JSR SUB2, will be treated in a similar manner. STX ADDRSS is translated into 2 bytes corresponding to the op code, DF, and to the address, 50. HERE BRA HERE generates two code words corresponding to the op code, 20, and the address offset, in this case FE. During execution, this instruction will be executed repeatedly until the computer is halted by some other means, e.g., by an interrupt or a reset. This instruction is commonly used to terminate a program and prevent the computer from executing the undefined code stored in location 100E and so on.†

The next instruction, ORG $A0, resets the location counter. SUB1 LDA 0,X assigns the value 00A0 to the label SUB1 and generates a 2-byte machine-language instruction containing the op code, A6, and the address offset, 00. RETRN1 RTS generates a 1-byte machine-language instruction specifying the op code. The label on this instruction is unnecessary but is included to allow us to distinguish the RTS instructions in tracing the execution of this program later.

SUB2 COMA is the first instruction in the subroutine SUB2. It assigns the value 00A3 to the label SUB2 and generates a 1-byte machine-language instruction code. The next instruction, JSR SUB3, is treated just like the other JSR instructions; the op code, BD, is placed in the first byte, and 2 bytes are reserved for the as yet undefined address. Each of the next two instructions, INX and RETRN2 RTS generates a 1-byte machine-language instruction containing their op codes, 08 and 39, respectively.

The assembler directive ORG $5000 resets the location counter to 5000. SUB3 STA 0,X assigns the value 5000 to the label SUB3 and generates a 2-byte machine-language instruction containing the op code, A7, and the address offset, 00. RETRN3 RTS generates a single code word, its op code, 39. The END directive indicates that the entire program has been processed.

Since we have completed the entire program, let us return and fill in the code words defining the addresses in the three JSR instructions. In the first, JSR

---

† An equivalent instruction is BRA *, where the symbol * in the operand field indicates the current contents of the location counter.

SUB1, the second and third bytes become 00 A0 since that value was assigned to the label SUB1. Similarly in JSR SUB2 and JSR SUB3 the second and third bytes become 00 A3 and 50 00, respectively.

Let us now trace the execution of the program listed in Table 7-14. Since we wish to illustrate subroutine linkage with this example, we shall trace only the contents of the program counter (PC), the stack pointer (SP), and the memory space used for the stack. Before execution, the program counter must be set to 1000, the address of the first instruction in the program EXAMPL.

Table 7-15 summarizes the tracing of this program. The first instruction in the main program, EXAMPL LDS #STACK, loads the stack pointer with 20FF, the value assigned to the label STACK; the contents of the program counter are increased by 3 since this is a 3-byte instruction. Figure 7-6a shows the condition of the stack after executing this instruction. It indicates that the stack is empty and that the stack pointer contains the address of the first location assigned to the stack. LDX ADDRSS loads the index register with the value 0200 and increases the contents of the program counter by 2. The third instruction, JSR SUB1, pushes the return address, that is, 1008, onto the stack, decrements the stack pointer twice, and loads the program counter with 00A0, the address of the first instruction of the subroutine SUB1. Figure 7-6b indicates that after executing this instruction, the return address has been pushed into the upper two locations assigned to the stack and the stack pointer has the address of the next empty location.

The first instruction in the subroutine SUB1 loads accumulator A using the indexed addressing mode and increments the program counter twice. The second, and final, instruction in this subroutine, RETRN1 RTS, restores the return

Table 7-15 Tracing the program listed in Table 7-14

Program listing			PC	SP	Addressed locations
EXAMPL	LDS	#STACK	1003	20FF	
	LDX	ADDRSS	1005	—	
	JSR	SUB1	00A0	20FD	08 → LOC 20FF; 10 → LOC 20FE
SUB1	LDAA	0,X	00A2	—	
RETRN1	RTS		1008	20FF	
	JSR	SUB2	00A3	20FD	0B → LOC 20FF; 10 → LOC 20FE
SUB2	COMA		00A4	—	
	JSR	SUB3	5000	20FB	A7 → LOC 20FD; 00 → LOC 20FC
SUB3	STAA	0,X	5002	—	
RETRN3	RTS		00A7	20FD	
	INX		00A8	—	
RETRN2	RTS		100B	20FF	
	STX	ADDRSS	100D	—	
HERE	BRA	HERE	100D	20FF	
HERE	BRA	HERE	100D	20FF	

:

	20FB	*		20FB	*		20FB	*
	20FC	*		20FC	*		20FC	*
	20FD	*	SP →	20FD	*		20FD	*
	20FE	*		20FE	10		20FE	10
SP →	20FF	*		20FF	08	SP →	20FF	08

(a)   (b)   (c)

	20FB	*	SP →	20FB	*		20FB	*
	20FC	*		20FC	00		20FC	00
SP →	20FD	*		20FD	A7	SP →	20FD	A7
	20FE	10		20FE	10		20FE	10
	20FF	0B		20FF	0B		20FF	0B

(d)   (e)   (f)

	20FB	*
	20FC	00
	20FD	A7
	20FE	10
SP →	20FF	0B

(g)

* Undefined value.

Figure 7-6 Condition of stack after executing selected instruction in EXAMPL: (a) after LDS STACK, (b) after JSR SUB1, (c) after RETRN1 RTS, (d) after JSR SUB2, (e) after JSR SUB3, (f) after RETRN3 RTS, (g) after RETRN2 RTS.

address by transferring the last two entries on the stack to the program counter. In the process the stack pointer is incremented twice. Figure 7-6c indicates that after this instruction the stack is empty, and the stack pointer contains the address of the first location again.

The next instruction executed in the main program is JSR SUB2. This instruction again pushes the return address onto the stack, decrements the stack pointer twice, and loads the program counter with 00A3, the address of the first instruction in the subroutine SUB2. Figure 7-6d indicates that the upper 2 bytes of the stack contain the return address and that the stack pointer contains 20FD, the address of the next empty location.

In the subroutine SUB2, the first instruction, SUB2 COMA, complements the contents of accumulator A and increments the program counter. The second instruction in this subroutine, JSR SUB3, pushes the return address, 00A7, onto the stack, decrements the stack pointer twice, and loads the program counter with 5000, the address of the subroutine SUB3. Figure 7-6e shows the condition of the stack after executing JSR SUB3. It now contains two return addresses arranged in such a way that the return address from SUB3, the subroutine currently being executed, will be pulled first, followed by the return address from SUB2 to the main program.

In the subroutine SUB3 the first instruction stores the contents of accumulator A using the indexed addressing mode and increases the contents of the program counter by 2. The next, and final, instruction in this subroutine, RETRN3 RTS, transfers the last two entries in the stack, 00 and A7, to the program counter; the stack pointer also is incremented twice. Figure 7-6*f* shows the condition of the stack after executing RETRN3 RTS.

The next instruction executed in the subroutine SUB2 is INX. After INX the next instruction executed is RETRN2 RTS. This transfers the next two entries in the stack to the program counter and increments the stack pointer twice. Figure 7-6*g* indicates that the stack is now empty.

The next instruction executed is STX ADDRSS in the main program EXAMPL. The final instruction, HERE BRA HERE is executed over and over until the computer is interrupted by some external control.

7-4-2 Input-Output Synchronization

Data transfers between external units and the computer system are synchronized through the input and output interfaces similar to those described in Figs. 5-6 and 5-8. There are two distinct ways for implementing this synchronization: program and interrupt control. With *program-controlled input-output transfers* the program defines when a data transfer is required, repeatedly tests the appropriate interface status flip-flop until the external unit is ready, and then performs the data transfer. With *interrupt-controlled input-output transfers* the interface defines when a data transfer is possible by generating an interrupt request, and when the processor acknowledges this request, the interrupt-service routine identifies which interface generated the interrupt request and then performs the data transfer. Thus, with program-control the program initiates the data transfer; while, with interrupt control, the external unit initiates the data transfer and the interrupt-service routine performs the transfer. In general, program control is simpler to implement, and it is used when the timing specifications on the input and output data transfers are not severe. On the other hand, interrupt control is more complicated to implement, and it is used when timing specifications are severe and cannot easily be met using program control.

Let us first consider assembly-language subroutines that synchronize input and output transfers under program control. Later we shall discuss an interrupt-service routine for dealing with analogous transfers under interrupt control. In this discussion, we shall use the input and output interfaces described in Figs. 5-6 and 5-8.

The input interface has two addresses assigned to it, one for the input data buffer and one for the status flip-flop. The status flip-flop, which is set by an external signal when input data are valid, is connected to line D_0 in the system data bus and to the IRQ (maskable-interrupt-request) line in the control bus. To perform an input data transfer under program control we use the subroutine INPUT. This subroutine repeatedly tests the status flip-flop until its output equals

1, indicating that the input data are valid. The subroutine then transfers the data to accumulator A and clears the status flip-flop. We shall assume that the addresses 8001 and 8000 are assigned to the input data buffer and the status flip-flop, respectively. Input data, a 7-bit ASCII code word, will be in accumulator A when returning from this subroutine.

The output interface also has two addresses assigned to it, one for the output data register and one for the status flip-flop. Again the status flip-flop, which is set by an external signal to indicate when the external unit is ready to accept data, is connected to line D_0 of the system data bus and to the IRQ line of the control bus. To perform an output data transfer the subroutine OUTPUT repeatedly tests the status flip-flop until its output equals 1, indicating that the external unit is ready. The subroutine then stores the output data in the port data register and clears the status flip-flop. We shall assume that the addresses 8003 and 8002 are assigned to the output data register and the status flip-flop, respectively. The output data, a 7-bit ASCII code word, will be in accumulator A when this subroutine is entered. In the subroutine we shall set the eighth bit since it provides a signal indicating valid data to the external unit.

Listings for the subroutines INPUT and OUTPUT are given in Table 7-16. Let us trace the order in which instructions in the subroutine INPUT are executed and at the same time point out the rationale for some of these instructions. INPUT LDAA P1STAT transfers the contents of the status flip-flop in the input interface to accumulator A. Since only line D_0 in the system data bus is connected to the

Table 7-16 Listing of subroutines INPUT and OUTPUT

	NAM	INOUT
	NAM	INOUT
P1STAT	EQU	$8000
P1DATA	EQU	$8001
P2STAT	EQU	$8002
P2DATA	EQU	$8003
	ORG	$2100
INPUT	LDAA	P1STAT
	ANDA	#1
	BEQ	INPUT
	LDAA	P1DATA
	CLR	P1STAT
	RTS	
OUTPUT	PSHA	
TEST	LDAA	P2STAT
	ANDA	#1
	BEQ	TEST
	PULA	
	ORAA	#$80
	STAA	P2DATA
	CLR	P2STAT
	RTS	
	END	

status flip-flop, bits 1 to 7 are undefined. The ANDA #1 instruction clears all but bit 0, which contains the value transferred from the status flip-flop by the previous instruction. Execution of this instruction sets or clears the Z bit in the condition code register based on the result of the AND operation. Thus if the status flip-flop was set, Z will be 0; conversely, if it was cleared, Z will be 1. The conditional branch instruction, BEQ INPUT, causes a branch to retest the status flip flop if Z = 1, the condition indicating that input data are not yet valid. This sequence of three instructions is executed repeatedly until the status flip-flop is set by the external signal. When this occurs, BEQ INPUT will not cause a branch and LDAA P1DATA will be executed, transferring the input data to accumulator A. CLR PISTAT resets the status flip-flop in the input interface so that it is ready to receive the signal indicating that another input is present. RTS causes a return from the subroutine INPUT with input data in accumulator A.

Now let us trace the execution of the subroutine OUTPUT. This subroutine assumes that a 7-bit ASCII code word is in accumulator A when the subroutine is entered. The first instruction pushes the ASCII code word onto the stack to free accumulator A for testing the status flip-flop in the output interface. The next three instructions repeatedly test the status flip-flop in a way identical to that used in the subroutine INPUT. Once the status flip-flop is set, the instruction PULA is executed transferring the ASCII code word from the stack to accumulator A. ORAA #$80 sets the most significant bit of accumulator A without changing the ASCII code word contained in the other 7 bits. STAA P1DATA transfers the modified code word to the output data register. CLR P1STAT resets the status flip-flop, and RTS causes a return from this subroutine.

Let us now consider an assembly-language interrupt-service routine for a maskable interrupt. We shall assume that only one input and one output interface are connected to the IRQ line and that they are assigned the same port data and status address as defined above. In this scheme the external input and output unit set the status flip-flop in the interface when they are ready for a data transfer. When either status flip-flop is set, the IRQ line becomes active; and if the I bit in the processor's condition code register is cleared, the processor will acknowledge this interrupt request by saving the contents of all processor registers and then loading the program counter with the address of the maskable-interrupt-service routine. This routine sequentially examines the status flip-flops in each interface to determine which produced the interrupt. Once the interface has been identified, the appropriate data-transfer routine is executed. After completing the input transfer the data must be stored in memory because the return from interrupt will write over all the internal processor registers. Similarly, on an output transfer, the data first must be fetched from some memory location. After the requested transfer has been completed, the return-from-interrupt instruction is executed.

Table 7-17 lists the maskable-interrupt-service routine to deal with a single input and output interface. Let us trace the execution of this subroutine when an interrupt is generated by the input interface and then by the output interface. The three executable instructions, IRQSER LDAA P1STAT to BEQ NOTIN, test the status of the input interface to determine whether it generated the interrupt

Table 7-17 Listing of maskable-interrupt-service routine

	NAM	IRQSER
P1STAT	EQU	$8000
P1DATA	EQU	$8001
P2STAT	EQU	$8002
P2DATA	EQU	$8003
INLIST	EQU	* * * †
OUTLST	EQU	* * * †
	ORG	$FFF8
IRQADR	FDB	$C000
	ORG	$C000
IRQSER	LDAA	P1STAT
	ANDA	#1
	BEQ	NOTIN
	LDAA	P1DATA
	LDX	INLIST
	STAA	0,X
	INX	
	STX	INLIST
	CLR	P1STAT
	BRA	EXIT
NOTIN	LDAA	P2STAT
	ANDA	#1
	BEQ	EXIT
	LDX	OUTLST
	LDAA	0,X
	INX	
	STX	OUTLST
	ORAA	#$80
	STAA	P2DATA
	CLR	P2STAT
EXIT	RTI	
	END	

† Enter value assigned by calling program.

request. If it did, the test condition $Z = 1$ will be false and the next instruction in the sequence, LDAA P1DATA, will be executed to transfer the input data word to accumulator A. The next four instructions load the index register with the address of the location where the input data will be stored, store the data, and increment and store the address so that it is ready for the next input transfer. The location where the address is stored must be common to both the main program processing the data and the interrupt-service routine transferring the data. The next instruction in the sequence, CLR P1STAT, resets the status register so that it is ready for another transfer. BRA EXIT transfers control to the last executable instruction in the sequence to return from the interrupt.

If the interrupt request was generated by the output interface, executing the first three instructions will result in a branch to the instruction labeled NOTIN.

The next three instructions are analogous to the first three and test the status of the output interface. If its status flip-flop is set, the test condition $Z = 1$ will be false and the next instruction in the sequence will be executed. The four instructions from LDX OUTLST to STX OUTLST load the index register with the address of the output data, transfer these data to accumulator A, and increment and store the address. This procedure is analogous to that used above in dealing with the input transfer. ORAA #$80 sets the most significant bit, and then the data word is stored and the status flip-flop cleared. Finally, the return from interrupt is performed.

At the beginning of the program in Table 7-17 are several data descriptors and assembler directives. The first four simply assign values to the labels used for the port data and status addresses. The next two define the values of the labels INLIST and OUTLST for assembling the IRQSER. Before actually assembling this routine, the actual values, which we assume will be defined when the main program is assembled, must be entered. The next two statements are assembler directives to remind us that the address of the maskable-interrupt-services routine, in this case, C000, must be stored in locations FFF8 and FFF9. The next assembler directive ensures that this routine is indeed stored in this location.

7-5 SOFTWARE SUPPORT

Earlier in this chapter we described how simple assembly-language programs can be converted into machine language by translating one instruction at a time. Assembling programs in this way is tedious and becomes impossible if the program is very large. Since the assembling process is fairly routine, computer programs have been written to perform the translation into machine language. These programs, called *assemblers*, accept an assembly-language program as input data and generate the corresponding machine language as output data.

Even with an assembler there are still two major difficulties: (1) the assembly-language program must be entered into the computer for processing by the assembler, and (2) the resulting machine code must be transferred to the memory unit in the microcomputer system. There are many levels of sophistication for dealing with these difficulties, some of which will be discussed in the following paragraphs.

One approach uses standard computer cards to transfer the assembly-language program into a large computer system and a standard printer to produce a listing of the machine-language version. This approach requires a key punch, a card reader, and a printer, all standard equipment on most large general-purpose computer systems. With this approach, each line of the assembly-language program is punched on a separate card using the same instruction format described earlier. Corrections are made by adding, removing, or replacing individual cards. With this approach the printed machine-language program must still be entered manually into the memory unit of the microcomputer system using a key pad or terminal. Since this is tedious and liable to error, alternatives have been developed.

Some large computer systems have paper-tape or magnetic-tape units, and the machine-language version of the program can be stored on this medium. If the microcomputer system has the corresponding unit for reading paper or magnetic tape, the machine language can be transferred to the microcomputer's memory unit using this medium. Some large computer systems can store the machine language directly in an integrated-circuit memory element, which is then physically transferred to the microcomputer system by plugging it into the appropriate socket. Alternatively there may be a third system which transfers the machine language stored on paper or magnetic tape to an integrated-circuit memory element. Finally there are systems where large computers are connected to smaller microcomputers so that the two essentially share a common memory unit. In such systems the large computer can assemble the program storing the machine code in the common memory unit, and the microcomputer can access the same memory unit while executing the machine-language program.

Some large computer systems can be used interactively, allowing the programmer to enter the assembly-language program directly into the large computer system, thereby eliminating the computer cards. This approach requires another support program, called an *editor*, which accepts the assembly-language program as text and converts it into a form that is suitable for the assembler. In general, editors allow the user to alter a previously entered assembly-language program. If a large computer system has an editor and an assembler, and if it is interfaced with the microcomputer system, an assembly-language program can be entered, assembled, and executed easily. Errors can be corrected quickly using the editor and the revised program reassembled and executed again. This makes program development much easier.

One final support program, called a *debugger*, simplifies program development by allowing machine-coded programs to be executed instruction by instruction. The contents of the internal processor registers and any addressable location can be examined after any instruction to help define programming errors. Values in these registers or locations can also be changed to evaluate possible corrections.

Up to this point our discussion has been based on using a large computer system in developing programs for a relatively simple microcomputer system. Many microcomputer systems are sophisticated enough to run their own editor, assembler, and debugger. These *development systems* are used to develop applications programs for later execution in a computer system similar to the development system but without all the general-purpose units and the support software. Once the application program has been developed and tested in the development system, it is transferred to a scaled-down version specifically configured for the application.

In addition to the support software we have just discussed, most computer systems are supplied with another type of program, generally referred to as a *monitor*. This program resides in the memory of the system and allows the user to enter commands through a standard terminal or through a more limited special keyboard to execute development or application programs stored in the system. The monitor can also display information on the terminal or on a more limited display. Monitor programs vary in complexity from a simple program for a single-board computer with a small keyboard and display consisting of a few digits to complex programs for large computer systems with several standard terminals and other peripheral devices.

7-6 CONCLUSION

In this chapter we have described a symbolic language, assembly language, used to write programs. Although our discussion has been restricted to assembly language for the 6800, the features and concepts in this particular language are representative of many other assembly languages.

In addition to assembly language and program syntax we have presented the assembling procedure, not because you will be required to assemble programs manually but to develop an accurate understanding of the relationship between this description and machine-language programs discussed in the previous two chapters.

We also introduced assembly-language program analysis. This includes determination of program and data memory requirements, timing requirements, and program execution steps from the assembly-language description rather than the more detailed machine-language description.

Typically many programs are required to support the orderly development of effective assembly-language programs. These programs were discussed briefly.

In the next chapter we shall use assembly language in writing programs in a disciplined and systematic way.

PROBLEMS

7-1 Define each of the following terms:

executable instruction
data descriptor
assembler directive
label field
operation field
operand field
comment field
assemble a program

location counter
label table
subroutine linkage
program-controlled input-output transfers
interrupt-controlled input-output transfers
assembler program
editor program

7-2 Describe the notation used to define all addressing modes for the 6800 assembly language presented in this chapter. Describe how hexadecimal, decimal, octal, and binary values are distinguished in this language. How are ASCII character code words specified?

7-3 Indicate all syntax errors in the following assembly-language statements:

(a)	LABEL1	LDA	#50		(b)	LABEL2	LDX	#9473
(c)		LDS	32		(d)	TEST	BEQ	END
(e)		JSR	SUB		(f)		NAM	TSTCHR
(g)		ADDA	OFFSET		(h)	START	INCA	PLUS1
(i)	DATA1	FCC	32		(j)		CLR	$53
(k)	LABEL3	EQU	LABEL4		(l)	DATA2	FDB	64,72,96

(*m*)		ORG	$9999	(*n*)		ANDB	MASK1
(*o*)		BLT	EXIT	(*p*) EXIT		END	
(*q*)	ADDRESS	FDB	10,20,30	(*r*) ADD		ADDA	#3
(*s*)		ROR	#102C	(*t*) INST10		ANDB	0,X

7-4 Indicate whether the assembly-language statements in Prob. 7-3 are executable instructions, data descriptors, or assembler directives.

7-5 Indicate the addressing mode used in each statement in Prob. 7-3.

7-6 Define the hexadecimal value and the 8-bit word assigned to each label in the program segment given below. Indicate the contents of all addressable locations defined by the program segments.

(*a*)

	NAM	CONST
	ORG	$52
DATA	FCB	$62,$7A,99,10
TABLE	RMB	30
MESSAG	FCC	'ERROR 23'
ADDRES	FDB	$726A,$9C,%10,1024
	.	
	END	

(*b*)

	NAM	QCT
	ORG	$10
MESS1	FCC	'INPUT DATA?'
MESS2	FCC	'NEW SET?'
TABLE	RMB	$20
PORT1	EQU	$8000
INDEX	FDB	$90
	.	
	END	

(*c*)

	NAM	DATADO
	ORG	$105
STACK	EQU	$300F
DATA	FCB	50,51,52,53,54,55,56
YES	FCC	'YES'
NO	FCC	'NO'
TABLE	RMB	15
ADDRES	FDB	$1000,$100,$10
	.	
	END	

7-7 Assemble the following programs and complete a label table.

(*a*)

	NAM	EXCER1
	ORG	$10
DATA1	FCB	10,20,30
RESULT	RMB	3
MESS	FCC	'DONE'
	ORG	$C370
EXCER1	LDAA	#20
I2	LDAA	#DATA1
I3	LDAA	DATA1
REPEAT	LDAA	DATA1+1
I5	STAA	RESULT+2
I6	LDX	#MESS
I7	LDAA	3,X
I8	LDAA	#'Q'
I9	LDAA	MESS+3
I10	CLR	$392
	END	

(*b*)

	NAM	EXCER2
	ORG	$90
TABLE	RMB	10
INDEX	FDB	30
	ORG	$1000
DATA	FDB	$92,$72,$A3,$67,$07
RESULT	RMB	1
MESS	FCC	'ERROR'
I1	LDAA	#10
I2	LDAA	DATA
I3	LDX	DATA
I4	LDAA	2,X
I5	LDAA	DATA+3
I6	LDAA	INDEX
I7	LDX	INDEX
I8	LDX	#MESS
I9	LDAA	3,X
I10	LDAA	#'7'
I11	LDX	#$3A
	END	

```
(c)              NAM   EXCER3
                 ORG   $1072
        DATA     FCB   $3C,64,52,7,0
        START    LDAA  DATA
                 LDAA  DATA+1
                 LDX   DATA
                 LDX   #DATA
                 LDAA  2,X
                 LDAA  #'3'
                 LDAA  DATA+4
                 END
```

7-8 Indicate the addressing mode used in all executable instructions in the programs given in Prob. 7-7.

7-9 Indicate the contents of the A accumulator and the index register after executing each instruction in the programs defined in Prob. 7-7.

7-10 Assemble the following subroutines and generate a label table.

```
(a)             NAM   PROG1              (b)             NAM   PROG2
                ORG   $9020                              ORG   50
        DATA    FCB   $02,$F0,$A3                DATA    FCB   1,2,3,4
        PROG1   LDAA  #31                        PROG2   LDX   #DATA
                ANDA  DATA                               LDAB  3,X
                ADDA  DATA+1                             ADDB  DATA
                STAA  $100                              STAB  0,X
                RTS                                      RTS
                END                                      END


(c)             NAM   PROG3              (d)             NAM   PROG4
                ORG   $1000                              ORG   $9FD
        DATA    FCB   $9A,53,6,0                 MESS    FCC   'YES'
        PROG3   LDX   #DATA                      PROG4   LDS   #MESS
                LDAB  2,X                                PULB
                ANDB  1,X                                ANDB  #'Y'
                CMPB  DATA                               LDAB  MESS+1
                CLR   DATA+3                             LDX   #MESS
                RTS                                      SUBB  2,X
                END                                      RTS
                                                         END


(e)             NAM   PROG5
                ORG   $D
        D       FCC   'D'
        PROB5   LDAA  D
                LDAA  #D
                LDAA  #'D'
                RTS
                END
```

7-11 Assemble the following subroutines and generate a label table.

(*a*)
```
        NAM   TEST
        ORG   $10
PORT    EQU   $8000
DATA    FCB   $50,$60
TEST    LDAA  PORT
        BNE   SKIP1
        ADDA  DATA
        BRA   SKIP2
SKIP1   LDAA  DATA+1
SKIP2   STAA  PORT+1
        RTS
        END
```

(*b*)
```
        NAM   OVRFLW
        ORG   $00
PORT    EQU   $8002
MESS    FCC   'Z = 1'
OVRFLW  LDAA  PORT
        BEQ   SKIP
        LDX   #MESS
        LDAA  0,X
        STAA  PORT
        LDAA  1,X
        STAA  PORT
        LDAA  2,X
SKIP    RTS
        END
```

(*c*)
```
        NAM   PROCES
        ORG   $90
DATA    FCB   10,20,30
PORT    EQU   $0532
        ORG   $F370
PROCES  LDAA  PORT
        CMPA  #01
        BNE   NOT1
        LDAB  DATA
        ANDB  DATA+1
        ANDB  DATA+2
NOT1    CMPA  #02
        BNE   NOT2
        LDAB  DATA
        ORAB  DATA+1
        ORAB  DATA+2
STORE   STAB  PORT+1
NOT2    RTS
        END
```

7-12 Assemble the following subroutines and generate a label table.

(*a*)
```
        NAM   MOVLST
        ORG   $0
COUNT   RMB   1
ADDR    FDB   $100
PORTA   EQU   $8005
MOVLST  LDX   ADDR
        LDAA  #$FF
        STAA  COUNT
LOOP    BEQ   EXIT
        LDAA  0,X
        STAA  $FF,X
        INX
        DEC   COUNT
        BRA   LOOP
EXIT    CLRA
        RTS
        END
```

(*b*)
```
        NAM   OUTMES
        ORG   $4050
OUTPRT  EQU   $8002
MESS15  FCC   'ERROR 15'
        FCB   0
        LDX   #MESS15
LOOP    LDAA  0,X
        BEQ   EXIT
        STAA  OUTPRT
        INX
        BRA   LOOP
EXIT    RTS
        END
```

(c)

```
          NAM   LOADM
          ORG   $1000
LOADM  LDAA  #0
          LDX   #0
LOOP   CPX   #$FF
          BEQ   EXIT
          STAA  0,X
          INX
          INCA
          BRA   LOOP
EXIT   RTS
          END
```

7-13 Assemble the following subroutines and generate a label table.

(a)

```
          NAM   DELAY1
          ORG   $6000
DELAY1 LDAA  #100
LOOP   BEQ   EXIT
          DECA
          BRA   LOOP
EXIT   RTS
          END
```

(b)

```
          NAM   DELAY2
          ORG   $C050
DELAY2 LDX   #$100
LOOP1  BEQ   EXIT1
          LDAA  #100
LOOP2  BEQ   EXIT2
          DECA
          BRA   LOOP2
EXIT2  DEX
          BRA   LOOP1
EXIT1  RTS
          END
```

(c)

```
          NAM   DELAY3
          ORG   $6700
COUNT  RMB   1
          LDAA  #$0A
          STAA  COUNT
LOOP   BEQ   EXIT
          DEC   COUNT
          BRA   LOOP
EXIT   RTS
          END
```

7-14 The subroutine shown below adds two multiple-precision BCD-coded values. Assemble the subroutine and generate a label table.

```
          NAM   BCDADD
          ORG   0
ADDR   RMB   2
NB     EQU   8
          ORG   $1000
BCDADD LDX   ADDR
          LDAB  #NB
          CLC
NEXT   BEQ   OUT
          LDAA  NB-1,X
          ADCA  2*NB-1,X
          DAA
          STAA  3*NB-1,X
          DEX
          DECB
          BRA   NEXT
OUT    RTS
          END
```

7-15 The following subroutine searches a list of five binary words for the value 10. Assemble the subroutine and generate the label table.

```
          NAM    SRCH10
          ORG    $10
ADDR      EQU    $50
COUNT     FCB    5
          ORG    $1000
SRCH10    LDX    #ADDR
          LDAB   COUNT
BACK      LDAA   4,X
          CMPA   #10
          BEQ    FOUND
          DEX
          DECB
          BNE    BACK
FOUND     RTS
          END
```

7-16 The subroutine shown below loads the index register with the address of a message that indicates whether a binary word represents a positive, negative, or zero value. Assemble this subroutine and generate the label table.

```
          NAM    SGNTST
          ORG    $100
MNEG      FCC    'NEGATIVE'
MPOS      FCC    'POSITIVE'
MZERO     FCC    'ZERO'
          ORG    $500
SGNTST    LDAA   0,X
          BNE    SKIP1
          LDX    #MZERO
          BRA    DONE
SKIP1     BGE    SKIP2
          LDX    #MNEG
          BRA    DONE
SKIP2     LDX    #MPOS
DONE      RTS
          END
```

7-17 The subroutine given below searches a list of 50 binary words and counts the number of times the ASCII code for the character A occurs. Assemble this program and generate the label table.

```
            NAM   ACNT
            ORG   $70
LIST        RMB   50
NUMB        RMB   1
COUNT       RMB   1
ACNT        LDX   #LIST
            LDDA  #50
            STAA  COUNT
NEXT        BEQ   DONE
            LDAA  0,X
            SUBA  #'A'
            BNE   SKIP
            INC   NUMB
SKIP        INX
            DEC   COUNT
            BRA   NEXT
DONE        LDAA  NUMB
            RTS
            END
```

7-18 The subroutine given below complements each element in a list, where the first element defines the number of elements to be complemented. Assemble the subroutine and generate the label table.

```
            NAM   SEARCH
            ORG   $50
STEMP       RMB   2
COUNT       RMB   1
STACK       EQU   $102
            ORG   $1000
SEARCH      STS   STEMP
            LDS   #STACK
            PULA
            STAA  COUNT
NEXT        BEQ   DONE
            PULA
            COMA
            PSHA
            INS
            DEC   COUNT
            BRA   NEXT
DONE        LDS   STEMP
            RTS
            END
```

7-19 The following subroutine either inputs or outputs a binary word depending on the code word transferred to the subroutine. Assemble this subroutine.

```
            NAM    INOUT
            ORG    $1000
PORTA       EQU    $FF0
INOUT       LDAA   0,X
            CMPA   #0
            BEQ    SKIP
            JSR    READ
            BRA    EXIT
SKIP        BSR    WRITE
EXIT        LDAA   #2
            STAA   0,X
            RTS
READ        LDAA   PORTA
            ANDA   #1
RNEXT       BEQ    RDONE
            LDAA   PORTA
            ANDA   #1
            BRA    RNEXT
RDONE       LDAA   PORTA+1
            STAA   1,X
            RTS
WRITE       LDAA   PORTA
            ANDA   #2
WNEXT       BEQ    WDONE
            LDAA   PORTA
            ANDA   #2
            BRA    WNEXT
WDONE       LDAA   1,X
            STAA   PORTA+2
            RTS
            END
```

7-20 Define the number of memory locations required to store the executable instructions and the data for the assembly-language program in:

    (1) Prob. 7-10   (2) Prob. 7-11   (3) Prob. 7-12

    (4) Prob. 7-14   (5) Prob. 7-15   (6) Prob. 7-16

    (7) Prob. 7-17   (8) Prob. 7-18   (9) Prob. 7-19

7-21 For the assembly-language programs given in Prob. 7-10 indicate the contents of all manipulated processor registers and addressable locations after each instruction is executed.

7-22 Repeat Prob. 7-21 for the assembly-language programs given in Prob. 7-11 if, when the subroutine is executed, (1) the initial contents of the location with the label PORT are equal to 01; (2) the initial contents of PORT are equal to 00.

7-23 For the assembly-language program given in Prob. 7-12, indicate the contents of all manipulated processor registers and addressable locations after executing each instruction. Continue until the instruction BEQ EXIT has been executed twice.

7-24 For the assembly-language program given in Prob. 7-15, indicate the contents of all manipulated processor registers and addressable locations after each instruction has been executed if the contents of locations 0050 to 0054 are C5, 0A, 10, 6C, 43.

7-25 For the assembly-language program given in Prob. 7-16 indicate the contents of all manipulated processor registers and addressable locations after each instruction is executed if the input word is (a) C0, (b) 35, and (c) 00.

7-26 For the assembly-language program given in Prob. 7-17 indicate the contents of all manipulated processor registers and addressable locations after each instruction has been executed. Continue the process until the instruction BRA NEXT is executed twice. The list contains the hexadecimal values 40, 41, 42, and so on.

7-27 For the assembly-language program given in Prob. 7-18, indicate the contents of all manipulated processor registers and addressable locations after each instruction. Locations 100 to 1FF contain 00 to FF, respectively.

7-28 For the assembly-language program given in Prob. 7-19 indicate the contents of all manipulated processor registers and addressable locations for the following conditions:

(a) The input code word is AA, and PORTA and PORTA + 1 contains 01 and 02.

(b) The input code word is 00 and PORTA and PORTA + 1 contains 02 and 01.

7-29 Define the maximum number of clock cycles required to execute the subroutine(s) listed in:

(1) Prob. 7-10   (2) Prob. 7-11   (3) Prob. 7-12

7-30 Define the time delay generated by the subroutine listed in Prob. 7-13 if the clock rate is 1 MHz.

7-31 Define the maximum number of clock cycles required to execute the subroutine defined in:

(a) Prob. 7-15   (b) Prob. 7-16   (c) Prob. 7-17

(d) Prob. 7-18   (e) Prob. 7-19

7-32 The subroutine given below counts the number of negative integers in a list. Define:

(a) The contents of all manipulated processor registers and addressable locations after each instruction is executed.

(b) The execution time if the clock operates at 500 kHz.

```
           NAM    COUNTN
LOOPCT    EQU    3
DATA      FCB    $32,$F2,$43
NEGCNT    RMB    1
COUNTN    LDX    #DATA
          CLR    NEGCNT
          LDAB   #LOOPCT
LOOP      BEQ    OUT
          LDAA   0,X
          BGE    ARND
          INC    NEGCNT
ARND      INX
          BRA    LOOP
OUT       RTS
          END
```

7-33 Indicate the contents of the program counter (PC), index register (X), B accumulator, and memory locations $0, $10, $100, $1000 after the following program has been executed:

```
           NAM    PRIME
           ORG    $1000
PRIME     LDAB   #0
          LDX    #0
LOOP      STAB   0,X
          INCB
          INX
          CPX    #$100
          BNE    LOOP
          RTS
          END
```

7-34 The following subroutine examines the contents of accumulator A and stores the word in a list if it represents an even integer and disregards the word if it represents an odd integer.

(*a*) Determine the maximum number of computer cycles required to execute this subroutine for any word in A.

(*b*) If the contents of accumulator A are $8B upon entering this subroutine, indicate the contents of accumulator A, the program counter (PC), the index register (X), the C bit (carry bit), and the N bit (negative bit) in the condition code register after executing each instruction.

```
          NAM   EVEN
          ORG   $2000
TEMP  FCB   0
EVEN  STAA  TEMP
          ASRA
          BCS   ODD
          LDAA  TEMP
          STAA  0,X
          INX
ODD   CLRA
          RTS
          END
```

7-35 The subroutine given below loads specific memory locations with certain values.

(*a*) Define the contents of both accumulators and the index register after the instruction labeled EXIT1 is executed the first, second, and last time.

(*b*) Define the contents of both accumulators and the index register after the instruction labeled EXIT2 is executed the first, second, and last time.

```
            NAM    PRIMEM
            ORG    $300
PRIMEM  LDS    #$400
            LDX    #$0
            LDAA   #2
            LDAB   #0
LOOP1   BEQ    EXIT1
LOOP2   BEQ    EXIT2
            STAB   0,X
            INX
            INCB
            CMPB   #$FF
            BRA    LOOP2
EXIT2   LDAB   #0
            DECA
            BRA    LOOP1
EXIT1   SWI
            END
```

7-36 For the subroutine given in Prob. 7-35, define:

(*a*) The contents of the two accumulators, index register, program counter, and stack pointer just before the instruction EXIT1 SWI is executed.

(*b*) The contents of the two accumulators, index register, program counter, and stack pointer after executing the entire program.

(*c*) The contents of locations $0000, $0001, $0010, $0100, $0200, $0300, and $0400 after executing the entire program.

7-37 For the subroutine given below define:
(a) The number of memory locations required to store the executable instructions and the data.
(b) The maximum number of computer cycles required for execution.

```
        NAM    LISTS
        ORG    $5000
TABLE   RMB    50
        ORG    $60
LGTH    EQU    50
POS     FCC    'P'
LISTS   LDX    #TABLE
        LDAB   #LGTH
NEXT    BEQ    DONE
        JSR    TEST
        INX
        DECB
        BRA    NEXT
DONE    RTS
        ORG    $1000
TEST    LDAA   0,X
        BMI    SKIP
        LDAA   POS
        BRA    STORE
SKIP    LDAA   #'N'
STORE   STAA   LGTH,X
        RTS
        END
```

7-38 For the subroutine given in Prob. 7-37, indicate the contents of the program counter, index register, stack pointer and A accumulator after executing each instruction until the instruction BRA NEXT has been executed twice. At the start of this subroutine the stack pointer contains 0050. The data in the table are 7C, FC, 60, 49....

7-39 Assemble the subroutine given in Prob. 7-37 and generate a label table.

7-40 Assemble the following subroutine:

```
            NAM    ADDLST
            ORG    $10
TABLE       RMB    50
SUM         RMB    1
COUNT       RMB    1
INPUT       EQU    $8700
OUTPUT      EQU    $8702
            ORG    $100
ADDLST      LDX    #TABLE
NEXT        LDAA   INPUT
LOOP        BNE    EXIT
            LDAA   INPUT
            BRA    LOOP
EXIT        CMPA   #'Y'
            BNE    SKIP
            JSR    YSUB
            BRA    DONE
SKIP        CMPA   #'N'
            BNE    DONE
            JSR    NSUB
DONE        RTS
            ORG    $800
NSUB        LDAB   SUM
            STAB   0,X
            ADDB   SUM
            STAB   1,X
            INC    COUNT
            RTS
YSUB        LDAB   SUM
            STAB   OUTPUT
            RTS
            END
```

7-41 For the subroutine given in Prob. 7-40, define:
  (a) The number of memory locations required to store the executable instructions and the data
  (b) The maximum number of clock cycles required to execute this subroutine
  (c) The minimum number of clock cycles required to execute this subroutine
  (d) The maximum number of clock cycles if the contents of INPUT are nonzero

7-42 For the subroutine given in Prob. 7-40, indicate the contents of the A accumulator, program counter, index register, and stack pointer after executing each instruction when the contents of the stack pointer are 00F0, the contents of SUM are 3A, and the contents of INPUT are (a) 59, (b) 49, (c) 4E, and (d) 01.

REFERENCES

Bishop, R.: "Basic Microprocessors and the 6800," Hayden, Rochelle, N.J., 1979.
Leventhal, L.: "6800 Assembly Language Programming," Osborne Associates, Berkeley, Calif., 1978.
_____ : "Introduction to Microprocessors: Software, Hardware, Programming," Prentice-Hall, Englewood Cliffs, N.J., 1978.
Motorola Staff: "M6800 Microprocessor Programming Manual," Motorola Inc., Phoenix, Ariz., 1976.

CHAPTER
EIGHT

WRITING PROGRAMS

In this chapter, we introduce the use of flowcharts as diagrammatic representations of programs and consider their use in developing an assembly-language program from a verbal program specification. After finishing this chapter the reader should be able to:

1. Define the terms in Prob. 8-1
2. Describe the order in which tasks in a flowchart description of a structured program are executed
3. Translate a flowchart description of a structured program into a sequence of assembly-language instructions, data descriptors, and assembler directives
4. Write structured programs from the verbal specification of a problem of limited complexity

8-1 FLOWCHARTS

The previous chapter discussed several assembly-language programs. In these programs some instructions manipulated data, for example, ADDA VALUE, while others controlled the order in which other instructions were executed, for example, BEQ SKIP. We used a schematic diagram, e.g., Fig. 7-2, to describe concisely how these two types of instructions interact to define the sequence in which instructions are executed. These diagrams define the "flow" of the program, and when they are made more pictorial they are called *flowcharts*.

In this section, we describe three elements used in flowcharts and define three of their basic configurations, called *structural units*. These structural units form the building blocks for all structured flowcharts.

8-1-1 Flowchart Elements

The three flowchart elements are the terminal, task, and decision elements, the symbols for each of which is shown in Fig. 8-1.

Terminal elements (Fig. 8-1a) are used to define the beginning and end of a flowchart. At the beginning of a flowchart the name of the program is placed in the terminal element. The last element contains END if the flowchart represents a main program or RETURN if the flowchart represents a subroutine or an interrupt-service routine.

The *task element* (Fig. 8-1b) represents some definable activity indicated by a representative name or a description of the activity written in the rectangle. This activity may be complicated, requiring many assembly-language instructions, e.g., ORDER THE LIST OF NUMBERS, or it may be a simple task requiring only a single assembly-language instruction, e.g., STORE A IN RESULT. Later we shall see how complicated tasks can be considered as subroutines and implemented as such.

The final flowchart element, the *decision element* (Fig. 8-1c) is symbolized by a diamond with a single input path and two output paths. The choice between the output paths is based upon an evaluation of the logical proposition specified in the diamond. Since this is a logical proposition, it must be either true or false and each of these possibilities is associated with one of the output paths. This element is used to define a logical decision that is made during program execution.

8-1-2 Basic Structural Units

The task and decision flowchart elements can be connected in many ways to form many different configurations, but to produce programs that are more likely to be

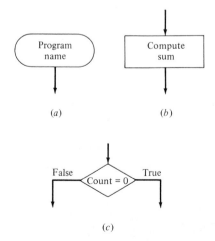

Figure 8-1 Three flowchart elements: (*a*) terminal element, (*b*) task element, and (*c*) decision element.

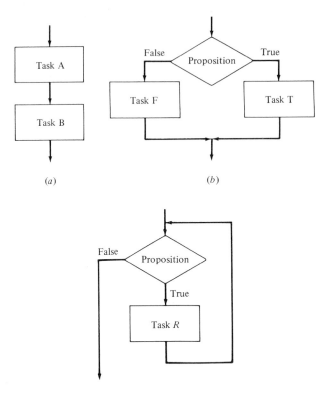

Figure 8-2 Three basic structural units: (*a*) sequential task, (*b*) alternative task, and (*c*) repeated task.

correct and more easily understood it is common to use only the three arrangements shown in Fig. 8-2.

The *sequential-task structural unit* (Fig. 8-2*a*) represents a subroutine or task followed sequentially in time by a second subroutine or task. The *alternative-task structural unit* (Fig. 8-2*b*) contains a decision element causing the single execution of one of two alternative tasks or subroutines. This structural unit also is called an IF THEN ELSE unit because its operation is defined by the statement "IF the specified proposition is true, THEN do task T, or ELSE do task F."

The *repeated-task structural unit*, or loop (Fig. 8-2*c*) also contains a decision element causing a single task or subroutine to be performed repeatedly while the specified proposition is true. The condition tested by the proposition must be altered during the repeated task in order to produce an exit. This structural unit is also referred to as a DO WHILE unit because its operation is defined by the statement "DO task R WHILE the specified proposition is true."

These three configurations are referred to as basic structural units because they are the building blocks used in constructing program flowcharts. They form a complete set, and any program can be defined by appropriate combinations of them. These three structural units have many advantages, one of the most important being their single input and single output paths. This feature facilitates the verification and modification of programs since each structural unit can be developed, exercised, and tested by itself, or it can be replaced in total without altering the remaining elements. When a flowchart for a program contains combinations of only the three basic structural units, it is called a *structured flowchart* and the corresponding program is called a *structured program*.

Example 8-1 Translate the sequence diagram of Fig. 7-3 into a structured flowchart. Show the proposition so that the convention of branching false is maintained.

SOLUTION The flowchart is shown in Fig. E8-1.

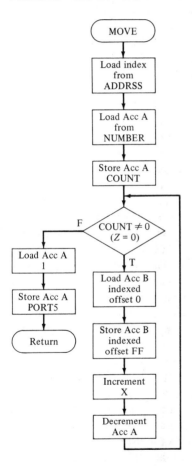

Figure E8-1 Solution flowchart.

8-2 THE SUBSTITUTION PROCESS

In the three basic structural units, various tasks may represent simple activities that can be implemented by a single assembly-language instruction or extremely complicated activities best defined as a subroutine. Between these two extremes there are tasks which can be implemented using several assembly-language instructions. It is often convenient to redraw the flowchart so that the complicated task is replaced by a set of simpler tasks that can be implemented by a single assembly-language instruction. This procedure of replacing a single task by a set of simpler tasks defined in one of the three basic structural units is referred to as the *substitution process*; it is the procedure we shall use in developing programs.

In Fig. 8-3c the PROCESS WORD AND INCREMENT COUNT task has been subdivided into three additional units, a GET WORD task, followed by an alternative-task structural unit and the INCREMENT COUNT task. In the alternative-task structural unit, the logical proposition tested to define which pathway is chosen is WORD < 0. If this proposition is true, the right-hand task, which negates and stores the modified word in its original location, is selected. If the proposition is false, the left-hand task, which in this case consists of no activity, is selected.

As an example, in Fig. 8-3b the PROCESS LIST task is subdivided into a sequential task, INITIALIZE COUNT, followed by a repeated-task structural unit in which the list is processed word by word. In the repeated task the logical proposition tested on each repetition is COUNT < LENGTH, where LENGTH defines the number of words in the list and COUNT defines the number of repetitions completed or the number of words processed. If this proposition is true, a word is processed and COUNT is incremented; if it is false, the flow continues from the repeated-task structural unit to the next task, OUTPUT LIST.

In Fig. 8-3c the PROCESS WORD AND INCREMENT COUNT task has been subdivided into three additional units, a GET WORD task, followed by an alternative-task structural unit and the INCREMENT COUNT task. In the alternative-task structural unit, the logical proposition tested to define which pathway is chosen is WORD < 0. If this proposition is true, the right-hand task, which negates and stores the modified word in its original location, is selected. If the proposition is false, the left-hand task, which in this case consists of no activity, is selected.

In general, with a complicated program many substitution steps are required to obtain tasks that can be implemented by single assembly-language instructions. However, this substitution process generally is terminated when the modified flowchart fills a single page of paper. This limit is maintained because a single-page description is easier to read and understand than a multipage description requiring the reader to turn a page while trying to remember the logical flow. In this convention, once a page is filled, all remaining complicated tasks are defined as subroutines, and each subroutine is expanded on a separate page. For example, if we wish to expand the description of the INPUT LIST task in Fig. 8-3c, instead of adding details to the present page, we can define the task INPUT LIST as a subroutine. When a task is defined as a subroutine, a new symbol is used for the task in the flowchart, as shown in Fig. 8-3c for the INPUT LIST and OUTPUT LIST tasks.

All subroutine descriptions are begun on a new page. The flowchart is started with a terminal element containing the name of the subroutine, e.g., INPUT LIST. All are terminated with a terminal element containing RETURN. The detailed tasks

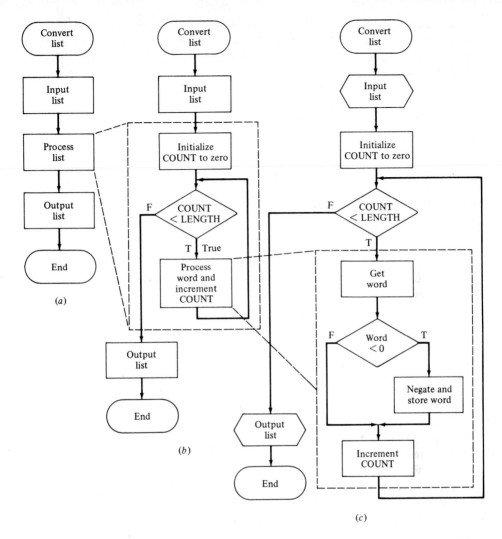

Figure 8-3 Flowchart development for a program to input a list of words, convert them into positive numbers, and output them: (*a*) initial, (*b*) intermediate, and (*c*) final program description.

in between are defined by the substitution process just as we did in expanding the PROCESS LIST task above. The expansion of each subroutine continues only until the description fills the new page. If further expansion is required, tasks from the second page requiring added detail are identified as subroutines, and a new page is begun for each task requiring additional development. This process of creating new pages is repeated as often as necessary. Assembly-language implementation of the program described in a single flowchart will include instructions to implement the tasks defined as rectangles and will include a subroutine calling sequence for the tasks defined as subroutines.

The substitution process is called *top down* when the first page defines the complete program, albeit in limited detail. Consequently, the first page is called a *top-level description*. Thus, the description in Fig. 8-3c represents a top-level description for the CONVERT LIST program. A *second-level description* represents an expansion of a subroutine found in the top level; a *third-level description* represents a subroutine found in a second level, and so on. In this scheme there is only one top-level description, while there typically will be many pages of descriptions for each subsequent level. Additional examples of the top-down substitution process will be given later in this chapter.

Example 8-2 Develop a second-level flowchart for the task UPDATE TIME VALUES found in the top-level flowchart for the program 12-HOUR CLOCK in

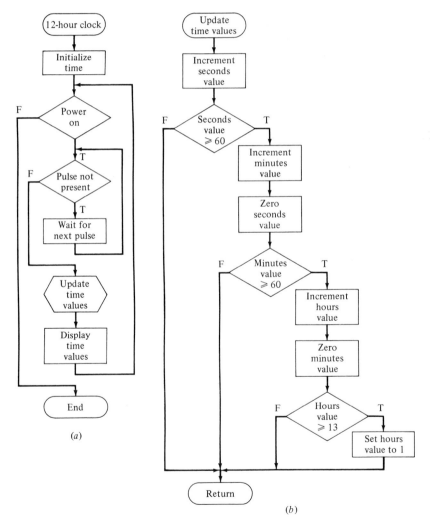

Figure E8-2 (*a*) Top-level description and (*b*) second-level flowchart.

Fig. E8-2*a*. The time of day is determined by counting a reference pulse with a 1-s period.

SOLUTION The flowchart is shown in Fig. E8-2*b*.

8-3 TRACING THE EXECUTION OF A FLOWCHART

In describing the procedure used to trace the execution of a program defined by a flowchart we must either be given the initial state for all test conditions used in the logical propositions in the decision elements or they must be defined by the execution of earlier tasks. We begin with the first element after the beginning terminal element and proceed task by task. At each decision element we evaluate the proposition to define the correct path. If a test condition is altered by executing any task, this fact must be noted. We illustrate this procedure using the flowchart in Fig. 8-4, which provides a top-level flowchart of a program for a microcomputer-based electronic instrument, a voltmeter-ohmmeter, and a second-level flowchart of the VOLTMETER FUNCTION subroutine.

This instrument has two selector knobs, a pair of input probes, and a digital display. One selector knob allows the user to select either the voltmeter function or the ohmmeter function. The other knob allows the user to select between a low and high range of values for the measurement. When the voltmeter function is selected, the low range is 0 to 1 V and the high range is 0 to 100 V. When the ohmmeter function is selected, the low range is 0 to 1 kΩ and the high range is 0 to 1 MΩ. In this example, we shall consider the case where the voltmeter function and the low range are selected.

The instrument's operation, defined by the top-level flowchart in Fig. 8-4*a*, begins with a decision element with POWER ON as the test condition for the logical proposition. This approach allows us to describe a continuously repeated operation using one of the basic structural units. The setting of the voltmeter-ohmmeter selector knob is then tested in a second decision element. In this example, the true path is selected, and the subroutine VOLTMETER FUNCTION is encountered and recognized as a subroutine by its special symbol. We then move to the second-level flowchart in Fig. 8-4*b*.

In the subroutine VOLTMETER FUNCTION the first task is to read the range-selector-knob setting. The value read is tested in the decision element, and in this case the maximum range is set to 1 V since the low range was selected. Next the input voltage is read and scaled according to the selected range. The resulting voltage value is converted into the appropriate display code word and displayed. The terminal element specifying RETURN, encountered next, transfers the flow back to the top-level flowchart at the output of the task defining the subroutine VOLTMETER FUNCTION. From here the flow is transferred back to the decision element testing POWER ON, and the cycle is repeated.

Example 8-3 For the flowchart in Fig. E8-3 define the sequence of tasks resulting during execution of the program if (*a*) P_1 is true, P_2 is true, and P_3 is

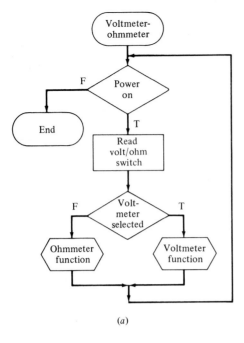

(a)

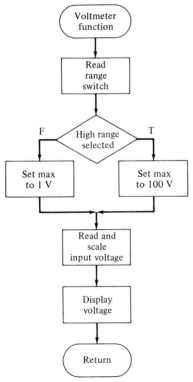

(b)

Figure 8-4 Flowchart for a voltmeter-ohmmeter program: (a) top-level flowchart and (b) second-level flowchart.

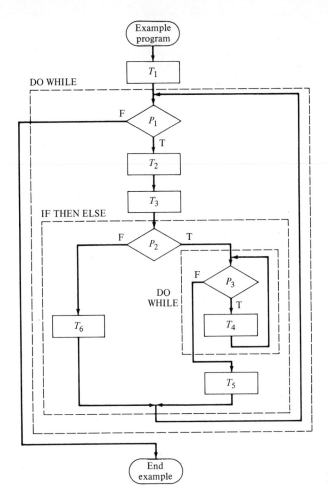

Figure E8-3 Flowchart.

true; (*b*) P_1 is true, P_2 is false, and P_3 is true; and (*c*) P_1 is true, P_2 is true, and P_3 is false.

SOLUTION (*a*) The resulting sequence of tasks is $T_1, T_2, T_3, T_4, T_4, \ldots$.
    (*b*) The resulting sequence of tasks is $T_1, T_2, T_3, T_6, T_2, T_3, T_6, \ldots$.
    (*c*) The resulting sequence of tasks is $T_1, T_2, T_3, T_5, T_2, T_3, T_5, \ldots$.

8-4 CONVERTING FLOWCHARTS INTO ASSEMBLY-LANGUAGE PROGRAMS

In this section we describe the procedure for converting flowcharts into assembly-language programs. In flowcharts for structured programs only three basic structural units occur, and so we need to discuss converting only these three structural units.

8-4-1 Sequential Tasks

Converting a sequential-task structural unit into assembly-language instructions is straightforward. If the task corresponds to a single instruction, the conversion is obvious. If it is a more complicated task, it is common to redefine it as a sequence of simpler tasks that correspond to assembly-language instructions. Consider the problem shown in Fig. 8-5. It requires that three values with the labels MASK1, MASK2, and VALUE be combined according to the logical expression MASK1·VALUE + MASK2·VALUE, where · and + are logical AND and OR operators, respectively. The result is stored in the location labeled RESULT.

A flowchart of the solution is shown as two sequential tasks in Fig. 8-5a. Whereas the task STORE RESULT can be implemented with a single assembly-language instruction and requires no refinement, the task PROCESS DATA must be

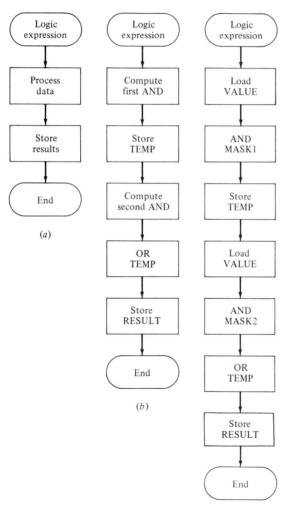

(a)

(b)

(c)

Figure 8-5 Flowchart implementing RESULT = MASK1·VALUE + MASK2·VALUE.

Table 8-1 Assembly-language program for flowchart in Fig. 8-5c†

	NAM	LOGIC	
	ORG	$100	
VALUE	FCB	· · ·	VALUE MUST BE PROVIDED
MASK1	FCB	· · ·	VALUE MUST BE PROVIDED
MASK2	FCB	· · ·	VALUE MUST BE PROVIDED
RESULT	RMB	1	STORAGEE FOR RESULT
TEMP	RMB	1	STORAGE FOR TEMP VALUE
	ORG	$300	
LOGIC	LDAA	VALUE	LOAD VALUE INTO ACC
	ANDA	MASK1	PERFORM "AND" OPERATION WITH MASK1
	STAA	TEMP	SAVE RESULT OF FIRST "AND"
	LDAA	VALUE	RELOAD VALUE INTO ACC
	ANDA	MASK2	PERFORM "AND" OPERATION WITH MASK2
	ORAA	TEMP	COMBINE RESULT OF TWO "AND" OPERATIONS
	STAA	RESULT	SAVE THE FINAL RESULT
	SWI		SOFTWARE INTERRUPT
	END		

† VALUE, MASK1, and MASK2 would be loaded with input data.

subdivided. The data processing involves two logical ANDs and a logical OR. According to the rules of boolean algebra, the program must perform the AND operations first and then the OR operation. This sequence is defined in the flowchart in Fig. 8-5b. Note that the result of the first AND operation is stored in a temporary location to free the accumulator for the second AND operation. The use of a temporary location is a common programming technique. In this second flowchart all tasks but COMPUTE FIRST AND and COMPUTE SECOND AND are instruction-level tasks. Figure 8-5c showing the flowchart with these two tasks subdivided, can be used in generating assembly-language instructions. Table 8-1 shows the assembly-language program for the flowchart in Fig. 8-5. We have chosen to store the first piece of data at location 100 and the first executable instruction at location 300, as indicated by the two ORG assembler directives. The problem statement included four labels, and we introduced a fifth (TEMP) while developing the flowchart; these labels are defined, just after the first ORG directive using the FCB descriptor to define the values of VALUE, MASK1, and MASK2 and the RMB descriptor to reserve a memory location for TEMP and RESULT. Executable instructions representing the sequential tasks start after the second ORG directive. The last line contains the assembler directive END.

8-4-2 Alternative-Task Structural Unit

Defining the sequence of assembly-language instruction for the alternative-task structural unit requires us to convert the two-dimensional flowchart into a one-dimensional sequence of instructions. In this section we first describe how this is accomplished using two branch instructions. Then we shall describe four types of test conditions which can be used in the proposition for this structural unit and illustrate how an example of each is converted into a sequence of assembly-language instructions.

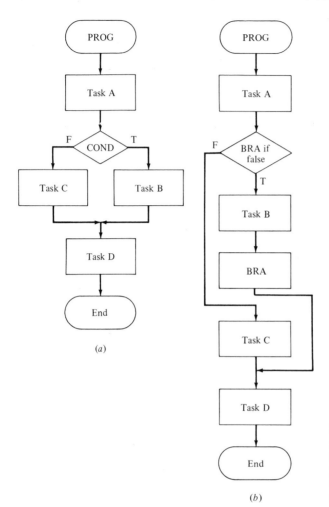

(a)

(b)

Figure 8-6 Alternative-task structural unit: (a) standard form; (b) redrawn to emphasize the one-dimensional nature of the instruction sequence.

In order to implement the alternative-task structural unit we use two branch instructions, one conditional and one unconditional. Figure 8-6 illustrates the scheme used to translate the two-dimensional geometrical flowchart for an alternative-task structural unit into a linear sequence of instructions. In this figure the flowchart is redrawn to emphasize the one-dimensional nature of the sequence of instructions. Since the alternative-task structural unit also is referred to as the IF...THEN...ELSE structure, we shall adopt the convention of using an instruction that branches if the test condition is false, as shown in Fig. 8-6b.

Table 8-2 presents a skeleton program for the flowchart in Fig. 8-6. The BRANCH IF CONDITION FALSE instruction (BCF) transfers control to the first instruction in task C if the test condition is false and skips all the instructions in task B. Otherwise, the first instruction in task B is executed. After the last

Table 8-2 Instruction sequences corresponding to flowchart in Fig. 8-6

	⋮		
TASKA	INST		FIRST INSTRUCTION IN TASKA
	⋮		
	INST		LAST INSTRUCTION IN TASKA
	BCF	TASKC	BRANCH TO TASKC IF CONDITION IS FALSE
TASKB	INST		FIRST INSTRUCTION IN TASKB
	⋮		
	INST		LAST INSTRUCTION IN TASKB
	BRA	TASKD	UNCONDITIONAL BRANCH TO SKIP TASKC
TASKC	INST		FIRST INSTRUCTION IN TASKC
	⋮		
	INST		LAST INSTRUCTION IN TASKC
TASKD	INST		FIRST INSTRUCTION IN TASKD
	⋮		
	INST		LAST INSTRUCTION IN TASKD
	END		

instruction in task B has been executed, an unconditional branch instruction transfers control to the first instruction in task D and skips all the instructions in task C.†

Flowcharts are not usually redrawn as shown in Fig. 8-6b; this version is presented here only to emphasize that the flowchart must be translated into a linear sequence of instructions. The reader should develop the ability to write assembly-language instructions for the alternative-task structural unit directly from the flowchart in Fig. 8-6a.

Although the test condition in the alternative-task structural unit can assume many forms, it must be expressed as a logical proposition that can be transformed into a proposition involving one or more bits in the condition code register. We now describe four types of test conditions, present an example of each, and show the corresponding assembly-language instructions.

The first type of test condition is based on the result of a previous operation and uses propositions like "the result was positive," "the result was negative," or "an arithmetic overflow was generated." As an example, Fig. 8-7 shows a flowchart for an alternative-task structural unit which adds the contents of memory location NUMB to the accumulator and IF no arithmetic overflow occurs ($V = 0$) THEN it stores the result, ELSE it transfers the condition code register to the accumulator and stores it. To implement the convention of branching when

---

† There is an equally valid alternative using a BRANCH IF CONDITION TRUE instruction. However, since consistency is an important attribute of good programs, we strongly recommend that the reader adopt one approach and use it exclusively, and we suggest that ours is more consistent with the IF...THEN...ELSE statement.

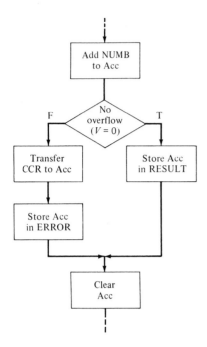

Figure 8-7 Flowchart showing an alternative-task structural unit based on result of previous operation (in this case ADD NUMB TO ACC).

the proposition is false, the conditional branch instruction should branch if $V = 1$, and so the appropriate instruction is BVS (branch if overflow set).

Table 8-3 shows the sequence of instruction for this flowchart. The BVS (branch if overflow set) instruction transfers control to the instruction labeled SKIP IF $V = 1$. If $V \neq 1$, the branch does not occur and the instruction following

Table 8-3 Sequence of assembly-language instructions corresponding to flowchart in Fig. 8-7

		⋮	
NUMB	FCB	· · ·	VALUE MUST BE PROVIDED
RESULT	RMB	1	STORAGE FOR RESULT
ERROR	RMB	1	STORAGE FOR ERROR COUNT
		⋮	
	ADDA	NUMB	ADD CONTENTS OF NUMB TO ACC
	BVS	SKIP	BRANCH IF OVERFLOW SET
	STAA	RESULT	STORE IN LOCATION RESULT
	BRA	NEXT	UNCONDITIONAL BRANCH
SKIP	TPA		TRANSFER COND. CODE REG. TO ACC
	STAA	ERROR	STORE ACC IN LOCATION ERROR
NEXT	CLRA		CLEAR ACC
		⋮	

the BVS is executed. The BRA (unconditional branch) instruction is used to bypass the second alternative task if the first was executed.

A test condition based on the relative magnitude of two binary words represents a second type of proposition that can be used in an alternative-task structural unit. This type takes the form IF WORD1 greater than WORD2, THEN do task 1, ELSE do task 2. As an example, consider the alternative task in which we compare two words in locations WORD1 and WORD2 and save the one representing the larger integer in location LARGE; that is, IF WORD1 is greater than or equal to WORD2, THEN store WORD1 in LARGE, ELSE store WORD2 in LARGE. Figure 8-8*a* shows a flowchart implementing this task; Fig. 8-8*b* shows the corresponding instruction-level flowchart using a subtract instruction to accomplish the comparison. This alternative-task structural unit now becomes IF result greater than or equal to zero (N = 0) THEN store WORD1, ELSE store WORD2. To implement our convention of branching when the proposition is false, the conditional branch instruction should branch if N = 1, and so the appropriate instruction is BMI (BRANCH IF MINUS). Note that since the task to store the accumulator in LARGE was common to both alternative pathways it was removed from the alternative-task structural unit and placed in sequence with it.

Figure 8-8*c* shows the analogous flowchart using a compare instruction. The last instruction simulates a subtraction; i.e., it sets the condition-code register as if

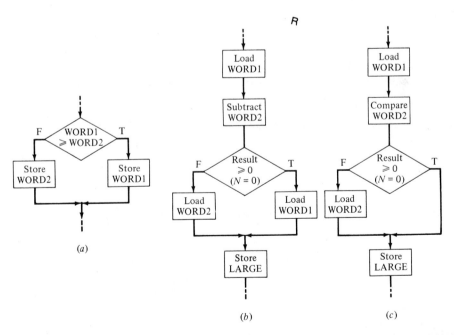

Figure 8-8 (*a*) Flowchart showing an alternative-task structural unit based on relative magnitude of two words; (*b*) refined version of (*a*) using instruction-level task with subtraction for comparison; (*c*) like (*b*) except that COMPARE instruction is used instead of subtraction.

Table 8-4 Sequences of assembly language instructions corresponding to flowcharts in Fig. 8-8*b* and *c*

			Using SUBTRACT instruction
		:	
		:	
WORD1	FCB	· · ·	VALUE MUST BE PROVIDED
WORD2	FCB	· · ·	VALUE MUST BE PROVIDED
LARGE	RMB	1	STORAGE FOR LARGER VALUE
		:	
		:	
	LDAA	WORD1	LOAD WORD1 IN ACC
	SUBA	WORD2	SUBTRACT WORD2 FROM ACC
	BMI	SKIP	BRANCH IF RESULT LESS THAN ZERO
	LDAA	WORD1	LOAD WORD1 IN ACC
	BRA	NEXT	BRANCH TO STORE WORD1
SKIP	LDAA	WORD2	LOAD WORD2 IN ACC
NEXT	STAA	LARGE	TRANSFER LARGER WORD FROM ACC TO LARGE
		:	
		:	

			Using COMPARE instruction
		:	
		:	
WORD1	FCB	· · ·	VALUE MUST BE PROVIDED
WORD2	FCB	· · ·	VALUE MUST BE PROVIDED
LARGE	RMB	1	STORAGE FOR LARGER VALUE
		:	
		:	
	LDAA	WORD1	LOAD WORD1 IN ACC
	CMPA	WORD2	COMPARE WORD2 USING WORD1 MINUS WORD2
	BMI	SKIP	BRANCH IF RESULT LESS THAN ZERO
	BRA	NEXT	BRANCH TO STORE WORD1
SKIP	LDAA	WORD2	LOAD WORD2 IN ACC
NEXT	STAA	LARGE	TRANSFER LARGER WORD FROM ACC TO LARGE
		:	
		:	

a subtraction were performed without changing the accumulator. Table 8-4 shows the sequence of assembly-language instructions for the flowcharts in Fig. 8-8*b* and *c*.

A third type of test condition is based on whether a specific bit in a word is set or cleared. This is especially important in synchronizing input and output transfers, for example, see Sec. 7-4-2. Another example is shown in Fig. 8-9*a*. This flowchart describes an alternative-task structural unit described by IF the contents of DATA are odd, THEN store the ASCII code word for the character O in CODE, ELSE store the ASCII code word for the character E. Figure 8-9*b* to *d* shows three instruction-level flowcharts using three different approaches for setting or clearing bits in the condition-code register. All three approaches are

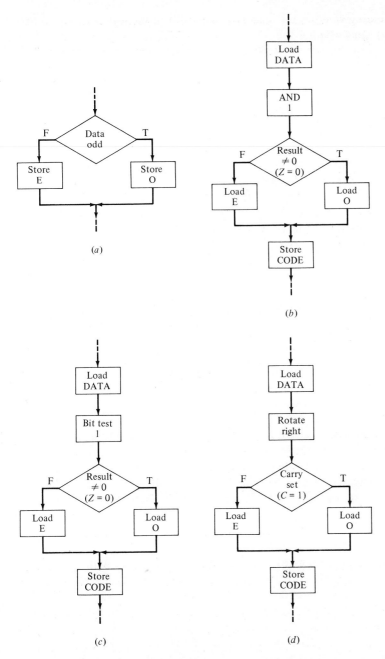

Figure 8-9 (*a*) Flowchart showing alternative-task structural unit based on the condition of a specific bit; (*b*) refined version using instruction-level tasks with logical AND instruction used to test bit; (*c*) like (*b*) except that BIT-TEST instruction is used in place of logical AND; (*d*) like (*b*) except that ROTATE RIGHT instruction used to test bit.

based on determining whether the least significant bit in the test word is a 0 or 1 since this bit indicates whether the word is even or odd, respectively. In Fig. 8-8*b* a logical AND with the hexadecimal value 01 sets all but the least significant bit in the accumulator to zero; thus the result is 0 if the test word is even or 1 (nonzero) if it is odd. This alternative-task structural unit now becomes IF result is nonzero ($Z = 0$) THEN store ASCII code for O, ELSE store ASCII code for E. To implement the convention of branching when the proposition is false, the conditional branch instruction should branch when $Z = 1$, and so the appropriate instruction is BEQ (BRANCH IF EQUAL). In Fig. 8-8*c*, a bit-test instruction replaces the logical AND instruction. The bit test simulates a logical AND by setting the condition-code register as if a logical AND were performed without altering the contents of the accumulator. The same conditional branch instruction is used.

The third approach, Fig. 8-8*d*, rotates the bit of interest into the C bit, which then is tested. The alternative-task structural unit now becomes, IF carry bit is set ($C = 1$) THEN store ASCII code for O, ELSE store ASCII code for E. To implement the convention of branching when the proposition is false, the conditional branch instruction should branch when $C = 0$, and so the appropriate instruction is BCC (BRANCH IF CARRY CLEAR).

Table 8-5 shows the sequence of assembly-language instructions for these three flowcharts. Note that in these three programs, different instructions were used to load the ASCII code for the characters O (0100 1111 in binary and 4F in hexadecimal), and the character E (0100 0101 in binary and 45 in hexadecimal).

A fourth type of test condition for an alternative-task structure involves the recognition of particular bit pattern or code word; e.g., the ASCII code word for a specific character. Figure 8-10*a* shows a flowchart that determines whether the contents of CHAR represent the ASCII code for a Y, an N, or neither, and then increments the appropriate counter located at YCNT, NCNT, and ERROR, respectively. Note that this flowchart contains two alternative-task structures, each with a single input and single output. The function of the flowchart is IF the character is a Y, THEN increment YCNT, ELSE do the alternative task, where the alternative task is IF the character is an N, THEN increment NCNT, ELSE increment ERROR.

An instruction-level flowchart is shown in Fig. 8-10*b*. To determine whether the test word represents a Y or an N, the actual code words for these characters are subtracted from the test word and the result is compared with zero. After subtracting the ASCII code word for Y, the first alternative-task structural unit now becomes IF result is zero ($Z = 1$), THEN increment YCNT, ELSE do the alternative task. To implement the convention of branching when the proposition is false, the conditional branch instruction should branch when $Z = 0$, and so the appropriate instruction is BNE (BRANCH WHEN NOT EQUAL ZERO). Similarly, after subtracting the ASCII code word for N, the second alternative-task structural unit becomes IF result is zero ($Z = 1$), THEN increment NCNT, ELSE increment ERROR. Again the BNE is the appropriate instruction. The sequence of assembly-language instructions for the flowchart in Fig. 8-10*b* is shown in Table 8-6. COMPARE instructions could be used in place of the two SUBTRACT

Table 8-5 Sequence of assembly-language instructions corresponding to flowcharts in Fig. 8-9b to d

---

Using AND instruction

```
              ⋮
DATA    FCB      . . .         VALUE MUST BE DEFINED
CODE    RMB      1             STORAGE FOR CHAR CODE
              ⋮
        LDAA     DATA          LOAD DATA INTO ACC
        ANDA     #01           ISOLATE FIRST BIT USING IMMED MODE
        BEQ      SKIP          BRANCH IF ZERO
        LDAA     #'O'          LOAD ASCII CODE FOR O
        BRA      NEXT          BRANCH TO STORE O CODE
SKIP    LDAA     #'E'          LOAD ASCII CODE FOR E
NEXT    STAA     CODE          STORE CODE
              ⋮
```

Using BIT-TEST instruction

```
              ⋮
DATA    FCB      . . .         VALUE MUST BE DEFINED
CODE    RMB      1             STORAGE FOR CHAR CODE
              ⋮
        LDAA     DATA          LOAD DATA INTO ACC
        BITA     #01           TEST FIRST BIT
        BEQ      SKIP          BRANCH IF ZERO
        LDAA     #$4F          LOAD ASCII CODE FOR O
        BRA      NEXT          BRANCH TO STORE O CODE
SKIP    LDAA     #$45          LOAD ASCII CODE FOR E
NEXT    STAA     CODE          STORE IN CODE
              ⋮
```

Using ROTATE instruction

```
              ⋮
DATA    FCB      . . .            VALUE MUST BE DEFINED
CODE    RMB      1                STORAGE FOR CHAR CODE
              ⋮
        LDAA     DATA             LOAD DATA INTO ACC
        RORA                      ROTATE RIGHT USING CARRY BIT
        BCC      SKIP             BRANCH IF CARRY CLEAR
        LDAA     #%01001111       LOAD ASCII CODE FOR O
        BRA      NEXT             BRANCH TO STORE O
SKIP    LDAA     #%01000101       LOAD ASCII CODE FOR E
NEXT    STAA     CODE             STORE IN CODE
              ⋮
```

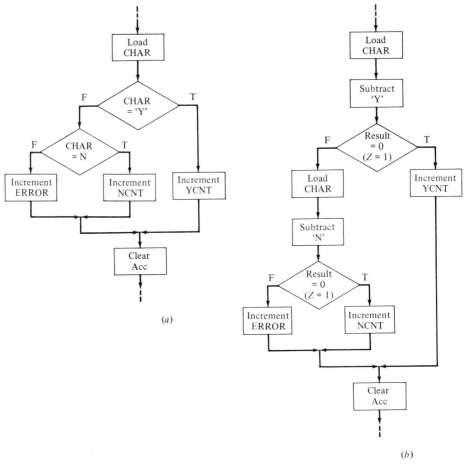

Figure 8-10 (*a*) Flowchart showing an alternative-task structural unit based on the recognition of a particular code word; (*b*) revised version using instruction-level tasks.

instructions, eliminating the need for reloading the test word before testing to see whether it represents an N.

8-4-3 Repeated-Task Structural Unit

Just as with the alternative-task structural unit, we must convert the two-dimensional flowchart for the repeated-task structural unit into a one-dimensional sequence of instructions. The repeated-task structural unit has two basic forms, depending on whether the number of repetitions is prespecified and controlled by a counter or unspecified and controlled by an external event. The conversion is slightly different for these two forms.

The repeated-task structural unit in which the repeated task is performed a prespecified number of times uses a loop counter, generally defined in memory,

Table 8-6 Sequence of assembly-language instructions corresponding to the flowchart in Fig. 8-10

	⋮		
CHAR	FCC	⋯	VALUE MUST BE DEFINED
YCNT	RMB	1	STORAGE FOR Y COUNT
NCNT	RMB	1	STORAGE FOR N COUNT
ERROR	RMB	1	STORAGE FOR ERROR COUNT
	⋮		
	LDAA	CHAR	LOAD UNKNOWN CODE INTO ACC
	SUBA	# 'Y'	SUBTRACT ASCII CODE FOR Y
	BNE	NOTY	BRANCH IF RESULT IS NOT ZERO; UNKNOWN NOT Y
	INC	YCNT	INCREMENT Y COUNTER
	BRA	EXIT	BRANCH TO CLEAR ACC
NOTY	LDAA	CHAR	RELOAD UNKNOWN CODE INTO ACC
	SUBA	# 'N'	SUBTRACT ASCII CODE FOR N
	BNE	NOTN	BRANCH IF RESULT IS NOT ZERO; UNKNOWN NOT N
	INC	NCNT	INCREMENT N COUNTER
	BRA	EXIT	BRANCH TO CLEAR INSTRUCTION
NOTN	INC	ERROR	INCREMENT ERROR COUNTER
EXIT	CLRA		CLEAR ACC
	⋮		

although one of the internal processor registers may be used. This counter must be initialized before entering the loop; then it must be tested and altered during each repetition. There are many methods for implementing this structure. Figure 8-11a and b shows two in which the counters are decremented and incremented, respectively. Figure 8-11c and d shows corresponding flowcharts in which the initialization and alteration of the counter are defined with instruction-level tasks. In Fig. 8-11a and c, the location COUNT is loaded with the number of repetitions and is decremented in the loop until its contents equal zero. With the second approach, the location COUNT is initially set to zero and is incremented until its contents equal the specified number of repetitions. When comparing the two detailed flowcharts in Fig. 8-11c and d, we see that the first approach requires fewer instructions to control the counter and does not use the accumulator during the looping. The latter feature offers a definite advantage with programs that retain results from one iteration to the next in the accumulator. Thus, we shall use the structure defined in Fig. 8-11a and c.

Figure 8-12 shows an alternative representation of the flowchart in Fig. 8-11c emphasizing the one-dimensioned nature of the instruction sequence. Table 8-7 contains the assembly-language instructions to implement this arrangement. The instruction BRANCH IF EQUAL ZERO (BEQ) transfers control out of the loop if $Z = 1$; if this is not the case, the first instruction in the repeated task is executed. The last instruction in the repeated task decrements the counter, and control is transferred back to the BEQ instruction with an unconditional branch (BRA).

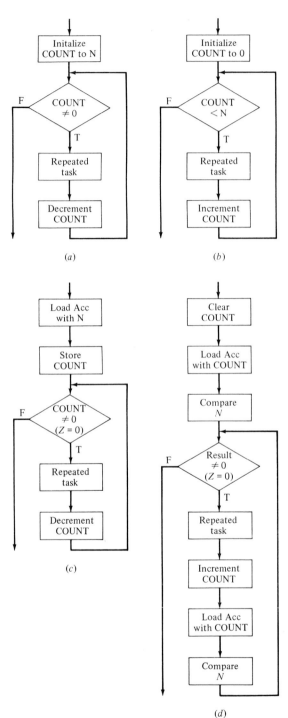

Figure 8-11 Repeated task structural unit where counter is (*a*) decremented and (*b*) incremented on each repetition. (*c*) Refined version of (*a*). (*d*) Refined version of (*b*).

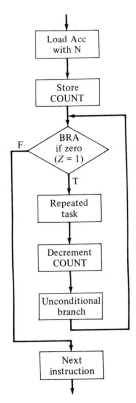

Figure 8-12 Rearrangement of Fig. 8-11c to show linear sequence of instructions.

This structure is also referred to as a DO WHILE structure since its function is described by DO the repeated task WHILE the contents of COUNT are nonzero.

One important feature of this structure is that it will function correctly regardless of the value stored in NUMB and will handle the unusual case where this value is zero. Although it may seem ridiculous to specify zero repetitions, it is essential to consider all unusual cases since this repeated-task structural unit may

Table 8-7 Sequence of assembly-language instructions corresponding to flowchart in Fig. 8-12

NUMB	FCB	. . .	NUMBER OF REPETITIONS MUST BE DEFINED
COUNT	RMB	1	LOOP COUNTER
	LDAA	NUMB	LOAD NUMBER OF REPETITIONS INTO ACC
	STAA	COUNT	STORE IN COUNT
LOOP	BEQ	EXIT	BRANCH TO NEXT TASK IF COUNT ZERO
	INST		FIRST INSTRUCTION IN REPEATED TASK
	⋮		
	INST		LAST INSTRUCTION IN REPEATED TASK
	DEC	COUNT	DECREMENT THE COUNTER
	BRA	LOOP	BRANCH TO CONDITIONAL BRANCH
EXIT	INST		FIRST INSTRUCTION OF NEXT TASK

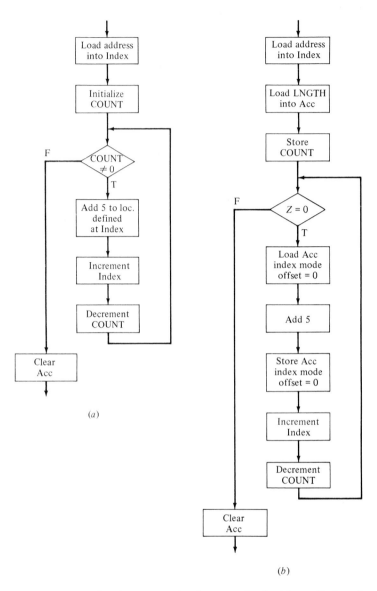

Figure 8-13 Flowchart for a repeated-task structural unit with specified number of iterations.

be used in the middle of some complex program where the number of repetitions is computed.

As a specific example of a repeated-task structure, Fig. 8-13a shows a flowchart for a program that will add 5 to all elements in a list of words stored in memory. The length of the list, i.e., the number of elements in the list, is stored in location LNGTH, and the address of the first element is stored in locations FIRST and FIRST + 1. Figure 8-13b shows the corresponding flowchart with

Table 8-8 Sequence of assembly-language instructions corresponding to flowchart in Fig. 8-13

```
          ⋮
FIRST   FDB    ⋯       ADDRESS OF FIRST ELEMENT
LNGTH   FCB    ⋯       LENGTH OF LIST
COUNT   RMB    1       COUNTER TO TRACK NO. OF REPETITIONS
          ⋮
        LDX    FIRST   LOAD INDEX WITH ADDRESS OF FIRST ELEMENT
        LDAA   LNGTH   LOAD ACC WITH LENGTH OF LIST
        STAA   COUNT   STORE IN COUNT
NEXT    BEQ    EXIT    BRANCH IF EQUAL ZERO
        LDAA   0,X     LOAD ACC FROM LIST
        ADDA   #5      ADD 5
        STAA   0,X     STORE ACC IN LIST
        INX            INC INDEX
        DEC    COUNT   DEC COUNT
        BRA    NEXT    BRANCH TO TEST AND PROCESS NEXT ELEMENT
EXIT    CLRA           CLEAR ACC
          ⋮
```

instruction-level tasks; Table 8-8 lists the corresponding sequence of assembly-language instructions. We use both a counter (location COUNT) to tally the number of repetitions and an index (the index register) to select the appropriate element in the list. The control tasks in this structure are subdivided into initializing the counter and index before entering the loop and updating them on each repetition of the loop. To eliminate the need for extra COMPARE instructions, we order these control tasks so that manipulating the counter is the last task in both the initializing and the updating procedures. This ordering ensures that the Z bit in the condition code register will reflect the condition of the counter when the BRANCH IF ZERO instruction is executed. In the assembly-language instructions in Table 8-8, we used three instructions to perform the repeated task. Each element in the list is loaded into the accumulator using the indexed addressing mode, increased by 5, and then stored using the indexed addressing mode.

A slight variation of the previous program results when the first element in the list defines the number of words to be processed, the second element in the list represents the first word to be processed, and so on. Figure 8-14 shows a flowchart with instructional-level tasks for a program using this approach. The contents of the location LIST define the address of the first element in the list. Table 8-9 lists the corresponding sequence of assembly-language instructions. There are two differences between these instructions and the sequence in Table 8-8. The initialization of the counter is accomplished using the index, and the instruction to increment the index is moved ahead of the instructions performing the repeated task.

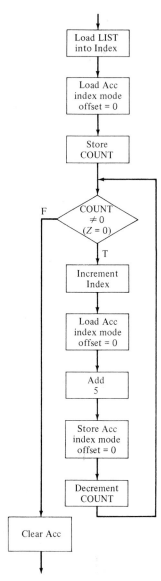

Figure 8-14 Flowchart similar to Fig. 8-13*b* except that the first element in the list defines its length.

Table 8-9 Sequence of assembly-language instructions corresponding to flowchart in Fig. 8-14

```
                    .
                    .
                    .
LIST    FDB    ···      DEFINES ADDRESS OF FIRST ELEMENT IN LIST
COUNT   RMB    1        COUNTER TO TRACK NUMBER OF REPETITIONS

                    .
                    .
                    .
        LDX    LIST     LOAD INDEX WITH ADDRESS OF THE LENGTH
        LDAA   0,X      LOAD ACC WITH LENGTH OF LIST
        STAA   COUNT    STORE IN COUNTER
NEXT    BEQ    EXIT     BRANCH IF EQUAL ZERO
        INX             INCREMENT INDEX
        LDAA   0,X      LOAD DATA ELEMENT FROM LIST
        ADDA   #5       ADD 5
        STAA   0,X      RETURN TO LIST
        DEC    COUNT    UPDATE COUNTER
        BRA    NEXT     BRANCH TO TEST AND PROCESS NEXT ELEMENT
EXIT    CLRA            CLEAR ACC

                    .
                    .
                    .
```

As a second example of a repeated-task structure with an explicit number of iterations, Fig. 8-15 shows two stages of a flowchart for a repeated task that counts the number bits set in an 8-bit word. The test word is stored in location VALUE and the number bits that are set are stored in TALLY. Table 8-10 lists the corresponding sequence of instructions. The initialization involves setting TALLY to zero, loading the test word in the accumulator, and then setting the counter to 8. The counter is initialized last so that the Z bit in the condition code register reflects the content of COUNT and not TALLY or VALUE when the conditional branch instruction is executed the first time. In the loop, the counter is decremented last for the same reason. This repeated-task structural unit is described by DO the repeated task WHILE COUNT is nonzero. In the repeated task, each bit of the test word is rotated into the C bit in the condition-code register. An alternative-task structural unit is used to test the C bit and increment TALLY if it is set. This unit is described by IF the carry is set ($C = 1$), THEN increment TALLY, ELSE do nothing. The instruction that branches when the proposition is false is BCC (BRANCH IF CARRY CLEAR). Since the alternative task is to do nothing, the unconditional branch used to skip this task is unnecessary.

In the second major form of the repeated-task structural unit the number of iterations is not explicitly defined but is controlled by external events. This structural unit is extremely important in controlling the transfer of data through the input and output interfaces. As an example, consider the problem of repeatedly checking the fourth bit in the word stored in location TEST until it is set. Figure 8-16 shows flowcharts for two different implementations of this

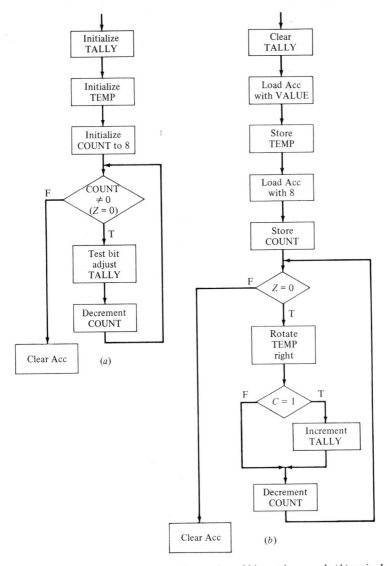

Figure 8-15 (*a*) Flowchart to count the number of bits set in a word; (*b*) revised version.

Table 8-10 Sequence of assembly-language instructions corresponding to flowchart in Fig. 8-15b

	⋮		
TALLY	RMB	· · ·	DEFINE LOCATION TO TALLY NO. OF ONES
VALUE	FCB	· · ·	WORD TO BE TESTED
TEMP	RMB	1	TEMPORARY LOCATION TO STORE WORD
COUNT	RMB	1	COUNTER TO TRACK NO. OF REPETITIONS
	⋮		
	CLR	TALLY	SET TALLY TO ZERO
	LDAA	VALUE	LOAD ACC WITH TEST WORD
	STAA	TEMP	STORE IT IN TEMPORARY LOCATION
	LDAA	#8	LOAD ACC WITH 8
	STAA	COUNT	STORE IN COUNTER
NEXT	BEQ	EXIT	BRANCH IF EQUAL ZERO
	ROR	TEMP	ROTATE TO RIGHT THROUGH CARRY BIT
	BCC	SKIP	BRANCH IF CARRY CLEAR
	INC	TALLY	INCREMENT TALLY
SKIP	DEC	COUNT	DECREMENT COUNTER
	BRA	NEXT	BRANCH FOR NEXT BIT
EXIT	CLRA		CLEAR ACC

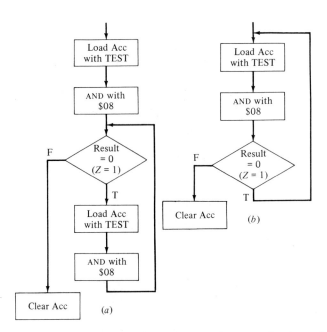

Figure 8-16 (*a*) Flowchart for a repeated-task structural unit terminated by an external event; (*b*) nonstandard representation.

Table 8-11 Two sequences of assembly-language instructions corresponding to flowcharts in Fig. 8-16a and b

For Fig. 8-16a

```
TEST        FCB         ...         LOCATION OF TEST WORD

            LDAA        TEST        LOAD TEST WORD INTO ACC
            ANDA        #$08        LOGICAL AND TO ISOLATE BIT 3
AGAIN       BNE         DONE        BRANCH IF NOT ZERO—BIT 3 IS SET
            LDAA        TEST
            ANDA        #$08
            BRA         AGAIN       BRANCH TO RETEST BIT
DONE        CLRA                    CLEAR ACC—NEXT INSTRUCTION
```

For Fig. 8-16b

```
TEST        FCB         ...         LOCATION OF TEST WORD

AGAIN       LDAA        TEST        LOAD TEST WORD INTO ACC
            ANDA        #$08        LOGICAL AND TO ISOLATE BIT 3
            BEQ         AGAIN       BRANCH TO RETEST—NOT SET
            CLRA                    CLEAR ACC—NEXT INSTRUCTION
```

repeated-task structural unit. Figure 8-16a represents the standard structure with some initialization, a conditional branch instruction, and then a loop with the repeated task. In this case, the initializing tasks are identical to those in the loop, and so the nonstandard implementation shown in Fig. 8-16b is frequently used. Table 8-11 lists the sequence of assembly-language instructions for each of these flowcharts.

Example 8-4 The flowchart in Fig. E8-4a represents a program which searches a list for the smallest value and places its address in SADDR and its value in SMALL. The first element in the list is stored in location LIST and defines the number of elements to be searched. Translate the flowchart into a sequence of assembly-language instructions.

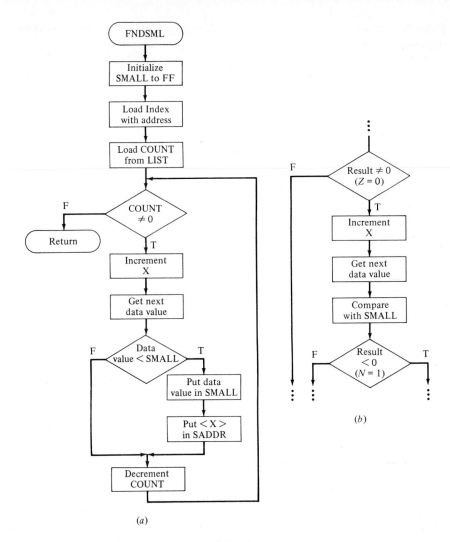

Figure E8-4 (*a*) Flowchart and (*b*) refined flowchart segment.

SOLUTION First we convert the propositions in the two decision elements to ones involving bits in the condition-code register. A portion of the flowchart is redrawn in Fig. E8-4b showing this revision. The assembly-language instructions are given in Table E8-4:

Table E8-4 Sequence of assembly-language instructions corresponding to flowcharts in Fig. E8-4

	:		
	:		
LIST	FCB	. . .	DATA MUST BE PROVIDED
COUNT	RMB	1	ITERATION COUNT
SMALL	RMB	1	
SADDR	RMB	2	
	:		
	:		
FNDSML	CLR	SMALL	ZERO SMALL
	COM	SMALL	SMALL IS NOW $FF
	LDX	#LIST	ADDR OF LIST TO X
	LDAA	0,X	
	STAA	COUNT	INITIALIZE COUNT
ELOOP	BEQ	EXIT	
	INX		POINT X TO NEXT DATA VALUE
	LDAA	0,X	NEXT DATA VALUE IN A
	CMPA	SMALL	COMPARE NEXT TO SMALL
	BGT	SKIP	BRA IF NEW VALUE IS LARGER
	STAA	SMALL	NEW SMALL VALUE
	STX	SADDR	ADDR OF NEW SMALL VALUE
SKIP	DEC	COUNT	DECREMENT LOOP COUNT
	BRA	ELOOP	BRA TO TEST AND REPEAT
EXIT	RTS		

8-5 TRANSFERRING DATA TO AND FROM SUBROUTINES

As explained earlier, we shall use top-down programming, where flowcharts are restricted to one page and complicated tasks are defined as subroutines. Transferring data from the calling program to the subroutine and vice versa represents the one major complication introduced by the use of subroutines. As in all programming problems, there are many solutions; we present one that is fairly standard and adaptable to many microcomputer systems. In this approach, the data, also called parameters or arguments, are loaded into consecutive memory locations to form a list. The address of the first element in the list is loaded into the index register before branching to a subroutine or returning from one.

As an example of the use of subroutines, we shall consider a program that accepts a sequence of binary words, interprets the first word as a binary number specifying the number of other elements, and generates two output words representing the high- and low-order bytes, respectively, of the sum of these elements. The inputs are interpreted as positive integers; a program to handle

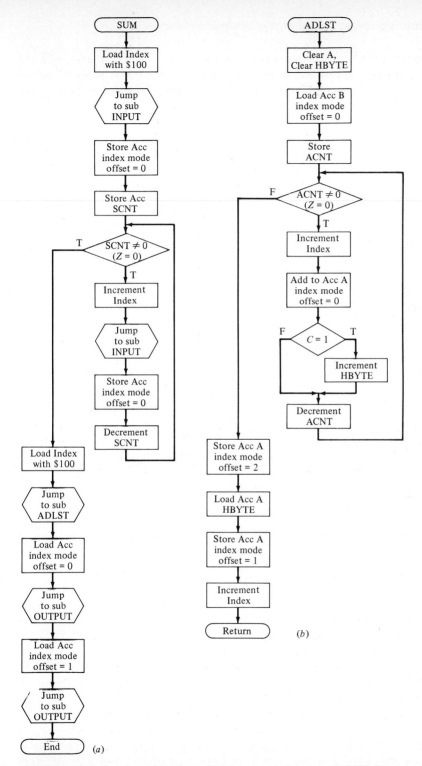

Figure 8-17 Flowchart for main program (SUM) and one subroutine (ADLST) for a program to input and add list of numbers and then output results.

signed integers would introduce more complicating details than we wish to consider at present. Figure 8-17*a* shows the flowchart for this program called SUM. Three subroutines, INPUT, OUTPUT, and ADLST (add list), are used. The subroutines INPUT and OUTPUT involving the input and output units are described in Table 7-16 and will not be developed further here. However, in assembling the routines SUM and ADLIST we must define the values assigned to these two labels using the two EQU directives. For our purpose here, we recall that INPUT loads the accumulator with the input data and OUTPUT transfers the data in the accumulator to the output unit. A flowchart for the third subroutine, ADLST, is shown in Fig. 8-17*b*. Table 8-12 contains the sequence of assembly-language instructions for SUM and ADLIST along with necessary assembler directives to reserve memory locations for various labels used in these two routines. Since the same label cannot appear in two different routines, we used SCNT and ACNT for the counter in the routines SUM and ADLIST, respectively. Similarly, different labels are used with the branch instructions, e.g., SNEXT and ANEXT. Also, note that the name of the subroutine must be the label for the first executable instruction in the subroutine.

In tracing through the main program, we see that the index register is initialized with the value $100; this represents the address of the list used to transfer data to subroutine ADLST. The first execution of the subroutine INPUT obtains a word defining the number of words that will be summed. This number is stored in the first location in the list and in a counter (SCNT) in the main program. The actual data values are then obtained using the subroutine INPUT and stored in the list using a repeated-task structural unit. As before, the counter is initialized and updated just before executing the conditional branch instruction so that the Z bit in the condition-code register reflects the status of the counter contents. Just before branching to the subroutine ADLIST, the index register must be reinitialized to a value of $100. When returning from this subroutine, the sum is stored in the next two locations at the end of the list and the index register contains the address of the first. These values are then transferred to the output unit using the subroutine OUTPUT.

The subroutine ADLIST contains a repeated-task structural unit in which the repeated task contains an alternative-task structural unit. During the initialization the sum is cleared and the first element in the list is transferred to the counter with the label ACNT. The repeated task sums one word at a time and increments HBYTE, the high byte of the sum, each time the addition generates a carry. After all repetitions have been completed, the high byte of the sum, which is stored in HBYTE, is transferred to the first empty location at the end of the list and the low byte of the sum which is in the A accumulator is transferred to the second empty location at the end of the list. Just before the return to the main program, the index register is adjusted so that it contains the address of the high byte of the sum.

Example 8-5 Modify the sequence of assembly-language instructions given in Table 8-10 so that the modified version represents a complete subroutine.

Table 8-12 Assembly-language programs for flowcharts shown in Fig. 8-17

```
          NAM    SUM
          ORG    $1000
INPUT     EQU    · · ·        VALUE DEFINED BY SUBROUTINE INPUT
OUTPUT    EQU    · · ·        VALUE DEFINED BY SUBROUTINE OUTPUT
SCNT      RMB    1            DEFINE LOCATION FOR MAIN PROG
SUM       LDX    #$100        LOAD INDEX WITH 100
          JSR    INPUT        JUMP TO SUB INPUT—GET LENGTH
          STAA   0,X          STORE LENGTH OF LIST IN FIRST LOC
          STAA   SCNT         INITIALIZE MAIN PROGRAM COUNTER
SNEXT     BEQ    SEXIT        BRANCH IF EQUAL ZERO—LIST INPUT
          INX                 INCREMENT INDEX
          JSR    INPUT        JUMP TO SUB INPUT—GET ELEMENT
          STAA   0,X          STORE IN LIST
          DEC    SCNT         DECREMENT MAIN PROGRAM COUNTER
          BRA    SNEXT        RETEST—INPUT NEXT ELEMENT
SEXIT     LDX    #$100        INITIALIZE INDEX FOR TRANSFER TO SUBROUTINE
          JSR    ADLST        JUMP TO SUBROUTINE ADLST
          LDAA   0,X          GET HIGH BYTE OF SUM
          JSR    OUTPUT       JUMP TO SUB-OUTPUT HIGH BYTE
          LDAA   1,X          GET LOW BYTE OF SUM
          JSR    OUTPUT       JUMP TO SUB-OUTPUT LOW BYTE
          SWI                 EXIT TO SYSTEM
HBYTE     RMB    1            DEFINE LOCATION FOR HIGH BYTE OF SUM
ACNT      RMB    1            DEFINE LOCATION FOR COUNTER IN ADLST
ADLST     CLR    HYBTE        CLEAR HIGH BYTE OF SUM
          CLRA
          LDAB   0,X          GET LENGTH OF LIST FROM FIRST LOC
          STAB   ACNT         STORE IN ADLST COUNTER
ANEXT     BEQ    AEXIT        BRANCH IF EQUAL ZERO—LIST COMPLETE
          INX                 INCREMENT INDEX
          ADDA   0,X          ADD ELEMENT TO ACC
          BCC    ASKIP        BRANCH IF CARRY CLEAR
          INC    HBYTE        INCREMENT HIGH BYTE OF SUM
ASKIP     DEC    ACNT         DECREMENT ADLST COUNTER
          BRA    ANEXT        BRANCH TO RETEST AND ADD NEXT ELEMENT
AEXIT     STAA   2,X          STORE LOW BYTE OF SUM IN LIST
          LDAA   HBYTE        GET HIGH BYTE OF SUM
          STAA   1,X          STORE HIGH BYTE OF SUM IN LIST
          INX                 INCREMENT INDEX—POINTS TO HIGH BYTE
          RTS                 RETURN
          END
```

Data will be transferred in the standard way using the index register. Name the subroutine PTALLY.

SOLUTION Two instructions must be added at the beginning of the sequence of executable instructions to provide a label for the subroutine and to transfer the word to be searched to the location labeled VALUE:

```
PTALLY    LDA A    0,X
          STA A    VALUE
```

Two instructions must be added at the end of the sequence to place the address of the result in the index register and to return from the subroutine:

LDX   #TALLY

RTS

8-6 PROGRAM DEVELOPMENT

Program development involves defining an appropriate algorithm in a flowchart, refining this flowchart to obtain a flowchart containing instruction-level tasks, and translating this refined flowchart into assembly-language instructions. The first step represents the creative process requiring insight and experience which are achieved by solving many problems. The second and third steps rely on the concepts developed earlier in this chapter. In order to provide the reader with some experience in program development and to use some of the concepts presented in this chapter, we shall describe program solutions for three problems. These programs will be specified as subroutines to provide more experience in dealing with this aspect of programming.

The definition of the algorithm is more or less independent of the microprocessor used, although the availability of certain instructions can affect the choice between alternative algorithms. As the flowchart becomes more and more detailed, the development becomes very dependent on the microcomputer used. The final step, the translation into assembly language, must be based on a specific microcomputer and a specific assembler. We shall use the 6800 assembly language described in Chap. 7.

8-6-1 Binary Multiplication

In this section we develop a subroutine that will multiply two unsigned 8-bit binary numbers. When control is transferred to the subroutine, the index register contains the address of the multiplier and the multiplicand is stored in the next memory location. The product will be 16 bits; when this subroutine is completed, the index register will contain the address of the high byte with the low byte in the next location.

Before discussing this solution, we need to describe a multiplication method using binary words. This approach uses the standard binary add and shift operations. It is advantageous since it requires fewer data storage locations than the traditional approach. Figure 8-18a shows the multiplication of two 4-bit binary words using standard arithmetic. There are four partial products; the first, from the least significant bit of the multiplicand, is unshifted, the second is shifted one position to the left, and so on. These partial products are summed to generate the result, which in general has twice as many bits as the multiplier and multiplicand. Figure 8-18b shows the procedure when the add and shift opera-

```
    0110   Multiplicand
    1101   Multiplier

    0110   First partial product
 0  000    Second partial product
0 1  10    Third partial product
0 1 1  0   Fourth partial product

0 1 0 0  1110  Result
          (a)
```

```
0 1 1 0  Multiplier
1 1 0 1  Multiplicand
```

	0 0 0 0 0 0 0 0	Initial result
1 × 0 1 1 0 →	0 1 1 0	Add 1st partial product
	0 1 1 0 0 0 0 0	Intermediate result
	0 0 1 1 0 0 0 0	Rotate right
0 × 0 1 1 0 →	0 0 0 0	Add 2d partial product
	0 0 1 1 0 0 0 0	Intermediate result
	0 0 0 1 1 0 0 0	Rotate right
1 × 0 1 1 0 →	0 1 1 0	Add 3d partial product
	0 1 1 1 1 0 0 0	Intermediate result
	0 0 1 1 1 1 0 0	Rotate right
1 × 0 1 1 0 →	0 1 1 0	Add 4th partial product
	1 0 0 1 1 1 0 0	Intermediate result
Final result →	0 1 0 0 1 1 1 0	Rotate right

(b)

Figure 8-18 Comparison of multiplication approaches: (a) traditional multiplication; (b) multiplication using addition and rotation.

tions are used. There are two basic differences between this method and that shown in Fig. 8-18a: (1) the partial products are added to the result as they are generated, and (2) the partial products are added to the more significant positions and then shifted to the right. In the beginning the result is set to zero, and the first partial product is added to the more significant positions. Note that after this addition the result eventually is shifted four positions to the right so that, in effect, the first partial sum is added to the four less significant positions. Similarly, the second partial product is added to the more significant positions and then eventually shifted 3 times; this is equivalent to adding this partial sum to the fifth through second bits. The treatment of the third and fourth partial products is similar. This approach can be implemented using a repeated-task structural unit in which the repeated task consists of an alternative-task structural unit and several sequential tasks. The alternative-task structural unit tests the least significant bit in the multiplier; if it is set, the multiplicand is added to the high byte of the product. Otherwise nothing is done. The sequential tasks shift the product and the multiplier one position to the right.

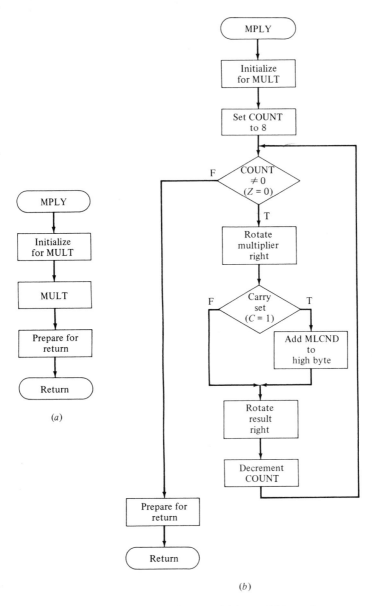

Figure 8-19 Flowcharts for subroutine to multiply two 8-bit words.

As shown in Fig. 8-19a, the subroutine MPLY is divided into three sequential subtasks, initializations for multiplication, multiplication, and preparation for return from the subroutine. Figure 8-19b shows a more detailed flowchart indicating that multiplication is performed bit by bit in a repeated-task structural unit. Figure 8-20 shows a second refinement of the flowchart containing instruction-level tasks. The initialization task includes loading the multiplier and multi-

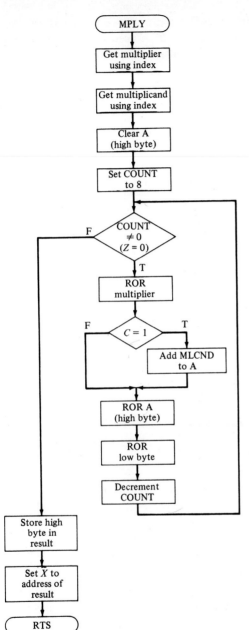

Figure 8-20 Instruction-level flowchart for a subroutine to multiply two 8-bit words refined from Fig 8-19.

plicand using the index register, setting the value 8 into the counter with the label COUNT, and clearing the accumulator since it will be used for the high byte of the product. As a part of the repeated task, an alternative-task structural unit is used to determine whether the multiplicand is added or not on each repetition. Shifting the partial product is slightly complicated since it is a 2-byte word and thus it must be shifted in two steps. In the first step, the high byte, stored in the accumulator, is rotated with its least significant bit going into the C bit of the condition-code register. This rotation also adjusts for any carries generated in adding the multiplicand. In the second step the low byte is rotated and the C bit shifted into the most significant bit.

Preparation for return involves loading the high byte of the product into memory and then loading the index register with this address. The low byte of the result is in the next location. Table 8-13 shows the corresponding program.

8-6-2 Ordering a List

The second problem will be developing a subroutine RDLST that will rearrange a list of 8-bit words in order of decreasing magnitude. The words are interpreted as unsigned integers. When control is transferred to the subroutine, the address of

Table 8-13 Assembly language for 8-bit multiply subroutine Fig. 8-20

```
            NAM    MLPY
            ORG    0
COUNT   RMB    1              LOOP COUNTER
RSLTH   RMB    2              RESULT HIGHBYTE AND LOWBYTE
MLPR    RMB    1              MULTIPLIER
MLCND   RMB    1              MULTIPLICAND
            ORG    $100
MLPY    LDAA   0,X            GET MULTIPLIER
            STAA   MLPR
            LDAA   1,X            GET MULTIPLICAND
            STAA   MLCND
            CLRA                  ZERO HIGH BYTE IN A
            LDAB   #8             INITIALIZE LOOP COUNT
            STAB   COUNT
MLOOP   BEQ    MEXIT          LOOP TEST
            ROR    MLPR           LEAST SIG BIT TO C
            BCC    MSKIP
            ADDA   MLCND          IF C = 1 ADD MULTIPLICAND TO HIGH BYTE
MSKIP   RORA                  ROTATE A WHICH IS HIGH BYTE
            ROR    RSLTH + 1      ROTATE LOW BYTE WITH CARRY FROM HIGH BYTE
            DEC    COUNT
            BRA    MLOOP
MEXIT   STAA   RSLTH          STORE HIGH BYTE OF RESULT
            LDX    #RSLTH         LOAD INDEX WITH ADDRESS OF RESULT
            RTS
            END
```

the list will be in the index register. The first element in the list defines the length of the list and is followed by the input words.

As shown in Fig. 8-21a, the subroutine RDLST can be subdivided into three sequential tasks, initialization for the ordering, the actual ordering of the words, and the preparation for return from the subroutine. Figure 8-21b indicates that the middle task is a repeated task which moves the smallest word in the list to the bottom. The counter COUNT1 is used to control the number of repetitions of this loop.

Figure 8-21c shows a further refinement of the flowchart for the subroutine RDLST and indicates that the task ORDER ONE WORD also requires a repeated task which compares two successive words and places the smaller second. The counter COUNT2 is used to control the number of repetitions in this inner loop. On the first repetition of the outer loop, all elements in the list are compared using the inner loop, and the smallest is moved toward the bottom. At the end of the first repetition of the outer loop the smallest value is at the bottom of the list. On each successive repetition the length of the list to be searched is diminished by 1 and the next smallest value is moved to the bottom of the shorter list. Each repetition of the outer loop results in pairwise comparisons of the as yet unordered values in the list using the inner loop. After $N - 1$ iterations of the outer loop, all elements are ordered.

A flowchart showing sufficient detail for writing the assembly-language program is shown in Fig. 8-22, and the program is given in Table 8-14. Initially the number of elements in the list is stored in COUNT1, the counter for the first repeated-task structural unit, i.e., the outer loop. The index register then is incremented so that it points to the first word in the list to be ordered, and this address is stored in LSTADR. The outer loop must be repeated $N - 1$ times since the process of ordering $N - 1$ elements automatically orders the Nth; as a result, COUNT1 is decremented before entering the loop. The RLOOP1 BEQ REXIT1 instruction is the exit for the outer loop. Inside this loop, the index register is loaded with the address of the top of the list, a task that is required to restore the index register for subsequent repetitions. With the indexed addressing mode the first entry is loaded into accumulator A. COUNT2 is set to the same value as COUNT1 since on each repetition of the outer loop this value defines the number of unordered elements in the list.

The COUNT2 value is tested with RLOOP2 BEQ REXIT2 for the exit from the inner loop. Inside this loop, the value in accumulator A is compared with the next entry in the list. If the result of this comparison is greater than or equal to zero, the next entry is smaller or the same, and so the list is unaltered and the smaller value is loaded into accumulator A. If the result of the comparison is less than zero, the next entry is larger; the two entries in the list are therefore interchanged, and the value in accumulator A is unaltered. After ordering each pair of elements, the index register is incremented to point to the next element to be ordered. The loop counter, COUNT2, is decremented, and the result is tested to determine whether another repetition is required.

When the inner loop has been repeated the appropriate number of times, the smallest remaining value has been moved to its proper place in the list. The loop

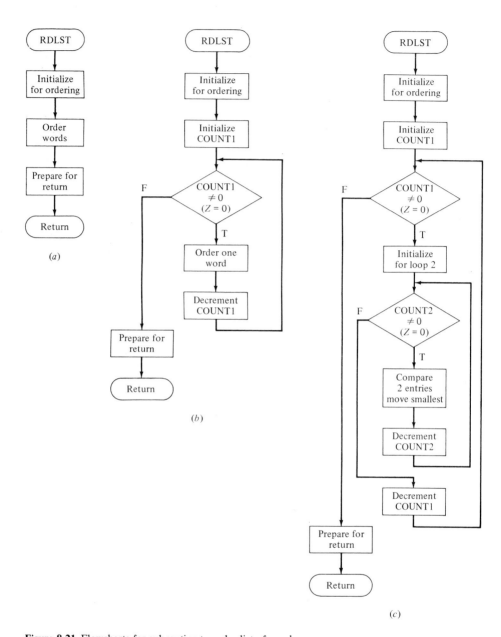

Figure 8-21 Flowcharts for subroutine to order list of words.

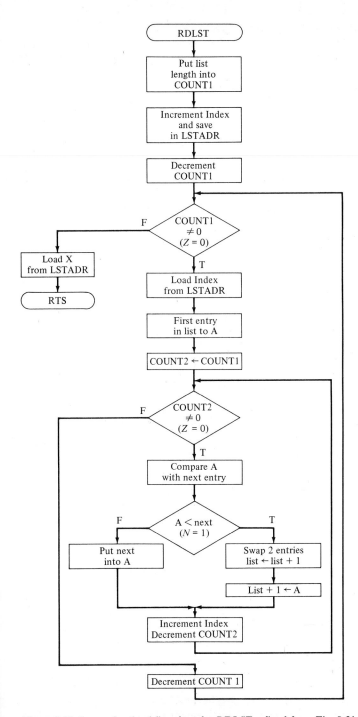

Figure 8-22 Instruction-level flowchart for RDLST refined from Fig. 8-21.

Table 8-14 Assembly-language program for flowchart, Fig. 8-22

	NAM	RDLST	
	ORG	0	
COUNT1	RMB	1	OUTER LOOP COUNTER
COUNT2	RMB	1	INNER LOOP COUNTER
LSTADR	RMB	2	LIST ADDRESS
	ORG	$100	
RDLST	LDAA	0,X	PUT LIST LENGTH IN COUNT1
	STAA	COUNT1	
	INX		
	STX	LSTADR	SAVE INDEX POINTING TO TOP
	DEC	COUNT1	REPEAT LOOP 1 LENGTH-1 TIMES
RLOOP1	BEQ	REXIT1	EXIT LOOP1
	LDX	LSTADR	INDEX POINTS TO TOP OF LIST
	LDAA	0,X	FIRST ENTRY IN A
	LDAB	COUNT1	GET NO. OF UNORDERED ELEMENTS
	STAB	COUNT2	INITIALIZE COUNT2 WITH THIS NUMBER
RLOOP2	BEQ	REXIT2	EXIT LOOP2
	CMPA	1,X	CHECK TWO ENTRIES
	BGE	RSKIP1	BRANCH IF A IS LARGER
	LDAB	1,X	GET LARGER ENTRY
	STAB	0,X	MOVE IT UP IN LIST
	STAA	1,X	MOVE SMALLER DOWN IN LIST
	BRA	RSKIP2	
RSKIP1	LDAA	1,X	MOVE SMALLER TO A
RSKIP2	INX		NEXT LIST PAIR
	DEC	COUNT2	DEC LOOP2 COUNTER
	BRA	RLOOP2	TO TOP LOOP2
REXIT2	DEC	COUNT1	DEC LOOP1 COUNTER
	BRA	RLOOP1	TO TOP LOOP1
REXIT1	LDX	LSTADR	INDEX AT TOP OF LIST
	RTS		RETURN
	END		

counter for the outer loop, COUNT1, is decremented, and the result is tested to determine whether another repetition is required.

When the outer loop has been repeated $N - 1$ times, all elements have been ordered. The last task is to load the index register with the address of the first element in the list.

8-6-3 Hexadecimal-to-ASCII Conversion

In this section we develop a subroutine that will convert a list of 8-bit words into a list of ASCII code words for the hexadecimal characters representing the input list. When the subroutine is entered, the address of the parameter list is in the index register. The first two elements of the parameter list contain the address where the output list of ASCII characters is to begin. The third element of the parameter list contains the length of the input list which begins with the fourth element. The subroutine need not return the address of the output list in the index register, and the contents of the internal processor registers need not be preserved.

As shown in Fig. 8-23a, this subroutine can be divided into two sequential tasks, initialization and conversion of the list of values. As shown in Fig. 8-23b, the CONVERT LIST task can be expanded as a repeated-task structural unit in which each element in the list is processed individually. In Fig. 8-24 the initialization and word-conversion tasks are refined further to obtain a one-page top-level description. The initialing tasks consist of getting and saving the address of the output list and transferring the length of the list to the loop counter. The CONVERT WORD task is more complicated. First the address of the input list is updated and saved, and one word is obtained from the input list. A subroutine, CWORD, is used to convert this word into two ASCII code words. Next the address of the output list is transferred to the index register, and the two ASCII code words are stored in the output list. The address of the output list then is updated and stored, and the address of the input list is transferred to the index register.

The subroutine CWORD converts a binary word into two ASCII code words. When the subroutine is entered, the index register contains the address of the input word. When returning from the subroutine the ASCII code words for the more and less significant characters are stored in the next two locations, respectively. Figure 8-25a shows a flowchart for this subroutine. The procedure is to get the word and process the more significant 4 bits and then the less significant 4 bits. Figure 8-25b shows a refinement of this subroutine defining the processing in more detail. First, the less significant 4 bits are set to zero to isolate the more significant 4 bits, which are shifted four positions to the right converted into an

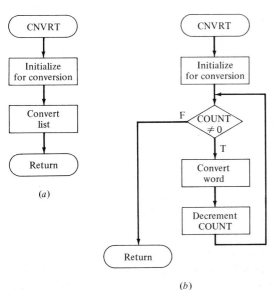

(a)

(b)

Figure 8-23 Flowcharts for subroutine to convert list of hexadecimal values into ASCII coded characters.

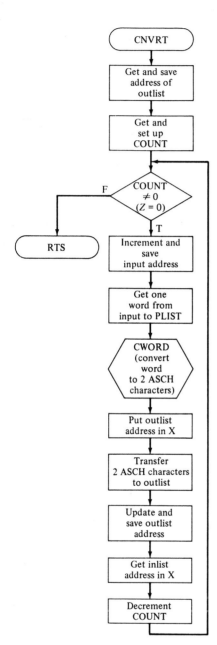

Figure 8-24 Top-level flowchart for CNVRT refined from Fig. 8-23.

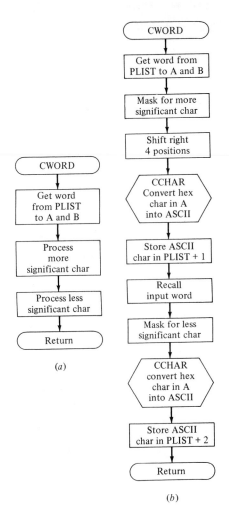

Figure 8-25 Flowchart for CWORD subroutine used in CNVRT routine (Fig. 8-24).

ASCII code word using the subroutine CCHAR, and stored in the location just below the input word. Next, the original word is obtained again, and the more significant 4 bits are set to zero to isolate the less significant 4 bits, which are converted again using CCHAR and stored in the second location below the input word.

The subroutine CCHAR replaces the 4-bit word in the lower half of accumulator A with the ASCII code for the equivalent hexadecimal character. Since this subroutine will be used only by the routine CWORD, and since only one parameter is transferred back and forth, we choose to transfer parameters directly in accumulator A instead of transferring their addresses in the index register. This subroutine is essentially a code converter where the input words and corresponding output words are shown in Table 8-15. Using a look-up table represents the most general approach for code conversion, but in this case there is a

Table 8-15 Table of corresponding hexadecimal and ASCII code-word values

Character	Hexadecimal input word	ASCII output word	Character	Hexadecimal input word	ASCII output word
0	00	30	8	08	38
1	01	31	9	09	39
2	02	32	A	0A	41
3	03	33	B	0B	42
4	04	34	C	0C	43
5	05	35	D	0D	44
6	06	36	E	0E	45
7	07	37	F	0F	46

systematic relationship between the input and output words. For the first 10 entries, i.e., values 0 to 9, the output word equals the input word plus the hexadecimal value 30, and for the last 6 entries the output word equals the input word plus the hexadecimal value 37. Thus the conversion is accomplished with an alternative-task structural unit implementing the statement IF value greater than 9, THEN add $37, ELSE add $30. The flowchart for this program is shown in Fig. 8-26.

The sequence of assembly-language instructions and data descriptors for the subroutines CNVRT, CWORD, and CCHAR is shown in Tables 8-16 and 8-17, respectively. There are two approaches for ensuring that the addresses of all subroutines will be available when assembling the calling programs. In the first approach the subroutines are assembled with the calling program. A single NAM directive is placed at the beginning and a single END directive is used at the very end. Alternatively, the subroutines can be assembled independently with a NAM,

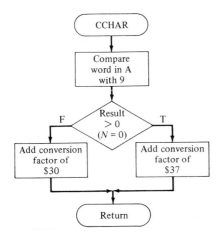

Figure 8-26 Flowchart for subroutine CCHAR used in CWORD routine (Fig. 8-25).

Table 8-16 Assembly-language program for top-level flowchart, Fig. 8-24

	NAM	CNVRT	
	ORG	0	
OUTADR	RMB	2	OUTPUT LIST ADDRESS
INADR	RMB	2	INPUT LIST ADDRESS
COUNT	RMB	1	LOOP COUNTER
PLIST	RMB	3	PARAMETER LIST FOR CWORD
CWORD	EQU	$200	ADDRESS OF CWORD SUBROUTINE
	ORG	$100	
CNVRT	LDAA	0,X	GET HIGH BYTE OUTPUT LIST ADDRESS
	STAA	OUTADR	SAVE HIGH BYTE OUTPUT ADDRESS
	INX		
	LDAA	0,X	GET LOW BYTE OUTPUT LIST ADDRESS
	STAA	OUTADR+1	SAVE LOW BYTE OUTPUT LIST ADDRESS
	INX		
	LDAA	0,X	GET LENGTH OF INPUT LIST
	STAA	COUNT	SETUP LOOP COUNT
CLOOP	BEQ	CEXIT	TEST LOOP EXIT
	INX		
	STX	INADR	SAVE ADDRESS OF INPUT LIST
	LDAA	0,X	GET WORD FROM INPUT LIST
	STAA	PLIST	PUT WORD IN PARAMETER LIST
	LDX	#PLIST	GET ADDRESS OF PARAMETER LIST
	JSR	CWORD	CONVERT WORD TO 2 ASCII
	LDX	OUTADR	GET OUTPUT LIST ADDRESS
	LDAA	PLIST+1	GET FIRST ASCII CHAR
	STAA	0,X	STORE IN OUTPUT LIST
	LDAA	PLIST+2	GET SECOND ASCII CHAR
	STAA	1,X	STORE IN OUTPUT LIST
	INX		UPDATE OUTLIST ADDRESS
	INX		BY TWO
	STX	OUTADR	SAVE OUTPUT LIST ADDRESS
	LDX	INADR	GET INPUT LIST ADDRESS
	DEC	COUNT	DEC LOOP COUNT
	BRA	CLOOP	DO LOOP AGAIN
CEXIT	RTS		RETURN
	END		

ORG, and END directive used for each. In this second approach an EQU directive must be added to each calling routine to define the starting addresses that were assigned when the subroutines were assembled. In the present example the subroutine CNVRT is assembled as one program and the subroutines CWORD and CCHAR are assembled together. Thus in CNVRT the directive CWORD EQU $200 is included to define the starting address of the subroutine CWORD.

We have developed the subroutine CNVRT as a top-level program using other subroutines at two lower levels. This development has been independent of other programs which might ultimately make use of the subroutine CNVRT. This

Table 8-17 Assembly language for second-level flowcharts, Figs. 8-25 and 8-26

	NAM	CWORD	
	ORG	$200	
CWORD	LDAA	0, X	GET INPUT WORD
	TAB		SAVE INPUT WORD IN B
	ANDA	#$F0	MASK FOR MORE SIG. BITS
	LSRA		RIGHT JUSTIFY
	LSRA		
	LSRA		
	LSRA		
	JSR	CCHAR	CONVERT MORE SIG. CHAR. TO ASCII
	STAA	1, X	STORE ASCII CODE IN PLIST + 1
	TBA		RECALL INPUT WORD
	ANDA	#$0F	MASK FOR LESS SIG. BITS
	JSR	CCHAR	CONVERT LESS SIG. CHAR TO ASCII
	STAA	2, X	STORE ASCII CODE IN PLIST + 2
	RTS		RETURN
CCHAR	CMPA	#9	NUMERIC OR ALPHA
	BLE	C1	BRANCH IF CHAR IS 9 OR LESS
	ADDA	#$37	ALPHA SYMBOL— ADD $37
	BRA	C2	
C1	ADDA	#$30	NUMERIC SYMBOL— ADD $30
C2	RTS		RETURN
	END		

independent development is made possible by carefully specifying the input and output parameter lists. Similarly, the subroutine CWORD is a second-level program in relation to the subroutine CNVRT, while the subroutine CCHAR is a third-level program with respect to the subroutine CNVRT. Each of these subroutines, CNVRT, CWORD, and CCHAR, may represent other levels with respect to programs which call the subroutine CNVRT.

This example stresses the importance of restricted complexity and modularity in program development. The careful specification of module interfaces, parameter-list structures, and program behavior allows concurrent independent development of simple program modules that are later integrated to solve complex problems.

Earlier, when we first discussed the subroutine CCHAR, we mentioned that using a look-up table was the most general approach for implementing a code converter. Now we shall redefine this subroutine to illustrate the use of a look-up table. In this approach, the two-column table identifying corresponding code words, Table 8-15, must be converted into a one-column look-up table so that it can be stored in memory. The most effective configuration is to alternate entries in such a way that the odd-numbered entries represent input code words and the even-numbered entries represent output code words. Thus the reorganized look-up table derived from Table 8-15 would contain 00, 30, 01, 31, 02, 32..., 0E, 45, 0F, and 46.

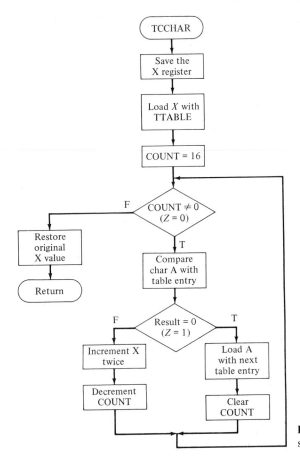

Figure 8-27 Table-look-up version of subroutine to convert character.

The flowchart for the look-up-table solution to the subroutine CCHAR is shown in Fig. 8-27. When the subroutine is entered, the hexadecimal value to be converted is in the A accumulator and the corresponding ASCII code word will be returned in the same register. First, the contents of the index register are saved. Then the index register is loaded with TTABLE, the address of the first entry in the look-up table. Then, the loop count is initialized to 16, the number of pairs of entries in the look-up table. A repeated-task structural unit is used for a sequential comparison of the value in the A accumulator with the odd-numbered entries in the look-up table until a match is found. In the repeated task the value in the A accumulator is compared with each odd-numbered entry in the look-up table addressed by the index register. If the two values are equal, the next entry in the look-up table, which is the code word corresponding to the input word, is loaded into the A accumulator and the loop-counter value is set to zero to terminate the repetitions; otherwise the index register is incremented twice, to address the next odd-numbered entry, and the loop counter is decremented.

Table 8-18 Assembly-language subroutine for table-look-up version of CCHAR, Fig. 8-27

	NAM	TCCHAR	
	ORG	$10	
TTABLE	FCB	$0, $30, $1, $31, $2, $32	
	FCB	$3, $33, $4, $34, $5, $35	
	FCB	$6, $36, $7, $37, $8, $38	
	FCB	$9, $39, $A, $41, $B, $42	
	FCB	$C, $43, $D, $44, $E, $45	
	FCB	$F, $46	TABLE WITH HEX. AND ASCII CODE
TXSAVE	RMB	2	STORAGE FOR ORIGINAL X REG
TCOUNT	RMB	1	LOOP COUNTER
TCCHAR	STX	TXSAVE	SAVE X REG VALUE
	LDX	#TTABLE	TABLE ADDRESS TO X
	LDAB	#16	COUNT FOR LOOP = 16
	STAB	TCOUNT	
TLOOP	BEQ	TEXIT	EXIT WHEN TCOUNT = O
	CMPA	0, X	COMPARE A TO TABLE ENTRY
	BNE	T1	NOT EQUAL. SKIP TO T1
	LDAA	1, X	ASCII IS NEXT ENTRY
	CLR	TCOUNT	NO MORE REPETITIONS
	BRA	T2	BRA TO END OF LOOP
T1	INX		INCR INDEX TO NEXT PAIR
	INX		
	DEC	TCOUNT	DECR LOOP COUNTER
T2	BRA	TLOOP	BRA TO LOOP TEST
TEXIT	LDX	TXSAVE	RESTORE X REG VALUE
	RTS		RETURN
	END		

When the correct table entry has been found and the corresponding ASCII code word obtained, the loop is terminated and the original value of the index resister restored. Finally, the subroutine returns to the calling program. The assembly-language program for the flowchart of Fig. 8-27 is given in Table 8-18.

8-7 CONCLUSION

In this chapter we have examined the process of writing programs. This process is restricted and disciplined by using only three distinct structural units and a well-defined substitution rule. Programs developed in this way are called structured programs. The complexity of any single program module is limited by restricting the module description to a single page.

We have used flowcharts as the model for program module development and description. Many high-level languages, such as PL/M and PASCAL, have features well suited to the development and description of structured programs.

Since we can now translate any structured program into assembly language, the material of this chapter is linked with the material of the last two chapters. The most important topic we have discussed is the systematic method for transforming a problem specification into a structured program. In the next chapter we turn again to hardware elements to study their behavior and interconnection in order to construct a microcomputer system capable of executing the program solutions derived here.

PROBLEMS

8-1 Define each of the following terms:

flowchart	alternative-task structural unit	top-level description
terminal element	IF-THEN-ELSE statement	second-level description
task element	repeated-task structural unit	third-level description
decision element	DO WHILE statement	substitution process
basic structural units	structured flowchart	top-down development
sequential-task structural unit	structured program	

8-2 Discuss how the configurations shown in Fig. P8-2 differ from the structural units defined in this chapter.

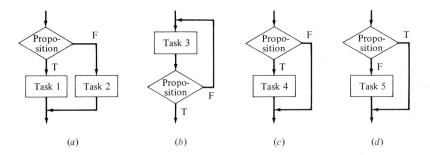

(a)   (b)   (c)   (d)

Figure P8-2 Flowcharts.

8-3 Using standard flowchart elements, redraw:
(a) Fig. 7-2   (b) Fig. 7-4   (c) Fig. 7-5

8-4 Draw a structured instruction-level flowchart for the assembly-language program shown in:
(1) Prob. 7-11   (2) Prob. 7-12   (3) Prob. 7-13
(4) Prob. 7-14   (5) Prob. 7-15   (6) Prob. 7-16
(7) Prob. 7-17   (8) Prob. 7-18

8-5 Draw structured flowcharts for all subroutines for the assembly-language program shown in:
(a) Prob. 7-19   (b) Prob. 7-34
(c) Prob. 7-35   (d) Prob. 7-40

8-6 For the flowcharts in Fig. P8-6, define the order the tasks are executed when:
(a) DATA contains 41, SUM contains D2, and accumulator A contains 59
(b) DATA contains B2, SUM contains 05, and accumulator A contains 37

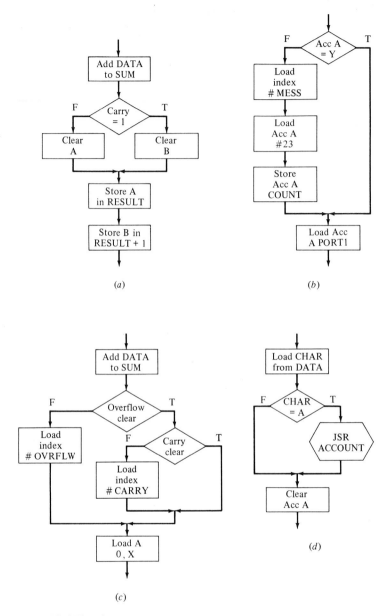

(a)

(b)

(c)

(d)

Figure P8-6 Flowcharts.

8-7 For the flowcharts in Fig. P8-7, define the order the tasks are executed when:
   (a) DATA contains 53 and SUM contains E7
   (b) DATA contains E3 and SUM contains 02
   (c) DATA and SUM contain 00

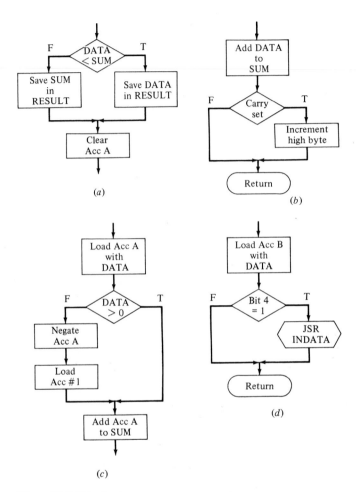

Figure P8-7 Flowcharts.

8-8 For the flowcharts shown in Fig. P8-8, define the order the tasks are executed when:
   (1) TEST1 contains 03   (2) TEST1 contains 00   (3) TEST1 contains 02

8-9 Define the sequence of assembly-language instructions to implement the flowcharts and make a list of all labels that must be defined for:
   (1) Fig. P8-6   (2) Fig. P8-7   (3) Fig. P8-8

8-10 Define the sequence of assembly-language instructions to implement the flowcharts shown in Fig. P8-10. Define all labels used in the subroutine.

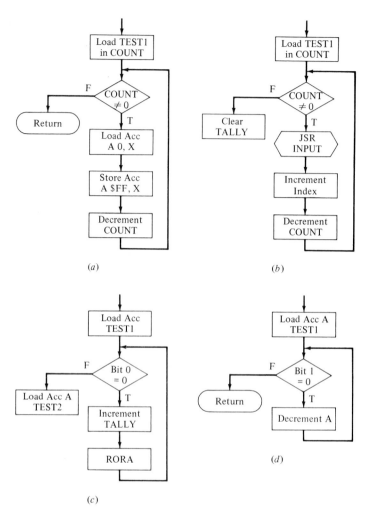

Figure P8-8 Flowcharts.

8-11 Draw the flowchart and write the corresponding assembly-language instructions to implement the following task descriptions:

(*a*) If DATA positive THEN store A in RESULT, ELSE store B in RESULT. The next task is increment X.

(*b*) IF overflow occurred, THEN store contents of A using the indexed addressing mode with an offset of 0 and jump to subroutine OVRFLW, ELSE do nothing. The next task is store X in ADDRES.

(*c*) IF contents of ALPHA is not ASCII Q, THEN do nothing, ELSE load A from PORT and jump to subroutine QCHAR. The next task is the subroutine TSTDAT.

(*d*) IF contents of ALPHA is ASCII Q, THEN load A from PORT and jump to subroutine QCHAR, ELSE do nothing. The next task is increment COUNT.

8-12 Draw the flowchart and write the corresponding assembly-language instructions to implement the following task descriptions:

(*a*) IF contents of A is greater than B, THEN transfer accumulators, ELSE do nothing. The next task is increment X.

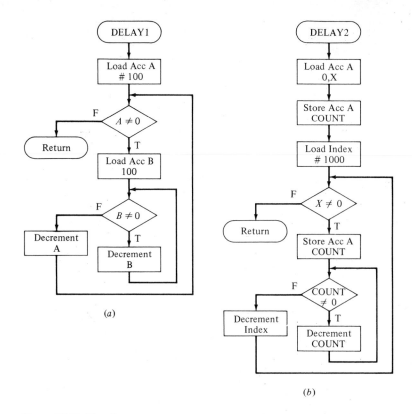

Figure P8-10 Flowcharts.

(*b*) IF contents of A is less than B, THEN do nothing, ELSE transfer accumulators. The next task is store A in RESULT.

(*c*) IF bit 4 of TEST is set, THEN increment X, ELSE decrement X and jump to subroutine AGAIN. The next task is increment COUNT.

(*d*) IF bit 7 of DATA is set, THEN jump to subroutine BITSET, ELSE jump to subroutine BITRST. The next task is increment X.

8-13 Draw the flowcharts and write the corresponding assembly-language instructions to implement the following task descriptions:

(*a*) DO decrement A WHILE A is nonzero. The next task is increment X.

(*b*) DO increment A WHILE A is not equal $50. The next task is decrement B.

(*c*) DO test bit 4 of PORT WHILE bit 4 of PORT is zero. The next task is load A from DATA.

(*d*) DO rotate DWORD to the left and decrement COUNT WHILE COUNT is nonzero. The next task is the subroutine TCASE.

8-14 Draw the flowchart and write the corresponding assembly-language instructions to implement the following task descriptions:

(*a*) DO clear memory using the indexed addressing mode and decrement X and COUNT WHILE COUNT is nonzero. The next task is load X from SAVE.

(*b*) DO increment X, jump to subroutine XDATA, and decrement COUNT WHILE COUNT is nonzero. The next task is the subroutine YDATA.

(*c*) DO increment X and test the memory location whose address is contained in X WHILE the contents of memory are nonzero. The next task is store X in SAVE.

(*d*) DO jump to subroutine INPUT, store A in list using the indexed addressing mode with a 0 offset, jump to subroutine OUTPUT, increment X, and decrement COUNT WHILE COUNT is nonzero. The next task is a subroutine TESTD.

8-15 Discuss the rationale of branching when the test condition is false, which we used consistently in translating both the alternative-task structural unit and the repeated-task structural unit into assembly-language instructions.

8-16 For the program defined by Fig. 8-17*b*, verify that the correct result is produced if:

 (*a*) The list contains one element with the value 00.

 (*b*) The list contains $03, $FC, $82, and $3E.

8-17 For the program defined by Fig. 8-22 verify that the correct result is produced if the input list contains $03, $03, $1C, and $0E.

8-18 For the program CNVRT defined by Figs. 8-24 to 8-26 verify that the correct result is produced for the input list (*a*) $03, $0C, $01, and $C3 and (*b*) $05, $F3, $03, $02, $7C, and $50.

8-19 Draw a structured flowchart and write the corresponding assembly-language program for a subroutine that will search a list of words in memory and count the number of bits that have a value of 1. When entering the subroutine the index register contains the address on the first element of the list. This first element defines the number of elements to be searched. When returning from the subroutine the total should be placed at the end of the list and its address stored in the index register. Use a separate subroutine to count the 1s in each word.

8-20 Draw a structured flowchart and write the corresponding assembly-language program for a subroutine that will load the index register with an address of a list containing the ASCII code words for a message. The message is based on input data which are in accumulator A when the subroutine is entered. The message should be CARRIAGE RETURN if the data represent the ASCII code word for a carriage return; it should be LINE FEED if the data represent the ASCII code word for a line feed; and it should be NEITHER if the data represent neither. When returning from this subroutine, accumulator A must contain a value that defines the number of characters in the message.

8-21 Draw a structured flowchart and write the corresponding assembly-language program for a subroutine that will add two BCD-coded values. When the subroutine is entered, the index contains the address of the first value; the second value is stored in the next location. On return from the subroutine, the sum is stored using BCD code in the next highest memory location. The contents of the index registers should not be changed by this subroutine.

8-22 Draw a structured flowchart and write the corresponding assembly-language program for a subroutine that requires 100 computer cycles for execution and then returns with the same data in all internal processor registers.

8-23 Draw a structured flowchart and write the corresponding assembly-language program for a subroutine that requires $100N$ computer cycles and then returns with the same data in all internal processor registers. When entering the subroutine, accumulator A contains the value N as an unsigned binary-value code word.

8-24 Draw a structured flowchart and write the corresponding assembly-language program for a subroutine that will search a list and count and identify the addresses of all elements that are identical to the first element in the list and store the addresses of all identical elements. When entering the subroutine, the index register contains the address of the first element. The second element defines the number of elements that must be compared. When returning from the subroutine, the total count is stored at the bottom of the list and the addresses of identified elements are stored in subsequent memory locations. The index register should contain the address of the total.

8-25 Draw a structured flowchart and write the corresponding assembly-language program for a subroutine that will search a list for its most negative value. Elements in the list are interpreted using the signed binary-value two's-complement code. The first element in the list defines the number of elements to be searched. When returning the index register should contain the address of the identified element.

8-26 Draw a structured flowchart and write the corresponding assembly-language program for a subroutine that will interpret a list of words as BCD-coded decimal values and generate an output list representing the corresponding seven-segment display code words. Each input word contains two BCD characters. In the output code the most significant bit must be 0 and bits 6 to 0 represent a to g, respectively (see Fig. 2-26). When entering the subroutine, the index register contains the address of the first element in the list. This element defines the number of words that must be converted. The output list should be stored just below the input list. When returning from this subroutine, the index register must contain its original address. Use a separate subroutine to do the actual code conversions.

8-27 Draw a structured flowchart and write the corresponding assembly-language program for a subroutine that will convert a BCD word present at the input port assigned the address $30C4 into the corresponding seven-segment code word and put the result in the output port assigned the address $503C. The status bits for the input port and output port are assigned the addresses $30C5 and $503D, respectively. Use a separate subroutine for the actual code conversion.

8-28 Draw a structured flowchart and write the corresponding assembly-language program for a subroutine that will input an 8-bit data word and a 3-bit data-selection code word from the input ports assigned the address $80F2 and $80F4, respectively. The input status bit, assigned the address $80F3, is used to synchronize both input transfers. The data-selection code-word pattern defines a particular bit of the 8-bit data word for output; e.g., the pattern 011 defines bit 3 of the data word. The defined input data bit is then stored in bit 5 of the output port assigned the address $3000. The status bit used to synchronize the output transfer is assigned the address $3001.

8-29 Draw a structured flowchart and write the corresponding assembly-language program for a subroutine that will input an 8-bit data word, a 3-bit input selection code word, and a 3-bit output selection code word from input ports assigned the addresses $80F2, $80F4, and $80F6, respectively. The input status bit assigned to the address $80F3 is used to synchronize these input transfers. The input-selection code-word pattern is used to define a particular bit of the 8-bit data word, e.g., the pattern 011 defines bit 3 of the data word. In a similar way the output-selection code pattern defines the bit in the output port assigned address $3000 where the selected input data bit is to be stored. The status bit used to synchronize the output transfer is assigned the address $3001.

8-30 Draw a structured flowchart and write the corresponding assembly-language program for a subroutine that will input an 8-bit data word and a 3-bit rotation control code word from the input ports assigned the addresses $80F2 and $80F4, respectively. The input status bit used to synchronize both input transfers is assigned the address $80F3. The binary value of the rotation control word defines the number of positions the input data word must be rotated to the right. For example, a rotation control word of 011 defines a rotation of three positions to the right. The rotated result is to be stored in the output port assigned the address $3000. The status bit used to synchronize the output transfer is assigned the address $3001.

8-31 Draw a structured flowchart and write the corresponding assembly-language program for a subroutine that will merge two previously ordered lists into a single ordered list. The lists are in descending order. When entering the subroutine, the index register contains the address of the location defining the length of input LIST1, the address of the first element in LIST1, the length of LIST2, the address of the first element in LIST2, and the address where the first element in the output list of ordered words is to be placed. Others are stored in subsequent locations. The entries in LIST1 and LIST2 are already in descending order and are to be merged into a single output list.

REFERENCES

Horowitz, E., and S. Sahni,: "Fundamentals of Data Structure," Computer Science Press, Potomac, Md., 1976.

IBM Corporation, Structured Programming: Textbook and Workbook, IBM Corporation SR20-7921, 1974.

McCracken, D. D.: "A Guide to PL/M Programming for Microcomputer Applications," Addison-Wesley, Reading, Mass., 1978.

Wester, J. G., and W. D. Simpson: "Software Design for Microprocessors," Texas Instruments, Inc., Dallas, Tex., 1976.

Winkel, D., and F. Prosser: "The Art of Digital Design: An Introduction to Top-Down Design," Prentice-Hall, Englewood Cliffs, N.J., 1980.

Wirth, N.: "Systematic Programming: An Introduction," Prentice-Hall, Englewood Cliffs, N.J., 1973.

Yourdon, E.: "Techniques of Program Structure and Design," Prentice-Hall, Englewood Cliffs, N.J., 1975.

―――― and L. Constantine: "Structured Design: Fundamentals of a Discipline of Computer Program and Systems Design," Prentice-Hall, Englewood Cliffs, N.J., 1979.

6800 MICROCOMPUTER FAMILY HARDWARE

In this chapter we shall describe several physical devices or packages used in configuring a 6800 microcomputer system. By the end of this chapter you should be able to:

1. Define the terms listed in Prob. 9-1
2. Draw an input-output model and a block diagram for the MCM6810 and the MCM6830 memory packages
3. Draw a schematic diagram for a memory unit to meet any size and addressing specification, using the two family memory devices described, and show all connections between the memory unit and the system bus
4. Draw the input-output model for the MC6821 peripheral interface package, describe the purpose of each user-accessible register, and define the code words for appropriate registers for a specific application
5. Draw a schematic diagram for an input-output unit to meet any size and addressing specification using the parallel input-output devices, and show all connections between the input-output unit and the system bus

9-1 MICROPROCESSOR FAMILIES

In Chap. 5 we discussed microcomputer hardware in terms of four basic units: the processor, memory, input, and output units. We also pointed out that these units contain many individual logic elements and modules. In practice these units are constructed and packaged using integrated circuits. Current integrated-circuit manufacturing technology places many logic elements and modules on a single chip. Consequently, a single package can include several computer functions or even a complete computer system of limited capability. Packages that contain a large number of logic elements, typically more than 100 gates, are referred to as *large-scale-integration* (LSI) packages. A *microcomputer* is a complete computer constructed from LSI circuit packages. A *microprocessor* is a computer processor unit constructed from LSI circuit packages.

Ideally, a manufacturer would like to market a single microprocessor along with a selection of compatible memory and support devices and would like these devices to be effective in meeting the needs of a broad set of applications, thus increasing the potential market. Since this has proved to be impractical, manufacturers offer a group of related devices referred to as a family. A microcomputer family is a number of processor devices with varying capabilities along with a selection of compatible memory and support devices that can be used with a standard system bus. With few exceptions, all processors in a family can execute the same instruction set and thus the same programs. This allows a user to select the processor device that is most effective for each application while eliminating the support costs and learning time associated with changing to a completely new device. From the manufacturer's point of view the advantages of a family of devices are the wider market potential for all devices and lower development cost because of the similarity of the devices and a more limited amount of support software and documentation.

The 6800 family includes microprocessors, microcomputers, memories, and various support packages, like clocks and input-output interfaces. Although there are many different packages in the 6800 family, we shall limit our discussion to those listed in Table 9-1. These packages are representative of the family and will provide ample opportunity for discussing the principles of operation and interconnection. By properly selecting and connecting packages from this list we shall be able to create microcomputer systems with a wide range of capabilities and thus configure microcomputer systems for a wide range of applications.

9-2 MICROPROCESSOR HARDWARE

This section discusses four microprocessor devices, the MC6800, MC6800A, MC6800B, and MC6802. The first three contain only the basic 6800 processor unit and operate with maximum clock rates of 1.0, 1.5, and 2.0 MHz, respectively. The MC6802 contains the basic 6800 processor along with an internal clock and 128 bytes of memory assigned to address block 0000 to 007F. The maximum clock rate for the MC6802 is 1.0 MHz.

Figure 9-1 shows the signal-to-pin assignment and the input-output model for the MC6800, MC6800A, and MC6800B. The internal architecture was described in Chap. 5. The device has 16 address pins (A_0 to A_{15}), 8 data pins (D_0 to D_7), a read-write control pin (R/W), a valid-memory-address pin (VMA), a reset pin

Table 9-1 Representative 6800 family packages

Package type	Number	Description
Microprocessor	MC6800	8-bit microprocessor unit
Microprocessor	MC6802	8-bit microprocessor with clock and RAM
Memory	MCM6810	128 × 8 static RAM
Memory	MCM6830	1024 × 8 masked ROM
Input-output	MC6821	Peripheral interface adapter
Microcomputer	MC6801	8-bit microcomputer unit

($\overline{\text{RESET}}$), a maskable-interrupt-request pin ($\overline{\text{IRQ}}$), a nonmaskable-interrupt-request pin ($\overline{\text{NMI}}$), a halt pin ($\overline{\text{HALT}}$), two clock signal pins (ϕ_1 and ϕ_2), a three-state control pin (TSC), a data-bus-enable pin (DBE), and a bus-available pin (BA). These pins are connected to the corresponding lines in the 6800 system bus. Although we discussed the nature of most of these signals, we have not yet discussed the TSC, DBE, and BA signals. They are used to coordinate the control of the address and data buses in systems where data transfers can be initiated by units other than the processor. Since we shall not consider any systems with this

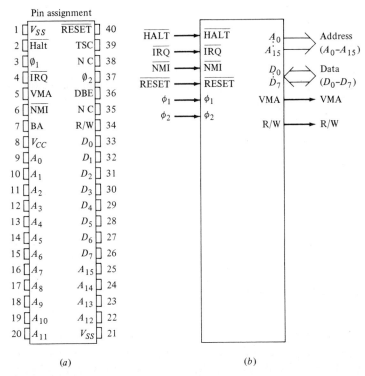

Pin assignment

(a)   (b)

Figure 9-1 MC6800 package description: (*a*) signal-to-pin assignment; (*b*) input-output model.

Table 9-2 Summary of some processor control signals

$\overline{\text{HALT}}$	All processor activities halted as long as this signal is low
$\overline{\text{RESET}}$	Loads program counter with contents of location FFFE and FFFF to execute the restart routine
$\overline{\text{NMI}}$	Completes current instruction, saves all processor registers, and loads program counter with contents of FFFC and FFFD to execute nonmaskable-interrupt-service routine
$\overline{\text{IRQ}}$	
	I bit = 1: Completes current instruction and continues
	I bit = 0: Completes current instruction, saves all processor registers, and loads program counter with contents of FFF8 and FFF9 to execute maskable-interrupt-service routine

capacity, these signals will not be discussed further and are omitted from the input-output model in Fig. 9-1*b*.

In Fig. 9-1 the symbol describing the signal on some pins contains an overbar. This notation implies that the signal connected to that pin is considered active when low; i.e., the signal connected to that pin uses the negative-logic assumption. To be consistent with the M6800 processor unit, the signals on the reset, halt, and maskable- and nonmaskable-interrupt-request lines in the 6800 system bus must be at the low level when active. Other devices connected to these lines must be consistent with this logic assumption.

Table 9-2 summarizes the activity of the processor unit when the four input control signals, HALT, RESET, NMI, and IRQ, are active, i.e., at the low level. The HALT signal simply stops the processor as long as it is active. The RESET signal aborts the program being executed and causes the execution of the restart routine whose address is stored in locations FFFE and FFFF. The NMI signal allows completion of the current instruction, saves the contents of all processor registers on the stack so that execution of the current program can continue after the interrupt is served, and causes the execution of the nonmaskable-interrupt-service routine whose address is stored in locations FFFC and FFFD. The IRQ signal is ignored if the I bit in the condition-code register is set, but if this bit is cleared, the IRQ signal allows completion of the current instruction, saves the contents of all processor registers on the stack so that the current programs can be continued, and causes execution of the maskable-interrupt service routine whose address is stored in locations FFF8 and FFF9.

Figure 9-2 shows the signal-to-pin assignment and the input-output model for the MC6802 microprocessor. Most pins on this device are identical to those on the MC6800 device. The three exceptions are the memory-enable pin (RE), the enable pin (E), and the memory ready pin (MR). The signal on the RE pin connects the 128 bytes of internal memory to the address, data, and read-write control lines. The signal on the E pin is used to provide timing information to other devices on the system bus in place of the ϕ_2 clock signal. The signal on the MR pin is used when nonstandard devices are connected to the system bus to help synchronize data transfers; it will not be discussed further. As with the

Pin assignment

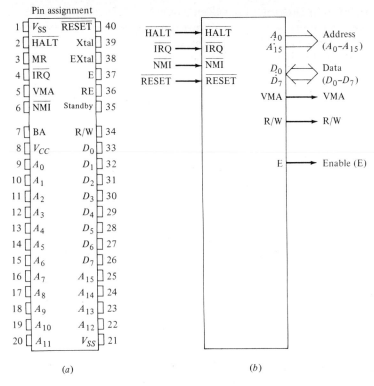

(a)   (b)

Figure 9-2 MC6802 package description: (*a*) signal-to-pin assignment; (*b*) input-output model.

M6800 the $\overline{\text{HALT}}$, $\overline{\text{IRQ}}$, $\overline{\text{NMI}}$, and $\overline{\text{RESET}}$ pins again must be connected to signals using the negative-logic assumption.

9-3 MEMORY HARDWARE

In this section we shall limit our discussion to memory devices constructed with semiconductor material, omitting those constructed from magnetic materials. After giving a general discussion of some of the types of memory devices that are available we shall describe the behavior of two representative memory devices in the 6800 family. Finally we shall outline a procedure for designing a memory unit with a specified capacity and address space.

9-3-1 Memory Technologies

Semiconductor memories are available in a wide range of capacities and characteristics. *Volatile memory devices* lose stored data when electric power is lost, while *nonvolatile memory devices* retain their data when power is lost. The term *random-access memory* (RAM) is used for volatile memory and *read-only memory* (ROM) for nonvolatile memory. In general, RAM devices are used to store data manipulated by the programs, and ROM devices are used to store the programs.

RAM devices can be divided further into two classes, static and dynamic. A static RAM device uses a flip-flop circuit for each bit. Data stored in the flip-flop circuit are retained until they are altered by writing in that location or by losing electric power. A dynamic RAM device uses a capacitor-like element for each bit. Since the charge on a capacitor decays with time, dynamic RAM devices must be recharged or *refreshed* periodically. Dynamic memory devices are attractive because they require fewer circuit elements per bit and consequently can be packaged more densely at a lower cost per bit. They are unattractive because they require special circuitry to control the refreshing process.

The nonvolatile data storage characteristic of ROM devices can be achieved in a number of ways. The data stored in a *masked ROM* device are defined by the interconnection of the circuit elements on the chip when it is manufactured. Thus, the user must define the stored data before ordering the part and typically must make a large purchase because of the high cost of developing the masks used in the manufacture of an integrated circuit. A user would choose masked ROM devices when the application programs are tested completely and a large market is anticipated.

A second alternative is to use ROM devices which can be altered by the user after manufacture. When purchased, these devices contain either 1s or 0s in every bit, but they are made so that each bit can be switched selectively to the opposite state. These devices are referred to as *programmable read-only memory* (PROM), and the procedure for loading specific data into the device is referred to as *programming* the PROM.

In one type of PROM device each bit is "fused," and the user selectively "blows" these fuses to store data. A special piece of hardware, a *PROM programmer*, is used to address each memory location sequentially and provide adequate current into the data output lines to blow the appropriate fuse, thereby changing the value stored in that location. These *fusable-link ROMs* are attractive since it is not necessary to commit to a large purchase.

A second type of PROM device uses capacitors with decay times of several years to store the data. With a PROM programmer, the user selectively charges these capacitors to store data. In addition, these devices have a window for applying high-energy ultraviolet light to accelerate the charge decay, thereby erasing present data. Because of this feature, these devices are called *erasable-programmable read-only memories* (EPROM). In general, EPROM devices are significantly more expensive than fusable-link PROMs and are used while developing application programs. For both fusable-link PROM devices and EPROM devices programming is accomplished off-line from the actual microcomputer system in which the memory is used. Newer ROM devices can be programmed in place, either by extending the duration of the write cycle or by applying higher voltage at the inputs during the write cycle. The read cycle is significantly faster than the write cycle, and the contents are nonvolatile. The devices have been dubbed *read-mostly memories*, a special type of EPROM.

In the next two sections we shall discuss two typical memory devices from the 6800 family, the MCM6810 RAM and the MCM6830 ROM.

9-3-2 MCM6810 RAM Package

The MCM6810 is a 128×8 RAM device. Figure 9-3 shows its signal-to-pin assignment, input-output model, and block diagram. The package has six chip-select pins (CS_0 to CS_5), seven address pins (A_0 to A_6), eight data pins (D_0 to D_7), and a read-write control pin (R/W).

Signals on the six chip-select pins are ANDed inside the package to create a signal which uniquely selects or activates the package. If all six chip-select signals are at the appropriate level, we say the package is selected. Signals on the seven address pins are decoded internally to produce signals that enable one of the memory locations in the package. The R/W input determines the direction of data flow at the eight data pins. Signals from the data pins are connected to a three-state buffer similar to that described in Figs. 3-29 and 3-30. If the package is selected and the signal on the R/W pin is high, the contents of the location enabled by the address decoder are passed to the data pins. Conversely, if the package is selected and the signal on the R/W pin is low, the pattern on the data pins is stored in the location enabled by the address decoder. If the package is not selected, the three-state buffers are in the high-impedance state and the data pins appear to be open circuits. There is an overbar on the symbols associated with the four chip-select pins, $\overline{CS_1}$, $\overline{CS_2}$, $\overline{CS_4}$, and $\overline{CS_5}$, indicating that the signals connected to these pins will be interpreted using the negative-logic assumption; i.e., they will be interpreted as active when at the low level. When the signal actually uses a positive-logic assumption, as with the 6800 address signals, a value of 0 on that signal will be considered as active. We shall use *true* and *false inputs* to designate pins designed for the positive- and negative-logic assumptions, respectively.

To illustrate the connection of the MCM6810 package to the 6800 system bus let us define the connection to provide 128 bytes of RAM at locations \$0400 to \$047F. The required connections are shown in Fig. 9-4. The data lines and the read-write control line of the system bus are connected to the corresponding data and read-write control pins on the package. Address lines A_6 to A_0 of the system bus are connected to the corresponding address pins on the package. Using the low-order address lines ensures that the memory locations on the device will be assigned consecutive addresses. When the M6800 processor is used, the valid-memory-address signal (VMA) and the ϕ_2 clock signal are ANDed externally and connected to the CS_0 pin to provide the required timing information. When the M6802 processor is used, the enable signal (E) is used instead.

The nine remaining address lines in the system bus, A_{15} to A_7, are available for connection to the five remaining chip-select pins on the package, CS_5 to CS_1,

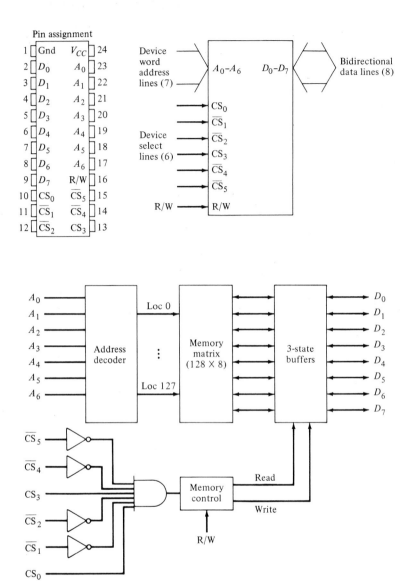

Figure 9-3 MCM6810 RAM device: (*a*) signal-to-pin assignment, (*b*) input-output model, and (*c*) block diagram.

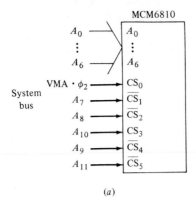

(a)

	Unconnected lines	Connected to chip-select pins	Connected to address pins
Address lines	$A_{15}A_{14}A_{13}A_{12}$	$A_{11}A_{10}A_9A_8A_7$	$A_6A_5A_4A_3A_2A_1A_0$
Recognized value	d d d d	0 1 0 0 0	d d d d d d d

(b)

Value of A_{15}–A_{12}	Smallest address in block	Largest address in block
0000	0000 0100 0000 0000 (0400)	0000 0100 0111 1111 (047F)
0001	0001 0100 0000 0000 (1400)	0001 0100 0111 1111 (147F)
0010	0010 0100 0000 0000 (2400)	0010 0100 0111 1111 (247F)
. . .	. . .	. . .
1111	1111 0100 0000 0000 (F400)	1111 0100 0111 1111 (F47F)

(c)

Figure 9-4 MCM6810 RAM package address assignment: (a) signal connections, (b) complete address, and (c) address blocks specified.

to ensure that the package is selected for the desired address block. One approach is to use external AND gates to combine these address lines before connecting to the chip-select pins, but this complexity is frequently unnecessary and often the decoding can be done by connecting selected address lines directly to the chip-select pins. This approach is called *partial decoding*. In this case five address lines are connected to the five chip-select pins and the remaining four address lines are left unconnected. This approach simplifies the connections but complicates the address assignment for other packages, as we shall see later. Figure 9-4a shows one connection for partial decoding in which address lines A_{11}, A_9,

A_{10}, A_8, and A_7 are connected to pins $\overline{CS_5}$, $\overline{CS_4}$, CS_3, $\overline{CS_2}$, and $\overline{CS_1}$, respectively. Thus, when the pattern 01000 appears on address bus lines A_{11} to A_7, the package will be selected regardless of the pattern on address lines A_{15} to A_{12}.

With partial address decoding, unconnected address signals must be considered as don't-care conditions (d) since they may be either 0 or 1. Thus, the pattern dddd 0100 0 on the address bus lines A_{15} to A_7 will select this package. Since each of the 4 unspecified bits can assume either of 2 values there are a total of $2^4 = 16$ distinct address blocks to which this package will respond. These address blocks can be defined by substituting each of the 16 possible patterns the d's can assume, as shown in Fig. 9-4c. For example, when the pattern on A_{15} to A_{12} is 0000, the resulting address block is \$0400 to \$047F. These addresses are computed by inserting the value 0000 for A_{15} to A_{12}, the permanently assigned values (0010 0) for A_{11} to A_7, and the smallest value (000 0000) and largest value (111 1111) for A_6 to A_0. Inserting the value 0001 for A_{15} to A_{12} defines the second address block \$1400 to \$147F; and inserting the value 1111 defines the sixteenth and last address block \$F400 to \$F47F. Thus this device will respond to 16 address blocks.

Example 9-1 Two MCM6810 packages are connected to the address bus as shown in Fig. E9-1. (*a*) How many words of memory are provided? (*b*) How many address blocks are recognized by each of these packages? (*c*) List the address blocks recognized by these two packages.

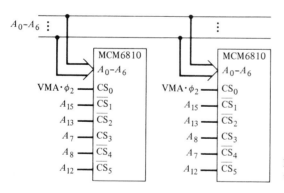

Figure E9-1 Address-bus connection for two RAM packages.

SOLUTION (*a*) Each package contains 128 words, so 256 words are provided.

(*b*) The patterns 0d00 ddd0 1 and 0d00 ddd1 0 on address lines A_{15} to A_7 will select these two packages. The total number of blocks of addresses is determined by the number of d's in the address patterns from unconnected address lines, and thus each will respond to $2^4 = 16$ different address blocks.

(*c*) The blocks of addresses are found by substituting the 16 possible patterns 0000 to 1111. The results are

$0080–$017F	$4080–$417F
$0280–$037F	$4280–$437F
$0480–$057F	$4480–$457F
$0680–$077F	$4680–$477F
$0880–$097F	$4880–$497F
$0A80–$0B7F	$4A80–$4B7F
$0C80–$0D7F	$4C80–$4D7F
$0E80–$0F7F	$4E80–$4F7F

9-3-3 MCM6830 ROM Device

The MCM6830 is a 1024 × 8 ROM device. Figure 9-5 shows its signal-to-pin assignment, input-output model, and block diagram. The package has four chip-select pins (CS_0 to CS_3), ten address pins (A_0 to A_9), and eight data pins (D_0 to D_7). There is no read-write control line since this device is a read-only memory. The four chip-select lines are ANDed internally to create a signal which uniquely activates or selects the package. Unlike those in the MCM6810 RAM device described in the previous section, the chip-select inputs can be designated either true or false at the time of purchase. The 10 address lines are decoded to produce a signal that enables one of the 1024 memory locations in the package. When the package is selected, the contents of the location enabled by the address decoder are passed to the data pins. If the device is not selected, the data pins are in the high-impedance state.

Suppose we are connecting an MCM6830 device to the 6800 system bus in order to provide 1024 words of ROM at locations $0400 to $07FF. The data lines of the system bus are connected to the corresponding data pins on the package. Address lines A_0 to A_9 in the system bus are connected to the corresponding address pins on the package. The use of the low-order address lines again ensures that memory locations on this device will be assigned consecutive addresses. When the M6800 processor is used, the valid-memory-address signal (VMA) and the ϕ_2 clock signal are ANDed and connected to the CS_0 pin to provide the required timing. When the M6802 processor is used, the enable signal (E) is connected to the CS_0 pin.

The seven remaining address lines, A_{15} to A_{10}, are available for connection to the package chip-select pins CS_3 to CS_1 to ensure that the package will be selected for the desired block of address. In this example we have defined CS_0 and CS_1 as true inputs and CS_2 and CS_3 as false inputs. Since there are only three chip-select pins remaining to decode the six remaining address signals, partial address decoding is used. Figure 9-6*a* shows one connection for partial decoding in which address lines A_{12}, A_{11}, and A_{10} are connected to $\overline{CS_3}$, $\overline{CS_2}$, and CS_1, respectively.

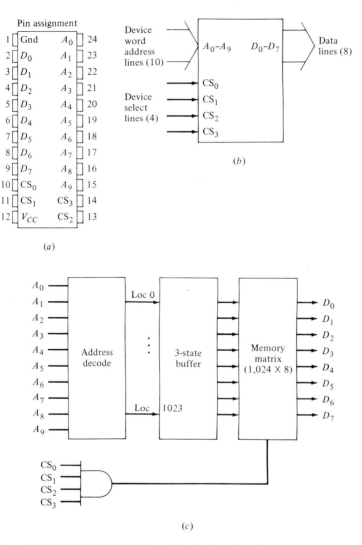

Figure 9-5 MCM6830 ROM device: (*a*) signal-to-pin assignment; (*b*) input-output model; and (*c*) block diagram. The active level of the CS inputs are defined by the customer.

Thus, when the pattern 001 appears on the address bus lines A_{12} to A_{10}, the device will be selected regardless of the pattern for address lines A_{15} to A_{13}.

Partial decoding again means that the device will respond to several address blocks. These address blocks are represented by the pattern ddd0 01 on the address bus lines A_{15} to A_{10}. Since the 3 unconnected lines can assume either of 2 values, there are a total of $2^3 = 8$ distinct address blocks to which this package will respond. For example, when the pattern on A_{15} to A_{13} is 000, the resulting block of addresses is $0400 to $07FF. These addresses are computed by inserting 000 for A_{15} to A_{13}, the permanently assigned value (001) for A_{12} to A_{10}, and the

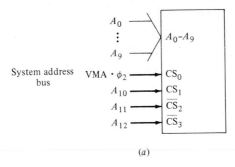

(a)

	Unconnected lines	Connected to chip-select pins	Connected to address pins
Address lines	$A_{15}A_{14}A_{13}$	$A_{12}A_{11}A_{10}$	$A_9A_8A_7A_6A_5A_4A_3A_2A_1A_0$
Recognized value	d d d	0 0 1	d d d d d d d d d d

(b)

$A_{15}\text{-}A_{13}$	Smallest address in block	Largest address in block
000	0000 0100 0000 0000 (0400)	0000 0111 1111 1111 (07FF)
001	0010 0100 0000 0000 (2400)	0010 0111 1111 1111 (27FF)
$\vdots$	$\vdots$	$\vdots$
111	1110 0100 0000 0000 (E200)	1110 0111 1111 1111 (E7FF)

(c)

Figure 9-6 MCM6830 ROM package address assignment: (*a*) signal connections, (*b*) complete address, and (*c*) address blocks specified.

smallest (00 0000 0000) and the largest (11 1111 1111) values for A_9 to A_0, as shown in Fig. 9-6c. The other blocks of addresses are computed in a similar way and are also shown in Fig. 9-6c.

9-3-4 Memory-Unit Design

In this section we consider the design of a memory unit for a microcomputer system using several RAM and ROM devices. In general, timing information is provided to each package by connecting the chip-select pin CS_0 to the enable signal (E) or to a signal obtained by ANDing the valid-memory-address signal (VMA) and the ϕ_2 clock signal. The low-order address lines are connected to the corresponding address pins on all devices to ensure that consecutive addresses will be assigned to each location on each device. The high-order address lines are connected in a unique way to the chip-select pins on each device to ensure that a single memory device will be activated for each valid address.

In assigning the high-order address lines to the chip-select lines in a partial decoding scheme, it is common to use one address line to distinguish between addresses assigned to RAM and ROM devices. Thus one address line is connected to a true-input chip-select pin on all devices of one type and to a false-input chip-select pin on all devices of the other type. In selecting this address line it is important to recall two facts about the organization of the 6800 microcomputer system: (1) the address of the interrupt-service and restart routines are stored in locations with the highest address, and thus this memory needs to be ROM so that these addresses will not be lost when power is disconnected; (2) it is convenient to use locations with the lowest address for data storage since this allows use of the direct addressing mode, which requires less memory and execution time than the extended addressing mode. Thus memory with the lowest address needs to be RAM for storing data. As a result, one of the more significant address bits, usually A_{15}, is used to distinguish RAM and ROM addresses and is connected to a true chip-select input on the ROM and a false chip-select input on the RAM.

Other address lines for partial decoding of RAM devices are selected to ensure that RAM addresses will start at 0000 and will be consecutive. This feature is assured by using the next more significant address lines above those connected to the address pins. For example, for the MCM6810, RAM device, A_0 to A_6 are connected to the address pins, and so A_7, A_8, and so on, would be used in the partial decoding. These lines would be connected to true and false chip-select inputs so that each RAM device would have unique but consecutive address blocks.

Figure 9-7a shows the connections for three RAM devices. In this configuration A_{15} is used to distinguish RAM and ROM addresses and is connected to $\overline{\text{CS}_1}$ on all three RAM devices. A_7 and A_8 are used to distinguish the three RAM devices from each other. On RAM1, they are both connected to false chip-select inputs, $\overline{\text{CS}_5}$ and $\overline{\text{CS}_4}$; on RAM2, A_7 is connected to a true input CS_3 and A_8 to a false input $\overline{\text{CS}_5}$; on RAM3, A_7 is connected to a false input $\overline{\text{CS}_4}$ and A_8 to a true input CS_3.

Figure 9-7b shows the complete address blocks with don't-care conditions and the designated address blocks for all three devices. The complete address blocks are obtained as described earlier, with 1s used for address lines connected to true chip-select inputs, 0s used for address lines connected to false chip-select inputs, d's used for all unconnected address lines, and either all 0s or all 1s for the lines connected to the address inputs of the devices. In this case, the designated address blocks are obtained by replacing the d's with 0s. Thus RAM1 is assigned the first 128 addresses, $0000 to $007F; RAM2 the second 128 addresses, $0080 to $00FF; and RAM3 the third 128 addresses, $0100 to $01FF. In summary, RAM memory is assigned the address block from $0000 to $01FF.

Other address lines for partial decoding of the ROM device are selected to ensure that ROM addresses will end with the last address, $FFFF, and will be consecutive. Again, using the next more significant address lines above those connected to the address pins meets these requirements. For example, for the MCM6830 ROM device, A_0 to A_9 are connected to the address pins, and so $A_{10}, A_{11}, \ldots$, would be used in a partial decoding scheme. These address lines

	Address line							
	A_{15}	A_{14}	...	A_9	A_8	A_7	A_6	...	A_0
RAM1	$\overline{CS_1}$	X	...	X	$\overline{CS_5}$	$\overline{CS_4}$	A_6	...	A_0
RAM2	$\overline{CS_1}$	X	...	X	$\overline{CS_5}$	CS_3	A_6	...	A_0
RAM3	$\overline{CS_1}$	X	...	X	CS_3	$\overline{CS_4}$	A_6	...	A_0

(*a*)

RAM1	
Complete address block	0ddd ddd0 0000 0000–0ddd ddd0 0111 1111
Designated address block	$0000–$007F

RAM2	
Complete address block	0ddd ddd0 1000 000–0ddd ddd0 1111 1111
Designated address block	$0080–$00FF

RAM3	
Complete address block	0ddd ddd1 0000 0000–0ddd ddd1 0111 1111
Designated address block	$0100–$017F

(*b*)

Figure 9-7 Partial decoding of three RAM devices: (*a*) device-pin-to-address-line connections; (*b*) assigned address. X indicates that this address line is not connected to this device.

would be connected to true and false chip-select inputs so that each ROM device would have unique but consecutive address blocks.

Figure 9-8*a* shows the connections for four ROM devices. Note that the CS_2 and CS_3 inputs are specified in three different ways for these devices. In this configuration, A_{15} again is used to distinguish RAM and ROM addresses, and so it is connected to CS_1 on all four ROM devices. A_{10} and A_{11} are used to distinguish the four ROM devices from each other. On ROM1, they are both connected to true chip-select inputs; on ROM2, A_{11} is connected to a true input while A_{10} is connected to a false input; on ROM3, A_{11} is connected to a false input and A_{10} to a true one; and on ROM4, both are connected to false inputs.

Figure 9-8*b* shows the complete address blocks with don't-care conditions and the designated address blocks for all four devices. Complete address blocks are obtained as discussed for the RAM memory. The designated address blocks were defined by replacing all d's with 1s, so that the highest addresses were obtained. Thus ROM1 is assigned the last 1024 addresses, $FC00 to $FFFF; ROM2 the next lowest 1024 addresses, $F800 to FBFF, ROM3 the next lowest 1024 addresses, $F400 to $F7FF; and ROM4 the next lowest 1024 addresses,

				Address lines					
	A_{15}	A_{14}	A_{13}	A_{12}	A_{11}	A_{10}	A_9	...	A_0
ROM1†	CS_1	X	X	X	CS_3	CS_2	A_9	...	A_0
ROM2‡	CS_1	X	X	X	CS_3	$\overline{CS_2}$	A_9	...	A_0
ROM3‡	CS_1	X	X	X	$\overline{CS_2}$	CS_3	A_9	...	A_0
ROM4§	CS_1	X	X	X	$\overline{CS_3}$	$\overline{CS_2}$	A_9	...	A_0

† Specified with CS_2 and CS_3 as true inputs.
‡ Specified with CS_2 as a false input and CS_3 as a true input.
§ Specified with CS_2 and CS_3 as false inputs.

(a)

ROM1	
Complete address block	1ddd 1100 0000 0000– 1ddd 1111 1111 1111
Designated address block	$FC00–$FFFF

ROM2	
Complete address block	1ddd 1000 0000 0000– 1ddd 1011 1111 1111
Designated address block	$F800–$FBFF

ROM3	
Complete address block	1ddd 0100 0000 0000– 1ddd 0111 1111 1111
Designated address block	$F400–$F7FF

ROM4	
Complete address block	1ddd 0000 0000 0000– 1ddd 0011 1111 1111
Designated address block	$F000–$F3FF

(b)

Figure 9-8 Partial decoding of four ROM devices: (a) device-pin-to-address-line connections; (b) assigned address.

$F000 to $F3FF. In summary, ROM memory is assigned the address block $F000 to $FFFF.

Figure 9-9 shows a block diagram for the memory unit we have designed. This figure summarizes the connection between the system bus and the three RAM and four ROM devices. The reader is encouraged to verify that each memory package responds uniquely to the desired address blocks.

In designing the memory unit in this section we use partial decoding to avoid adding an external decoder package to the unit. The scheme shown will work properly as long as none of the address blocks is assigned to the same addresses either in the designated or undesignated address blocks. Although partial decoding eliminates the need for a decoder, it consumes the available system addresses

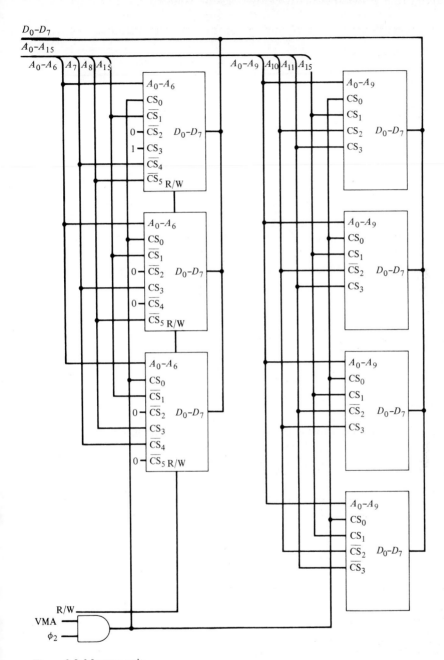

Figure 9-9 Memory unit.

much more rapidly than full decoding. In the present example, the RAM packages were connected to all but six of the address lines, and so each package consumed $2^6 = 64$ address blocks. Since each address block contained 128 addresses, each RAM consumed $64 \times 128 = 8K$ addresses. The ROM devices were connected to all but three of the address lines, and so each consumed $2^3 = 8$ address blocks. Since each block contained 1K addresses, each ROM consumed $8 \times 1K = 8K$ addresses. Thus the three RAM packages in this memory unit consume 24K addresses, and the four ROM packages consume 32K addresses for a total of 56K of the 64K available addresses. Thus, partial decoding is effective as long as the number of memory packages in the system is small, typically, on the order of eight or fewer.

Example 9-2 Using a partial decoding scheme, design a memory unit that contains 6K of ROM and 1K of RAM using a 2K $\times$ 8 ROM device and a 512 $\times$ 8 RAM device. The ROM device has 11 address pins (A_0 to A_{10}) and five chip-select pins (CS_0 to CS_4); CS_0, CS_1, CS_2 and CS_3 are true inputs, and $\overline{C_4}$ is a false input. The RAM device has nine address pins (A_0 to A_8) and five chip-select pins (CS_0 to CS_4); CS_0 and CS_1 are true inputs, and $\overline{CS_2}$, $\overline{CS_3}$, and $\overline{CS_4}$ are false inputs.

SOLUTION Three ROM devices and two RAM devices are required. The signal obtained by ANDing the valid memory address signal with the ϕ_2 clock signal will be connected to the CS_0 pin on all devices to provide timing information. Line A_{15} will be used to distinguish RAM and ROM addresses; it will be connected to a true chip-select input on the ROM devices and a false chip-select input on the RAM devices. Lines A_{11} and A_{12} will be used to select one of the three ROM devices, while lines A_9 and A_{10} will be used to select one of the two RAM devices. The table below shows the connections. The complete address block for the ROM is 1dd0 1000 0000 0000 to 1dd1 1111 1111 1111, and the designated block is $E800 to $FFFF. The complete address block for the RAM is 0ddd d000 0000 0000 to 0ddd d011 1111 1111, and the designated block is $0000 to $03FF.

	Address lines									
	A_{15}	A_{14}	A_{13}	A_{12}	A_{11}	A_{10}	A_9	A_8	$\ldots$	A_0
ROM1	CS_1	X	X	CS_2	CS_3	A_{10}	A_9	A_8	$\ldots$	A_0
ROM2	CS_1	X	X	CS_2	$\overline{CS_4}$	A_{10}	A_9	A_8	$\ldots$	A_0
ROM3	CS_1	X	X	$\overline{CS_4}$	CS_2	A_{10}	A_9	A_8	$\ldots$	A_0
RAM1	$\overline{CS_2}$	X	X	X	X	$\overline{CS_3}$	$\overline{CS_4}$	A_8	$\ldots$	A_0
RAM2	$\overline{CS_2}$	X	X	X	X	$\overline{CS_3}$	CS_1	A_9	$\ldots$	A_0

Example 9-3 The memory unit described in Figs. 9-5 to 9-7 uses 56K of the 64K addresses. Identify the unused address blocks.

SOLUTION The address blocks used by the ROM devices are defined by

1ddd 0000 0000 0000– 1ddd 1111 1111 1111

Substituting all possible combinations for the d's produces the following hexadecimal address blocks:

Don't-cares	000	001	...	111
Address block	8000–8FFF	9000–9FFF	...	F000–FFF

Thus the ROM consumes all addresses from 8000 to FFFF. The address blocks used by the RAM devices are defined by

0ddd ddd0 0000 0000– 0ddd ddd1 0111 1111

Substituting all possible combinations for the d's produces the following hexadecimal address blocks:

Don't-cares	000000	000001	000010	...	111110	111111
Address blocks	0000–017F	0200–037F	0400–057F	...	7C00–7DFF	7E00–7F7F

Thus the unused address blocks are

$$0180–01FF$$
$$0380–03FF$$
$$0580–05FF$$
$$\vdots$$
$$7D80–7DFF$$
$$7F80–7FFF$$

The number of packages that can be connected to any line in the system bus also is limited by electrical considerations. Dealing with this problem is simplified if we consider each package as one load and recognize that only a certain number of loads can be connected directly to the bus. For the 6800 microcomputer bus, 10 loads is a typical maximum. When a system contains more than the allowed number of packages, buffers must be added. The inputs of these buffers, which represent one load, are connected to the system bus lines, and their outputs are capable of driving several additional packages, typically 10. Buffer packages are available in most microcomputer families.

In more complex microcomputer systems, the memory unit often contains more than 10 packages. In such units, full decoding is used, and the memory packages usually are organized in 1K, 2K, or even larger modules. Figure 9-10 shows the memory decoding for a memory unit organized in 1K units. Decoding is accomplished with a decoder device that has an enable input (E), three coded inputs (C_0 to C_2) and eight decoded outputs (D_0 to D_7). If the enable input is

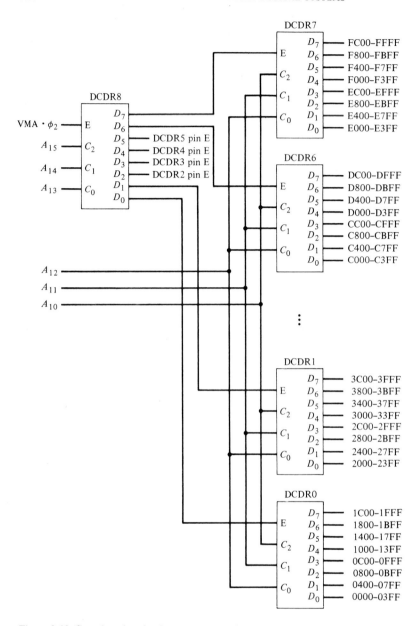

Figure 9-10 Complete decoder for a memory unit organized with 1K modules.

inactive, all outputs are inactive; and if the enable input is active, only one output is active. The active output is defined by interpreting the pattern on the coded inputs as a binary value; e.g., when C_2 is active and C_1 and C_0 are inactive, the active output is D_4.

Nine decoders are used in the memory unit. One, DCDR8, is used to decode address lines A_{15}, A_{14}, and A_{13} with the signal obtained by ANDing the valid-memory-address signal and the ϕ_2 clock signal connected to its enable input. The other eight packages decode address lines A_{12}, A_{11}, and A_{10}. The enable inputs on these eight packages are provided from the outputs from DCDR8 processing A_{15}, A_{14}, and A_{13}. Thus, only one of these eight decoders will be enabled and so only one of the 64 output signals can be active at a time. These signals separate the 64K addresses into 1K blocks, some of which are defined in Fig. 9-10. For example, the D_7 signal from DCDR7 is active when 111 is on A_{15} to A_{17} and 111 is on A_{12} to A_{10}, corresponding to the address block

$$1111\ 1100\ 0000\ 0000 - 1111\ 1111\ 1111\ 1111$$

or \$FC00 to \$FFFF in hexadecimal. The D_6 signal from DCDR7 is active when 111 is on A_{15} to A_{13} and 110 is on A_{12} to A_{10}, corresponding to the address block \$F800 to \$FBFF. As a final example, the D_3 signal from DCDR5 (not shown in the figure) is active when 101 is on A_{15} to A_{13} and 011 is on A_{12} to A_{10}, corresponding to the address block \$AC00 to \$AFFF.

Example 9-4 In Fig. 9-10 define the address blocks designated by the signals from D_6 of DCDR1 and D_0 of DCDR2.

SOLUTION D_6 of DCDR1 is active when 001 is on A_{15} to A_{13} and 110 is on A_{12} to A_{10}, and so the address block is \$3800 to \$3BFF. D_0 of DCDR2 is active when 010 is on A_{15} to A_{13} and 000 is on A_{12} to A_{10}, and so the address block is \$4000 to \$43FF.

The decoding scheme in Fig. 9-10 represents full address decoding and allows much more efficient use of the system addresses than the partial decoding scheme discussed earlier. There are many intermediate schemes in which one or two decoders are used to increase the number of memory packages beyond the limit imposed by partial decoding.

Memory modules containing 1K, 2K, or even more words of memory are often available on individual circuit boards. Each board is connected to all address lines, and an address block is assigned to each board by setting mechanical switches on the board. These boards contain a decoder so that the address space can be used more efficiently. They also contain buffers so that each board appears as a single load to the system bus. This organization allows users to expand the size of the memory unit in a very efficient way as requirements change. Memory boards are available for most microcomputer families.

9-4 PARALLEL-INTERFACE HARDWARE

In Chap. 5 we described simple input and output interfaces to synchronize the connection of external signals to the system data bus through an input or output port. In practice many types of external units must be interfaced with a microcomputer system, and to meet all these requirements the device manufacturers have designed general-purpose interface devices whose behavior can be altered to suit the user's specific needs. We shall focus on one of these packages, the MC6821 peripheral interface adapter.

9-4-1 MCM6821 Parallel Interface

In the 6800 family an important interface device is the MC6821, referred to as the *peripheral interface adapter* (PIA). It has two separate 8-bit ports which can function as either input or output ports. In fact, individual lines in each port can be designated as input or output lines. In addition to the eight data lines, each port has two control lines which can be connected to the external unit and used to synchronize data transfers between the external unit and the microcomputer system. The two ports are referred to as port A and port B. The operation of both ports is nearly identical, and we shall not consider the distinctions. Figure 9-11 shows the signal-to-pin assignment and the input-output model for the MC6821. There are eight data input pins (D_0 to D_7) for connection to the data bus, three chip-select input pins (CS_0 to CS_2), an enable-input pin (E), two register-select pins (RS_0 and RS_1), a read-write control pin (R/W), a reset pin ($\overline{RESET}$), an interrupt-request pin from each port ($\overline{IRQA}$ and $\overline{IRQB}$), eight external data pins

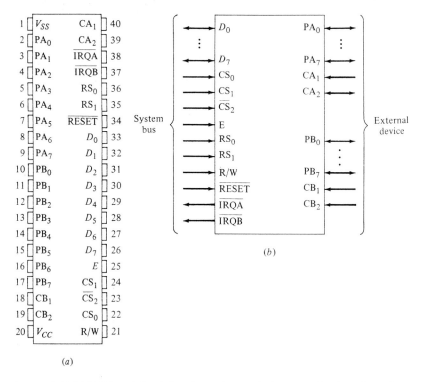

Figure 9-11 MC6821 peripheral interface adapter device: (*a*) signal-to-pin assignment and (*b*) input-output model.

for each port (PA_0 to PA_7 and PB_0 to PB_7) and two external control pins for each port (CA_1, CA_2, CB_1, and CB_2). Signals on the three chip-select pins and on the enable pin are ANDed internally to produce a signal which activates or selects the device.

Each port contains three 8-bit registers: a peripheral data register, a data direction register, and a control register. The *peripheral data register* serves as the output data register when the port is used as an output interface or as the input data buffer when it is used as an input interface. The contents of the *data direction register* define whether the external data lines are used as input or output lines. The external data line is an input line when the corresponding bit in the data direction register is cleared, and it is an output when the corresponding bit in the data direction register is set. The *control register* is really a control and status register. In this register 2 bits serve as status flip-flops for the two external control inputs connected to CA_1 and CA_2 in port A and CB_1 and CB_2 in port B. The remaining bits are selectively set or cleared to control the behavior of the interface. The function of each bit in the control register will be described below.

With a partial decoding scheme the three chip-select pins are connected to the address bus in a way that assigns a unique block of addresses to this device. The enable pin is connected to the enable signal on the bus or to a signal generated by ANDing the valid memory address signal with the ϕ_2 clock signal to provide the needed timing information. The two register-select signals RS_0 and RS_1 are decoded internally to provide signals to enable one of the six registers in the device. Since there are six registers and only four possible combinations of signals on the two register-select inputs, special decoding is required. The special decoding involves the third bit (bit 2) in each of the two control registers which in essence adds a third bit to the code word defining which register is addressed. The code used in defining the selected register is shown in Table 9-3. If the signal on RS_0 equals 0, one of the registers in port A is enabled; if it equals 1, one of the registers in port B is enabled. If the signal on RS_1 equals 1, one of the control registers is enabled; if it equals 0, one of the peripheral data registers or one of the data direction registers is enabled and the choice depends on bit 2 in the control registers. If this bit is set, the peripheral data register is selected; if it is cleared, the data direction register is selected.

The read-write control pin and the reset pin usually are connected to the corresponding lines in the control bus. The two interrupt-request pins may be connected to the same interrupt-request lines in the system bus, or one may be connected to the maskable-interrupt-request line and one to the nonmaskable-interrupt-request line, depending on the nature of the external signal.

The four external control pins, CA_1, CA_2, CB_1, and CB_2, can be connected to synchronizing signals from the external unit. Signals connected to CA_1 and CB_1 must be input signals to the microcomputer system from the external unit and an active transition on these lines sets the corresponding status bit in the control register. This active transition also may activate the signal connected to the corresponding interrupt-request pin if the interrupt capability is enabled. Signals connected to the CA_2 and CB_2 pins may be input signals like those

Table 9-3 Register-select decoding

RS_0	RS_1	Control register A (bit 2)	Control register B (bit 2)	Register
0	0	0	d	Data direction register A
0	0	1	d	Peripheral data register A
0	1	d	d	Control register A
1	0	d	0	Data direction register B
1	0	d	1	Peripheral data register B
1	1	d	d	Control register B

connected to the CA_1 and CB_1 pins, or they may be output signals from the microcomputer system to the external system. The interpretation on these two pins is controlled by bits 3 to 5 of the control register. In this presentation, however, we shall always consider the signals on CA_2 and CB_2 as inputs; this behavior is defined by placing a 0 in bit 5 of the control register.

Table 9-4 describes the function of each bit in control register A; the definitions for control register B are identical. Bit 0 in the control register (IRQA1 ENABLE) serves as an interrupt enable. If this bit is set, an active transition on an external control input will activate the line connected to the interrupt-request pin. Bit 1 in the control register (CA1 POS) defines whether the external control signal is interpreted with the positive- or negative-logic assumption. A 1 in bit 1 implies the positive-logic assumption where the low-to-high transition is the active one; correspondingly a 0 in this bit implies a negative-logic assumption where the high-to-low transition is the active one. Bit 2 (PDRA SEL) is used in decoding the

Table 9-4 Definition of bits in control register A†

Bit	Designation	Control or status function
0	IRQA1 ENABLE	If bit 0 = 1, $\overline{IRQA}$ activated when CA_1 activated
1	CA1 POS	If bit 1 = 1, CA1 uses positive-logic assumption
2	PDRA SEL	If bit 2 = 1, peripheral data register selected
3	IRQA2 ENABLE	If bit 3 = 1, $\overline{IRQA}$ activated when CA_2 activated
4	CA2 POS	If bit 4 = 1, CA_2 uses positive-logic assumption
5	CA2 OUT	If bit 5 = 1, CA_2 is output signal‡
6	CA1 STATUS	Status bit for CA_1
7	CA2 STATUS	Status bit for CA_2

† The definitions of all bits in control register B are analogous.

‡ The interpretation of bits 3 and 4 is more complicated when bit 5 = 1. We shall always set this bit to 0.

register-select signals to define whether the data direction register (bit $2 = 0$) or the peripheral data register (bit $2 = 1$) is selected. Bit 3 is analogous to bit 0 and serves as the interrupt enable for CA_2. Similarly, bit 4 is analogous to bit 1 and defines the active transition in CA_2. Bit 5 (CA2 OUT) defines whether the signal connected to the CA_2 pin is an input (bit $3 = 0$) or an output (bit $3 = 1$). In this presentation we shall always place a 0 in bit 3. Bit 6 (CA1 STATUS) is the status bit for the input signal connected to the CA_1 pin. Bit 6 is set by an active transition of the signal on the CA_1 pin. Bit 7 (CA1 STATUS) is the status bit for the signal connected to CA_2. If the signal on CA_2 is configured as an input, this bit is set by an active transition on the CA_2 pin. Bits 6 and 7 are cleared automatically when the peripheral data register is read.

All bits in the control and data direction register are under programmer control; i.e., they can be set or cleared selectively by storing the appropriate code word in these registers. In a typical application the control registers are loaded with binary words to define the operation of the external control signals, CA_1, CA_2, CB_1, and CB_2. Then the data direction registers are loaded with binary words defining the direction of the data flow for each bit of the peripheral data registers. After these two registers have been loaded, any store operation to a peripheral data register results in data being stored only into the bits designated as output bits, and any load operation from a peripheral data register results in a transfer of only the bits designated as input bits.

9-4-2 Design of a Computer-Terminal Interface

In considering the use of an MC6821 as an interface for a standard computer terminal we first describe the specification of the terminal signals. Then we discuss how these specifications define the connections to the MC6821, the code words for configuring its behavior, and the software for loading these code words and for performing input and output data transfers.

Figure 9-12a shows an input-output model for a simple computer terminal containing a keyboard and printer. When a key is pressed, the 7-bit ASCII code for that character appears on the keyboard data lines, KB_0 to KB_6, and the keyboard strobe signal, STROBE, goes high, as indicated in the timing diagram shown in Fig. 9-12b. These signal levels remain stable as long as the key is depressed.

Printing is a separate activity controlled by the computer, and so pressing a key does not print the character. In general, when the computer reads a character from the keyboard, it echoes the character back to the printer for printing. The printer timing diagram is given in Fig. 9-12c. In order to print a character, the ASCII code for the character must be placed on the printer data lines, PB_0 to PB_6, and after they are stable, the print control line, PRINT, must undergo a low-to-high transition. The printer responds by putting the low level on its ready line, READY, to indicate that the character is being printed. When printing is completed the printer returns the READY line to the high level. Signals on the printer data lines must be stable as long as the READY line is low.

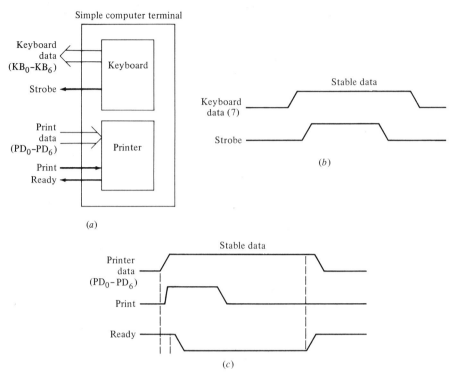

Figure 9-12 Simple terminal: (*a*) block diagram, (*b*) keyboard signals, and (*c*) printer signals.

The terminal can be connected to a microcomputer using a single MC6821 package since the terminal has fewer than 16 data lines and fewer than 4 control lines. The keyboard is assigned to port A, and the 7 data lines from the keyboard are connected to pins PA_0 to PA_6, and the STROBE line is connected to the CA_1 pin, as shown in Fig. 9-13. The printer is assigned to port B and its 7 data lines are connected to PB_0 to PB_6 pins, the PRINT line is connected to PB_7, and the READY line is connected to pin CB_1.

The MC6821 is connected to most lines in the system bus in the standard way, as shown in Fig. 9-13. The system data bus is connected to pins D_0 to D_7, the read-write control line is connected to pin R/W, the reset line to the $\overline{\text{RESET}}$ pin. The valid memory address signal is ANDed with the ϕ_2 clock signal and connected to pin E. The interrupt request pins for both ports, $\overline{\text{IRQA}}$ and $\overline{\text{IRQB}}$, are tied together and then connected to the maskable interrupt line, $\overline{\text{IRQ}}$, in the system bus.

We shall connect the address bus to this device so that the six registers have the following addresses:

$C000   Peripheral data register A and data direction register A
$C001   Control register A
$C002   Peripheral data register B and data direction register B
$C003   Control register B

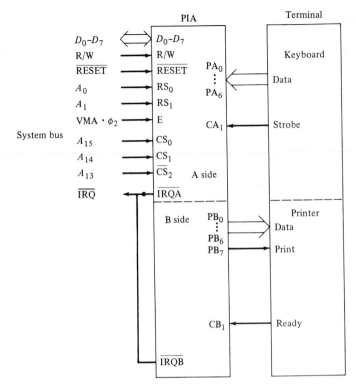

Figure 9-13 Connections to MC6821 for interfacing the simple computer terminal in Fig. 9-12.

To implement this, address lines A_1 and A_0 are connected to the register-select pins RS_1 and RS_0, respectively, so that consecutive addresses are used. We use partial decoding in defining the connection to the three chip-select pins. There are many choices; those shown in Fig. 9-13 connect the A_{15}, A_{14}, and A_{13} address lines to chip-select pins CS_0, CS_1, and $\overline{CS_2}$, respectively. Thus, when the pattern 110 appears on these lines, the device will be enabled, regardless of the pattern on lines A_{12} to A_2. Since the 11 unconnected lines must be considered as don't-care conditions in defining the address blocks to which this PIA will respond, this device will respond to $2^{11} = 2048$ different address blocks. They are described in Fig. 9-14 using the same approach as that used earlier in defining the address blocks for the RAM and ROM devices.

Next we must define the code words that are loaded into the two data direction registers and the two control registers to provide the desired behavior. Since all seven external data signals connected to PA_6 to PA_0 are input signals to the interface, bits 6 to 0 in data direction register A must be cleared. Since PA_7 is not used, the value loaded into bit 7 in the data direction register is arbitrary. Thus either the code word 00 or the code word 80 must be stored in the data direction register A; we arbitrarily choose 00, as shown in Table 9-4. Similarly, since all seven external data signals connected to PB_6 to PB_0 are output signals

	Connected to chip-select pins			Unconnected												Connected to address pins	
Address lines	A_{15}	A_{14}	A_{13}	A_{12}	A_{11}	A_{10}	A_9	A_8	A_7	A_6	A_5	A_4	A_3	A_2		A_1	A_0
Recognized value	1	1	0	d	d	d	d	d	d	d	d	d	d	d		d	d

(a)

Value of $A_{12}-A_2$	Smallest address in block	Largest address in block
0 0000 0000 00	1100 0000 0000 0000 (C000)	1100 0000 0000 0011 (C003)
0 0000 0000 01	1100 0000 0000 0100 (C004)	1100 0000 0000 0111 (C007)
0 0000 0000 10	1100 0000 0000 1000 (C008)	1100 0000 0000 1011 (C00B)
⋮	⋮	⋮
1 1111 1111 11	1101 1111 1111 1100 (DFFC)	1101 1111 1111 1111 (DFFF)

(b)

Figure 9-14 MC6821 PIA address assignment: (a) complete address; (b) address blocks specified.

from the interface, and since PB_7 is used as an output timing signal, all bits in data direction register B must be set; so the code word is FF.

In defining the contents of the two control registers, we must consider two situations. When the data direction registers are being addressed, the PDRA SEL and PDRB SEL bit must be cleared, and since all other bits are unimportant, we arbitrarily use all 0s. Thus the code words for both control registers when data direction registers are being loaded is 00, as shown in Table 9-5.

When the peripheral data registers are being addressed, the situation is slightly more complicated since we must load the control registers so that the interfaces are consistent with the specifications on the two synchronizing signals, STROBE and READY, connected to pins CA_1 and CB_1, respectively. STROBE is an input signal to the interface. It uses the positive-logic assumption since it is active at the high level; thus the CA1 POS bit must be set. Similarly, READY is an input

Table 9-5 Code words for data direction register and control registers for computer-terminal interface

Data direction register A	00
Data direction register B	FF
Control register A (when addressing data direction register A)	00
Control register B (when addressing data direction register B)	00
Control register A (when addressing peripheral data register A)	06
Control register B (when addressing peripheral data register B)	06

using the positive logic assumption so the CB1 POS bit also must be set. In addition we must define whether or not we wish to allow the keyboard or printer to generate an interrupt request, i.e., whether the IRQA1 and the IRQB1 bits are set or cleared. In this example, we choose to disable the interrupt capability, and so bit 0 in both control registers must be cleared. Finally we adopt the policy of placing 0s in all unused bits. Thus the code words for both port A and port B are 0000 0110, or 06 in hexadecimal, and these also are listed in Table 9-5.

Now let us consider the software to support this interface. First we need a routine for initialization of the interface. This routine must load 00 in data direction register A, FF in data direction register B, 06 in control register A, and 06 in control register B. The assembly-language subroutine ITERML shown in Table 9-6 performs these tasks. The first two executable instructions load 00 into the data direction register of port A to make it an input port. The next three load FF into the data direction register of port B to make it an output port. The next four instructions load 06 into the control registers in ports A and B. This subroutine will be used in the RESTART routine, and it should be assembled with that routine. The RESTART routine and thus the ITERML routine will be executed each time the reset line in the system bus is activated. Since this line always is activated when electric power is applied, the terminal interface will be initialized each time the microcomputer system is turned on.

The subroutine for reading a character from the keyboard READKB and for printing characters through the terminal PRINT are given in Table 9-7. It is most

Table 9-6 Subroutine for initializing terminal interface

	NAM	INTERM	
	ORG	· · ·	TO BE DEFINED
KWORD	EQU	$06	CODEWORD FOR CRA, PDR SELECTED
PWORD	EQU	$06	CODEWORD FOR CRB, PDR SELECTED
KDATA	EQU	$C000	ADDRESS ASSIGNED TO PDRA AND DDRA
KDRCTN	EQU	KDATA	
KCNTRL	EQU	$C001	ADDRESS ASSIGNED TO CRA
PDATA	EQU	$C002	ADDRESS ASSIGNED TO PDRB AND DDRB
PDRCTN	EQU	$C003	
PCNTRL	EQU	$C003	ADDRESS ASSIGNED TO CRB
INTERM	CLR	KCNTRL	CLEAR CRA, SELECT DDRA
	CLR	KDRCTN	CLEAR DDRA, MAKE INPUT PORT
	CLR	PCNTRL	CLEAR CRB, SELECT DDRB
	CLR	PDRCTN	CLEAR DDRB
	COM	PDRCTN	SET DDRB, MAKE OUTPUT PORT
	LDAA	#KWORD	CODEWORD FOR CRA, FOR DATA TRANSFERS
	STAA	KCNTRL	INITIALIZE CRA, SELECT PDRA
	LDAA	#PWORD	CODEWORD FOR CRB FOR DATA TRANSFERS
	STAA	PCNTRL	INITIALIZE CRB, SELECT PDRB
	RTS		
	END		

Table 9-7 Subroutines for reading and printing with terminal

	NAM	READKB	
	ORG	· · ·	TO BE DEFINED
KDATA	EQU	$C000	ADDRESS ASSIGNED PDRA AND DDRA
KCNTRL	EQU	$C001	ADDRESS ASSIGNED TO CRA
PDATA	EQU	$C002	ADDRESS ASSIGNED PDRB AND DDRB
PCNTRL	EQU	$C003	ADDRESS ASSIGNED TO CRB
READKB	LDAA	KCNTRL	LOAD PORTA CONTROL REG
	ANDA	#$40	ISOLATE CA1 STATUS, STROBE ACTIVE?
	BEQ	READKB	BRANCH IF STROBE = 0
	LDAA	KDATA	TRANSFER DATA IN THROUGH PDRA
	STAA	0, X	STORE CHAR FOR CALLING ROUTINE
	RTS		
PRINT	CLR	PDATA	PUT PRINT LINE TO LOW LEVEL
PTST	LDAA	PCNTRL	LOAD PORT B CONTROL REG
	ANDA	#$40	ISOLATE CA1 STATUS BIT, PRINTER RDY?
	BEQ	PTST	BRANCH IF READY = 0
	LDAA	0, X	GET CHAR FROM CALLING ROUTINE
	ORAA	#$80	SET MOST SIGNIFICANT BIT
	STAA	PDATA	TRANSFER DATA OUT THROUGH PDRB
	RTS		
	END		

likely that these two routines would be assembled independent of any calling routines since they will be used in many different calling routines. The values assigned to the labels READKB and PRINT would be supplied to all calling routines using EQU directives in each.

The READKB routine defines when the keyboard's STROBE signal is active and then transfers the character code word into the microcomputer system. The first three instructions of KBREAD repeatedly test bit 6 in control register A, the status bit for the CA_1 input signal, until it is set. This condition indicates that the STROBE signal from the keyboard is active. The next two instructions load the data word from the peripheral data register A and store it using the indexed addressing mode. This last instruction transfers the data back to the calling program. The final instruction causes a return from this subroutine.

The subroutine for printing a character, PRINT, is also shown in Table 9-7. This subroutine deactivates the PRINT signal for a short time, defines when the printer's READY signal is active, and transfers the code word to the printer. The first instruction deactivates the PRINT line so that it can be reactivated when the output data are valid. The next three instructions repeatedly test bit 6 in control register B, the status bit for the CB_1 input signal, until it is set. This condition indicates that the READY signal from the printer is active. The next three instructions get the data word, set the most significant bit, and store it in peripheral data register B. The final instruction returns to the calling routine.

Example 9-5 Define code words for the data direction registers and the control registers in an MC6821 device for the following conditions:

PA_0 to PA_3 are connected to input signals.
PA_4 to PA_7 are connected to output signals.
PB_0 to PB_6 are connected to output signals.
PB_7 is connected to an input signal.
CA_1 is active on the low-to-high transition and must generate an interrupt request.
CB_1 is active on the high-to-low transition and must not generate an interrupt request.
CB_2 is an input signal active on the low-to-high transition and must generate an interrupt.

SOLUTION The code words for data direction registers A and B are F0 and 7F, respectively. When the data direction register is selected, the code word for both control registers is 00. When the peripheral data registers are selected, the following patterns must be in the two control registers:

IRQA1 ENABLE $= 1$	IRQB1 ENABLE $= 0$
CA1 POS $= 1$	CB1 POS $= 0$
PDRA SEL $= 1$	PDRB SEL $= 1$
IRQA2 ENABLE $= d$	IRQB2 ENABLE $= 1$
CA2 POS $= d$	CB2 POS $= 1$
CA2 OUT $= d$	CB2 OUT $= 0$
CA1 STATUS $= d$	CB1 STATUS $= d$
CA2 STATUS $= d$	CB1 STATUS $= d$

We shall arbitrarily set all d's to zero. Thus the code words for control registers A and B are 07 and 1C, respectively.

Example 9-6 An MC6821 PIA device must be added to the microcomputer system that contains the memory unit described by Figs. 9-5 to 9-7. Define a connection between the address bus and the MC6821 devices that assigns it a unique address block using a partial decoding scheme.

SOLUTION Lines A_1 and A_0 are connected to pins RS_1 and RS_0, respectively. There are only three chip-select pins, and they must be connected to three address lines to assign a unique block of addresses to the device. The table given below summarizes the address blocks assigned to the four ROM devices and the three RAM devices; all unspecified entries represent don't-care conditions.

	A_{15}	A_{14}	A_{13}	A_{12}	A_{11}	A_{10}	A_9	A_8	A_7
RAM1	0							0	0
RAM2	0							0	1
RAM3	0							1	0
ROM1	1				1	1			
ROM2	1				1	0			
ROM3	1				0	1			
ROM4	1				0	0			

Since lines A_{14}, A_{13}, A_{12}, and A_9 are don't-care conditions in all addresses assigned to the memory devices, they cannot be used to specify the address block for the PIA uniquely. Thus only lines A_{15}, A_{11}, A_{10}, A_8 and A_7 can be used. Since there are only three RAM devices, there is one combination, $A_{15} = 0$, $A_8 = 1$, $A_7 = 1$, in the RAM address space that is unused and can be assigned to the PIA device. Thus, lines A_{15}, A_8, and A_7 are connected to $\overline{CS_2}$, CS_1, and CS_0, respectively. The corresponding address block is 0ddd ddd1 1ddd dd00 to 0ddd ddd1 1ddd dd11. In designating a specific address we shall set all d's to 0s; the designated address block is therefore $0180 to $0183. This corresponds to the unused addresses, as we saw in Example 9-3.

9-5 MC6801 MICROCOMPUTER DEVICE

As large-scale integrated-circuit technology advances and gate density increases, more elements of the microcomputer system can be provided in a single package. The MC6801 is an example of a complete, albeit limited, microcomputer system in a single package.

This device contains a 6800 processor unit, 128 bytes of RAM, 2048 bytes of ROM, 4 input-output ports which can be programmed either as input or output signals, and several other functions. This device is also available in two options: depending on whether the application requires a single-package computer or an expanding system containing other packages in the family. We consider only the single-package computer option; its signal-to-pin assignment and the input-output model are shown in Fig. 9-15.

The MC6801 will execute all standard instructions and offers several new instructions that help to improve system performance. These new instructions, described in Table 9-8, provide several 16-bit operations and an 8-bit multiply. Thus, MC6801 programs using these new instructions are not compatible with the two processors discussed in Sec. 9-2. In addition, the execution times for many key instructions in the MC6801 are faster than in the other two processors, and so the timing performance of a program executing in the MC6801 will not be compatible with the other two.

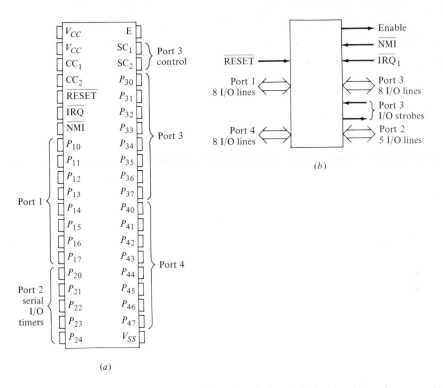

(a)

(b)

Figure 9-15 MC6801 microcomputer package description: (a) signal-to-pin assignment, (b) input-output model, single-chip mode.

For comparison, Fig. 9-16 shows an MC6800-based microcomputer system which has approximately the same capability as the MC6801 device. This system is of interest because it represents about the maximum number of packages which can be interconnected without buffer packages to eliminate loading problems on the system bus and without decoder packages to accommodate increased density in address assignment. The capacity of this system is 2K bytes of ROM for program storage, 384 bytes of RAM for data storage, 32 bidirectional lines for parallel input-output data along with 8 control lines, and a serial input-output interface.

In addition to the nine LSI devices pictured in Fig. 9-16, some other packages are required, e.g., the clock network, TTL buffer for ϕ_2, the AND gate used to form VMA$\cdot\phi_2$, and the power-on switch circuit driving the processor RESET signal.

9-6 CONCLUSION

The number of different microprocessor and microcomputer models available increases constantly. In this chapter we have described several members of the

Table 9-8 MC6801 new instructions

ABX	Adds 8-bit unsigned accumulator to 16-bit X register, taking into account possible carry out of low-order byte of X register	$IX \leftarrow IX + ACCB$
ADDD	Adds double-precision ACCAB† to double-precision value $M:M+1$ and places the results in ACCAB	$ACCAB \leftarrow ACCAB + M:M + 1$
ASLD	Shifts all bits of ACCAB one place to left; bit 0 is loaded with zero; C bit is loaded from most significant bit of ACCAB	$ACCAB_i \leftarrow ACCAB_{i-1}; i = 1, \dots 15$ $ACCAB_0 \leftarrow 0; C \leftarrow ACCAB_{15}$
LDD	Loads contents of double-precision memory location into double accumulator $A:B$; condition codes set according to data	$ACCAB \leftarrow M:M + 1$
LSRD	Shifts all bits of ACCAB one place to right; bit 15 loaded with zero; C bit loaded from least significant bit to ACCAB	$ACCAB_{i-1} \leftarrow ACCAB_i; i = 1, \dots 15$ $ACCAB_{15} \leftarrow 0; C \leftarrow ACCAB_0$
MUL	Multiplies 8 bits in accumulator A with 8 bits in accumulator B to obtain 16-bit unsigned number in $A:B$; ACCA contains MSB of result	$ACCAB \leftarrow ACCA * ACCB$
PSHX	Contents of index register pushed onto stack at address contained in stack pointer; stack pointer decremented by 2	$M_{SP}:M_{SP-1} \leftarrow X, SP \leftarrow SP - 2$
PULX	Index register pulled from stack beginning at current address contained in stack pointer $+1$; stack pointer incremented by 2 in total	$X \leftarrow M_{SP+2}:M_{SP+1}, SP \leftarrow SP + 2$
STD	Stores contents of double accumulator $A:B$ in memory; contents of ACCAB remain unchanged	$M:M + 1 \leftarrow ACCAB$
SUBD	Subtracts contents of $M:M+1$ from contents of double accumulator AB and places result in ACCAB	$ACCAB \leftarrow ACCAB - M:M + 1$

† ACCAB is the ACCA and ACCB used as a 16-bit accumulator.

Motorola M6800 family as examples. Although the specifics of signal names, pin designations, and architecture vary from one device model and one manufacturer to the next, the concepts underlying the Motorola M6800 family change very little in other models or manufacturers.

We have described only two representative memory packages, but the package-selection and address-assignment concepts are common to many other

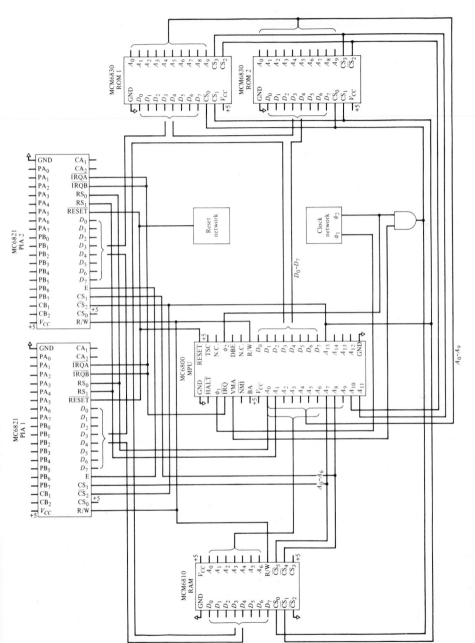

Figure 9-16 Typical multipackage M6800 microcomputer system.

memory devices. The system-bus–to–memory-package signal connections required to create a memory unit with a specified number of words and bits per word are similar for many different packages, just as they were for the RAM and ROM we considered.

The standard parallel package presented is typical of devices provided by many manufacturers. This interface is representative of the most important and widely used interface occurring in microcomputer systems.

PROBLEMS

9-1 Define each of the following terms:
large-scale integration
microcomputer
microprocessor
microcomputer family
volatile
nonvolatile
RAM
ROM
masked ROM
PROM
fusable-link PROM
EPROM
read-mostly memories
partial decoding
peripheral interface adapter
peripheral data register
data direction register
control register

9-2 Discuss differences and similarities in how the MC6800 processor handles an active signal on the HALT, RESET, IRQ, and NMI pins. How does the MC6802 differ from the MC6800 in dealing with these signals?

9-3 Summarize the difference between the MC6800, MC6800A, MC6800B, and MC6802 processors.

9-4 Will programs written for a computer system containing the MC6800 processor package run on systems containing the MC6800A, the MC6800B, or the MC6802 processor package? Discuss your answer.

9-5 Discuss why ROM devices generally are used to store programs while RAM devices generally are used to store data.

9-6 Define the advantages and disadvantages of masked, fusable-link, and erasable ROM.

9-7 Define the voltage level on all pins of the MCM6810 to perform the following data transfers:
(*a*) Write 7C in the first location
(*b*) Write the ASCII code word for the character T in the tenth location
(*c*) Clear the twentieth location
(*d*) Read from the last location
(*e*) Read from the twelfth location

9-8 In an MCM6810 device the value 00 is in the first location, 01 in the second, and so on, so that 7F is in the last location. Define the voltage level on all pins for the following data transfers:

(*a*) Read from the tenth location

(*b*) Read from the first location

(*c*) Read from the sixtieth location

(*d*) Write the ASCII code word for the character S into last location

(*e*) Write the ASCII code word for the character 8 in the thirtieth location

9-9 List all address blocks recognized by the MCM6810 devices shown in Fig. P9-9.

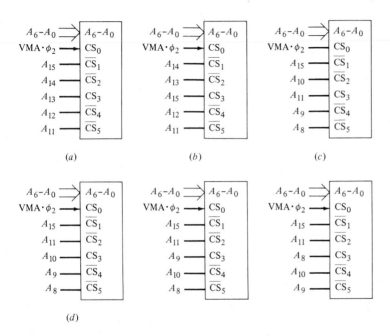

Figure P9-9 Address-bus connections for MCM6810 devices.

9-10 List the address blocks that are not used by the MCM6810 devices shown in Fig. P9-9.

9-11 Indicate which of the MCM6810 devices shown in Fig. P9-9 will respond to the following address:

(*a*) 0273

(*b*) 8332

(*c*) 0193

(*d*) 0000

(*e*) FFFF

(*f*) 2222

9-12 Indicate which of the MCM6810 devices shown in Fig. P9-9 will respond to the following patterns on the address bus:

(*a*) All lines at the low level

(*b*) All lines at the low level

(*c*) A15 and A9 at the high level and all others at the low level

(*d*) A13 and A9 at the high level and all others at the low level

(*e*) A13 and A8 at the high level and all others at the low level

9-13 Draw a schematic diagram showing all connections to the address bus for all MCM6810 devices required for the following memory units:

(*a*) 128 words starting at address 1000
(*b*) 256 words starting at address 0200
(*c*) 256 words starting at address of 0100
(*d*) 384 words starting at address F000
(*e*) 384 words starting at address 0400

9-14 List all addresses consumed by the memory unit you specified in Prob. 9-13.

9-15 Define the voltage level on all pins of MCM6830 to perform the following data transfers:

(*a*) Read the contents of the first location
(*b*) Read the contents of the fortieth location
(*c*) Read the contents of the hundredth location
(*d*) Write B2 in the last location
(*e*) Clear the thirtieth location

9-16 List the addresses recognized by the MCM6830 devices shown in Fig. P9-16.

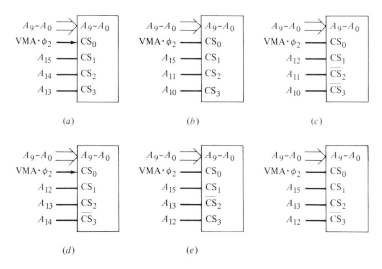

(*a*) (*b*) (*c*)

(*d*) (*e*)

Figure P9-16 Address-bus connections for MCM6830 devices.

9-17 In an MCM6830 device the value 00 is in the first location, 01 is in the second, and so on, so that FF is in the 256th location. The remaining locations contain 00. Define the voltage levels on all pins for the following data transfers:

(*a*) Read from the 256th location
(*b*) Read from the fifth location
(*c*) Read from the last location
(*d*) Write the ASCII code word for the character G in the twentieth location
(*e*) Clear the 256th location

9-18 List all address blocks that are not used by the MCM6830 packages shown in Fig. P9-16.

9-19 Indicate which of the MCM6830 devices shown in Fig. P9-16 will respond to the following patterns on the address bus:

(*a*) All lines at the low level
(*b* All lines at the high level

(c) A15 and A14 at the high level and all others at the low level

(d) A15 and A13 at the high level and all others at the low level

(e) A15 and A12 at the high level and all others at the low level

9-20 Indicate which of the MCM6830 devices shown in Fig. P9-16 will respond to the following addresses:

(a) FFFF

(b) 3022

(c) 0000

(d) C17C

(e) 1111

9-21 Draw a schematic diagram showing the connection to the address bus for all MCM6830 devices required for the following memory units:

(a) 1024 words starting at address F000

(b) 3072 words starting at address 1000

(c) 4096 words starting at address 0000

(d) 4K words starting at address 3000

(e) 8K words starting at address 0800

9-22 List all addresses consumed by the memory unit you specified in Prob. 9-21.

9-23 Draw a schematic diagram showing all connections to the address bus for all MCM6810 and MCM6830 devices required for the following memory units:

(a) 1024 words of ROM ending at address FFFF and 128 words of RAM starting at address 0000

(b) 2K words of ROM ending at address FFFF and 256 words of RAM starting at address 0080

(c) 3K words of ROM starting at address 1000 and 384 words of ROM starting at address 0020

(d) 4K words of ROM starting at address 2000 and 384 words of RAM starting at address F000

(e) 3K words of ROM starting at address 0000 and 384 words of RAM ending at address FFFF

9-24 List all addresses consumed by the memory unit you specified in Prob. 9-23.

9-25 Describe the differences between partial and full address decoding in a memory unit. Discuss the advantages and disadvantages of both approaches.

9-26 Define which decoder output lines in Fig. 9-10 are active when the value on the address bus is:

(a) 7C24

(b) 037D

(c) F726

(d) 54CD

(e) 0092

9-27 Define the address block designated by the following signals in Fig. 9-10:

(a) D4 of DCDR5

(b) D2 of DCDR0

(c) D7 of DCDR1

(d) D4 of DCDR2

(e) D0 of DCDR7

9-28 Define the connections between the DCDR7 decoder in Fig. 9-10 and all MCM6830 devices required to form 8K words of ROM memory responding only to the address block E000 to FFFF. Define the connection to all other pins on each MCM6830 device.

9-29 Define the connections between DCDR0 in Fig. 9-10 and all MCM6810 devices to form 1K words of RAM memory which responds only to the address block 0000 to 03FF. Define the connections to all other pins on each MCM6810.

9-30 Define the voltage level on all pins of the MC6821 to perform the following data transfers:

(a) Read the peripheral data register in port A

(b) Read the control register in port B

(c) Write the code word 7C in the control register in port A

(d) Write the code word 0F in the data direction register in port B

(e) Write 73 in the peripheral data register in port B

9-31 Define the voltage level on all pins of the MC6821 to perform the following data transfers:

(a) Read the peripheral data register in port B

(b) Read the control register in port A

(c) Write the code word C7 in the control register in port B

(d) Write the code word F7 in the data direction register in port A

(e) Write A6 in the peripheral data register in port A

9-32 Define the code words for all registers in an MC6821 device for the following conditions:

(a) Both ports are inputs; CA_1, CB_1, CA_2, and CB_2 are input signals, all synchronizing signals are active on the low-to-high transition, and all interrupts are disabled

(b) The same as part (a) except that CA_1 and CB_1 are active on the high-to-low transition

(c) The same as part (a) except that CA_1 and CB_2 should cause an interrupt

(d) The same as part (a) except that port B is an output port

(e) The same as part (a) except that CA_2 is active on the high-to-low transition and should cause an interrupt

9-33 Define the code words for all registers in an MC6821 device for the following conditions:

(a) PA_0 is connected to an input line, all other external data lines are outputs; CA_1, CB_1, and CB_2 are connected to input signals, all synchronizing signals are active on the high-to-low transition, and all interrupts are enabled

(b) The same as part (a) except that PA_7 is connected to an output line

(c) The same as part (a) except that CA_2 is active on the low-to-high transition

(d) The same as part (a) except that the interrupt for CB_1 should be disabled

(e) The same as part (a) except that CB_2 is active on the low-to-high transition and should not cause an interrupt

9-34 List all addresses recognized by the MC6821 devices shown in Fig. P9-34

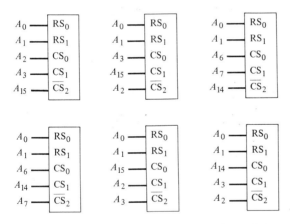

Figure P9-34 Address-bus connections for MC6821 devices.

9-35 Indicate which MC6821 devices in Fig. P9-34 will respond to the following addresses:

(a) 707C

(b) FD8E

(c) 8888

(d) FFFF

(e) 5C65

9-36 Define a connection between the address bus and an MC6821 so that it will respond to the following addresses:

   (*a*) 4 to 010

   (*b*) 100C to 100F

   (*c*) CCC8 to CCCB

   (*d*) 0000 to 0003

9-37 Define a connection between the address bus and four MC6821 devices so that the devices are assigned consecutive addresses starting at:

   (*a*) 0000

   (*b*) 0800

   (*c*) 1000

   (*d*) 0400

   (*e*) 0080

9-38 Modify the assembly language subroutines in Table 9-5 so that they are compatible with the PIAs defined in Prob. 9-32.

9-39 Modify the assembly-language subroutines in Table 9-6 so that they are compatible with the MC6821 device defined in Prob. 9-32.

9-40 Define a connection to the address bus for an MC6821 device that is compatible with the memory unit you defined in Prob. 9-23.

9-41 Define a connection between the address bus and an MC6821 device that is compatible with the memory unit defined in Example 9-2.

9-42 Define the address bus connections using a partial decoding scheme for an input-output unit that uses MC6821 devices and is compatible with the memory unit defined in Example 9-2. The unit should have:

   (*a*) 4 input and 8 output lines

   (*b*) 16 input lines

   (*c*) 25 output lines

   (*d*) 10 input and 10 output lines

   (*e*) five 8-bit ports

9-43 Two terminals like that described in Fig. 9-12 are connected to two MC6821 interface packages. The interface for terminal 1 is assigned addresses C000 to C003, and that for terminal 2 is assigned addresses C004 to C007. All data transfers are under interrupt control using the $\overline{\text{IRQ}}$ line.

   (*a*) Define the code word for all registers in these two devices

   (*b*) Write a subroutine to initialize these two devices

   (*c*) Write an interrupt-service routine to perform these data transfers. In this routine the addresses for storing input words are stored in locations READ1 and READ2; similarly addresses for output words are stored in locations PRINT1 and PRINT2

9-44 Write a subroutine that uses program control to transfer data through the two terminals defined in Prob. 9-43. The subroutine should alternately test the two terminals to determine which has valid data and then jump to one of two subroutines titled TRMNL1 or TRMNL2 to perform the data transfer.

9-45 Repeat Prob. 9-43 using:

   (*a*) Addresses 0100 to 0103 and 0104 to 0107

   (*b*) Three terminals at addresses 2000 to 2003, 2004 to 2007, and 2008 to 200B

9-46 Write a subroutine that uses program control to transfer data through the three terminals defined in part (*b*) of Prob. 9-45. The subroutine should sequentially test the three terminals to determine which has valid data and then jump to one of three subroutines titled TRMNL1, TRMNL2, and TRMNL3 to perform the data transfer.

9-47 Define how many MC6800, MCM6810, MC6821, and MCM6830 packages must be used in a computer system that has equivalent capability to the MC6801 package.

9-48 Can programs written for the MC6800 processor run on the MC6801 microcomputer system and vice versa? Discuss your answer.

9-49 Write a subroutine for the M6800 microprocessor that performs the same operation as the following instructions in the M6801 microcomputer system:

(*a*) ABX
(*b*) ASLD
(*c*) LSRD
(*d*) PSHX
(*e*) PULX

9-50 Write a subroutine for the M6800 microprocessor that performs the same operation as the following instructions in the M6801 microcomputer system where the operand is specified using the extended addressing mode:

(*a*) ADDD
(*b*) LDD
(*c*) STD
(*d*) SUBD

9-51 Repeat Prob. 9-49 using the M6802 microprocessor.

REFERENCES

Garland, H.: "Introduction to Microprocessor System Design," McGraw-Hill, New York, 1979.

Klingman, E. E.: "Microprocessor System Design," Prentice-Hall, Englewood Cliffs, N.J., 1977.

Kraft, G. D., and W. N. Toy: "Mini/Microcomputer Hardware Design," Prentice-Hall, Englewood Cliffs, N.J., 1979.

Osborne, A.: "An Introduction to Microcomputers," Vol. II, "Some Real Products," Osborne Associates, Berkeley, Calif., 1977.

Motorola Staff: "M6800 Microprocessor Applications Manual," Motorola, Inc., Phoenix, Ariz., 1975.

Motorola Staff: "The Complete Microcomputer Data Library," Motorola, Inc., Phoenix, Ariz., 1978.

DESIGN OF MICROCOMPUTER-BASED DIGITAL NETWORKS

In Chap. 4 we presented the traditional logic design procedure. In this chapter we present the microcomputer-based design procedure as a series of steps that transform an informal specification into a program and a microcomputer system hardware configuration. After finishing this chapter the reader should be able to:

1. Develop an input-output model from a problem specification including the definition of binary variables and the association of input and output signal wires with the binary variables
2. Derive a flowchart for a top-level structured program depicting, on a single page, the time-ordered relationship of the major functions required to produce a solution and define flowcharts for additional levels of structured programs which refine tasks in the top-level programs
3. Translate all flowcharts into M6800 assembly-language programs
4. Define the number of memory devices required by the system and their connection to the system bus
5. Define the number of input-output devices required by the system, their connection to the system bus, and their configuration code words
6. Analyze the performance of a solution, including timing, to determine whether the problem specification has been met

10-1 VENDING-MACHINE CONTROL UNIT

Here we describe the design of a vending-machine control unit meeting the same specifications as those used in designing the traditional system in Chap. 4. By repeating this problem we shall acquire some understanding of the distinctions between the traditional and microcomputer-based design procedures. Before beginning to design the microprocessor system let us review the description of the vending-machine operation and the specifications for the control unit.

The major units in a hypothetical vending machine are shown in Fig. 4-1. Our objective is to design the control unit to accept inputs from the coin input unit and produce outputs controlling the coin-input, change-dispensing, and drink-dispensing units. As before, the three units not our primary concern are called auxiliary units. Their input-output behavior must be carefully considered because it directly affects the design of the control unit. A summary of the auxiliary-unit input-output signal specifications is given in Table 4-1.

Although the operation of a vending machine is familiar to us all, let us review a typical transaction considering the activities in a more technical way. A series of coins, restricted to nickels, dimes, or quarters, is inserted, one at a time, into the machine. For each valid input, the coin-input unit briefly activates one of its output lines, producing a single pulse indicating the denomination of the coin inserted. We define 35 cents as the cost of a drink. The buyer may push the coin-return lever at any time before completion of a transaction, generating a signal to the control unit indicating that all money has been returned. As soon as a coin causes the sum in the present transaction to equal or exceed 35 cents, the control unit will generate output signals to collect the coins and to dispense the proper change and a drink.

This narrative description, along with the information contained in Fig. 4-1 and Table 4-1, constitutes the problem specification. We now proceed through a six-step design procedure to produce a formal, unambiguous solution consisting of a program and a microprocessor configuration.

Step 1 In step 1 we identify an input-output model for the microcomputer system and carefully define each input and output signal. For the vending-machine control unit this is done in Fig. 4-1 and Table 4-1. Next we tentatively assign each input and output signal to a specific bit in an input-output port. Since there are only eight external signals in this system, one input-output port is sufficient. We arbitrarily assign the four input signals to the four lower-order bits and the four output signals to the four higher-order bits, as shown in Fig. 10-1.

Step 2 In step 2 the solution algorithm is developed. We begin this development by assuming that all input and output data transfers will be under program control. Later if the timing analysis in step 4 indicates problems, we shall consider interrupt control of the input and output data transfers. Nevertheless, a program control, if adequate, is preferred because the timing behavior is simpler to analyze than interrupt control.

A flowchart for the top-level program (VMCU) for the vending-machine control unit is given in Fig. 10-2. The flowchart begins by initializing the system when power is applied. This includes storing the correct code words in the data direction and control registers of the input-output port, setting the stack pointer

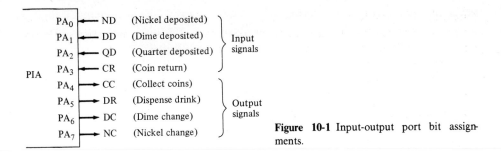

Figure 10-1 Input-output port bit assignments.

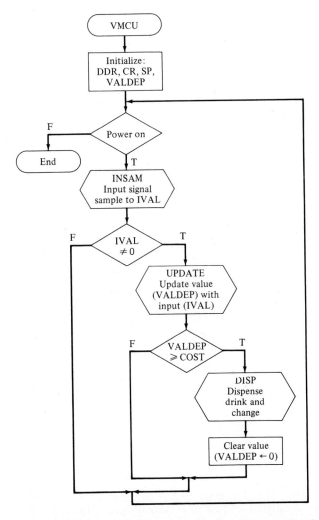

Figure 10-2 Top-level flowchart for vending-machine control unit.

to the proper address, and clearing the value on deposit. The next element, the DO WHILE POWER ON structural unit, establishes a repeated task structure for continuously monitoring the input signals and dispensing drinks.

Next, the subroutine INSAM is used to obtain a reliable sample of the input signals ND, DD, QD, and CR. This subroutine, which will be defined later, returns one parameter, a code word with bits 0 to 3 indicating the condition of ND, DD, QD, and CR, respectively. In the top-level program this code word will be stored in IVAL. In this flowchart we have omitted all tasks required for transferring parameters between the top-level program and the subroutines. When we translate this flowchart into an assembly-language program, these instructions must be included.

Once a code word has been transferred to IVAL, it is tested; if it is not zero, the subroutine UPDATE is executed; otherwise nothing is done, and the input signals are reexamined. The subroutine UPDATE accepts two parameters; one is the code word defining the condition of the input signals, and the other is a code word defining the value deposited before the current input. This subroutine returns one parameter defining the updated value deposited. In the top-level program the value deposited is stored in VALDEP.

After the value in VALDEP has been updated, it is compared with the cost of a drink. If the value is greater than or equal to the cost of a drink, the subroutine DISP is executed and VALDEP is cleared; otherwise nothing is done and the input signals are reexamined. The subroutine DISP accepts one parameter defining the value deposited and dispenses a drink and the appropriate change.

Let us discuss each subroutine in more detail before going on to the next step in the design procedure. The subroutine INSAM obtains a reliable estimate of the condition of the input signals. A flowchart for this subroutine is shown in Fig. 10-3. First, we obtain two samples of the input condition separated by a short time interval. Then a repeated-task structural unit is used to ensure that the two samples of the input condition are identical. Comparing two samples of the input condition greatly reduces the possibility of detecting an invalid condition resulting from spurious noise on the input signals. Upon entering the loop, the original two samples are compared; if they are the same, the loop is exited. Otherwise a new sample is obtained until two consecutive samples are identical. Next, another repeated-task structural unit is used to ensure that the detected input signal returns to a low level before returning from this subroutine. This ensures that a pulse on an input signal is detected only once. Finally, the detected input condition is placed in the parameter list and a return occurs.

A flowchart for the subroutine UPDATE is shown in Fig. 10-4. This subroutine first moves the code words defining the input condition and the value deposited from the parameter list to accumulators B and A, respectively. Then using a series of alternative-task structured units, the subroutine decodes the input condition and adjusts the value deposited to reflect the new input. If bit 0 of accumulator B is set, a nickel was deposited and so 5 is added to accumulator A; if bit 1 is set, a dime was deposited and so 10 is added; and if bit 3 is set, a quarter was deposited and so 25 is added. If bit 4 in accumulator B is set, the

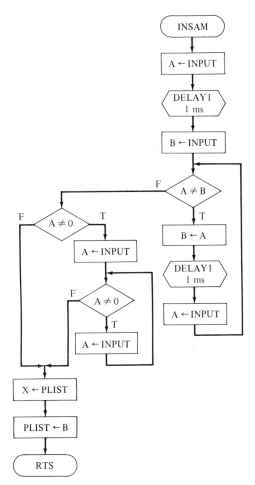

Figure 10-3 Flowchart for subroutine INSAM.

coin-return button was pushed, and so the value deposited, which is stored in accumulator A, is set to zero. Finally the subroutine transfers the adjusted value deposited from accumulator A to the parameter list and a return occurs.

A flowchart for the subroutine DISP is shown in Fig. 10-5. In the first step the value deposited is transferred from the parameter list to accumulator A, and the cost of a drink is subtracted. Next a series of alternative-task structural units is used to activate the correct output signals to dispense a drink and the correct change. If the difference between the value deposited and the cost of a drink is 20, the code word to collect the coins and dispense a drink and a dime is stored in the output port. A third-level subroutine DELAY2 is used to hold this output condition for 50 ms, and then the output port is cleared. After another 50-ms delay the code word to dispense a dime is stored, and the program continues. The second alternative-task structural unit in the series determines whether the difference is 15, in which case the code word to collect the coins and dispense a

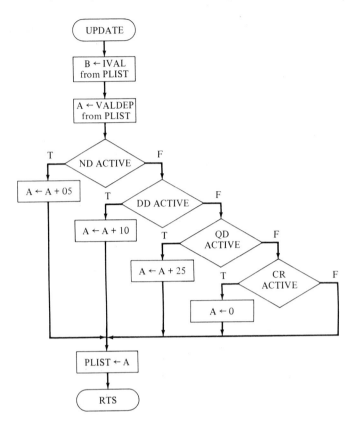

Figure 10-4 Flowchart for subroutine UPDATE.

drink, a dime, and a nickel is stored. If the difference is 10, the code word to collect the coins and dispense a drink and a dime is stored. In the last alternative-task structural unit if the difference is 5, the code word to collect the coins and dispense a drink and a nickel is stored; otherwise, the code word to collect the coins and dispense a drink is stored. After this series of alternative-task structural units, the subroutine DELAY2 is executed to hold the outputs active for 50 ms, after which the output is cleared and a return occurs.

Step 3 Step 3 involves translating the flowcharts into assembly-language programs. This procedure requires an initial estimate of both RAM and ROM memory requirements. Tentative address spaces must be assigned to these devices and to the input-output port. Tentative starting addresses must be defined for the top-level program and all subroutines.

Table 10-1 shows the assembly-language program implementation of the flowchart in Fig. 10-2. In developing this program we made an initial guess of the memory requirement. Since there are only four flowcharts, we guess that the program can be stored in one 1K ROM device, and since there are a limited

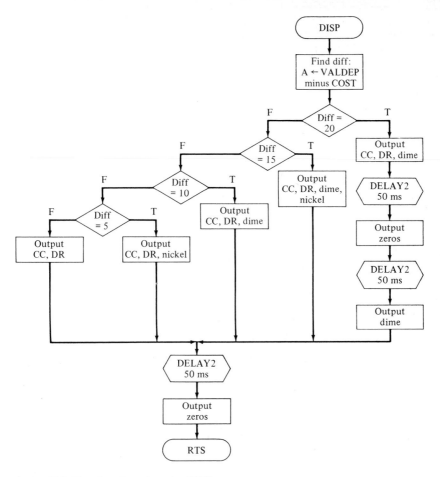

Figure 10-5 Flowchart for subroutine DISP.

number of data storage requirements, we initially use only one 128-byte **RAM** device. As discussed in Chap. 9, there are reasons for assigning addresses S0000 to $007F to the RAM device and addresses $FC00 to $FFFF to the ROM device. We arbitrarily use addresses $8000 and $8001 for the input-output interface because they will be easy to decode.

This program starts with the NAM directive, followed by a brief description of the program operation. Each line in this description starts with an asterisk, indicating that what follows is interpreted as a comment.

In Table 10-1 the first two directives after the comments assign $FC and 00 to memory locations $FFFE and $FFFF, since $FC00 is the starting address of the top-level program. This is done because the 6800 system transfers the contents of $FFFE and $FFFF to the program counter every time the RESET line in the system bus is activated. In the vending-machine control unit the RESET line will be connected to a special circuit that generates a pulse whenever the power is turned

Table 10-1 Top-level solution for vending-machine control unit

```
                    NAM     VMCU
*THIS PROGRAM EXAMINES INPUT SIGNALS ND, DD, QD, AND CR ASSIGNED TO
*BITS 0–3 OF INPUT-OUTPUT PORT, RESPECTIVELY. THE PORT IS
*ASSIGNED TO ADDRESSES $8000 AND $8001. THE VALUE OF THE DEPOSITED COIN IS
*ADDED TO THE VALUE ON DEPOSIT, VALDEP. WHEN THE VALUE ON DEPOSIT
*EQUALS OR EXCEEDS THE COST OF A DRINK, THEN ALL COINS ARE COLLECTED
*AND A DRINK AND THE CORRECT CHANGE ARE DISPENSED BY ASSIGNING VALUES
*TO THE OUTPUT SIGNALS CC, DD, DC, AND NC ASSIGNED TO BITS 4–7
*INPUT-OUTPUT PORT, RESPECTIVELY.
                    ORG     $FFFE
        RESTRT      FDB     $00FE
        INSAM       EQU     $FD00        DEFINE STARTING ADDRESS FOR INSAM
        UPDATE      EQU     $FE00        DEFINE STARTING ADDRESS FOR UPDATE
        DISP        EQU     $FF00        DEFINE STARTING ADDRESS FOR DISP
        PORTDR      EQU     $8000        ADDR FOR PORT DATA REG
        PORTDD      EQU     PORTDR       ADDR FOR PORT DATA DIR REG
        PORTCR      EQU     $8001        ADDR FOR PORT CONTROL REG
        DDCODE      EQU     $F0          PORT DATA DIR REG CODE WORD
        CRCODE      EQU     $04          PORT CONTROL REG CODE WORD
        STACK       EQU     $007F        ADDRESS OF STACK
        COST        EQU     35           COST OF DRINK
        VALDEP      RMB     1            VALUE ON DEPOSIT
        IVAL        RMB     1            INPUT SAMPLE VALUE
        PLIST       RMB     2            PARAMETER LIST FOR SUBROUTINE
                    ORG     $FC00
        VMCU        CLR     PORTCR       SELECT DATA DIR REG
                    LDAA    DDCODE       GET CODE WORD FOR PORT DDR
                    STAA    PORTDD       STORE IN PORT DATA DIR REG
                    LDAA    CRCODE       GET CODE WORD FOR PORT CR
                    STAA    PORTCR       STORE IN PORT CONTROL REG
                    CLR     PORTDR       OUTPUTS ALL INACTIVE
                    LDS     #STACK       INIT STACK POINTER
                    CLR     VALDEP       SET VALUE ON DEPOSIT TO ZERO
        VLOOP       LDX     #PLIST       SET X FOR SUBROUTINE
                    JSR     INSAM        INPUT CODE WORD
                    LDAA    0,X          GET INPUT CODE WORD FROM PLIST
                    STAA    IVAL         STORE CODE WORD IN IVAL
                    BEQ     VSKIP        IF IVAL = 0, SKIP
                    LDX     #PLIST       SET X FOR SUBROUTINE
                    LDAA    VALDEP       GET VALUE DEPOSITED
                    STAA    3,X          PLACE ON PARAMETER LIST FOR SUBROUTINE
                    LDAA    IVAL         GET INPUT CODE WORD
                    STAA    1,X          PLACE ON PARAMETER LIST FOR SUBROUTINE
                    JSR     UPDATE       UPDATE VALUE WITH INPUT
                    LDAA    0,X          GET VALUE DEPOSITED FROM PLIST
                    STAA    VALDEP       STORE VALUE ON DEPOSIT
                    CMPA    #COST        IS VALUE > COST?
                    BLT     VSKIP        IF LESS SKIP
                    LDX     #PLIST       SET X FOR SUBROUTINE
                    LDAA    VALDEP       GET VALUE DEPOSITED
                    STAA    0,X          PLACE ON PLIST FOR SUBROUTINE
                    JSR     DISP         DISPENSE DRINK AND CHANGE
                    CLR     VALDEP       SET VALUE DEPOSITED TO ZERO
        VSKIP       BRA     VLOOP
                    END
```

on. This ensures that the initialization tasks will be performed each time power is applied to the system.

The next three instructions are assembler directives defining the address of the subroutines: INSAM, UPDATE, and DISP. If these three subroutines were assembled with the top-level program, these three directives will be unnecessary.

Initially we arbitrarily allow 256 bytes for the main program and for each subroutine. Since the main program starts at $FC00, starting addresses for the three subroutines will be $FD00, $FE00, and $FF00. Later they can be modified based on the analysis of memory requirements.

The next five directives assign addresses to the input-output interface and define the code words for the data direction and control registers in this interface. The code word for the data direction register is 1111 0000 to define the four higher-order bits as outputs and four lower-order bits as inputs. Since the code word for the control register is defined to select the peripheral data register, bit 2 must be set. All other bits are arbitrary, so we set them to 0, thus the code word is $04.

The rest of the assembler directives define addresses and constants and reserve memory locations. We shall start the stack at the highest address in RAM, and so its initial address is $007F. The cost of a drink is defined as 35 cents. Memory locations are reserved for VALDEP, IVAL, and PLIST. Two bytes are reserved for PLIST since that is the maximum number of parameters transferred to or from a subroutine.

The executable instructions are started at location $FC00. The first eight executable instructions initialize the input-output port, the stack pointer, and the value deposited. The remainder of the instruction represents a straightforward implementation of the DO WHILE structural unit shown in the flowchart in Fig. 10-2. The translation of the jump of subroutine tasks requires a little explanation. For example, transferring to the subroutine UPDATE requires eight instructions starting with the LDX #PLIST instruction just after the BEQ VSKIP instruction. In this sequence the first five instructions are used to set up the input parameter list for the subroutine and the last 2 are used to retrieve the output parameters from the subroutine.

Table 10-2 shows an assembly-language-program implementation of the subroutine INSAM, for which the flowchart is shown in Fig. 10-3. The first instruction after the comments is an assembler directive defining the value of the PORTDR for this subroutine. Although this label was defined in the top-level program in Table 10-1, we must redefine it here because we shall assemble these two routines independently. The ORG $FD00 places the first executable instruction in location FD00, the address we arbitrarily assigned earlier in the top-level program in Table 10-1.

The translation of the flowchart in Fig. 10-4 into executable instructions is straightforward. This subroutine does use another subroutine DELAY1. The program for DELAY1 is listed just after the RTS instructions for INSAM. This delay routine is simply a loop where the index register is loaded with some initial value and decremented on each repetition. The exit occurs when zero is reached.

Table 10-2 Subroutine INSAM

	NAM	INSAM	

*THIS SUBROUTINE SAMPLES THE INPUT SIGNALS AND RETURNS THE INPUT CODEWORD.
*TWO SUCCESSIVE SAMPLES OF THE INPUTS MUST AGREE TO INSURE A
*STABLE INPUT SIGNAL. IF ANY INPUT SIGNAL IS ACTIVE, THEN THE SUB-
*ROUTINE WAITS UNTIL THE END OF THE PULSE BEFORE PROCEEDING SO THAT
*NO PULSE WILL BE READ TWICE.

Label	Op	Operand	Comment
PORTDR	EQU	$8000	ADDRESS PORT DATA REG
	ORG	$FD00	STARTING ADDRESS FOR INSAM
INSAM	LDAA	PORTDR	GET A SAMPLE
	JSR	DELAY1	WAIT 1 MS
	LDAB	PORTDR	GET ANOTHER SAMPLE
ILOOP1	CBA		ARE THEY EQUAL?
	BEQ	IEXIT1	EXIT IF YES
	TAB		OLD SAMPLE TO B
	JSR	DELAY1	WAIT 1MS
	LDAA	PORTDR	NEW SAMPLE TO A
	BRA	ILOOP1	GO SEE IF EQUAL
IEXIT1	BEQ	IEXIT2	EQUAL SAMPLES = ZERO?
	LDAA	PORTDR	LOAD INPUTS TO TEST FOR ZERO
ILOOP2	BEQ	IEXIT2	INPUT EQUAL ZERO?
	LDAA	PORTDR	LOAD INPUT TO TEST FOR ZERO
	BRA	ILOOP2	BRA TO TEST FOR ZERO
IEXIT2	LDX	#PLIST	RELOAD ADDRESS OF PARAMETER LIST
	STAB	0, X	STORE SAMPLE IN PLIST
	RTS		RETURN
COUNT1	EQU	82	INITIAL VALUE FOR COUNT FOR 1 MS DELAY
DELAY1	LDX	#COUNT1	INITIALIZE INDEX WITH COUNT
D1LOOP	BEQ	D1EXIT	BRANCH IF COUNT = 0
	DEX		DEC COUNT
	BRA	D1LOOP	BRANCH TO TEST COUNT
D1EXIT	RTS		
	END		

The initial value is defined by COUNT1, which is assigned the decimal value 82. The justification for this choice is presented later in the timing analysis. Since the delay routine uses the index register, it is necessary to load it with the address of the parameter list before returning from INSAM; this is accomplished by the instruction ISKIP2 LDX #PLIST.

Table 10-3 shows the assembly-language program implementing the subroutine UPDATE whose flowchart is shown in Fig. 10-4. The first four instructions after the comments are assembler directives defining the labels for the four possible input patterns that must be decoded. The ORG $FE00 places the first executable instruction in location FE00, the address we arbitrarily assigned earlier in the top-level program in Table 10-1. Translating the flowchart into executable instructions is straightforward and will not be discussed.

Table 10-3 Subroutine UPDATE

	NAM	UPDATE	
*THIS SUBROUTINE ADDS THE MONETARY VALUE DEFINED BY (IVAL) TO THE			
*VALUE ON DEPOSIT (VALDEP).			
NDWORD	EQU	$01	CODE WORD FOR ND
DDWORD	EQU	$02	CODE WORD FOR DD
QDWORD	EQU	$04	CODE WORD FOR QD
CRWORD	EQU	$08	CODE WORD FOR CR
	ORG	$FE00	STARTING ADDRESS FOR UPDATE
UPDATE	LDAB	1, X	GET IVAL FROM PLIST
	LDAA	0, X	GET VALDEP FROM PLIST
	BITB	#NDWORD	ISOLATE ND BIT
	BEQ	NOTND	BRANCH IF ND IS INACTIVE
	ADDA	#5	ADD 5 TO VALDEP
	BRA	UEXIT	VALDEP UPDATED, BRA FOR RETURN
NOTND	BITB	#DDWORD	ISOLATE QD BIT
	BEQ	NOTDD	BRANCH IF QD IS INACTIVE
	ADDA	#10	ADD 25 TO VALDEP
	BRA	UEXIT	VALDEP UPDATED, BRA FOR RETURN
NOTDD	BITB	#QDWORD	ISOLATE DD BIT
	BEQ	NOTQD	BRANCH IF DD IS INACTIVE
	ADDA	#25	ADD 10 TO VALDEP
	BRA	UEXIT	VALDEP UPDATED, BRA FOR RETURN
NOTQD	BITB	#CRWORD	ISOLATE CR BIT
	BEQ	UEXIT	BRANCH IF CR INACTIVE
	CLRA		VALDEP = 0
UEXIT	STAA	0, X	PUT VALDEP IN PLIST
	RTS		RETURN
	END		

Table 10-4 shows the assembly-language program implementing the flowchart for DISP in Fig. 10-5. The first seven statements after the comments assign values to labels used in this subroutine. The ORG $FF00 again places the first executable instruction in the location chosen earlier. The executable instructions are obtained directly from the flowchart. This subroutine uses another subroutine DELAY2, which is listed just after the RTS instruction for DISP. DELAY2 is identical to DELAY1 except that the initial decimal value is 4166, which results in a 50-ms delay, as we shall see later in the timing analysis.

Step 4 In step 4 we analyze the solution to determine whether it is compatible with the initial specification and tentative assignment of memory. With regard to specifications, timing and synchronization are the primary questions of interest. Is there any chance that an input pulse can be missed? Is there any chance that an input pulse can be read more than once? Do the output signals meet the timing specifications?

Table 10-4 Subroutine DISP

```
                NAM         DISP
*THE SUBROUTINE COMPUTES THE AMOUNT OF CHANGE REQUIRED FROM (VALDEP)
*AND (COST), OUTPUTTING THE PROPER CODE WORD TO ACTIVATE THE SIGNALS CC, DR, DC,
*AND NC.
        PORTDR  EQU         $8000           PORT DATA ADDRESS
        COST    EQU         35              COST OF DRINK
        CHNG10  EQU         $70             CODE TO ACTIVATE CC, DR, AND DC
        DIME    EQU         $40             CODE TO ACTIVATE DC
        CHNG15  EQU         $F0             CODE TO ACTIVATE CC, DR, DC, AND NC
        CHNG5   EQU         $B0             CODE TO ACTIVATE CC, DR, AND NC
        DRINK   EQU         $30             CODE TO ACTIVATE CC AND DR
                ORG         $FF00           STARTING ADDRESS FOR DISP
        DISP    LDAA        0, X            GET VALDEP FROM PLIST
                SUBA        #COST           DIFF = VALDEP-COST
                CMPA        #20             IS DIFF = 20?
                BNE         NOT20           BRANCH IF DIFF NOT 20
                LDAB        #CHNG10         GET CODE FOR CC, DR, AND DC
                STAB        PORTDR          OUTPUT CODE
                JSR         DELAY2          WAIT 50 MS
                CLR         PORTDR          INACTIVATE OUTPUTS
                JSR         DELAY2          WAIT 50 MS
                LDAB        #DIME           GET CODE FOR DC
                STAB        PORTDR          OUTPUT CODE
                BRA         DEXIT
        NOT20   CMPA        #15             IS DIFF = 15?
                BNE         NOT15           BRA IF DIFF NOT 15
                LDAB        #CHANG15        GET CODE FOR CC, DR, AND DC
                STAB        PORTDR          OUTPUT CODE
                BRA         DEXIT
        NOT15   CMPA        #10             IS DIFF = 10?
                BNE         NOT10           BRANCH IF DIFF NOT 10
                LDAB        #CHNG10         GET CODE FOR CC, DR, AND DC
                STAB        PORTDR          OUTPUT CODE
                BRA         DEXIT
        NOT10   CMPA        #5              IS DIFF = 5?
                BNE         NOT5            BRANCH IF DIFF NOT 5
                LDAB        #CHNG5          GET CODE FOR CC, DR, AND NC
                STAB        PORTDR          OUTPUT CODE
                BRA         DEXIT
        NOT5    LDAB        #DRINK          GET CODE FOR CC AND DR
                STAB        PORTDR          OUTPUT CODE
        DEXIT   JSR         DELAY2          WAIT 50 MS
                CLR         PORTDR          INACTIVATE OUTPUTS
                RTS
        COUNT2  EQU         4166            INITIAL VALUE FOR COUNT2 FOR 50 MS DELAY
        DELAY2  LDX         #COUNT2         INITIALIZE INDEX WITH COUNT
        D2LOOP  BEQ         D2EXIT          BRANCH IF COUNT = 0
                DEX                         DEC COUNT
                BRA         D2LOOP          BRANCH TO TEST COUNT
        D2EXIT  RTS
                END
```

In determining whether it is possible to miss an input pulse we must consider two alternatives. In the first, the pulse is missed because it becomes active just after the inputs are sampled and becomes inactive before two samples can be obtained. To verify that this will not happen we must show that two samples can be obtained during the specified input pulse width of 50 ms. The time between input samples is defined by the subroutine INSAM, and Table 10-5 shows the analysis defining the number of cycles between the first two samples, the second two samples, and any two samples after the second. All three conditions include one execution of the subroutine DELAY1, and the timing analysis for this subroutine is shown in Table 10-6. The combined analysis shows that 1025 is the maximum number of cycles between two successive samples. With a 1-MHz clock rate, this corresponds to 1.025 ms, and so approximately 50 samples will be obtained during the 50-ms duration of the input pulse. Thus it is highly unlikely that any input pulses will be missed because of failure to sample the input frequently enough.

Table 10-5 Maximum number of cycles between input samples

		First two samples agree	
INSAM	LDAA	PORTDR	4
	JSR	DELAY1	9
	(Subroutine DELAY1)†		996
	LDRB	PORTDR	4
			1013 cycles

		Second two samples agree	
	LDAB	PORTDR	4
	CBA		2
	BEQ	IEXIT1	4
	TAB		2
	JSR	DELAY1	9
	(Subroutine DELAY1)†		996
	LDAA	PORTDR	4
			1021 cycles

		Any two samples after second agree	
	LDAA	PORTDR	4
	BRA	ILOOP1	4
ILOOP1	CBA		2
	BEQ	IEXIT1	4
	TAB		2
	JSR	DELAY1	9
	(Subroutine DELAY1)†		996
	LDAA	PORTDR	4
			1025 cycles

† See Table 10-6.

Table 10-6 Number of cycles required to execute DELAY1

			Cycles for execution	Number of executions	Number of cycles
DELAY1	LDX	#COUNT1	3	1	3
D1LOOP	BEQ	D1EXIT	4	83	332
	DEX		4	82	328
	BRA	D1LOOP	4	82	328
D1EXIT	RTS		5	1	5
					996

The subroutine DELAY was introduced to separate the two samples so that both would not be in error due to the same noise spike on one of the input lines. The choice of 1-ms separation was arbitrary and could be adjusted. Earlier, in discussing the assembly-language program INSAM, we deferred indicating how the initial value for the counter for DELAY1 was defined. From Table 10-6 we see that 12 cycles are required for one repetition of the loop in the subroutine DELAY1. For a delay of 1 ms with a clock rate of 1 MHz, this sequence of instruction must be executed approximately 83 times

$$\frac{1000 \ \mu s}{12 \ \mu s/\text{repetition}} = 83.3 \text{ repetitions}$$

We shall choose 82 to allow for the execution of the initialization and return instructions in this subroutine.

The second way of missing an input pulse is if one occurs while a drink and change are being dispensed due to a previous sequence of inputs. To verify that this will not happen we must show that the maximum time to decode an input and dispense a drink and the proper change is less than the specified input pulse separation, 250 ms. Table 10-7 shows a timing analysis defining the maximum time required to dispense a drink and the correct change after the last coin input. This sequence starts with the first instruction in the top-level program after the subroutine INSAM and proceeds through the subroutines UPDATE, DISP, and INSAM. Execution times listed for these three subroutines represent the maximum number of cycles required for their execution, as defined in the timing analysis in Tables 10-8, 10-9, and 10-5, respectively.

For the subroutine UPDATE, this maximum occurs if the last coin deposited was a quarter, since the flowchart in Fig. 10-4 indicates that this subroutine first tests for a nickel, then a dime, and then a quarter.† Table 10-8 lists the sequence in which the instructions are executed if the input is a quarter. This analysis indicates that the maximum number of cycles for executing UPDATE is 45.

The analysis of the subroutine DISP is slightly more involved. At first glance it appears that the maximum number of cycles will occur when either 35 or 40

† Although the last test in the subroutine UPDATE is for a coin return, this last condition does not represent the overall worst case, since the subroutine DISP is not executed.

Table 10-7 Maximum number of cycles required to dispense drink and correct change

	Instruction sequence		Number of cycles
	LDAA	0,X	5
	STAA	IVAL	4
	BEQ	VSKIP	4
	LDX	#PLIST	3
	LDAA	VALDEP	3
	STAA	0,X	6
	LDAA	IVAL	3
	STAA	1,X	6
	JSR	UPDATE	9
	(Subroutine	UPDATE)†	45
	LDAA	0,X	5
	STAA	VALDEP	4
	CMPA	#COST	2
	BLT	VSKIP	4
	LDX	#PLIST	3
	LDA	VALDEP	3
	STAA	0,X	6
	JSR	DISP	9
	(Subroutine	DISP)‡	150,087
	CLR	VALDEP	6
VSKIP	BRA	VLOOP	4
VLOOP	LDX	#PLIST	3
	JSR	INSAM	9
	(Subroutine	INSAM)§	1,025
			151,258

† See Table 10-8.
‡ See Table 10-9.
§ See Table 10-6.

Table 10-8 Maximum number of cycles for execution of subroutine UPDATE

	Instruction sequence		Number of cycles
UPDATE	LDAB	1,X	5
	LDAA	0,X	5
	BITB	#NDWORD	2
	BEQ	NOTND	4
NOTND	BITB	#DDWORD	2
	BEQ	NOTDD	4
NOTDD	BITB	#QDWORD	2
	BEQ	NOTQD	4
	ADDA	#25	2
	BRA	UEXIT	4
UEXIT	STAA	0,X	6
	RTS		5
			45

Table 10-9 Maximum number of cycles for execution of subroutine DISP

Instruction sequence			Number of cycles
DISP	LDAA	0,X	5
	SUBA	#COST	2
	CMPA	#20	2
	BNE	NOT20	4
	LDAB	#CHNG10	2
	STAB	PORTDR	5
	JSR	DELAY2	9
	(Subroutine	DELAY2)†	50,004
	CLR	PORTDR	6
	JSR	DELAY2	9
	(Subroutine	DELAY2)†	50,004
	LDAB	#DIME	2
	STAB	PORTDR	5
	BRA	DEXIT	4
DEXIT	JSR	DELAY2	9
	(Subroutine	DELAY2)†	50,004
	CLR	PORTDR	6
	RTS		5
			150,087

† See Table 10-10.

cents is deposited since this is the last condition for which the subroutine tests. However, if 55 cents is deposited, two separate outputs are required and each involves the execution of the subroutine DELAY2, which requires 50,004 cycles for execution, as shown in Table 10-10. Since all other deposited values require only one output, and since DELAY2 requires many more cycles than any of the series of compare and branch instructions used to define the output, the maximum number of cycles occurs when 55 cents is deposited. Table 10-9 shows the analysis for this condition and indicates that the maximum number of cycles is 150,087.

Table 10-10 Number of cycles required to execute DELAY2

Instruction sequence			Cycles per execution	Number of executions	Number of cycles
DELAY2	LDX	#COUNT2	3	1	3
D2LOOP	BEQ	D2LOOP	4	4167	16,668
	DEX		4	4166	16,664
	BRA	D2LOOP	4	4166	16,664
D2EXIT	RTS		5	1	5
					50,004

When these values are entered into Table 10-7, we see that the maximum number of cycles required to dispense a drink and correct change is 151,258. Again with a 1-MHz clock, this corresponds to approximately 152 ms. Since this is less than the specified interval between input pulses, none will be missed while dispensing a drink and change.

The second question listed earlier is concerned with the possibility of detecting the same input pulse more than once. This problem was eliminated by the design of the subroutine INSAM, since after an active input is detected in the first loop (Fig. 10-3), the subroutine enters another loop to detect the disappearance of the input before returning to the top-level program. Thus it is highly unlikely that an input pulse will be detected more than once.

The third question concerned the timing of the output pulses which must be active for 50 ms and inactive for 50 ms between pulses. Table 10-9 shows the sequence in which the instructions in DISP are executed for 55 cents deposited. The duration of the first output pulse is defined by the sequence in lines 7 to 9, that is, JSR DELAY2, the subroutine DELAY2, and CLR PORTDR. The number of cycles is 50,019, which with a 1-MHz clock rate corresponds to approximately 50 ms. The duration of the second output pulse is defined by the sequence in lines 14 to 17, that is, BRA DEXIT to CLR PORTDR. The number of cycles is 50,023, which again with a 1-MHz clock rate corresponds to approximately 50 ms. Since this second sequence of instructions is used in the other paths in DISP, the output pulse will always be approximately 50 ms.

Except when 55 cents is deposited, the output lines are activated only once during each transaction. Since input pulses must be separated by at least 250 ms, the interval between output pulses will exceed 50 ms. When 55 cents is deposited, two output pulses are generated and the interval between them is defined by the sequence of instructions in lines 10 to 13 in Table 10-9, that is, JSR DELAY2 to STAB PORTDR. Thus the number of cycles required is 50,020, and so with a 1-MHz clock rate the interval exceeds 50 ms.

The subroutine DELAY2 in essence defines the duration of the output pulse and the separation between the two output pulses when 55 cents is deposited. Since both times were specified to be 50 ms, we designed DELAY2 so that it required 50 ms, or 50,000 cycles, for execution. The initial value for the loop counter was defined by

$$\frac{50,000 \text{ cycles}}{12 \text{ cycles/repetition}} = 4166.7$$

and we choose 4166.

A second consideration in the analysis of the program is to determine whether the initial memory selection and address assignment is compatible with the derived programs. This is accomplished by assembling the one top-level program and the three second-level subroutines to make sure they fit in the address space allotted to each. In this case the top-level program requires 76 bytes and so it uses addresses FC00 to FC4B. The subroutines INSAM, UPDATE, and DISP require 48, 36, and 81 bytes, respectively, and so they also fit in the address space allotted to them. Thus one ROM device and the assigned addresses are adequate.

In analyzing the RAM requirements, we note that 4 bytes are required for parameters. Also since only two levels of subroutines are used and no interrupts are used, the stack will contain at most 4 bytes. Thus the one RAM device is adequate.

Step 5 In step 5 we refine the solution to correct any design errors discovered during the analysis in step 4. In this example, the initial program satisfied all the specifications for input and output timing and fit into the memory and address spaces selected. Actually we did not generate this completely acceptable solution on the first pass; it was derived during several repetitions of the procedure defined in steps 2 to 5. Our original idea was to describe the evolution of this solution, but the presentation appeared so contrived that we simply presented an acceptable solution. We emphasize, however, that developing an acceptable solution generally requires several repetitions of these steps.

Step 6 In step 6 we complete the microcomputer hardware configuration by defining specific devices and their connection to the system bus. In this system we use the MC6800 processor, one MCM6810 RAM device, one MCM6830 ROM device, and one MC6821 PIA device. The MC6800 is connected to the system bus in the standard way, but it is not necessary to connect the two interrupt-request pins, the halt pin, and the two pins TSC and DBE used in synchronizing bus sharing.

The eight data pins for the RAM, ROM, and PIA devices are connected to the corresponding lines in the system bus. The R/W signal is connected to the corresponding pin on the RAM and PIA devices. The valid-memory-address signal again is ANDed with the ϕ_2 clock signal; the resulting signal is connected to the CS_0 pin on the RAM and ROM devices and to the enable (E) pin on the PIA device. The remaining chip-select pins on the memory and PIA devices are connected to the high-order bit lines in the address bus to implement a partial decoding scheme. Table 10-11 shows the address assigned to each of these three devices and the connection of lines A_{15} and A_{14} to specify each device uniquely.

Table 10-11 Address assignments and address-line connections for vending-machine control unit

Device	Assigned address	Address bus line	
		A_{15}	A_{14}
RAM1	0000–007F	$\overline{CS_1}$	
ROM1	FC00–FFFF	CS_1	CS_2
PIA1	8000–8001	CS_1	$\overline{CS_2}$

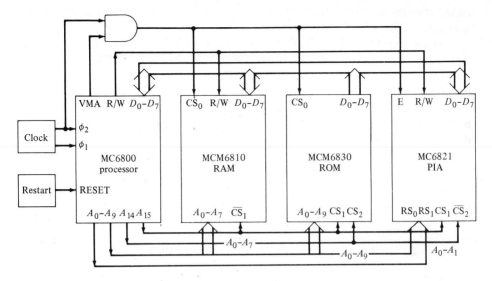

Figure 10-6 Block diagram for microcomputer system, vending-machine control unit.

The address pins on the RAM and ROM devices and the register-select pins on the PIA are connected to the low-order bit in the address bus.

Figure 10-6 shows a block diagram for vending-machine control unit and defines all connections to the four standard devices used in the design. Two additional modules, the clock and the restart unit, also are shown.

10-2 DIGITAL VOLTMETER

In this section we describe the design of a microcomputer-based digital voltmeter, using the same steps as in designing the vending-machine control unit. The primary difference will be the use of interrupts to synchronize the microcomputer with the auxiliary units of the voltmeter.

The digital voltmeter to be designed represents a simplified version of currently available commercial instruments. It operates as follows. An operator selects one of three ranges for use in measuring and displaying the analog input signal measured with the probes. The three ranges are ± 1 V, ± 10 V, and ± 100 V. The analog signal value is scaled according to the range selection, converted into digital form, and displayed using four digits with the appropriate algebraic sign and decimal point.

The major units in the digital voltmeter are the operator input unit, the display unit, the analog comparator unit, and the computation unit, as shown in Fig. 10-7.

The operator input unit has three buttons for selecting one of three voltage ranges. The three output signals indicating which range currently is selected are

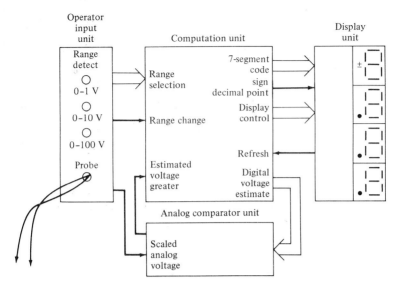

Figure 10-7 Block diagram for simplified digital voltmeter.

connected to the computation unit. An additional output signal is active (V_H) for 25 μs whenever the voltage range is changed. The operator unit also contains an analog network to scale the input signal to the ± 1-V range if one of the higher ranges is selected. The scaled analog voltage is connected to the analog comparator unit.

The display unit contains four seven-segment displays with an algebraic sign to the left of the most significant digit and a decimal point to the left of the other three digits. The display accepts two input-code words, a 4-bit word defining which digit is addressed and an 8-bit word defining which segments in the addressed digit are energized. In the 8-bit code word the eighth bit defines the status of the algebraic sign in the most significant digit and that of the decimal point in the other three digits. This arrangement makes use of the persistence of the displays and multiplexes the 8-bit code word between the four digits. The display unit generates a pulse indicating that the next digit in the sequence needs refreshing. This signal is activated once every millisecond.

The analog comparator unit accepts an analog signal in the range ± 1 V and an 11-bit code word which is interpreted as a numerical value using the twos-complement binary-value code. This unit generates one binary signal that is active when the digital value is greater than the analog value. This signal is valid 25 μs after the digital value is stable.

Our objective is to design the computation unit to accept inputs from the operator input unit and the analog comparator unit and to produce outputs for the display unit and analog comparator unit. The input-output behavior of these three auxiliary units must be carefully considered because they affect the design

Table 10-12 Auxiliary-unit signal specifications

	Operator input unit
R_1, R_2, R_3	Binary output signals indicating that range ± 1, ± 10, or ± 100 V, respectively, is selected; only one may be active (V_H) at any time
RCHANGE	Output binary signal active (V_H) for 25 μs whenever voltage range changes
SAV (scaled analog voltage)	Analog output signal scaled to ± 1-V range

	Display unit
SIGN DEC	Binary input signal connected to algebraic sign in most significant display digit and to decimal point in other three display digits; in the first case, a plus sign is displayed when this signal is active (V_H) and a minus sign when it is inactive (V_L); in the second case, the decimal point is energized when the signal is active (V_H)
SEGA, SEGB, SEGC SEGD, SEGE, SEGF, SEGG	Binary input signals connected to segments a to g in a standard seven-segment display (Fig. 2-26); when one of these signals is active (V_H), the corresponding segment is energized
$DIG_1, DIG_2, DIG_3, DIG_4$	Binary input signals indicating that the 8 bits of display are directed to the least through most significant display digits, respectively; only one may be active (V_H) at a time
REFRESH	Binary output signal that is activated (V_H) for 25 μs each ms; signal indicates that a new digit must be displayed

	Analog comparator unit
SAV (scaled analog voltage)	Analog input signal scaled to ± 1-V range
$DV_{10}-DV_0$	Binary input signals representing estimated voltage for comparison with analog input signal; estimated voltage is represented using the twos-complement binary value code, DV_{10} being most significant bit; signals are active at high level
EVG (estimated voltage greater)	Binary output signal that is active (V_H) when digitally coded voltage is greater than analog voltage; signal valid 25 μs after signals on $DV_{10}-DV_0$ are stable

of the computation unit directly. A summary of the input-output signal specifications for the auxiliary units is given in Table 10-12.

This narrative description along with the information contained in Fig. 10-7 and Table 10-12 constitutes the problem specification. We shall proceed through the six-step design procedure to produce a solution consisting of a program and a microcomputer configuration.

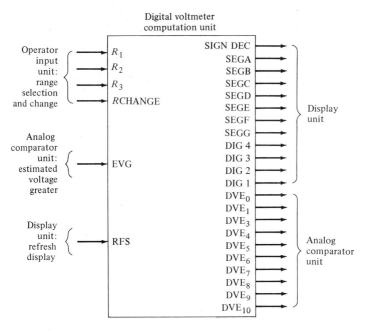

Figure 10-8 Input-output model for computation unit.

Step 1 In Step 1 we derive an input-output model for the digital-voltmeter computation unit (Fig. 10-8). The unit has a total of 6 input signals and 23 output signals. We shall use two peripheral interface adapter packages to connect these signals to the microcomputer system. Twenty-seven of the signals are assigned to peripheral data pins, as shown in Fig. 10-9. The RCHANGE and REFRESH signals are not connected to peripheral data lines, but they are connected to port control pins CA_1 and CA_2, respectively, so that an active transition of either signal will generate an interrupt.

Step 2 In step 2 the solution algorithm is developed. Interrupts will be used to indicate a change in the range selection and a request for a new digit to display. Consequently, the interrupt-service routine will take care of these two tasks. The main program will convert the input analog voltage into a digital representation and formulate code words for the display unit.

The flowchart for the interrupt-service routine INTSVR is shown in Fig. 10-10. We plan to connect the IRQA pin for the port connected to the RCHANGE and REFRESH signals to the IRQ line of system bus. Thus if the I bit in the condition code register is clear, an interrupt request on this line will be acknowledged and this routine will be entered. This will occur when a new voltage range is selected or when the display unit needs a new character to display. The display-refresh interrupt bit is tested first. If it is active, the 4-bit code word to

PIA1		
PA_0	Range select, Low range	R_1
PA_1	Range select, Mid range	R_2
PA_2	Range select, High range	R_3
PA_3	Estimated voltage greater	EVG
PA_4–PA_7	Unused	
CA_1	Range change	RCHANG
CA_2	Refresh display	REFRESH
PB_0	Display segment g	SEGG
PB_1	Display segment f	SEGF
PB_2	Display segment e	SEGE
PB_3	Display segment d	SEGD
PB_4	Display segment c	SEGC
PB_5	Display segment b	SEGB
PB_6	Display segment a	SEGA
PB_7	Sign and decimal point	SIGN DEC
CB_1	Unused	
CB_2	Unused	

PIA2		
PA_0	Digital voltage estimate, bit 8	DV_8
PA_1	Digital voltage estimate, bit 9	DV_9
PA_2	Digital voltage estimate, bit 10	DV_{10}
PA_3	Unused	
PA_4	Digit selection, fourth digit	DIG_4
PA_5	Digit selection, third digit	DIG_3
PA_6	Digit selection, second digit	DIG_2
PA_7	Digit selection, first digit	DIG_1
CA_1	Unused	
CA_2	Unused	
PB_0	Digital voltage estimate, bit 0	DV_0
PB_1	Digital voltage estimate, bit 1	DV_1
PB_2	Digital voltage estimate, bit 2	DV_2
PB_3	Digital voltage estimate, bit 3	DV_3
PB_4	Digital voltage estimate, bit 4	DV_4
PB_5	Digital voltage estimate, bit 5	DV_5
PB_6	Digital voltage estimate, bit 6	DV_6
PB_7	Digital voltage estimate, bit 7	DV_7
CB_1	Unused	
CB_2	Unused	

Figure 10-9 Input-output port bit assignments.

select the next display digit, and the 8-bit code word for the appropriate character are transferred to DIG_4 to DIG_0, SIGN DEC, and SEGA to SEGG. The display-list address is updated to the next character to be displayed when the REFRESH signal generates the next interrupt. The range-change-interrupt bit is then tested; if it is active, a sample of the range-select signals is obtained and stored. Finally, the interrupt-service routine returns to the interrupted program.

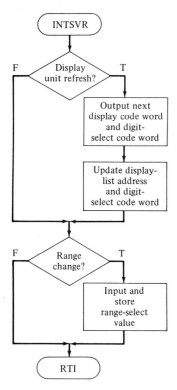

Figure 10-10 Flowchart for the interrupt-service routine.

The flowchart for the top-level program VCOMP is shown in Fig. 10-11. The flowchart begins with an initialization task that is executed when power is applied. This includes storing the code words required in the data direction and control registers of the input-output interfaces, initializing the stack pointer, and defining the beginning address for the display list.

The next task in VCOMP, a repeated-task structural unit, described by DO WHILE POWER ON, repeatedly converts the input voltage into a list of code words for the display unit.

The first task in this loop is the subroutine VCONV, used to derive the binary value of the input voltage by successive approximations. This subroutine, described later, returns two code words defining the value of the input voltage using an 11-bit twos-complement code. As before, the index register will contain the address of the parameter lists transferred from one routine to another. The next task, the subroutine DCONV, is then used to translate these two code words into four 8-bit code words for the four display digits. When entering this subroutine, the index register contains the address of the two input words, and when returning, the index register contains the address of the first of the four display code words. This subroutine also will be discussed later. The final two tasks in the loop, store the proper sign in the most significant bit of the first display code

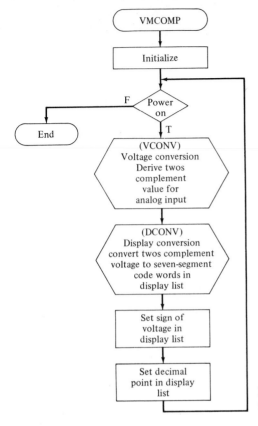

Figure 10-11 Top-level flowchart for voltage computation unit.

word and the decimal point, determined by the range selected, in the most significant bit of the appropriate display code word.

The flowchart for the subroutine VCONV is shown in Fig. 10-12. The sign of the measured analog voltage is established by transferring an 11-bit binary value of zero to the analog comparator unit. If the EVG signal from the analog comparator is a 1, the measured value is negative and the most significant bit of the 11-bit code word is set; otherwise this bit is cleared.

A repeated-task structural unit is used to determine the next 10 bits of the binary value. On each repetition 1 bit is set to 1, and the new estimate is transferred to the analog comparator unit. After a delay of approximately 30 μs the EVG signal is tested. If this signal is a 1, the estimate is too large and the bit, presently being resolved, is cleared. Otherwise the bit is left set. This process is repeated, from the most significant to the least significant bit, until all the bits have been determined. The final result is an 11-bit code word representing the input voltage with the two's-complement signed-binary-value code. After exiting from this loop, the address of the first of the two code words is loaded into the index register and the subroutine returns to the calling program.

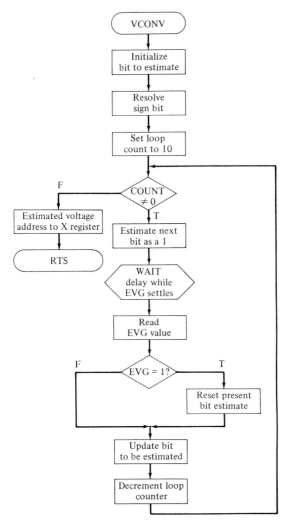

Figure 10-12 Flowchart for voltage-conversion subroutine, VCONV.

The flowchart for the subroutine DCONV (Fig. 10-13) first converts the 11-bit twos-complement representation of the input voltage to four BCD-coded values. It then uses another subroutine, SSCONV, to convert the four BCD code words into four display code words. The first task forms the magnitude of the binary value of the input voltage. Then initialization includes storing the address of the BCD conversion table in the index register, clearing a flag used in the conversion, setting the least significant bit in the test word, and clearing the BCD value. Next a loop counter is loaded with the value 10 so that a repeated-task structural unit can be used to convert separately each bit in the 10-bit code word representing the magnitude of the input voltage as a binary number.

In the loop for DCONV the first task tests the bit being converted; if it has the value 1, the BCD code word for the corresponding decimal value of the bit is

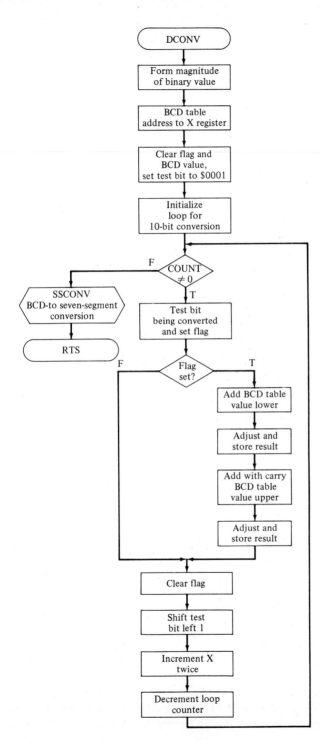

Figure 10-13 Flowchart for subroutine to convert binary values to display codewords, DCONV.

added to the accumulated BCD value. This process requires four steps because the addition is a BCD addition, using the decimal add adjust instruction, and because the addends are 2 bytes. The last four tasks in the loop are clear the flag for the next repetition, shift the test bit one position to the left, increment the index register twice for the next BCD value, and decrement the loop counter. When the loop exit is taken, the subroutine used to convert the four BCD code words into four display code words is executed. This is followed by the return to the calling program.

The flowchart for the subroutine SSCONV (Fig. 10-14) accepts the four BCD code words and returns the corresponding four display code words. First the

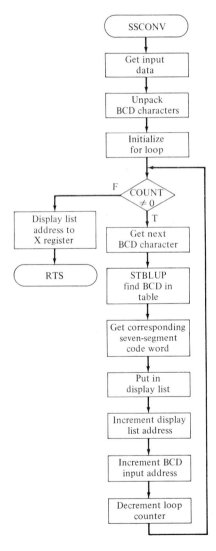

Figure 10-14 Flowchart for BCD-to-seven-segment conversion subroutine, sscONV.

BCD code words are obtained and unpacked into 4 bytes, each containing a single BCD-coded value in the four least significant positions. Each of these code words will be converted separately using a repeated-task structural unit. The loop initialization includes defining the address of the list of BCD code words to be converted, defining the address of the list of display code words, and loading the loop counter with the value 4.

The first task in the loop for SSCONV gets the next BCD character to be converted. The subroutine STBLUP is then executed to find the BCD value in a table. This subroutine accepts a BCD code word and returns the address of the BCD character being converted. This address is used to access a second table containing the seven-segment code words ordered according to the corresponding BCD characters. The subroutine STBLUP is straightforward, and its flowchart is omitted because it is very similar to Fig. 8-27.

The last four tasks in the loop of the subroutine SSCONV store the seven-segment code word in the appropriate place in the display list, increment the address of the display list, increment the address of the BCD character to be converted, and decrement the loop counter. After exiting from this loop, the index register is loaded with the address of the display list and the subroutine returns to the calling program.

Step 3 Step 3 involves translating the flowcharts into assembly-language programs. This procedure requires an initial estimate of both RAM and ROM memory requirements and a tentative assignment of address spaces to all memory devices as well as the input-output interface devices. Tentative starting addresses must be assigned for the interrupt-service routine, the top-level program, and all subroutines.

In developing these programs we made an initial estimate of the memory storage requirement. Since the five flowcharts developed in step 2 will generate approximately 100 bytes each, a $1K \times 8$ ROM will be more than adequate for program storage. This ROM package will be assigned addresses $FC00 to $FFFF with the interrupt-service routine assigned the address $FC00. The data requirements of the programs for this example are limited, and we estimate that the data and stack storage will require less than one 128×8 RAM package. This package will be assigned the addresses $0000 to $007F. The two input-output interface packages required are assigned the addresses $5000 to $5003 and $6000 to $6003, respectively.

Table 10-13 shows the assembly-language program implementation for the interrupt service called INTSVR, defined by the flowchart in Fig. 10-10.

This program begins with a NAM directive followed by an ORG directive assigning it to the first available ROM address $FC00. Some labels used in this program are not defined in it. Since these labels are defined with the program VMCOMP, these two programs must be assembled together.

The first three executable instructions in INTSVR read the control register from the input port to which REFRESH and RCHANGE are connected, test the CA_2 status bit to determine whether the REFRESH signal caused the interrupt

Table 10-13 Assembly language for interrupt-service routine†

	NAM	INTSVR	
	ORG	$FC00	
INTSVR	LDAA	PI1CRA	GET RFRESH AND RCHANGE STATUS BITS
	BITA	#$80	CHECK FOR DISP UNIT IRQ
	BEQ	INT1	IF ZERO, NOT DISP UNIT
	LDX	NDISP	GET ADDR OF NEXT CHAR
	LDAB	0,X	GET NEXT CHAR
	STAB	PI1DRB	OUTPUT CHAR
	LDAB	PI1DRA	GET DIGIT SELECT PORT
	ANDB	#$0F	SAVE OTHER BITS
	ORAB	DIGVAL	GET DIGIT SELECT CODE WORD
	STAB	PI2DRA	OUTPUT DIGIT SELECTION
	ASLB		NEXT DIGIT SELECT CODE WORD
	BCC	INT2	IF CARRY CLEAR NO WRAP AROUND
	LDAB	#$10	WRAP AROUND, START AGAIN
	STAB	DIGVAL	
	LDX	#DLIST	REINITIALIZE DISPLAY ADDR
	STX	NDISP	
	BRA	INT1	
INT2	ANDB	#$E0	SAVE DIGVAL
	STAB	DIGVAL	
	INX		NEXT DISP LIST ENTRY
	STX	NDISP	
INT1	BITA	#$40	CHECK FOR RANGE CHANGE IRQ
	BEQ	INT3	IF ZERO, NO RANGE CHANGE
	LDAA	PI1DRA	GET RANGE SELECTION VALUE
	ANDA	#$07	
	STAA	RSEL	SAVE RANGE SELECT VALUE
INT3	RTI		RETURN FROM INTERRUPT
	END		

† This routine must be assembled with VMCOMP. Only one NAM and END should be included.

request, and skip to the instruction with the label INT1 if the CA_2 status bit is clear. If the display unit requested the interrupt, the next seven instructions output the code words defining the next display character and selected digit. In this procedure the index register is loaded with the address of the next display character; this character is loaded into the B accumulator and stored in the appropriate output port. The port with the previous digit-select code word is then read and ANDed with the value $0F to retain the digital voltage estimate bits which share the same port. The new digit-select code word is then ORed with the bits saved and the value stored in the appropriate output-port data register.

The next 11 instructions update the display-list address and digit-select code word for the next display-unit interrupt. The digit-select code word is shifted left. If the shift results in a shift out of the most significant bit, the display code word must be reinitialized to $01 and the display-list address set to the first entry. If a shift out does not occur, the shifted value is saved and the display-list address incremented.

The instruction labeled INT1 tests the CA1 status bit to determine whether the RCHANGE signal generated the interrupt request. If it is active, the next three instructions read the input port and store the new value in the location labeled RSEL. Otherwise the RETURN FROM INTERRUPT instruction is executed, restoring the values of the registers and returning to the interrupted program.

Table 10-14 shows the assembly-language program for the top-level program VMCOMP. The ORG directive followed by four FDB data descriptors assigns the addresses required for the IRQ, SWI, NMI, and RESET functions. When an interrupt request is acknowledged, the value assigned to the label INTSVR, i.e., the address of the routine, is loaded into the program counter. The SWI and NMI functions are not used in this system. When a RESET occurs, the value assigned to the label VMCOMP, i.e., the address of this routine, is loaded into the program counter and program execution begins. The next several statements are EQU directives assigning values to labels used in the program.

The second ORG directive defines the beginning address for the data-storage area. The five RMB data directives set aside storage for various data elements used in the program. The comments appearing with the data descriptors explain the use of each assignment.

The third ORG directive defines the first address used by the program VMCOMP. The next 15 instructions take care of the initialization required each time power is applied to the system. This initialization includes defining the stack address, loading the data direction and control registers for the four ports, loading the beginning address of the display list, storing the initial display digit-select code word, and enabling the interrupt.

The instruction label VMLOOP defines the beginning of the repeated-task structural unit used to process the input voltage continuously. No initialization is required before calling the subroutine VCONV. Upon returning from this subroutine the index register contains the address of the binary-valued code word defining the input voltage. The next four instructions save this 2-byte code word. Next the subroutine DCONV is called with the index register already initialized by the last subroutine. This subroutine converts the binary-valued code words for the input voltage into the corresponding display code words and returns the address of the list of these code words in the index register. The next six instructions test the sign of the binary-coded input voltage saved earlier and set the most significant bit in the first display code word in the list. When this entry is transferred to the display unit, a 1 in this bit illuminates the plus sign and a 0 illuminates the minus sign.

The 16 instructions beginning at the label VM1 test the range selection value and set the appropriate decimal sign in the display list. If the low range is selected, the most significant bit in the second display code word in the list is set. If the midrange is selected, the most significant bit in the third display code word in the list is set. Finally, if the high range is selected, the most significant bit in

Table 10-14 Assembly-language for top-level VMCOMP

	NAM	VMCOMP	
	ORG	$FFF8	
IRQADR	FDB	INTSVR	ADDR FOR IRQ
SWIADR	FDB	0	UNUSED
NMIADR	FDB	0	UNUSED
RESADR	FDB	VMCOMP	ADDR FOR RESET
PI1CRA	EQU	$5002	ADDR FOR PIA1, CRA
PI1CRB	EQU	$5003	ADDR FOR PIA1, CRB
PI2CRA	EQU	$6002	ADDR FOR PIA2, CRA
PI2CRB	EQU	$6003	ADDR FOR PIA2, CRB
PI1DRA	EQU	$5000	ADDR FOR PIA1, DATA & DIR REGA
PI1DRB	EQU	$5001	ADDR FOR PIA2, DATA & DIR REGB
PI2DRA	EQU	$6000	ADDR FOR PIA2, DATA & DIR REGA
PI2DRB	EQU	$6001	ADDR FOR PIA2, DATA & DIR REGB
STACK	EQU	$007F	INITIAL ADDR FOR STACK
CR1AB	EQU	$1F04	VALUE FOR CRA & CRB(PIA1)
CR2AB	EQU	$0404	VALUE FOR CRA & CRB(PIA2)
VCONV	EQU	$FE00	ADDR OF VCONV SUB
DCONV	EQU	$FF00	ADDR OF DCONV SUB
	ORG	$00	
RSEL	RMB	1	RANGE SELECTION VALUE
DLIST	RMB	4	DISPLAY LIST
BVOLTS	RMB	2	BINARY VOLTAGE VALUE
NDISP	RMB	2	ADDR OF NEXT DISP WORD
DIGVAL	RMB	1	DIGIT SELECTION CODE WORD
	ORG	$FD00	
VMCOMP	LDS	#STACK	INITIAL STACK ADDR
	CLR	PI1DRA	PIA1 DIRA FOR INPUT PORT
	LDAA	#$FF	
	STAA	PI1DRB	PIA1 DIRB FOR OUT PORT
	STAA	PI2DRA	PIA2 DIRA FOR OUT PORT
	STAA	PI2DRB	PIA2 FOR OUT PORT
	LDX	#CR1AB	CONTROL REG VALUE PIA1
	STX	PI1CRA	STORE CRA & CRB AT ONCE
	LDX	#CR2AB	CONTROL REG VALUES, PIA2
	STX	PI2CRA	STORE CRA & CRB AT ONCE
	LDX	#DLIST	INITIALIZE DISP LIST ADDR
	STX	NDISP	
	LDAA	#$10	INIT DIGIT SELECT VALUE
	STAA	DIGVAL	
	CLI		ENABLE INTERRUPTS
VMLOOP	JSR	VCONV	GET BINARY VOLTAGE
	LDAA	0, X	SAVE BINARY VOLTAGE
	STAA	BVOLTS	
	LDAA	1, X	
	STAA	BVOLTS+1	
	JSR	DCONV	CONVERT BINARY TO DISP LIST
	LDAA	0, X	SET SIGN TO DISP LIST
	LDAB	BVOLTS	
	BITB	#$04	CHECK BINARY SIGN
	BEQ	VM1	IF ZERO SIGN IS PLUS
	ORAA	#$80	SET MINUS SIGN

Table 10-14 (Continued)

	STAA	0,X	PUT BACK TO DISP LIST
VMI	LDAA	RSEL	TEST RANGE SELECT, SET DEC PT
	BITA	#$01	CHECK FOR LOW RANGE
	BEQ	VM2	IF ZERO—NOT LOW RANGE
	LDAB	1,X	LOW—DECIMAL LEFT OF D3
	ORAB	#$08	
	STAB	1,X	
	BRA	VM3	
VM2	BITA	#$02	CHECK FOR MID RANGE
	BEQ	VM4	IF ZERO—NOT MID RANGE
	LDAB	2,X	MID RANGE—DEC LEFT OF D2
	ORAB	#$80	
	STAB	2,X	
	BRA	VM3	
VM4	LDAB	3,X	HIGH RANGE—DEC LEFT OF D1
	ORAB	#$80	
	STAB	3,X	
VM3	BRA	VMLOOP	GO AGAIN
	END		

the fourth display code word in the list is set. The last instruction branches to the beginning of the loop, VMLOOP.

Table 10-15 shows the assembly-language program for the subroutine VCONV, which produces a binary value of the analog measured voltage by successive approximations. The first ORG directive places the data storage used by this subroutine after those already assigned. The comments appearing with the three RMB data descriptors describe the use of these locations.

The second ORG directive assigns the first instruction to an unused portion of the ROM. The first three instructions initialize the bit position to be estimated. The next 11 instructions resolve the sign of the input voltage by first estimating the voltage as zero and then testing the EVG signal. The input port containing the three most significant bits of the estimate are read and the four digit-select bits sharing this port are retained unchanged. The zero estimate is output and the WAIT subroutine is called to delay about 30 μs while the EVG signal settles. The EVG signal is then read and tested. If it is 0, the analog voltage is positive and the sign remains 0; otherwise the sign is set to 1 for minus. The next two instructions initialize a loop counter for 10 repetitions of a repeated-task structural unit which resolves each of the remaining 10 bits.

The first six instructions in the repeated task set the next more significant bit to be estimated and output the new estimate to the appropriate ports. Again, the subroutine WAIT is executed to delay while the EVG signal settles. The next three instructions read and test the EVG signal value. If it is 0, the estimate is low and the bit being resolved remains set. If the EVG signal is 1, the estimate is too large, so the next instructions reset the bit being resolved. The four instructions

Table 10-15 Assembly-language for VCONV subroutine

	NAM	VCONV	
	ORG	$0B	
VEBIT	RMB	2	NEXT BIT POSITION TO ESTIMATE
VCOUNT	RMB	1	LOOP COUNT
VEST	RMB	2	BINARY VOLTAGE ESTIMATE
	ORG	$FD80	
VCONV	LDAA	#$02	BIT POSITION TO ESTIMATE NEXT
	STAA	VEBIT	
	CLR	VEBIT+1	
	LDAB	PI2DRA	DO NOT DISTURB PORT BITS
	ANDB	#$F0	ZERO ALL OTHER BITS
	STAB	PI2DRA	
	CLR	PI2DRB	ZERO LOWER BITS IN PORT
	BSR	WAIT	WAIT FOR EVG SIGNAL TO SETTLE
	LDAB	PI1DRA	GET EVG SIGNAL
	BITB	#$08	
	BEQ	VARND1	IF EVG = 0, ANALOG VOLTAGE IS+
	LDAB	PI2DRA	
	ORAB	#$04	
	STAB	PI2DRA	SET MINUS SIGN
VARND1	LDAA	#10	SET LOOP COUNT FOR TEN BITS
	STAA	VCOUNT	
VLOOP	BEQ	VEXIT	EXIT LOOP
	LDAB	PI2DRA	DO NOT DISTURB BITS 4–7
	ORAB	VEBIT	OR IN NEXT BIT TO ESTIMATE, BITS 8–10
	LDAA	PI2DRB	GET ESTIMATE–LOWER 8 BITS
	ORAA	VEBIT+1	OR IN NEXT BIT TO ESTIMATE, BITS 0–7
	STAB	PI2DRA	OUTPUT ESTIMATE, BITS 8–10
	STAA	PI2DRB	OUT ESTIMATE, BITS 0–7
	BSR	WAIT	WAIT FOR EVG SIG TO SETTLE
	LDAA	PI1DRA	GET EVG SIGNAL VALUE
	BITA	#$08	
	BEQ	VARND2	IF EVG = 0 EST OK SO FAR
	LDAB	PI2DRA	DO NOT DIST BITS 4–7
	EORB	VEBIT	CHANGE NEXT BIT TO ESTIMATE
	LDAA	PI2DRB	GET PRESENT ESTIMATE, BITS 0–7
	EORA	VEBIT+1	CHANGE NEXT BIT TO ESTIMATE
	STAB	PI2DRA	OUTPUT ESTIMATE, BITS 8 – 10
	STAA	PI2DRB	OUTPUT ESTIMATE, BITS 0–7
VARND2	LSR	VEBIT	SHIFT TO NEXT BIT TO ESTIMATE
	ROR	VEBIT+1	
	DEC	VCOUNT	DECREMENT LOOP COUNT
	BRA	VLOOP	GO AGAIN
VEXIT	LDAB	PI2DRA	GET FINAL ESTIMATE
	ANDB	#$07	
	STAB	VEST	
	LDAA	PI2DRB	
	STAA	VEST+1	
	LDX	#VEST	
	RTS		
WAIT	NOP		DO NOTHING BUT DELAY
	NOP		

Table 10-15 (Continued)

```
NOP
NOP
NOP
NOP
NOP
RTS
END
```

begining with the label VARND2 shift the bit to be estimated right one position, decrement the loop counter, and branch to the beginning of the loop.

When an exit from the loop occurs, the final value of the binary coded input voltage is read from the appropriate ports and stored. In addition, the address of the first byte is loaded into the index register. This subroutine then returns to the calling program.

The WAIT subroutine executes seven no-operation (NOP) instructions to delay 14 μs. This delay time, along with the 15 μs of the JSR and RTS, provides an adequate delay while the EVG signal settles.

Table 10-16 shows the assembly-language program for the display conversion subroutine DCONV. The first ORG directive defines the beginning address for the data values beyond those already assigned. The BINBCD table contains the BCD-coded values corresponding to the binary value of each bit position in the binary coded value being converted. For example, the first entry corresponds to the least significant binary bit and has a BCD-coded value of 1, the second has a BCD-coded value of 2, the third is 4, and so on. If a bit is active in the binary-coded value, the BCD-coded value from the table is added to an accumulated BCD-coded value stored in BCDVAL. The comments beside the other data descriptors define their use.

The second ORG directive assigns the subroutine to an unused portion of the ROM. When this subroutine is entered, the binary-coded value is in the A and B accumulators. The first two instructions test the sign of the binary-coded value. If it is minus, the twos-complement is formed by first complementing and then incrementing the lower byte in the A accumulator and, if a carry results, incrementing the upper byte in the B accumulator. The resulting magnitude is then stored by the next two instructions.

The next seven instructions initialize several values for the loop that follows; this includes loading the index register with the address of the BINBCD table, clearing the location FLAG, setting the first bit to be converted, and clearing the accumulated BCDVAL. Two more instructions set the value of the loop counter to 10.

In the loop the first nine instructions of the repeated-task test 1 bit in the binary-coded value being converted. This involves testing 2 bytes and results in setting a flag location if the tested bit is active. If FLAG is zero when the instruction labeled DC2 is executed, nine instructions are skipped. If FLAG is

Table 10-16 Assembly language for display conversion subroutine DCONV†

```
           NAM    DCONV
           ORG    $10
BINBCD     FDB    $0001        BCD FOR BIT-0 ACTIVE
           FDB    $0002        BCD FOR BIT-1 ACTIVE
           FDB    $0004        BCD FOR BIT-2 ACTIVE
           FDB    $0008        BCD FOR BIT-3 ACTIVE
           FDB    $0016        BCD FOR BIT-4 ACTIVE
           FDB    $0032        BCD FOR BIT-5 ACTIVE
           FDB    $0064        BCD FOR BIT-6 ACTIVE
           FDB    $0128        BCD FOR BIT-7 ACTIVE
           FDB    $0256        BCD FOR BIT-8 ACTIVE
           FDB    $0512        BCD FOR BIT-9 ACTIVE
BCDVAL     RMB    2            4 DIGITS OF BCD
BINVAL     RMB    2            11 BITS OF BINARY
TBIT       RMB    2            BIT BEING TESTED
FLAG       RMB    1            FLAG SET WHEN BIT IS ACTIVE
DCOUNT     RMB    1            LOOP COUNTER
           ORG    $FE00
DCONV      BITB   #$04         TEST FOR NEGATIVE
           BEQ    DCARND       GO AROUND IF POSITIVE
           COMB                FORM MAGNITUDE
           COMA                ONES COMPLEMENT
           INCA                PLUS 1
           BCC    DCARND       GO AROUND IF NO CARRY
           INCB                PLUS 1 TO B
DCARND     STAA   BINVAL+1     SAVE MAGNITUDE
           STAB   BINVAL
           LDX    #BINBCD      INITIALIZE TABLE ADDRESS
           CLR    FLAG         INITIALIZE FLAG
           CLR    TBIT
           LDAA   #$01         INITIALIZE TEST BIT
           STAA   TBIT+1
           CLR    BCDVAL       INITIALIZE BCD VALUE TO 0
           CLR    BCDVAL+1
           LDAA   #10          INITIALIZE LOOP COUNT FOR TEN BITS
           STAA   DCOUNT
DCLOOP     BEQ    DCEXIT       LOOP EXIT
           LDAB   BINVAL       GET BINARY VALUE
           LDAA   BINVAL+1
           ANDA   TBIT+1       TEST PRESENT BIT ACTIVE
           BEQ    DC1          NOT ACTIVE
           COM    FLAG         ACTIVE, SET FLAG
           BRA    DC2
DC1        ANDB   TBIT         TEST UPPER BITS
           BEQ    DC2          NOT ACTIVE
           COM    FLAG         ACTIVE, SET FLAG
DC2        TST    FLAG         TEST FLAG ACTIVE
           BEQ    DARND        NOT ACTIVE GO AROUND
           LDAB   BCDVAL       GET BCD VALUE
           LDAA   BCDVAL+1
           ADDA   1,X          ADD LOW PART OF TABLE VALUE
           DAA                 ADJUST FOR BCD ADD
```

408

Table 10-16 (Continued)

	STAA	BCDVAL+1	NEW BCDVAL LOWER
	TBA		UPPER BCD TO A, CARRY UNCHANGED
	ADCA	0,X	ADD WITH CARRY UPPER TABLE VALUE
	DAA		ADJUST FOR BCD ADD
	STAA	BCDVAL	NEW BCD VALUE UPPER
	CLR	FLAG	CLEAR FLAG FOR NEXT PASS
DARND	ASL	TBIT+1	ADJUST NEXT BIT TO CONVERT
	ROL	TBIT	
	INX		NEXT TABLE VALUE PAIR
	INX		
	DEC	DCOUNT	DEC LOOP COUNTER
	BRA	DCLOOP	GO AGAIN TOP OF LOOP
DCEXIT	LDX	#BCDVAL	SET X REG FOR BCD TO 7 SEG CONV
	JSR	SSCONV	SUBROUTINE FOR SEG CODE CONV
	RTS		
	END		

† This routine must be assembled with VMCOMP. Only one NAM and END directive should be included.

not zero, the appropriate BCD-coded value from the table is added to the accumulated BCD-coded value. This addition involves adding 2 byte operands and the use of the decimal adjust instruction. First the accumulated BCD-coded value is loaded into the two accumulators. Next the lower byte from the table is added to the A register and the decimal-adjust instruction is executed. This forms the first byte of the new BCD-coded value with a valid carry bit. The B register is transferred to the A register since the DAA instruction is only defined for the A register. The next byte is added with the carry bit included, and the decimal adjustment is made. The result is then stored. At the instruction labeled DARND the location FLAG is cleared, the test bit is rotated one position to the left for the next repetition, the table address in the index register is incremented twice to point to the next double-byte entry in the table, and the loop counter is decremented.

When the exit from the loop occurs, the address of the BCD- coded value is loaded into the index register and the subroutine SSCONV called to perform the final conversion to define the display code words. After returning from SSCONV, DCONV returns to the calling program.

Table 10-17 shows the assembly-language program for the conversion sub-routine SSCONV. The first ORG directive defines the beginning address for the data values beyond those already assigned. The BCDTBL table itemizes all possible BCD-coded values. The SSGTBL table is ordered so that each element represents the seven-segment code words for the corresponding element in the previous table. For example, the first entry in BCDTBL corresponds to the BCD character 0, and the first entry in SSGTBL contains the seven-segment code word for the character 0. The comments beside the other data descriptors define their use.

Table 10-17 Assembly language for seven-segment conversion subroutine

```
          NAM     SSCONV
          ORG     $30
BCDTBL    FCB     $00,$01,$02,$03,$04    BCD VALUES FOR LOOPUP
          FCB     $05,$06,$07,$08,$09
SSGTBL    FCB     $7E,$30,$CD,$79,3      7-SEG CODE WORDS, SAME ORDER
          FCB     $5B,$5F,$70,$7F,$73
BCDCH     RMB     4                     TABLE FOR UNPACKED BCD CHARS
DLIST     EQU     $0002                 OUTPUT TABLE FOR DISPLAY
DIN       RMB     2                     INPUT VALUES
BCDCHA    RMB     2                     ADDRESS OF BCD CHAR LIST
DLISTA    RMB     2                     ADDRESS OF DLIST
SLCOUN    RMB     1                     LOOP COUNTER
SCOUNT    RMB     1                     LOOP COUNTER FOR SUBROUTINE STBLUP
          ORG     $FF00
SSCONV    LDAA    0,X                   GET INPUT VALUES FROM PARAMETER LIST
          STAA    DIN
          LDAA    1,X
          STAA    DIN+1
          ANDA    #$0F                  GET FIRST BCD CHAR
          STAA    BCDCH+3
          LDAA    DIN+1
          ANDA    #$F0                  GET NEXT CHARACTER
          ASRA                          RIGHT JUSTIFY
          ASRA
          ASRA
          ASRA
          STAA    BCDCH+2
          LDAA    DIN
          ANDA    #$0F                  GET NEXT CHARACTER
          STAA    BCDCH+1
          LDAA    DIN
          ANDA    #$F0                  GET LAST BCD CHAR
          ASRA                          RIGHT JUSTIFY
          ASRA
          ASRA
          ASRA
          STAA    BCDCH
          LDX     #BCDCH                INITIALIZE BCDCH ADDR
          STX     BCDCHA
          LDX     #DLIST                INITIALIZE DISPLAY LIST ADDR
          STX     DLISTA
          LDAA    #$04                  SET LOOP COUNT TO 4
          STAA    SLCOUNSE
SLLOOP    BEQ     SLEXIT                LOOP EXIT
          LDX     BCDCHA                GET NEXT BCD CHAR
          LDAA    0,X
          BSR     STBLUP                SUBROUTINE FOR TABLE LOOKUP
          LDAA    10,X                  PICK UP CORRESPONDING ENTRY IN 7-SEG TBL
          LDX     DLISTA
          STAA    0,X                   PUT 7-SEG INTO OUTPUT
          INC     DLISTA                NEXT DISPLAY LIST ENTRY ADDR
          INC     BCDCHA                NEXT BCD CHAR ADDR
```

Table 10-17 (Continued)

	DEC	SLCOUN	DEC LOOP COUNTER
	BRA	SLLOOP	GO TO TOP OF LOOP
SLEXIT	LDX	#DLIST	SET INDEX TO OUTPUT FOR RETURN
	RTS		
STBLUP	LDX	#BCDTBL	INITIALIZE BCD TABLE ADDR
	LDAB	#10	INITIALIZE LOOP COUNT
	STAB	SCOUNT	
SLOOP	BEQ	SEXIT	LOOP EXIT
	CMPA	0,X	FIND BCD VALUE IN TABLE
	BEQ	SARND	FOUND
	INX		IF NOT, CHECK NEXT ENTRY
	DEC	SCOUNT	
	BRA	SEND	
SARND	CLR	SCOUNT	FORCE END OF LOOP
SEND	BRA	SLOOP	GO TO START OF LOOP
SEXIT	RTS		X REG HAS ADDR OF BCD TABLE MATCH
END			

The second ORG directive assigns this subroutine to an unused portion of the ROM. When this subroutine is entered, the address of the BCD-coded value to be converted is in the index register. The first four instructions get the two bytes containing the BCD-coded value. The next 19 instructions separate these 2 bytes into 4 bytes, each containing one BCD code word which has been shifted completely to the right.

The next six instructions initialize values for the loop that follows. This includes initializing the address of the BCD character to be converted, initializing the address of the display list where the resulting seven-segment code word is to be stored, and defining the loop counter value as 4.

In the loop the first two instructions load the A register with the next BCD character to be converted. The subroutine STBLUP is called to find the BCD character in the BCDTBL table. The next three instructions put the corresponding seven-segment code word in the appropriate entry in the display list. The next four instructions increment the address of the display list, increment the address of the BCD character to be converted, decrement the loop counter, and branch to the beginning of the loop.

When the exit from the loop occurs, the address of the display list is loaded into the index register and SSCONV returns to the calling program.

The subroutine STBLUP, also included in Table 10-17, searches BCDTBL to identify the address of the BCD character stored in the A register and returns this address to the calling program. The address is identified by setting up a loop and comparing the test word with each element in BCDTBL until it is found.

Step 4 In step 4 we shall analyze the solution to determine whether the requirements of the specification have been met. In this example we consider two questions in our analysis: How much execution time is used to service interrupts?

How much time is required to convert a measured analog voltage into binary-coded value?

In considering the first question, we know that the display unit interrupts the processor once every millisecond. In addition, the selection of a new range can also cause an interrupt. This latter interrupt will occur much less frequently but will occasionally cause a second interrupt to occur within a 1-ms interval. We shall analyze this worst-case condition where two interrupts occur in 1 ms. When the interrupt-service routine is executed and the display unit is requesting service, approximately 20 instructions are executed in the worst case. When the interrupt-service routine is executed due to a range-selection change, approximately 10 instructions are executed. Therefore, in the worst case, approximately 30 instructions are executed while servicing interrupts in 1 ms. If the approximation of four computer cycles per instruction is used, a total of approximately 120 computer cycles are used. If the clock frequency is assumed to be 1 MHz, the computer cycle time is 1 μs and the total execution time required for the interrupt service is approximately 120 μs = 0.12 ms. Another way of looking at this result is that, in the worst case, 12 percent of the available processing time is used for servicing interrupts. The best case, when the display unit alone causes an interrupt, approximately 8.5 percent of the available processing time is used for servicing interrupts.

The second question (How much time is required to estimate the measured analog voltage?) requires us to count the number of instructions required to execute the repeated-task structural unit in the program VMCOMP.

Most instructions are executed when the sign of the voltage is minus and the midrange voltage is selected. In this case 22 instructions are executed in this loop. In addition, the instructions executed by each of the subroutines called by VMCOMP must also be determined. In the subroutine VCONV, 400 instructions are executed in the worst case, including those in the subroutine WAIT. In the subroutine DCONV, 280 instructions are executed in the worst case, and the subroutine SSCONV is called. In the subroutine SSCONV, 375 instructions are executed in the worst case; this includes those of the subroutine STBLUP.

The total number of instructions executed in the program VMCOMP and the subroutines it calls, VCONV, DCONV, SSCONV, WAIT, and STBLUP, is approximately 1075. If an average of four computer cycles per instruction is used, then 4300 computer cycles are required for one complete execution of the program VMCOMP. If the computer clock frequency is 1 MHz, the resulting execution time required is 4.3 ms. The time required to service interrupts must be added. If 12 percent of the time is used to service interrupts in the worst case, the total time required to resolve a measured analog voltage is 4.3 + 0.5 ms = 4.8 ms, or approximately 5 ms. This amount of time delay will not be perceptible to the user and will provide a more than adequate response.

Step 5 In step 5 we refine the solution to correct any design errors discovered during the analysis in step 4. In this example, since the initial program satisfies the specification, no refinement is required. Actually we did not generate this

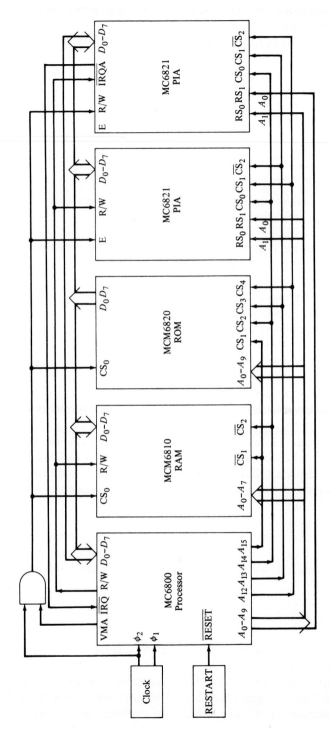

Figure 10-15 Block diagram for microcomputer-based voltmeter computation unit.

Table 10-18 Address assignments and address-line connections for the voltmeter computation unit

Package	Assigned addresses	Address-bus line			
		A_{15}	A_{14}	A_{13}	A_{12}
RAM1	0000–007F	$\overline{CS_1}$	$\overline{CS_2}$		
ROM1	FC00–FFFF	CS_1	CS_2	CS_3	CS_4
PIA1	5000–5003		CS_0	$\overline{CS_2}$	CS_1
PIA2	6000–6003		CS_0	CS_1	$\overline{CS_2}$

completely acceptable solution on the first pass; it was derived using several repetitions of the procedure defined in steps 2 to 5.

Step 6 In step 6 we complete the microcomputer hardware configuration by defining specific packages and their connection to the system bus. In this system we use the MC6800 processor, one MCM6810 RAM package, one MCM6830 ROM package, and two MC6821 PIA packages. The MC6800 is connected to the system bus in the standard way except that the NMI and HALT pins, along with the two pins used in synchronizing the sharing of the bus, TSC and DBE, are disabled.

The eight data pins on the RAM, ROM, and PIAs are connected to the corresponding lines in the bus. The R/W pin on the RAM and PIAs are connected to the R/W bus line. The valid-memory-address signal again is ANDed with the ϕ_2 clock signal and connected to the CS_0 Pin on the RAM and ROM packages and to the enable (E) pin on the PIA packages. The remaining chip-select pins are connected to the high-order lines in the address bus to implement a partial decoding scheme. Table 10-18 shows the address-bus connections used and the resulting addresses assigned to each of the four packages. The address pins on the RAM and ROM and the register-select pins on the PIAs are connected to the corresponding low-order lines in the address bus. The IRQA pin of the PIA with the input signals REFRESH and RCHANGE is connected to the IRQ line of the system bus. Figure 10-15 shows a block diagram for the voltmeter computation unit and defines all connections to the five standard packages used in the design. Two additional modules, the clock and restart unit, are also shown.

10-4 CONCLUSIONS

In this chapter we have demonstrated the microcomputer-based system design procedure by solving two example problems. Although simplified somewhat, they represent a systematic and useful design procedure. We have considered only restricted specifications and have ignored such issues as power, reliability, and packaging requirements in order to focus on the basic design process.

Treating the vending-machine control-unit example for a second time provided an opportunity to compare the microcomputer design process with the traditional design process. In addition the distinctions between the two realizations can be seen more clearly.

Since many systems incorporate several microcomputer systems in a single larger system, the interaction of multiple microcomputers is an important issue, left to more advanced textbooks.

PROBLEMS

10-1 Draw the timing diagram for all output signals from the vending-machine control unit when 55 cents is deposited. Do these signals satisfy the timing specifications?

10-2 (*a*) Discuss the changes required in the microcomputer-based vending-machine control unit if the price of a drink is raised to 40 cents.

(*b*) Compare these changes with those required to modify the traditional vending-machine control unit described in Chap. 4.

10-3 (*a*) Discuss the changes required in the vending-machine control units so that one of three brands of drinks can be selected. The cost of a drink remains at 35 cents.

(*b*) Compare these changes with those required to modify the traditional vending-machine control unit described in Chap. 4.

10-4 Discuss the changes required in the digital-voltmeter computation unit to add:

(*a*) A range of ± 0.1 V

(*b*) Another digit to the display

(*c*) An ohmmeter and ammeter functions. Assume that the operator input unit converts these signals into a voltage in the range ± 1 V.

10-5 For the sequential detector described in Prob. 4-7:

(*a*) Develop an input-output model

(*b*) Define signal assignments for all interfaces

(*c*) Define the code words for all PIA control and data direction registers

(*d*) Derive a flowchart for the top-level program and for all subroutines

(*e*) Translate the flowcharts into assembly-language programs

(*f*) Define the number of each type of device required by the system

(*g*) Define the connection of all devices to the system bus

10-6 Repeat Prob. 10-5 for:

(1) The seat-belt system described in Prob. 4-8

(2) The traffic-light controller defined in Prob. 4-9

(3) The combinational lock described in Prob. 4-10

(4) The elevator controller described in Prob. 4-11

(5) The bowling-pin-setter control unit in Prob. 4-12

REFERENCES

Fletcher, W.: "An Engineering Approach to Digital Design," Prentice-Hall, Englewood Cliffs, N.J., 1980.

Givone, D., and R. Roesser: "Microprocessors/Microcomputers: An Introduction," McGraw-Hill, New York, 1980.

Klingman, E.: "Microprocessor Systems Design," Prentice-Hall, Englewood Cliffs, N.J., 1977.

Kraft, G. D., and W. N. Toy: "Mini-Microcomputer Hardware Design," Prentice-Hall, Englewood Cliffs, N.J., 1979.

Krutz, R. L.: "Microprocessor and Logic Design," Wiley, New York, 1980.

Peatman, J.: "Microcomputer-Based Design," McGraw-Hill, New York, 1977.

Windel, D., and F. Prosser: "The Art of Digital Design," Prentice-Hall, Englewood Cliffs, N.J., 1980.

Yourdan, E., and L. Constantine: "Structured Design," Prentice-Hall, Englewood Cliffs, N.J., 1979.